DATE DUE FOR RETURN

D1611982

The Politics of Mental Health Legislation

CLIVE UNSWORTH

CLARENDON PRESS · OXFORD
1987

Oxford University Press, Walton Street, Oxford OX2 6DP
Oxford New York Toronto
Delhi Bombay Calcutta Madras Karachi
Petaling Jaya Singapore Hong Kong Tokyo
Nairobi Dar es Salaam Cape Town
Melbourne Auckland
and associated companies in
Beirut Berlin Ibadan Nicosia

Oxford is a trade mark of Oxford University Press

Published in the United States
by Oxford University Press, New York

British Library Cataloguing in Publication Data

Unsworth, Clive
The politics of mental health legislation.
1. Mental health laws—England—
History
I. Title
344.204'44 KD3412
ISBN 0-19-825512-8

Library of Congress Cataloging-in-Publication Data

Unsworth, Clive
The politics of mental health legislation.
Bibliography: p.
Includes index.
1. Mental health laws—Great Britain—History.
2. Insane—Commitment and detention—Great Britain—
History.   I. Title. [DNLM: 1. Commitment of Mentally
Ill—Great Britain—legislation.   2. Health Policy—
history—Great Britain.   3. Mental Disorders—Great
Britain—legislation.   4. Mental Health Services—
Great Britain—legislation.   WM 33 FA1 U5]
KD3412.U57 1987   344.4.'044   86-26813
ISBN 0-19-825512-8   344.10444

Set by Burgess and Son (Abingdon) Ltd
Printed in Great Britain by
Billing & Sons, Limited, Worcester

Acknowledgements

MY main thanks go to my supervisor, Margot Jefferys, Emeritus Professor of Medical Sociology, University of London, for her inspiration, unstinting help, and generous moral support. I am indebted to the Centre for Socio-Legal Studies, Wolfson College, Oxford, where I began the research on an SSRC studentship and especially to its Director, Donald Harris, whose encouragement and reassurance have been invaluable. I would also like to remember O. R. McGregor, formerly Director of the Centre, for acting as my supervisor in the early stages of the project. I am grateful to Kathleen Jones, Professor of Social Administration at the University of York, Phil Fennell of the Department of Law, University College, Cardiff, John Macnicol of the Department of Social Policy, Bedford College, London, and Nikolas Rose of the Department of Social Policy and Social Anthropology, Brunel University (who also kindly allowed me to see draft chapters of two books), for reading drafts of sections of the work at various stages in its development and providing me with useful comments and constructive criticisms. The same benefits have been conferred by the examiners of my D.Phil. thesis, Sarah McCabe, formerly of the Centre for Criminological Research, University of Oxford, and Larry Gostin, now of the Department of Public Health at Harvard, who also gave me access to MIND's papers and whose impact on modern English mental health legislation is an important part of the subject-matter of this book. The following contributed to the research by granting stimulating and informative interviews: Professor R. M. Jackson of St John's College, Cambridge, who was a member of the Percy Commission, Dr Alexander Walk, Honorary Emeritus Librarian of the Royal College of Psychiatrists, Kenneth Robinson, Christopher Mayhew, and Hugh Faulkner. I have been fortunate in receiving friendly assistance from the staff of a number of libraries and would like to thank in particular the staff of the Bodleian Law Library, the Radcliffe Science Library, and University College, Cardiff Law Library. Carol Black, Tracey Haslam, and Laura Brown were the long-suffering typists of the manuscript. Finally I would like to record my gratitude to David Staton, who first gave me an interest in this subject. Any remaining shortcomings are entirely my own responsibility.

CLIVE UNSWORTH
October 1985

Acknowledgements

Contents

Table of Cases

Table of Statutes

Introduction

THIS research was originally prompted in the mid-1970s by an interest in the growth at that time of a powerful critique by MIND (National Association for Mental Health) and other organizations of the comparative neglect in the Mental Health Act 1959 of formal legal procedures designed to function as judicial safeguards of patients' civil liberties. In the course of the research this critique has borne fruit in the Mental Health Act 1983 which returns the issue of civil liberties to the foreground. Developing and expanding the arguments advanced in my D. Phil thesis, 'Origins of the Mental Health Act 1959' (University of Oxford, 1983), and treating a succession of Acts—the Lunacy Act 1890, the Mental Treatment Act 1930, the Mental Health Act 1959 and the Mental Health Act 1983—this book seeks to account for the marked shifts in the level of importance attached to individual liberty and its legal protection which have taken place at each major legislative juncture in the last one hundred years. An attempt is made to set out the organizing assumptions of successive reworkings of the legal framework for mental health practices and to interpret the political, social, and psychiatric conditions which converted these assumptions into the ruling ones of their particular epoch. In doing so, it is hoped that the project of developing an adequate account of the politics of modern English mental health legislation, a project initiated by David Ewins' influential Master's thesis, 'The Origins of the Compulsory Commitment Provisions of the Mental Health Act 1959' (University of Sheffield, 1974), will be advanced and an alternative perspective to those recently offered by Geoffrey Baruch and Andrew Treacher,[1] Philip Bean,[2] and Tom Butler,[3] will be established.

The subject matter is selected, arranged, and interpreted around the civil liberation concerns of the 1970s and 1980s and is essentially confined to civil aspects of the treatment of mentally ill patients. It focuses particularly upon the changing form of admissions proce-

---

[1] *Psychiatry Observed*. London: Routledge and Kegan Paul, 1978, Chapter 1; 'Towards a Critical History of the Psychiatric Profession', in D. Ingelby (ed.), *Critical Psychiatry*. Harmondsworth: Penguin, 1981.

[2] *Compulsory Admissions to Mental Hospitals*. Chichester: John Wiley, 1980.

[3] *Mental Health, Social Policy and the Law*. London: Macmillan, 1985.

dures, since these have historically tended to provide the most
sensitive measure of movements toward and away from 'legalism', as,
for example, in the expansion of the scope of commitment orders
made by Justices in 1890 and the total abolition of the role of the
Justice in 1959. The limitation of the study to the civil dimensions of
legislation follows many precedents: in the early 1970s the historical
analysis of mental health legislation was carved up between Kathleen
Jones's *A History of the Mental Health Services* (1972)[4] and Nigel
Walker and Sarah McCabe's *Crime and Insanity in England, Volume 2*
(1973),[5] the former dealing with civil aspects and the latter with
mentally abnormal offenders. However, at certain points in the
history of civil provision, developments in relation to the role of
psychiatry in the criminal sphere have been significant and so receive
detailed treatment in the text. In terms of confining the study to the
mentally ill, modern legislation provides for mental disorders as a
generic category, subsuming under it mental impairment, severe
mental impairment, and psychopathy, as well as mental illness.
Nevertheless, each classification of mental disorder possesses, to a
greater or a lesser extent, its own distinctive social and legislative
history and lends itself to separate analysis. It must also be
recognized that the populations deemed to be appropriate subjects
for special legislation on grounds of mental abnormality or to fall
within the ambit of particular labels have not been static and that the
net of psychiatry has been spread increasingly wide during the period
under review. Again, at certain historical junctures developments
affecting mentally deficient or psychopathic patients have been
relevant to debates concerning the future of the mentally ill. This was
true, for example, in the period leading up to 1959. Instructive
historical comparisons can also be drawn between mental illness and
mental deficiency legislation: the Mental Deficiency Act 1913 is
covered in some detail in discussion of the context of the Mental
Treatment Act 1930.

The last mentioned statute is treated in greater depth because it
was with this enactment that the critical displacement of an
overriding preoccupation with the legal protection of individual
liberty in designing legislation took place. Many of the concepts in
legislation which provoked criticism from civil liberties activists in the
era of the 1959 Act were actually in position from 1930. As with

[4] London: Routledge and Kegan Paul.
[5] Edinburgh: Edinburgh University Press.

other turning points in the history of legislation for mental disorder, the objective of analysis has been to relate the evolution of state strategies systematically to the *general* political themes, debates, conflicts, and alignments at that conjuncture. Mental health legislation has too often been regarded as an isolated issue remote from 'real' politics, but this is an historically constructed perception strongly reinforced by the active depoliticization of certain sectors of social management as part of the post-Second World War accommodation between Labour and Conservative Parties based upon an acceptance of the 'givenness' of the philosophy of the Welfare State. In fact, different political ideologies can entail radically different strategies for mental disorder, which will be demonstrated in examinations of the views of individuals and by linking arguments specific to mental health legislation to the central issues of political debate: tracing, for example, the connections between the Mental Deficiency Act 1913 and the New Liberalism, or the Mental Treatment Act 1930 and Social Reconstruction. The intention is to chart in historical detail the relationship between the general social and political and the specific psychiatric and mental health conditions which have produced the alternating bold advances and submissive retreats of legal forms, procedures, and personnel which have constituted an important reality of the organization of control over mental disorders in the past century. Here there is material of interest to the Sociology of Law in that there has been a contested relationship between a field of social practice and the conventional legal order which has compelled the creation of a series of different strategies of mutual adaptation.

Many different disciplines and theoretical orientations within those disciplines are relevant to the ground covered by this research. From these different vantage points, accounts which differ in emphasis, selection, and content can be developed. My own particular entry into this area is from a legal background and inevitably this has helped to shape the treatment of the subject to be found in the following chapters. I hope that my handling of historical and sociological perspectives which illuminate the law will be read sympathetically by those who possess the advantage of having both feet planted in either history or sociology, and that this work can make some contribution to the development of a sociologically informed history of legal provision in the sphere of mental health.

1 Psychiatry, Law, and Politics

PSYCHIATRY is a realm where the appropriateness of mediating social relations by legal forms has been hotly contested for more than a century, and the debate is still unresolved. The central problem resides in a conflict of perspective between those who wish to subject the purveyors of mental health services, and especially psychiatrists, to a tight regime of legal rules, so defining the relationship between patients and professionals in terms of rights and duties, and those who insist that such an ambition mistakes the essentially individualized and discretionary nature of the therapeutic enterprise and threatens to impose a legal straight-jacket. In the former view, patients and professionals are perceived as polarized by potentially conflicting interests in relationships structured by a differential power which is at its most obvious in compulsory commitment and treatment: patients need legal rights to defend their civil liberty. In the latter view, however, patients and professionals are seen as bonded together in a common quest for successful treatment. The reconstruction of their relationship in adversarial legal terms is deemed irrelevant, obstructive, unscientific, and downright countertherapeutic: the substance of healing should not be sacrificed to the form of safeguarding abstract liberties.

In recent years, the civil libertarian advocates of patients' rights have won a partial but significant victory with the arrival on the statute book of the Mental Health (Amendment) Act 1982, consolidated with the Mental Health Act 1959 into the Mental Health Act 1983. However, in the wake of this victory there have been renewed arguments about the validity of this type of legislative strategy as a means of addressing the plight of the mentally ill and further doubts have been raised as to the ability of legal safeguards to perform their intended functions in psychiatric environments governed by alternative rationalities of therapy and discipline. Is authentic and effective legal protection a chimera after all?

In this chapter we will look at the opposed philosophies of mental health legislation which evaluate the contribution of law in such different terms, against the background of a closer examination of the multiplicity of functions that law can, and does, in fact, perform in psychiatric contexts.

Functions of Legislation in the Psychiatric Arena

It is a characteristic of the debate surrounding the relationship between law and psychiatry that it tends to counterpose medical discretion—in the interests of maximizing therapeutic success—and legal intervention to control this discretion—in the interests of protecting civil liberty. However, law is also involved in the regulation of mental health practices in the less invasive sense of constituting and defining the discretionary domain of mental health professionals in the first place. The complex provisions of Part IV of the Mental Health Act 1983 headed 'Consent to Treatment', for example, have both a negative and a positive function with respect to psychiatric power. In their negative aspect, they perform the inhibitive and restrictive function intended by the critics of the psychiatric profession, of debarring the administration of certain of the more serious medical treatments for mental disorder without the patient's consent and/or (depending upon the gravity of the treatment) a second opinion. But at the same time, in their positive aspect, these provisions equip the appropriate professionals with a legal mandate to deploy their expertise in the treatment of the mentally disordered, subject to compliance with the specified substantive and procedural limitations. The Mental Health Act 1983 recognizes the psychiatric, the social work, and the nursing professions, and accords them specific areas of competence. Law actually constitutes the mental health system, in the sense that it authoritatively constructs, empowers, and regulates the relationships between the agents who perform mental health functions. It is indeed a precondition of the operation of the complex and intricate mechanisms of control, surveillance, discipline, and reconstruction which assemble into an advanced mental health system. As Paul Hirst affirms in a critique of Michel Foucault's de-emphasis of law in the characterization of 'disciplinary society': 'There is no opposition between law and discipline . . . without a publicly assigned position and legally defined exclusiveness in the performance of their role, the key institutions and agents of the "disciplinary" region could not function: prisons, psychiatry, medicine, social work and so on.'[1]

Alternatives to legal regulation even at this basic level are imaginable. Strict regulation of the exercise of mental health skills dependent upon recognized qualifications and membership of

[1] P. Q. Hirst, 'Law, Socialism and Rights', in P. Carlen and M. Collison (eds.), *Radical Issues in Criminology*. Oxford: Martin Robertson, 1980, p. 92.

particular established professions could give way to a philosophy of 'let one hundred flowers bloom'. Exclusively voluntary and contractual relations could govern the supply of psychiatric services, with the public interest in controlling anti-social behaviour attributable to mental disorder being abandoned to the criminal law. Whatever the merits or demerits of such a marriage of anarchy and the market, the consequential social arrangements for solving the problem raised by mental pathology would not be recognizable as a mental health 'system' in its prevailing sense.

It is worth emphasizing the complementarity of law and medicine in the psychiatric sphere, of which this constitutive function of law is one instance. There is a long-standing tendency to treat legal and medical paradigms as antithetical, as in Kathleen Jones's *A History of the Mental Health Services*,[2] but this has more recently been balanced by an increasing appreciation of those features which they hold in common. As Roger Smith has demonstrated in his analysis of medico-legal conflict over the terms of the insanity plea in Victorian England,[3] the fundamentally deterministic discourse of medicine and the fundamentally voluntaristic discourse of law provide incompatible frameworks for a dialogue which, not surprisingly, is often unfruitful and acrimonious. Nevertheless, doctors and lawyers do possess the ability to play mutually supportive roles in the mental health system instead of becoming embroiled in conflicts of disciplinary perspective, and whether mutuality or antagonism predominates will tend to be dependent upon extrinsic social and political conditions.[4]

A number of general characteristics applicable to both professions suggest themselves. They include membership of the same social classes, a shared declaration of commitment to the ideals of professionalism and political conservatism. Toward the mentally disordered, both medical and legal approaches have traditionally adopted a posture of paternalism. In the legal approach this was the foundation of the jurisdiction over the person and property of lunatics and idiots originating in the medieval period. In medical approaches, it flows from the central contention that psychiatric

[2] K. Jones, *A History of the Mental Health Services*. London: Routledge and Kegan Paul, 1972, p. 153.

[3] R. Smith, *Trial by Medicine*. Edinburgh: Edinburgh University Press, 1981.

[4] Smith's analysis of conflict between doctors and lawyers in the nineteenth century is itself placed in the context of a recognition that 'at a more abstract and interpretative level, both sides and both discourses had fewer differences than they had things in common'. (p. 124.)

patients are afflicted by an illness which has the special character of depriving them of the ability to calculate their own best interests. Both legal and medical approaches are founded upon moral positions, albeit opposed. The legal position is one of concern to protect liberty unless there is good justification for its suppression, while the medical position is one of concern to alleviate the mental suffering inflicted by mental disorder. Both can therefore claim to be rooted in humane traditions, although the legal position is liable to attack from the medical perspective for insensitively subjecting the insane to procedural ordeals designed to meet the needs of the sane, and the medical from the legal for presumptuously imposing its ministrations upon the resistant. Furthermore, there exists a space for the notion of patients' rights in both discourses. The legal approach is a natural resort for patients anxious to protect their civil liberty against medical or other professional encroachment supported by therapeutic legitimations, but can also unite with the medical perspective to the extent that patients, as psychiatric consumers, assert their rights to an improved quality and range of psychiatric services. Patients who accept that their treatment is a medical province and recognize their own need for psychiatric care can proclaim their entitlement to services through the medium of legal rights. The co-operation of patients and their relatives within the National Schizophrenia Fellowship provides an example of patients becoming organized politically to pursue interests no more corrosive of medical prerogatives than kidney patients demanding more kidney machines. Finally, however uneasy their alliance, psychiatry and law are intimately interconnected and interdependent in the apparatuses of modern criminal justice, a relationship traceable to the emergence of a penality based upon the principles of the Enlightenment.[5] Psychiatric medicine has been one of the principal beneficiaries of what Michel Foucault describes as a fragmentation of the legal power to punish.[6] Law and psychiatry function as intersecting modalities of judgment and disposition in the control of crime.

A second main function of law in the psychiatric arena is that of determining the therapeutic division of labour, allocating their respective roles to the different sets of personnel engaged in mental health practices. In doing so, it accommodates competing profes-

[5] M. Foucault, *Discipline and Punish*. London: Allen Lane, 1977, pp. 16–23.
[6] Ibid., p. 21.

sional interests and establishes the hierarchy of professional authority in key areas of decision-making, especially those of commitment
and treatment. For example, while it does not seriously threaten the
hegemony of the medical profession, the Mental Health Act 1983
does reflect the weakened credibility of psychiatry since 1959 by
subjecting psychiatric decisions in relation to commitment, continued detention, and treatment to closer scrutiny and increased
review. By the same token, it accords new roles to other professions
working in the mental health services—social workers, clinical
psychologists, and nurses—in recognition of their growing strength
and status enhancement. Via the principle of multidisciplinary review
expressed in the consent to treatment provisions, and the complexion of the Mental Health Act Commission, the procedures and
structures erected to place a check upon psychiatric practitioners for
the protection of individual patients have simultaneously performed
the function of elevating other mental health professions.

Nikolas Rose has argued in a critique of the assault upon
psychiatric discretion by 'rights-strategists' that their victory does not
herald the liberation of the mentally disordered from social control
because 'the hidden agenda of such strategies entails a switch in
control from one agency to another—from doctors to psychothera-
pists, social workers or lawyers—or the advocacy of a new alignment
of professional sectors and powers'.[7] However, much depends upon
the content of the different knowledges which these alternative
arbiters of the fate of mental patients bring to bear in their
determinations. Whereas nursing, although it has its own traditions
and perspectives, is a paramedical profession, social work and clinical
psychology possess their own distinctive philosophies of the aetiology, nature, and treatment of mental disorder which are significantly
at odds with those of the medical profession. The dominant medical
orientation is still, as it was in the early nineteenth century, to a
concept of insanity as an organic pathology, whilst social work
stresses its sociogenic dimensions and clinical psychology the
psychopathological approach which has been relegated to a minority
influence within medicine. Furthermore, sections of those therapeutic professions and some lawyers, as extra-therapeutic monitors of
psychiatric practice, have taken on board elements of the theoretical
critiques of medical models of insanity which inform patients' rights

---

[7] N. Rose, 'Unreasonable Rights: Mental Illness and the Limits of the Law', *Journal of Law and Society* 12 (1985), p. 202.

movements. The theory is that they should therefore be able to provide a critical counterweight to medical rationality in hard cases, helping to promote a more liberal functioning of psychiatric power. It is in the achievement of an appropriate distribution of professional power within the mental health system that the route to increased individual liberty is seen to lie—a kind of Anti-Psychiatric translation of the checks and balances of Whig constitutionalism.

In the performance of this allocative function, law does not exclusively address the various professions jockeying for position, but also the question of the proper role to be accorded to the family. Amongst other provisions respecting the role of relatives, the Mental Health Act 1983 preserves the right of the patient's nearest relative to make an application for his compulsory admission to hospital or guardianship and his right to object to an application for admission for treatment or guardianship by a social worker.[8] It also extends the nearest relative's power of discharge to admission for assessment (formerly 'observation') as well as admission for treatment.[9] The family is thus assigned important rights and responsibilities in the operation of the compulsory powers under the Act. It can share responsibility for commitment but also reclaim the patient from psychiatric control. The role of the nearest relative as liberator is, however, critically restricted in that the responsible medical officer may furnish to the hospital managers a certificate of dangerousness which has the effect of barring this power of discharge.[10] Law draws the boundary line between the role of the family and that of the therapeutic professions, delimiting domestic and public spheres.

Thirdly, law performs that classic function most strongly advocated by lawyers and libertarians, of inhibiting and restricting psychiatric power in the interests of civil liberty and the accountability of the psychiatric profession as an agency of social control. The principle of the universality of the rule of law is pitted against a psychiatry characterized as a potentially arbitrary and oppressive concentration of power which threatens the legitimate autonomy of the individual. The concept of the rule of law emerged in seventeenth-century England and eighteenth-century Europe as an instrument in the political struggle to constitutionalize absolute monarchies. It is a

---

[8] Mental Health Act 1983, section 11(1), (4).

[9] Mental Health Act 1983, section 23(2)(a): compare Mental Health Act 1959, section 47(2)(a).

[10] Mental Health Act 1983, section 25.

defensive weapon which has generally been deployed to constrain that monopoly of legitimate force employed by the executive of the liberal state and exercised through the military, the police, penal institutions, and the bureaucracy in the form of direct coercive power—as in the refusal of the landed gentry of eighteenth-century England to countenance a standing army or a regular police force. However, it is advanced as an especially necessary check upon public psychiatry as a system of social control powerfully legitimated by justificatory therapeutic discourses which are not safely to be taken at face value. 'Soft' apparatuses of control, precisely because they function more by ideology, moral suasion, the generation of consent, images of healing, beneficence, and paternalism, may be said to require an acute legal scrutiny if the threats which they pose to civil liberty are to be successfully deflected. It is this role of law in relation to psychiatry which has been central to the confrontation between the guardians of professional discretion and the partisans of patients' rights, and which, when pressed beyond a certain minimal recognition, is liable to attract accusations of 'legalism'.

A fuller exploration of the issues raised by this inhibitory function will be undertaken below, but it may be noted at this stage that it is by no means the case that the legal measures championed by lawyers and libertarians are only capable of having a negative effect upon the standing of the psychiatric profession. Inhibition or restriction presupposes that there is a psychiatric dominion in place which must be subjected to controls. In terms of a radical Anti-Psychiatry it therefore follows that such 'legalism' is very much a second-best or half-way house. Thomas Szasz presents us with the vision of non-coercive 'contractual' psychiatry, responsive to the needs of its clients on the basis of market principles. This definition of liberation for the mentally disordered is economic rather than legal, with law operating as a framework for market relations. Elaborate legal safeguards surrounding commitment, forcible treatment, and other facets of coercion are necessary limits upon the persistently enduring structures of an 'institutional' psychiatry which it is his libertarian objective to supersede.[11] Some degree of legalism may be seen therefore as the price of survival for institutional psychiatry. Patients' rights fulfil much the same function in relation to the libertarian heaven of voluntarism as trade union rights of free collective

---

[11] T. Szasz, *Law, Liberty and Psychiatry*. London: Routledge and Kegan Paul, 1974, pp. 225–35.

bargaining within capitalism do in relation to the ultimate triumph of revolutionary socialism.

Furthermore, these very safeguards contribute to the execution of another legal function favourable to the psychiatric profession, namely the legitimation of psychiatric practices. At least three types of legitimating effect can be identified. Firstly, to the extent that the formal onus of the exercise of compulsory powers is shifted away from psychiatrists acting unilaterally and towards members of patients' families, social workers, magistrates, mental health review tribunals, or multidisciplinary panels, medical men themselves are absolved from responsibility and achieve a distance from the coercive operations of the mental health system. This effect helps to medicalize the psychiatrist's image, the role of healer being rendered more prominent at the expense of that of gaoler or technician of mental manipulation. It will be seen that the aspiration of medical men to resolve the apparent contradictions in the psychiatric mission between its therapeutic and custodial or control aspects plays an important part in explaining the positions they have adopted at various key stages in the evolution of modern mental health legislation. An example is *The Lancet's* at first sight surprising support in the 1880s for extending the requirement of a Justice's order before commitment from pauper to private patients, a reform to be embodied in the Lunacy Act 1890.

Secondly, the injection of greater legal safeguards against the excessive or unwarranted exercise of medical power tends to amount not to the transfer of effective decision-making from psychiatrists to other authorities, but to the increased mediation of psychiatrists' decisions by law. The validation of psychiatric decisions comes to depend not only upon their intrinsic medical merits, but upon their procedural rectitude. So, again invoking the consent to treatment provisions of the Mental Health Act 1983, if a psychiatrist wishes to prescribe a course of electroconvulsive therapy in a case falling within the relevant categories of detained patient, and that patient does not consent, he must obtain a second medical opinion and the second doctor must consult with a nurse and some other non-medical person professionally concerned with the patient's treatment.[12] Now, proper adherence to these procedural checks produces a powerful reason for public acceptance of such decisions. It is a classic instance of Max Weber's first type of legitimate domination, legal domination,

---

[12] Mental Health Act 1983, section 58.

in which obedience is accorded to decisions on the basis of their conformity to legality.[13] A 'legalistic' model of mental health legislation may encumber psychiatric prerogatives, but in doing so it commits decision-making to a formal, rule-bound pattern which is capable of generating legitimacy in its own right. In addition to this there is the substantively based legitimacy which flows from the (enforced) solicitation of medical second opinions (nearly always concurring in practice)[14] and consultation with representatives of other relevant disciplines. Psychiatry is enabled to bathe in the light of 'accountability' and to free itself from some of that degree of public suspicion which attaches to closed, exclusive, and autocratic orders in a society with vaunted liberal traditions.

Thirdly, legal challenges to monopolistic medical control of those patients whose care, even in the age of 'the community' as panacea, is still mental hospital based may actually have the effect of accelerating the medicalization of the asylum, so, paradoxically, sustaining its role. This is an argument advanced by Robert Castel and his co-authors, who maintain that legal struggles in Alabama in 1970 brought about

the improvement in living conditions, the increase in specialized personnel, and the greater rigour in deciding the validity of admissions (which) was . . . to assure the permanence of the asylum within the psychiatric landscape. Along with other similar legal forms of challenge to psychiatric autonomy within the asylum, what was achieved at least in part was a more precise specification of the conditions under which one of psychiatry's domains was to be guaranteed, an *aggiornamento* of the psychiatric hospital rather than its subordination to a variety of external controls.[15]

Similarly, Nikolas Rose has argued that the pursuit of decarceration via civil libertarian insistence upon a right to treatment in the 'least restrictive alternative'

effectively contributes to the modernization of psychiatry, by freeing it from those aspects of its social role which de-legitimize it. The use of mental hospitals as a repository for those whose only 'illness' is that they are unable to cope with the demands of a life outside casts doubt upon the therapeutic potential of psychiatry; their use as custodial institutions for those whose

[13] See M. Weber, *The Theory of Social and Economic Organization*. New York: Free Press, 1984, pp. 328 ff.
[14] See, *Biennial Report of the Mental Health Act Commission*, 1985, p. 38.
[15] P. Miller's review of F. Castel, R. Castel, and A. Lovell, *La Société Psychiatrique Avancée*: 'Psychiatry—the Renegotiation of a Territory', *Ideology and Consciousness* 8 (1981), pp. 102–3.

only 'illness' is that they are a 'danger to society' casts doubt upon the medical legitimacy of psychiatry. Hence the strategy forms one element in the annexation of psychiatry to general medicine ... and the utilization of non-medical institutions (from the prison to the social service group home) for the containment of those populations not amenable to therapy.[16]

Civil libertarianism may sharpen the boundary between the medical–psychiatric on the one hand and the penal–social defensive on the other. Pat Carlen observes in relation to the diagnosis of 'personality disorder' in her study of women imprisoned at Cornton Wood Prison in Scotland that

Psychiatrists have taken the anti-psychiatry movement's argument that the notion of illness must imply the possibility of treatment and they have turned it on its head. If they, *as psychiatrists*, do not *know* of any way of 'treating' the 'disturbed' person who is also an offender then they will use their privileged position *as psychiatrists* to make a *judicial* judgment—the person knew what she was doing, she needs a discipline setting; hospitals are for treatment not for discipline, therefore the disturbed offender must go to prison.[17]

Another positive function of legal regulation of the mental health system is to provide for the establishment of additional institutions and services. The creation of new legal powers and duties to provide particular services has figured prominently in all of the last three major items of English mental health legislation: the Mental Treatment Act 1930, the Mental Health Act 1959, and the Mental Health Act 1983. Each of these measures was founded upon a distinct dogma and was hailed in its turn, not as a self-executing revolution, but as an exciting threshold, an inspirational opportunity to implement a new philosophy. Thus, the Mental Treatment Act was the legislative embodiment of the conviction that 'there is no clear line of demarcation between mental and physical illness'[18] and therefore that the 'problem of insanity is essentially a public health problem to be dealt with on modern public health lines'.[19] The architects of the Mental Health Act 1959 looked forward to the decline of the mental hospital with the maximum decarceration of harmless 'chronic' inmates into facilities of 'Community Care'. The

[16] N. Rose, 'Unreasonable Rights', p. 211.
[17] P. Carlen, *Women's Imprisonment*. London: Routledge and Kegan Paul, 1983, p. 203.
[18] *Report of the Royal Commission on Lunacy and Mental Disorder* (Cmd. 2700, 1926), para. 38.
[19] Ibid., para. 50.

Mental Health Act 1983 enshrines the concept of patients' rights, not only in the sphere of formal liberties such as the right to resist irreversible and hazardous treatments, but also in the sense of positive or substantive rights, rights to treatment and services. Legal backing for the provision of appropriate therapeutic facilities was an integral feature of each of these dogmatic strategies for the promotion of national mental health. So, in the case of the Mental Treatment Act, local authorities were legally empowered, *inter alia*, to establish psychiatric clinics, preferably to be affiliated to general hospitals, and designed for the reception of incipient and recoverable cases of mental illness to be admitted as 'temporary' or voluntary patients without certification as of unsound mind. This represented an attempt to secure institutional assimilation of the treatment of early and curable cases of mental illness to that of the physically ill, giving a wide berth to the stigmatizing and deterrent presence of the asylum and easing the interaction of mental and physical medicine in the treatment of mentally ill patients.[20] It is interesting that in the largely quiescent House of Commons debates which preceded the adoption of the Mental Health Act 1959 one issue which sparked real controversy was whether the legal responsibilities of local authorities to provide alternative 'community' forms of care had effectively been rendered mandatory. The Percy Commission, reporting in 1957, had recommended a positive duty, proposing that a Ministerial directive be issued under section 28 of the National Health Service Act 1946 so that action need not await the passage of new legislation.[21] The Conservative Government complied with this, but then declined to follow the supporting recommendations in favour of special financial assistance to local authorities, in the face of strong Labour objections that the new block grant system of local government finance would subvert the supposedly mandatory basis of community mental health services.[22] The Mental Health Act 1983 instals a new duty in respect of non-hospital mental health facilities. Section 117 of the Act imposes a duty upon the district health authority and the local social services authority, 'in co-operation with relevant voluntary agencies', to provide after-care services for patients detained under an

---

[20] See Chapter 5 of the present work.

[21] *Report of the Royal Commission on the Law Relating to Mental Illness and Mental Deficiency* (Cmnd. 169, 1957), para. 715.

[22] This remained a point of contention at Third Reading: see the speech of Edith Summerskill from the Opposition Front Bench, *House of Commons Debates*, 605, cols. 410–11 (6 May 1959).

application for admission for treatment under section 3, together with certain categories of mentally abnormal offender. The Act reflects the principle that patients should be treated in the 'least restrictive alternative' championed by Larry Gostin in MIND's campaign for mental health law reform, not only as a libertarian argument for decarceration but also as the basis for a positive legal obligation upon Government to make available the consequentially necessary community alternatives.[23]

In the past, the most striking fact about this aspect of mental health legislation has been the signal failure of legal provisions to generate new services, falling prey to political and financial pressures. Reporting at the end of the first year's operation of the Mental Treatment Act 1930 the Board of Control (the mental health system's then legal watchdog and administrative overlord) bemoaned the fact that, albeit faced with practical and financial difficulties, local authorities had as yet failed to provide separate admission units within mental hospitals for the reception of new patients, recalling that 'when Parliament passed the Mental Treatment Act, it was an implied condition that suitable accommodation should be provided for recent cases, whether voluntary, temporary or certified patients . . . indeed in the case of temporary patients, the provision of suitable accommodation was made obligatory.'[24] At the Committee stage of the House of Lords debate on the Mental Health Bill in 1959, Lord Pakenham summarized a very general concern in relation to clause 6, dealing with local authority powers to develop community services:

But whether these powers we are conferring on local authorities have been hitherto mandatory, permissive or non-existent, or whether it is not quite clear what their status was, they have up till now been used on a scale which in no way matches up to what we all insist on in future as a necessity. We are, in fact, calling on local authorities to expand their services to a degree which virtually constitutes a new service.[25]

Yet in a devastating indictment of 'Community Care' in both Britain and the United States penned in 1983, Andrew Scull was able to instance 'the absence of the necessary infrastructure of services and

[23] Under this principle 'the use of compulsory powers must be the least invasive of individual liberty and autonomy as is necessary for the achievement of valid public objectives': see L. O. Gostin, 'Contemporary Social Historical Perspectives on Mental Health Reform', *Journal of Law and Society* 10 (1983), p. 50.
[24] *Annual Report of the Board of Control for the Year 1930*, pp. 10–11.
[25] *House of Lords Debates* 217, col. 104 (23 June 1959).

financial supports without which talk about community care is
simply a sham', referring to the mere £6.5 million spent on
residential and day-care services for patients outside hospital in
1973–4 in comparison with the £300 million reserved for the
institutional sector.[26] Whether an aggressive strategy of pursuing
the objective of adequate services through litigation on the basis of
individual patients' legal rights, as advocated by MIND, will
ameliorate this depressing situation can be gravely doubted, given
that in the United States a substantially more advanced development of such rights has not prevented the appearance there, in the
absence of appropriate public services, of what Scull describes as
nothing less than 'a new trade in lunacy, as entrepreneurial
industry resembling the private madhouse of eighteenth-century
England.'[27] The failure of governmental response to 'scandals' in
the treatment of the mentally disordered when the solution is new
capital investment is all too obvious from the slow pace at which
Regional Secure Units have materialized despite the frequency
with which sentencing judges have lamented the necessity to
dispatch mentally abnormal offenders to prison for lack of a
mental hospital able and willing to receive them.[28] In an era of the
virtual incorporation of the local state by central government in
the interests of rigid monetary discipline, the political and financial
barriers to the substantial expansion of local authority services for
the mentally ill are almost unprecedentedly daunting.

From perhaps the most immediately material category of legislative
functions we now turn to examine the ideological dimension of
mental health legislation as the statutory inscription of an official
conception of insanity. Given that the character of legislation is
normative rather than descriptive, it would not be expected to
incorporate definitive proclamations about insanity, but bodies of
statutory rules cohering into systems of regulation do necessarily
express underlying assumptions regarding their subject matter. The
Lunacy Act 1890 in its elaboration of a complex regime of
procedures to govern the compulsory institutionalization of the
insane offers an eloquent commentary upon the moral stigmatization

[26] A. T. Scull, *Decarceration*, 2n edn. Cambridge: Polity Press, 1984, p. 169.
[27] Ibid., p. 164.
[28] The first permanent Regional Secure Unit was opened at St. Luke's, Middlesbo-
rough, in November 1980. For further details of the early stages of implementation of
Regional Secure Unit policy, see *House of Commons Debates* 65, Written Answers, cols.
351–2 (1 August 1984).

of insanity prevalent in late nineteenth-century England and the correlative state of psychiatry: custodial, stagnant, and suspect. At a more innovative juncture, legislation may assume an almost missionary role as a vehicle for the authoritative public transmission of a specific reformist ideology of insanity. This was so in the case of the Mental Treatment Act 1930, which was strategic to the self-consciously enlightened campaign of the psychiatric profession, the Board of Control, and allied welfare organizations to propagate the conception of psychiatric disorder as a species of illness and appropriately treated in association with general medicine. The need to educate the populace to this view was essential to the work of destigmatizing psychiatric institutions and personnel as the prelude to a radical expansion of the frontiers of psychiatric medicine. Transformations of statutory language were one mechanism: 'asylum' became 'mental hospital' and 'pauper lunatic' became 'rate-aided patient of unsound mind'.[29] Such translations from an older discourse encrusted with antique and moralistic notions into the terms of a consistently medical discourse were the necessary recognition of a new official 'truth' about insanity and also functional to psychiatric expansion. Similarly, the title of a new measure of legislation, as its most frequently cited and therefore most widely resonant form of words, may be selected to encapsulate a particular message for mass consumption. The choice of the words 'mental health' rather than 'mental illness' or 'mental treatment' for the title of the 1959 Act reflected an acceptance of the broadening of psychiatric horizons beyond a narrow concern with the eradication of mental illness to extend to the much more ambitious and politically intoxicating aspiration of cultivating positive national mental health.[30]

The educative intent of mental health legislation may also be addressed specifically to those responsible for the day-to-day operation of the mental health system. Commended standards of practice and procedure may be accorded statutory force or enjoined by a Code of Practice, and their observance policed by Commissioners. The Mental Health Act 1983 adopted this approach of reliance upon a central supervisory body to promote good practice in preference to a more thoroughgoing entrenchment of individual

[29] Mental Treatment Act 1930, section 20.
[30] For comment on the significance of the title as a symbol of the positive and preventive reorientation of psychiatry, see E. Summerskill *House of Commons Debates* 598, col. 727 (26 January 1959).

patient rights,[31] and the production of a Code of Practice was allocated as one of its primary responsibilities to the new Mental Health Act Commission.[32]

A final function of law is to define the legal status of mental patients, determining how far they are constructed as legal subjects with the capacity to exercise an array of rights and how far their status is modified on the ground of the special characteristics of mental disorder, so that they become 'subjects' in the quite different sense that their freedom of choice is subordinated to professional judgment. Legal discrimination against mental patients may affect their civil and social status in respect of a whole range of matters—management of property, enfranchisement, access to the courts, jury service, correspondence, licence to drive—and in terms of the history of English mental health legislation such discrimination has been a feature common both to the 'legalistic' legislation of the late Victorian period and the early and mid-twentieth-century legislation which amended and then replaced it. It was, for example, at the high-water mark of 'legalism' that a procedural bar was introduced to restrict aggrieved patients' access to the courts for redress against those executing functions under lunacy legislation. With a special view to the protection of medical men from suit for signing certificates of insanity for the purpose of commitment, section 12 of the Lunacy Acts Amendment Act 1889 provided that the defendant might stay the proceedings by proving that there was no prima-facie case that he acted in bad faith or without reasonable care. The Mental Treatment Act 1930, which in most respects seriously undermined the legislative structures bequeathed in 1889–90, actually fortified this obstruction by shifting the onus to the plaintiff to obtain leave from the High Court before bringing proceedings and by increasing the standard of proof from prima-facie to substantial grounds.[33] It is only with the 1983 Act that the aim of enhancing the civil and social status of patients by minimizing their automatic legal disabilities has made a significant impact upon the shape of English mental health legislation.[34]

[31] See Kenneth Clarke, Minister of Health, *House of Commons Debates*, Special Standing Committee on the Mental Health Amendment Bill, 21st Sitting, col. 797 (29 June 1982).

[32] Mental Health Act 1983, section 118.

[33] Mental Treatment Act 1930, section 16.

[34] See L. O. Gostin, 'Contemporary Social Historical Perspectives', pp. 61–6.

Legalism

Although the relationship between law and psychiatry in the civil sphere is so multifaceted, the main conflict of view in relation to the philosophy of mental health legislation in England since the late nineteenth century has been over the extent to which legal intervention should inhibit psychiatric power, that is, how far legislation should be pervaded by 'legalism'. Kathleen Jones is to be credited with responsibility for the introduction of the term 'legalism' into the historical literature on mental health legislation. In *A History of the Mental Health Services* (1972), a revised and extended edition of two earlier studies, *Lunacy, Law and Conscience, 1744–1845* (1955) and *Mental Health and Social Policy, 1845–1959* (1960), she characterized the Lunacy Act 1890, because it was primarily addressed to preventing wrongful detention by the imposition of legal controls, as marking 'the triumph of legalism'.[35] In the same work she defines three approaches to legislation which have jostled for acceptance in recent history: the medical approach, 'blurring the distinction between mental health and physical disorders' and emphasizing physical treatment; the social approach, emphasizing human relations; and the legal approach, dominated by procedure and concerned with the protection of 'the liberty of the subject'.[36] These distinct shades of emphasis are presented as being associated with individual measures of legislation: the Lunacy Act 1890 is defined as reflective of the legal approach and the Mental Treatment Act 1930 as medical in orientation, while it is implied that the Mental Health Act 1959 combined medical and social approaches. The terms 'legalism' and 'legal approach' appear to denote the same concept.

Use of the term 'legalism' to describe an approach to mental health legislation is problematic. Kathleen Jones is a long-standing critic of the legal approach and 'legalism' is clearly employed pejoratively: in relation to the Lunacy Act 1890 it is described as 'piling safeguard upon safeguard to protect the sane against illegal detention, delaying certification and treatment until the person genuinely in need of care was obviously (and probably incurably) insane'.[37] These pejorative connotations cause difficulty if it is desired to use the term simply for definitional purposes. A variety of alternatives are available in the literature. Peter Sedgwick, in *Psycho Politics*, in discussion of the

[35] 'The Triumph of Legalism' is the title of Chapter 7, on the Lunacy Act 1890, and was previously the title of Part One of *Mental Health and Social Policy*.

[36] K. Jones, *A History of the Mental Health Services*, p. 153.

[37] Id.

emergence of the Mental Health Act 1983, although frequently
invoking 'legalism' also uses 'civil libertarianism'.[38] Peter Miller, in a
review article presenting Robert Castel's *L'Ordre Psychiatrique* for an
English language readership, renders the concept by 'juridism' as
well as 'legalism'.[39] Nikolas Rose, in a critique of MIND's campaign
leading up to the Mental Health Act 1983, employs the term 'rights-
based strategy,'[40] while Larry Gostin's concept of an 'ideology of
entitlement' could serve, once redefined to embrace formal civil
liberties as well as positive rights to mental health services.[41]
However, 'legalism' is now too well entrenched in discourse about
mental health legislation to be jettisoned. Certain of the possible
substitutes canvassed above would only be appropriate in the context
of the 1983 Act. Lord Halsbury, champion of lunacy reform in the
period prior to 1890, could hardly be designated a 'civil libertarian',
especially in the light of his attempt to block the establishment of
effective trade unionism at the turn of the century.[42] All the authors
just cited make some use of the term, and it will now be adopted,
rescued from quotation marks, and furnished with a definition for
present purposes.

A general definition of legalism has been provided by Judith
Shklar, who describes it as 'the ethical attitude that holds moral
conduct to be a matter of rule following and moral relationships to
consist of duties and rights determined by rules'.[43] In the psychiatric
context, this morality of rule-bound relationships is focused upon
relationships between mental health professionals, especially psychiatrists, and their patients or clients, and entails the superimposition of
legal duties and rights upon therapeutic and social responsibilities
and expectations, principally for the protection of the patient or
potential patient. The rule of law takes priority, if necessary at the
expense of other considerations, including that which is deemed to

---

[38] P. Sedgwick, *Psycho Politics*, London: Pluto Press, 1982: see especially pp. 212–21.
[39] P. Miller, 'The Territory of the Psychiatrist', *Ideology and Consciousness*, 7 (1980),
p. 63.
[40] N. Rose, 'Unreasonable Righrs, *passim*.
[41] L. O. Gostin, 'Contemporary Social Historical Perspectives', pp. 49–55, and 'The
Ideology of Entitlement: the Application of Contemporary Legal Approaches to
Psychiatry' in P. Bean (ed.), *Mental Illness: Changes and Trends*. Chichester: John Wiley,
1983, p. 27.
[42] See J. A. G. Griffith, *The Politics of the Judiciary*, 2nd edn. London: Fontana, 1981,
pp. 62–5.
[43] J. N. Shklar, *Legalism*. Cambridge, Mass.: Harvard University Press, 1964, p. 1.
See also C. N. Campbell, 'Legal Thought and Juristic Values', *British Journal of Law and
Society* 1 (1974), p. 21.

be optimally therapeutic by professionals. It is this which has produced the collision of perspectives with which this chapter began. Here law is performing its inhibitory function: psychiatry is in the dock. However, law itself is laid open to attack in performing this function by those like Kathleen Jones who invest the term 'legalism' with an emotive, accusatory inflection. As an accusation, legalism comprises a number of related charges. The foremost of these, and one which spokesmen for MIND were very anxious to deflect in their campaign to reform the Mental Health Act 1959, is the charge of legal formalism: that there is a misguided preoccupation with procedural correctness rather than, or at a cost to, the substantive goals which in its constitutive aspect law is intended to facilitate the mental health system in achieving. An associated notion is that of legal vandalism: that psychiatric processes are disrupted and damaged by legal interference. Another element is the insistence that to structure mental health legislation around the assumptions of legalism is sheer legal overkill: in practice, it is contended, there is only a minimal likelihood of abuse as the professions involved are trustworthy. Professional ethics all but solve the problem and legislation should not be designed with the exceptional case in mind if the effect is to impede the psychiatric enterprise in general. The charge of legal ignorance is a further powerful component of anti-legalism: that legal expertise is therapeutically irrelevant. The problem of liberty is only raised incidentally. Lawyers can make no direct contribution to treatment or cure and legal personnel and procedures should therefore be peripheral to the mental health system. This attitude is well illustrated by the view of Lord Dawson of Penn, an eminent physician, in the course of debate in the House of Lords on the Mental Treatment Bill in 1929:

It is true of medicine, as of any skilled calling, that it becomes so technical that you have to trust the people who have studied the calling. That is going to be a problem of government in the future . . . We are not going to have our skilled opinions overhauled by local magistrates who don't understand the A,B,C of our profession.[44]

One final charge, levelled, for reasons that will be examined later, against the Lunacy Act 1890 but not the Mental Health Act 1983, is that of legal stigmatization: that legalistic procedure imports a trial model into the commitment process which quasi-criminalizes the mental hospital population and thus conspires in their social ostracization.

[44] *House of Lords Debates* 75, col. 756 (28 November 1929).

Controversy over the extent to which solutions to a particular social problem should be mediated by legal forms, structures, concepts, and personnel is of course by no means confined to the sphere of mental health. In some departments of society, for example property relations, legalism is largely taken for granted, while in others, such as ordinary domestic family relations, it is regarded as so alien that its introduction can be the subject of comic fantasy.[45] But there are areas, of which mental health is one, where there exists a continuing debate about the merits of legal mediation. To take the case of the management of conflict in industrial relations, the extent to which different forms of industrial action and internal trade union organization should be controlled by the courts has been central to political debate since the late 1960s. On the very different question of how to channel compensation to accident victims the involvement of lawyers has also been seriously at issue. Critics of the tort system, where recovery is generally restricted by the precondition that the accident was fault caused, have argued for reform in the direction of a state-sponsored no-fault accident compensation scheme in which it is envisaged that routine bureaucratic processes would largely displace legal disputation and the enormous administrative costs associated with litigating fault would be cut out.[46] A further example is the subject of police powers, where the primary concern of the police with order maintenance rather than law enforcement has traditionally produced antipathy to what is seen as lawyers' diversionary obsession with procedural propriety in such matters as the collection of incriminating evidence. The Police and Criminal Evidence Act 1984, whilst it undoubtedly increases police powers, also formalizes them and has provoked considerable hostility from sections of the police who fear that it will become a lawyers' charter and a bureaucratic nightmare.[47]

Movements back and forth between the poles of legalism and anti-legalism in these areas where the role of law is controversial are

[45] As in W. Twining and D. R. Miers' employment of the figure of the legalistic child to illustrate problems of juristic technique in *How To Do Things with Rules*, 2nd edn. London: Weidenfeld and Nicolson, 1982.

[46] Annual administrative costs have been calculated as being as high as 45% of the total of actual compensation payments plus administration. See P. S. Atiyah, *Accidents, Compensation and the Law*, 3rd edn. London: Weidenfeld and Nicolson, 1980, p. 511; and see also D. R. Harris *et al.*, *Compensation and Support for Illness and Injury*. Oxford: Clarendon Press, 1984.

[47] The Home Secretary, Leon Brittan, faced a demonstration of such opposition at the 1985 Annual Conference of the Police Federation, the association of rank and file police officers.

instructive as indicators of broader social and political change. Rather as Emile Durkheim employed the changing form of legal sanctions as a 'visible symbol' of underlying shifts in the type of social solidarity, or moral integration, in a society,[48] so the degree of legalism in the regulation of certain key social practices may serve as an index of significant changes in the relationship between state and society. This is manifest in the instance of industrial relations. The graduated restoration of legalism achieved by the Conservative Goverment's Employment Acts 1980 and 1982, and Trade Union Act 1984 represents the rejection of the 1974–9 Labour Government's corporatist strategy, in which the leadership of the trade union movement were recruited to enforce government policies of industrial discipline and wage restraint by the mechanism of the Social Contract.[49] In its place has been planted a strategy, embodying the philosophy of economic liberalism, which is at once libertarian in its assertion of the rights of individual workers, whether unionized or not, and authoritarian in its harnessing of state power to protect those rights by the suppression of demonstrations of collective trade union strength. It is a strategy within which the rhetoric of 'the rule of law' and that of 'law and order' intersect, the trade unions being portrayed as potentially and often in actuality arbitrary and oppressive concentrations of power against which individuals need to be protected by the grant of rights to legal redress, and the police presence in industrial conflict being increased in order to ensure that expressions of this economic and legal individualism are respected.

Although the political contingency of legalism may not be so obvious in the case of mental health legislation, there are demonstrable links between the decline of legalism in the first half of the twentieth century and the growth of social intervention culminating in the creation of the welfare state. The recent revival of legalism may be interpreted as evidence of the disintegration of the political consensus upon which the institutional fabric of the welfare state was built and the emergence of an influential liberal individualist critique of its original paternalistic ethos. The Mental Health Act 1983 in fact provides a very good example of the reassertion of *gesellschaft* legal traditions, that is, forms of law associated with the market economy

---

[48]   E. Durkheim, *The Division of Labour in Society*. New York: Free Press, 1964, p. 64.

[49]   For a good analysis of the politics of the Employment Act 1980, see P. Kahn *et al.*, *Picketing: industrial disputes, tactics and the law*. London: Routledge and Kegan Paul, 1983.

and individualism and dominant in the nineteenth century, to which David Nelken has drawn attention in rebuttal of the argument that legal ideology is in crisis in face of the relentless expansion of mechanical bureaucratic–administrative regulation.[50]

If the political complexion of mental health legislation is to be properly understood, then it becomes necessary to explore further this political and historical basis of legalism. The controversy over legalism has its conditions of possibility in a tension in liberal social order as it emerged in late eighteenth- and early nineteenth-century Europe. It will be seen that it was this liberal epoch, marked by the expansion of the market economy with the rise of industrial capitalism, and the adaptation of the structures of the state to the requirements of constitutionalism and the early stages of democratization, that produced the foundations of the modern mental health system. The tension in liberal order lay between the commitment to the legal restraint of state power in the interests of individual liberty and the exertion of discipline in the prisons, workhouses, asylums, and other non-institutional mechanisms which in their different ways buttressed the essentials of that order: the sanctity of private property, the pliability of labour, the rigorous observance of bourgeois morality. It is a tension evident in the philosophy of Jeremy Bentham himself as the very embodiment of the governing values and also the governing contradictions of his age. Benthamism could be regarded as a monumental conceptual and programmatic systematization of *laissez-faire* and yet was later to be claimed as part of their intellectual heritage by the Fabian Socialists.[51] On the one hand, Bentham conceived the social order in starkly individualistic terms, social equilibrium being the product of individuals rationally pursuing their own self-interest within legal structures which by the appropriate distribution of deterrent sanctions channelled their energies away from activities which threatened the security of person or property. Bentham's hedonistic calculus, whereby motivation was understood as the maximization of pleasure and the minimization of pain, may be seen as very much the ethical and psychological counterpart of the calculation of profit and loss which was the motor of the ascendant free-market economy. On the other hand, Bentham was the secular archpriest of rational organization in public affairs.

---

[50] D. Nelken, 'Is there a Crisis in Law and Legal Ideology?', *Journal of Law and Society* 9 (1982), pp. 185–8.

[51] B. Webb and S. Webb, *English Poor Law History Part II: the last hundred years*. London: Longmans Green, 1929, p. 552.

The legislator was charged with maximizing the sum of individual happiness and he had to establish the conditions within which the interaction of rational individuals could be mechanically self-regulating. Bentham proposed Ministers for Indigence Relief, Interior Communications, Education, Health, and Preventive Services[52] and in his later writings was increasingly concerned with engineering the creation of minimum living standards.[53] He advocated the liberalization and rationalization of criminal penalties to render them predictable and proportionate to the crime, thus liberating the individual from the threat of arbitrary and oppressive state reprisal,[54] but was also the architect of the Panopticon, the prototype for the institutionally-mediated imposition of total discipline and surveillance 'to grind rogues honest and idle men industrious . . .'.[55] Although individuals were presumed to be autonomous and freely choosing, the principle upon which they exercised choice being known—namely the pursuit of pleasure and the avoidance of pain—so in the environment of the total institution they could be manipulated into a condition of determined docility.

This dochotomy in liberal social order has been characterized and explained in different ways. According to Karl Marx, it follows naturally from the structure of the capitalist mode of production in which labour-power itself, the capacity to labour, has become a commodity, a marketable quantity. The economy of capitalism consists of two spheres: the realm of production and the market, the site of distribution. In a much-cited passage of *Capital*, Marx refers ironically to 'the republic of the market':

This sphere . . . within whose boundaries the sale and purchase of labour-power goes on, is in fact a very Eden of the innate rights of man. There alone rule Freedom, Equality, Property and Bentham because both buyer and seller of a commodity, say labour-power, are constrained only by their own free will . . . Equality, because each enters into relations with the other, as with a simple owner of commodities and they exchange equivalent for equivalent. Property, because each disposes only of what is his own. And Bentham because each looks only to himself.[56]

[52] Id.

[53] D. J. Manning, *The Mind of Jeremy Bentham*. London: Longmans Green, 1968, pp. 91–2, 96.

[54] *Introduction to the Principles of Morals and Legislation*, ed. J. H. Burns and H. L. A. Hart. London: Methuen, 1982.

[55] Bentham to Brissot in *Works*, ed. J. Bowring. Edinburgh: Tait, 1843, x, p. 226, quoted in A. T. Scull, *Decarceration*, p. 26. See J. Bentham, *Panopticon*. London: Payne, 1791.

[56] K. Marx, *Capital*, volume 1. London: Lawrence and Wishart, 1970, p. 176.

The market is therefore a sphere of equality and freedom, albeit only formal, but this is contrasted with the sphere of production and the despotic realm of the factory. For it is in the process of production that the exploitation of labour takes place by the extraction of surplus value and it is here that substantive social inequalities are continually regenerated. In the market, the seller of labour-power is formally a free agent, but once his labour-power is sold he is at the disposal of the purchasing employer and enters a region of discipline. Thus, in a society in which the capitalist mode of production is dominant, there is an impetus to preserve the formal liberty, equality, and justice which are the counterpart of the market, but there is also an impetus to the creation and refinement of institutions and mechanisms which can perform repressive functions of social discipline over the labouring population.

Eugeny Pashukanis, the foremost Soviet legal theorist of the early post-revolutionary period, allocated law itself to the market sphere, developing a commodity-exchange theory of law in which the legal form of social relations was given a material basis in the capitalist mode of production. The formal values of the market satirized by Marx above are also the values enshrined in law. Pashukanis argued that the defining characteristics of legal personality—freedom, equality, will, the capacity to bear rights—are necessarily presupposed in the situation of exchange in the market. The legal subject is nothing other than 'the abstract owner of commodities raised to the heavens'[57] and bourgeois notions of natural law, legality, social contract, and common humanity but the universal idealizations of a transient form of distributive economic mechanism tied to a system which is, in its productive sphere of operation, exploitative and oppressive.

Michel Foucault also contrasts the spheres of law and discipline, but produces an account which avoids economic determinism and presents the growth of technologies of discipline as a precondition of capitalist success.[58] For Foucault, the burgeoning of elaborate disciplinary apparatuses in modern Europe undermines rather than, as might seem the case, realizes law: discipline should therefore be regarded as 'counter-law' rather than 'infra-law'. He offers a history of this antinomy in which the movement toward liberal individualism,

[57] E. B. Pashukanis, *Law and Marxism: A General Theory* (trans. B. Einhorn, ed. C. Arthur). London: Ink Links, 1978, p. 121.
[58] See H. L. Dreyfus and P. Rabinow, *Michel Foucault: Beyond Structuralism and Hermeneutics*. Brighton: Harvester Press, 1982, p. 135.

representative democracy, and the rule of law was accompanied by the development of the political rationality of *raison d'état*, the increase of state power over the subject population as an end in itself. This rationality was theorized from the Renaissance onwards in police and technical manuals and was reflected in the multiplication of new disciplinary technologies. Practised in such contexts as workshops, barracks, prisons, schools, and hospitals, they concerned the classification, spatial and temporal arrangement, intimate observation, recording, and behavioural modification of populations. Bentham's *Panopticon* serves Foucault as a characteristic programme for the imposition of such discipline. He observes:

Historically, the process by which the bourgeoisie became in the course of the eighteenth century the politically dominant class was masked by the establishment of an explicit, coded and formally egalitarian juridical framework, made possible by the organization of a parliamentary representative regime. But the development and generalization of disciplinary mechanisms constituted the other dark side of these processes... The 'enlightenment', which discovered the liberties also invented the disciplines... although the universal juridicism of modern society seems to fix limits on the exercise of power, its universally widespread panopticism enables it to operate, on the underside of the law, a machinery that is both immense and minute, which supports, reinforces, multiplies the asymmetry of power and undermines the limits which are traced around the law.[59]

The way in which 'the legal fiction of the work contract' is undermined by workshop discipline is given as but one example of this process of subversion.

In certain senses there is no real contradiction between Bentham's *laissez-faire* individualism and interventionist determinism, between Marx's two spheres, or between the juridical and the disciplinary as portrayed by Foucault. They function in mutual support to produce a particular type of social order. So Bentham's programmes for expanded public intervention and blueprints for total institutions were designed to optimize the conditions for the functioning of the market and a political order based on private property: to reproduce individuals who exhibited the autonomy and rationality definitive of

[59] M. P. Foucault, *Discipline and Punish*, pp. 222–3. For an interesting discussion of these two classic passages from Marx and Foucault see J. Lea, 'Discipline and Capitalist Development' in B. Fine (ed.), *Capitalism and the Rule of Law*. London: Hutchinson, 1979, p. 76. See also J. Palmer and F. Pearce, 'Legal Discourse and State Power: Foucault and the Juridical Relation' *International Journal of the Sociology of Law* 11 (1983), p. 361.

humanity in liberal theory, but only of types recognizable to and compatible with that order. In Marxist analysis, also, law as the repository of the values of formal liberty, equality, and justice derived from relations in the setting of the market provides an important medium through which bourgeois class interest can be projected as universal. In thus contributing to the maintenance of hegemony, it sustains the unfree, unequal, and expedient relations which confront the seller of labour-power in the setting of production. It has already been seen that law, although counterposed to discipline by Foucault, is also constitutive of the disciplinary region.[60]

The dichotomy between the juridical and disciplinary aspects of modern social order does not therefore amount to an antagonistic contradiction. But however reciprocal their relationship may be in certain practical respects, they remain sharply in conflict in the abstract, involving as they do quite polarized valuations of the individual founded in the contrasting politics of liberal individualism and *raison d'état*. Their coexistence opens up a whole terrain of debates surrounding the treatment of social problems from suicide to football hooliganism, and also the possibility of a range of conceptions of society, from an individualistic libertarianism, which displaces the liberal notion of the autonomous individual from its formal contractual context and attempts to reproduce it in fully social terms, to the negative Utopia of society as total institution. The potential for clashes between these discordant tendencies is minimized by the demarcation of the settings where juridical discourse is appropriate from those where discipline holds sway, but in many areas, including mental health, the boundaries are at issue and each sphere remains vulnerable to charges that its practices should be reconstructed in the terms of the other. Hence the problem of legalism, the unsettled question of to what extent psychiatric processes, as a department of the disciplines, should be evaluated and regulated in juridical terms.

It is possible to appreciate why the problem of legalism is so persistent by considering the history of civil commitment. The broad historical movement has been toward the displacement of judicial by medical control. Robert Castel has explained the origins of psychiatric dominion over the insane and the establishment of medical control of commitment in early nineteenth-century France in the

---

[60] See above, p. 5.

context of the requirements of the new liberal order then being erected in place of the *ancien régime*.[61] The abolition in March 1790 of the *lettres de cachet*, which had legitimated confinement of the insane on the basis of royal absolutism, necessitated the institution of a new mode of legitimation for incarceration consonant with the principles of the developing bourgeois society, in which individuals were bonded together by contract. The problem was that the insane, by definition irrational, were placed outside the framework of contractual exchange and could not, being irresponsible, be subject to penalties as criminals. The answer was to place the insane under a *relation de tutelle*, a regime of medical paternalism which could fill the space law was unable to enter. Castel describes liberal society and the total institution therefore as a 'dialectical couple'.[62] From 1802 onwards, a medical certificate was increasingly a prerequisite of asylum admission and the law of 1838 statutorily embodied an ensemble of elements which made up psychiatry's 'golden age', of which the dismissal of judicial in favour of medical control of admissions was one. By the 1860s, however, psychiatric 'despotism' was under attack and attempts were being made to restore active judicial participation in admissions processes which can be seen as prefigurations of modern Anti-Psychiatric critiques.[63]

The French experience cannot be directly generalized to the other nation states of Europe, but it is especially instructive because the Revolution of 1789 raised abruptly and in stark form the difficulties posed for the ascendant liberal political order by the existence of the insane. Castel's presentation of the effects of the transition from Bourbon absolutism to liberal order upon the procedure for commitment provides a basis for understanding the vulnerability of psychiatry to periodic revivals of aggressive legalism such as that endemic in states with developed asylum systems in the late nineteenth century. Applying the logic of Castel's analysis based upon the requirements of 'contractual society', the first threat of legalistic resurgence emanates from the fact that psychiatric coercion implicates inconsistent populations: the sane as well as the insane. At the gateway of the institution, when commitment is at stake, the possibility of medical error or corruption endangers the sane. But the sane are the proper bearers of contractual rights. This creates a space for dispute as to whether the commitment procedure should be

[61] P. Miller, 'The Territory of the Psychiatrist,' pp. 67–72.
[62] Ibid., pp. 71–2. Miller is here using the words of Castel.
[63] Ibid., pp. 90–1.

regarded as judicial or as an adjunct of the medically-dominated institutional domain.[64] The second threat is that posed by modern Anti-Psychiatry in the form of the argument that the insane, on the basis of their fundamental common humanity, should themselves be accepted into the contractual fold, endowed with rights, and benefit from the privileging assumption of juridical discourse. This is of course a more radical threat in its full implications, upsetting the basis of the *relation de tutelle* itself. It is the presence of these threats which has powerfully contributed to the instability and crisis in the history of mental health legislation in England as elsewhere. Legislation has, as we have seen, to arrive at an authoritative division of labour between the therapeutic professions. This is an important task, delimiting as it does the precise extent of the official mandate accorded by the political centre to each professional interest. It is also an intricate task: as David Ingleby states, 'the "therapeutic state" consists of a complex web of related professions, and its development is a story of territorial conquests, symbiotic alliances, secessions, (professional) assassinations, bartering and bullying—very much like the history of Europe itself.'[65] But legislation has also to determine the balance of power between the judicial and medical (and other therapeutic) instances, the extent to which the judicial encroaches upon disciplinary territory. How far this happens and how far therefore the legislation is pervaded by legalism, depends to a significant degree upon the political context. Legalism is the rendition in the psychiatric sphere of liberal individualism, and it will be seen that its historical fortunes have been closely tied to those of that particular politics.

The rootedness of legalism in liberal individualism means that it is liable to offend in all those various quarters where such a politics is regarded as repugnant. Larry Gostin and MIND's campaign for mental patients' legal rights, in asserting the autonomy of the patient against professional psychiatric power and demanding the enhancement of patients' civil and social status, was clearly reflective of a liberal individualist political philosophy and, as such, risked provok-

---

[64] This was the form of the argument at the end of the nineteenth century, when there was great concern that an expansive psychiatry placed the merely eccentric under threat of confinement. Admission was not the only point at which dispute could arise: the possibility of retention in an institution after recovery, for example, posed the question of whether discharge procedures should be basically under medical control or subject to judicial governance.

[65] D. Ingleby, 'Mental Health and Social Order', in S. Cohen and A. Scull (eds.), *Social Control and the State*. Oxford: Martin Robertson, 1983, p. 165.

ing the wrath of authoritarian conservatives, defenders of 'Fabian' 1940s Welfare State paternalism, and Socialists. To commence with the first of these anti-individualist ideological positions, Roger Scruton's *The Meaning of Conservatism*[66] is instructive. Scruton is a prominent ideologue of the Conservative Right, waging battle with that faction, currently dominant within the Conservative Party, who identify Conservatism with Manchester Liberalism. In sharp contradistinction from the market-oriented libertarian ideals fashionable in his Party, such as Frederick Hayek's concept of a 'catallaxy'—social order as the product of the total of mutually adjusting individual economies in a market[67]—Scruton holds to an organic view of society. He conceives of the social order as composed of sets of institutional traditions and symbols performing integrative functions and imposing upon individuals transcendent moral obligations which are not merely contractually assumed. In this respect society is the family writ large, for 'it would be absurd to think of family ties as contractual, or family obligations as in any way arising from a pure relinquishing of autonomy, or even of some unspoken bargain which rises into consciousness, so to speak, at some later stage'.[68] Scruton vehemently denies any notion that individual autonomy is essential, or prior to social order. The individual is not complete in himself and freedom is useless to a man 'who lives in a solipsistic vacuum, idly willing now this and now that, but with no conception of an objective order that would be affected by his choice.'[69] The idea of 'an individual united with no social order who has nothing to lose but his mental chains' is dismissed as a 'sublime illusion of the middle classes'.[70] It is the survival of the authoritative consensual institutional arrangements through which individuality takes on meaning, and not abstract individual liberty, which should be the preoccupation of government. In Scruton's definition of the meaning of conservatism the prime political task is the protection of the established order and the reassurance of the 'right-thinking' against those who threaten or subvert the bonds of society, not shying away

---

[66] R. Scruton, *The Meaning of Conservatism*, 2nd edn. London: Macmillan, 1984.

[67] F. A. Hayek, *Law, Legislation and Liberty*. London: Routledge and Kegan Paul, 1982, ii, pp. 108–9. Hayek cites the derivation of this term for the spontaneous order flowing from 'a network of interlaced economies' as R. Whatley's *Introductory Lectures on Political Economy* (1855). Hayek's conception is discussed by R. Cotterrell in *The Sociology of Law: An Introduction*. London: Butterworths, 1984, at p. 165.

[68] R. Scruton, p. 31.

[69] Ibid., p. 72.

[70] Ibid., p. 138.

from employing brutality where necessary to reassert authority. The liberal inheritance of the Enlightenment is scoffingly discarded in an atavistic reversion to the ideal of a stable order based upon duty which was historically embodied in feudalism.

Roger Scruton does not have anything to say about legalism, the MIND campaign, or the Mental Health Act 1983. However, he does excoriate the individualistic assumptions of the Anti-Psychiatry which inspired the logic of the patients' rights movement, selecting the works of R. D. Laing for special criticism. He characterizes the Laingian position as follows:

A natural attitude to mental illness is to suppose that the mentally ill are set apart from others and, if necessary, submitted to clinical treatment, as a *result* of their illness. This process of isolation is not thought of as an attempt to deprive the patient of his freedom; for, in his illness, freedom is already lost. The master thought of Laingian psychiatry consists in the reversal of that doctrine. It is the patient who becomes ill (and so sees himself not as person but as animal or object) because the clinical scientist treats him so. The patient has not lost his freedom: it has been stolen from him by the clinical refusal to treat him as a person.[71]

Scruton condemns this reversal of perspective as 'an extraordinary attempt on the part of alienated man to glamorize his condition'.[72] Rather than seeking the cure for the individual's alienation in reconciliation with those social institutions, primarily the family, within which individuals find belonging and meaning, Laing's project quests for a merely individual freedom of rescue from corruption by society. Along with other contributions to 'the theology of modern satanism' it subverts the values of family life, blaming as it does, not only the clinic as 'a kind of administrative "voice" ' of the established order, but the bourgeois family. Scruton defines the illness itself therefore as the negation of freedom and sees the solution in terms of successful social reintegration. Any search for the actualization of some mythical pre-social essential self must either reinforce alienation or be compromised by the reimportation of at least some basic constraining social values. Presumably, to advocate increased legal possibilities for mental patients to resist the guidance of the family and the clinic would be treated within this perspective as an outgrowth of the glamorization of alienation, perversely presenting as freedom the grant of legal rights which, in obstructing social

---

[71] Ibid., p. 135   [72] Ibid., p. 138.

reincorporation, fortify the imprisonment of being mentally ill. It is interesting that in launching this attack upon the liberal individualist basis of Anti-Psychiatry, Scruton chooses to focus upon Laing rather than his fellow conservative, Thomas Szasz, who manages to combine libertarianism with a stout adherence to the dominant order.[73]

Kathleen Jones is foremost amongst those opposed to liberal legalism from the quite different perspective of a basic sympathy with the social welfarist approach of the now partially discredited Mental Health Act 1959. For her, mental disorder is a social administrative problem, mental health is a department of 'social policy', and her welfare objective is to maximize the provision of effective mental health services: 'the provision of a good specialized community service backed by a good specialized (but much smaller) hospital service in which trained mental health professionals can be asked to exercise reasonable discretion in the interests of their patients'.[74] In a counterblast to MIND's campaign entitled 'The Limitations of the Legal Approach', published in 1980, she presents the essential evil of legalism as its anachronism, pinning it with Richard Titmuss's label 'resuscitated Diceyism'.[75] Law was tried in the shape of the Lunacy Act 1890, and it failed. The experience of that legislation demonstrated the limited purchase of law upon social reality, which she captures in the very true and telling observation that '[the] world of the psychiatric ward is a long way from the world of the Courts or of the House of Commons'.[76] The 'vicious subculture' which has been generated in mental hospitals by declining morale and conditions of work cannot be eradicated by the ponderous and formalistic machinery of the law. It is a problem of resources, the organization of social priorities, and training: economic, political, and technical, rather than legal. For this reason, legislation should be 'open-textured': a loose framework within which proper discretion can operate upon the essentially unpredictable course of mental disorder which renders mechanistic regulation especially inappropriate. What we have in this set of views is a projection into the 1980s of the assumptions of the post-Second World War political consensus, of which the Mental Health Act 1959 was one of the legislative progeny.

Finally, let us turn to the Left's critique of legalism and its liberal

[73] For a detailed analysis of the views of Thomas Szasz, see Chapter 10.
[74] K. Jones, 'The Limitations of the Legal Approach to Mental Health', *International Journal of Law and Psychiatry* 3 (1980), p. 14.
[75] Ibid., p. 10.
[76] Ibid., p. 11.

34 Psychiatry, Law, and Politics

individualist heritage. The place of law in Socialist political strategy in pre-Socialist societies and its role, if any, in the scheme of society envisioned as the end-product of that strategy has been, in part because of its individualism and formalism, the subject of fierce conflict at the level of both theoretical dispute and political action. In the historical development of Marxism, this conflict was exhibited in the rejection by both Austro-Marxists and Stalinists of the classical orthodoxy that the 'withering away' of law would be a concomitant of progress toward advanced communism, in favour of doctrines of 'Socialist Legality'.[77] Recently in this country there has been renewed debate about the validity of rights-based demands, with their associated legalism, as a part of Socialist political discourse, some contributors, notably Tom Campbell, arguing for a qualified rehabilitation of the concept of rights.[78] In *Psycho Politics*, Peter Sedgwick made an important Socialist intervention in the specific controversy surrounding patients' rights and the philosophy of legalism in the context of mental health.[79] The political content of Anti-Psychiatry in the 1960s and 1970s he identifies as highly ambiguous: 'as involved in setting the precedents for the burgeoning conservative right as in expressing the protests of a socially conscious left, as much (finally) Simon-pure individualist as it was collectivist in any shape or sense'.[80] This was, of course, most explicitly the case in the contributions of Thomas Szasz, whom Sedgwick accounts an intellectual descendant of Herbert Spencer. The civil libertarian legalism spawned by this type of perspective upon psychiatry is not condemned outright. Sedgwick concedes that it is a well-established and honourable tradition in the mental health field, and gives credit to MIND for certain of its campaigning positions: representation of patients at tribunals, the extension of patients' voting rights, and the provision of crisis intervention services—'one point at which libertarian lobbying has coincided with therapeutic good sense'.[81] However, the burden of his argument is that legalism, with its roots in liberal

---

[77] On Austro-Marxism, see R. Kinsey, 'Karl Renner on Socialist Legality', in D. Sugarman (ed.), *Legality, Ideology and the State*. London: Academic Press, 1983, p. 11; T. Bottomore, *Austro-Marxism*. Oxford: Clarendon Press, 1980. On Stalinism, see P. Beirne and R. Sharlet, 'In Search of Vyshinsky', *International Journal of the Sociology of Law* 12 (1981), p. 153.
[78] T. Campbell, *The Left and Rights*. London: Routledge and Kegan Paul, 1983. See especially pp. 35–57 on legalism.
[79] P. Sedgwick, Psycho Politics. London, Pluto Press, 1982.
[80] Ibid., p. 213.
[81] Ibid., p. 226.

individualism, is, *as a central strategy of mental health reform*, tragically misguided. Projects of 'forensic liberation' are a massive distraction from the real issues of 'how to create the economic means of employment, the material apparatus of housing, the ethical structures of fellowship and solidarity, for those who through various forms of disability cannot purchase these benefits as commodities in the market-place'.[82] The advocates of legalism condemn themselves to a necessarily negative role—they are part of a 'culture of resistance', a permanent reforming opposition:

... society concentrates in the hands of doctors the responsibility for the most fateful decisions concerning its mental deviants—and then sponsors a whole train of countervailing influences, in the subordinate professions and in the public generally, to moderate and protest this same power. The libertarian posture in mental health shields those who adopt it from demanding and assuming the responsibility for a continuing care for the disabled, whose concentration in other hands forms the target of their obloquy.[83]

Sedgwick argues that in challenging the validity of conceptualizing mental deviancy as illness rather than recognizing that somatic illnesses are themselves social constructs, critics of psychiatry have denied themselves the ability to campaign squarely on the terrain of illness and demand more progressive health practices and better health facilities. His own solution, invoking Kropotkin, is to build upon features of the mental health scene which can serve as prefigurative forms of communitarian provision in socialist society, of which he found the Belgian village community at Geel both the oldest and the most remarkable.

It is intriguing to detect in these critiques of legalism advanced from such divergent political positions certain basic common themes: the primacy of the social over the individual, of substance over form, of the concrete over the abstract. This compatibility is matched by the comparable spread of support for legalism—which in the 1970s stretched from the New Left to the New Right—and makes for some strange, even startling, alliances and counter-alliances. As we shall see, it has been a significant ingredient in the complex and erratic course of the political history of English mental health legislation.

[82] Ibid., p. 241.
[83] Ibid., pp. 220–1.

2 Mental Disorder and Legal Status

IN modern western legal thinking, the phenomenon of mental disorder carries a distinctive significance, producing a conceptualization irreducible to that found in other orders of discourse, be they medical, biological, psychological, or sociological. Legally, the mentally disordered rank as problematic and requiring special provision, as they may do in these other discourses, but the reasons for special treatment and the solutions arrived at are peculiarly legal in character. Evidence of mental disorder does not of itself divest an individual of legal status. Instead of relegating to the level of a mere object of legal intervention, it renders liable to certain legal disabilities, the cumulative effect of which is the imposition of a special subordinate legal status. It is true that proof of mental disorder can also shield its subject from legal liabilities and penalties but these immunities are really a corollary of legal incapacity rather than a mark of privilege.

To understand the subordinate status conferred on the mentally disordered, it is necessary to turn to a consideration of the nature of legal personality and to examine the reasons for their exclusion from full participation in its benefits. A convenient definition of legal personality is provided by Barry Hindess and Paul Hirst:

A legal personality is an entity which is legally free, legally responsible and which can appear as an autonomous party in legal actions and disputes. The legal personality is the support or carrier of the legal process; it is the subject which makes that process possible and necessary.[1]

Therefore, the definitive characteristics of legal personality are freedom, responsibility, and autonomy. Of course, legal personality is not confined in its application to human individuals: corporate entities are legal persons. Neither is it logically requisite that it should attach to all human individuals as such: under early Roman Law, for example, slaves had no legal personality and occupied the status of mere chattels. However, the European Enlightenment of the late seventeenth and eighteen centuries heralded the generalization legal status as an attribute of common humanity, and we need to

[1] B. Hindess and P. Q. Hirst, *Pre-Capitalist Modes of Production*. London: Macmillan, 1975, p. 111. See accompanying footnotes, pp. 329–30.

understand the failure of the mentally disordered to share in the rewards of this movement.

The Enlightenment must be credited with a far-reaching impact upon the development of modern western legal culture, and in particular with responsibility for the dominant constitutionalism and legalism of contemporary western political order. In this period, the remaining structures of European feudalism were challenged by the rising commercial and agrarian bourgeoisie, with the support of the peasantry and nascent proletariat, and it was in the course of these struggles that some of the essential foundations of liberal democracy were laid. At its most advanced, the programme of the politically ascendant classes was to break down the absolutism of the Continental European monarchies and to destroy the feudal privileges of aristocracy. European social order still largely reflected the feudal model of society as a pyramidic structure of personal relations of domination and submission, with the monarch at the apex as the personal repository of sovereignty, and absolutism reinforced this personal character of sovereignty. Thus the ultimate criminal offence was regicide, as graphically confirmed by the horrendous punishments inflicted upon Damiens in Paris in March 1757 for the attempted assassination of Louis XV.[2] Just as the social order reflected a hierarchy of privilege, so did the legal order, which is illustrated in England itself by the trial before her peers of the notorious Elizabeth Chudleigh, Countess of Bristol (1720–88) in April 1776. The Countess was found guilty of a bigamous marriage to the Duke of Kingston, a clergyable offence, for which she could have been branded on the hand, had she not been able to escape this indignity by successfully pleading the exemption of the peerage.[3]

Amongst the myriad reforming themes which gained currency during the Enlightenment were the doctrine of the rule of law—that sovereignty should be vested in the constitution, subjecting the apparatuses of the state to the impersonal governance of constitutional rules and conventions—and the conviction that hierarchical legal structures, with their graduated scales of privilege, should be dismantled and replaced with a system wedded to formal equality

[2] See M. P. Foucault, *Discipline and Punish*. London: Allen Lane, 1977, Chapter 1; P. Weiss, *The Persecution and Assassination of Marat as Performed by the Inmates of the Asylum of Charenton under the Direction of the Marquis de Sade*, 2nd edn. London: Calder and Boyars, 1966; J. Egret, *Louis XV et L'Opposition Parlementaire 1715–1774*. Paris: Armand Colin, 1970, pp. 82, 136.

[3] *Dictionary of National Biography*. London: Smith, Elder, 1887, x, pp. 300–1.

before the law. Monarchical despotism allowed the administration of punishment to be arbitrary, oppressive, and often savage, a personalized justice vacillating unpredictably between mercy and terror. Cesare Beccaria (1738–94), in his *Essays on Crime and Punishment* (1764) the *locus classicus* of the criminological theory of the Enlightenment, advocated the radical liberalization and rationalization of the penal system, with the injection of greater elements of publicity and democracy.[4] He argued that criminal penalties should be proportionate to the crime and enforced on a regular, predictable basis.[5] It was intended that the calculability of sanctions would promote their deterrent effectiveness, while the mechanical operation of punishment (symbolized so well by the French Revolutionary 'guillotine') would furnish a new ideological basis for its legitimacy, as explained by Jean Paul Marat:

The infliction of punishment should attempt to repair the offence as much as to expiate it. This is the triumph of liberty, because then punishment no longer arises out of the will of the legislator, but out of the very nature of crimes. Man is no longer committing violence against man.[6]

The realization of the desire to transform the relationship between law and society varied in nature, extent, and chronology in the different nation states of Europe. England's development had been idiosyncratic and its legal and political institutions were peculiarly advanced by the standards of the Enlightenment;[7] indeed, they were held up as examples in the France of the Revolutionary period, when the Third Estate pressed wide-ranging demands for legal reform on the crumbling Bourbon monarchy.[8] The constitutional struggles of the seventeenth century had already achieved a limited monarchy in England, and established the political ascendancy of the landed

---

[4] The English counterpart of the Essays was Jeremy Bentham's *Introduction to the Principles of Morals and Legislation*, first printed in 1780 and published in 1789.

[5] I. Taylor, P. Walton, and J. Young, *The New Criminology*. London: Routledge and Kegan Paul, 1973, Chapter 1.

[6] J. P. Marat, *Plan de Legislation Criminelle*. Paris, 1790, p. 33, quoted in R. Rusche and O. Kirchheimer, *Punishment and Social Structure*. London: Russell and Russell, 1968, p. 81.

[7] An adversarial, rather than inquisitorial, judicial process, and the incorporation of the magistracy and the jury system as potentially democratic lay elements marked England out from its Roman Law based continental neighbours. On the peculiarities of English legal development see M. Rheinstein (ed.), *Max Weber on Law in Economy and Society*. Cambridge, Mass.: Harvard University Press, 1954, pp. 78–81, 198–204, 315–18.

[8] The 1789 *Cahiers des États Généraux* reveal that these included public trials, free choice of a lawyer, trial by jury, suppression of torture, a clearly defined law of evidence, and protection against illegal imprisonment. See R. Rusche and O. Kirchheimer, p. 78.

interest, ushering in the era of the White Supremacy. The period which separates the Bill of Rights (1688) and the first Reform Act (1832) may be seen as representing the transition to modern liberal democratic legal order, as it comprised significant components of both personalized and impersonal justice. On the one hand, the landed élite buttressed the security of their estates by resort to the familiar technique of alternating terror and clemency: Walpole's infamous Black Act (1723) contributed to a quadrupling of predominantly property-related capital offences between 1688 and 1820,[9] but, partly as a result of the extensive deployment of the pardon, this in practice delivered comparatively few executions. On the other hand the landed gentry's power as a ruling class was exerted through their control of Parliament and the Courts, so that, in the eighteenth century, political hegemony became peculiarly dependent upon the observance of legality. There was a substantial growth in procedural regularity of judicial administration and there was an at least approximate even-handedness in the imposition of criminal penalties on members of different social classes.[10] Thus, the invocation of formal justice and equality before the law played an important role in the legitimation of the social order and the promotion of social consensus. Despite this, however, England's legal system was still seriously defective by Beccarian criteria. The gentry relied upon the savagery of penal sanctions as a deterrent rather than upon the dependability of the exaction of a more moderate scale of penalties, because they refused to countenance the introduction of the necessary machinery of enforcement, that is, a regular police force. Their apprehension was that such a force might be fashioned into a political police at the personal disposition of the sovereign in the manner of its counterparts in the despotisms of Continental Europe, and so create a base for the reassertion of royal power. The liberalization of the penal system and the associated establishment of a regular police force awaited the emergence in the early nineteenth century of a politically influential middle class with an interest in the protection of personal rather than landed wealth and whose power had not immediately been purchased at the expense of the royal prerogative.[11]

[9] D. Hay, 'Property, Authority and the Criminal Law', in D. Hay et al., Albion's Fatal Tree. London: Allen Lane, 1975, p. 18. For an account of the origins of the Black Act see E. P. Thompson, Whigs and Hunters. London: Allen Lane, 1975.
[10] D. Hay, pp. 33–9.
[11] See T. Bowden on the origins of the Metropolitan Police in Beyond the Limits of the Law. Harmondsworth: Penguin, 1978, pp. 215–18.

The Enlightenment bequeathed to the economic liberalism of early industrial capitalism distinctive conceptions of humanity, law, and society which became incorporated in the dominant ideology as political control passed into the hands of industrial and financial capital in the course of the nineteenth century. The classical conception of humanity postulated an essential human nature composed of fixed characteristics. Human beings were defined as autonomous, rational, self-determining, and therefore responsible for their own actions. It followed that at the level of common humanity they were, through the shared possession of these attributes, formally equal. Utilitarianism, the economic liberal rendition of this humanist position, conceived individuals as engaged in the rational pursuit of ends and goals, seeking happiness and avoiding pain as they might pursue profit and evade loss in an economic market, a felicific calculus which found legal and administrative expression in the New Poor Law test of less eligibility. Implicit in this teleological view of the organization of individual life was a view of social life as the aggregate of individual's intersecting life-plans.[12]

This conception of humanity assigns to law a pivotal role in the social order. In Roberto Unger's typological analysis of liberal societies—that is, those characterized by market economies, an open social hierarchy and equality of citizenship, and emergent in the early nineteenth century in Western Europe—law, in its insulation from politics and administration, provides 'the balance-wheel of social organization'.[13] Man's inherent competitive individualism is seen to necessitate law as a regulative framework within which the pursuit of individual goals must be contained if social order is to be preserved—law is thus *constitutive* of society, a barrier against anarchy. To the extent that a society is characterized by liberal forms, the ideological hegemony of the ruling class(es) controlling the state is based, in Max Weber's terms, upon legal domination, because popular political consent is purchased by the rulers' conformity to legality or the rule of law:

---

[12] Max Weber's seminal work on the development of a distinctively sociological methodology was based upon this presupposition: see P. Q. Hirst, *Social Evolution and Sociological Categories*. London: George Allen and Unwin, 1976, Chapter 3. For a Neo-Weberian examination of sociological philosophy see C. Grace and P. Wilkinson, *Sociological Inquiry and Legal Phenomena*. London: Collier Macmillan, 1978, pp. 214–15: 'Interpretive Sociology, the Lockean and Liebnizian vision of man'.

[13] R. M. Unger, *Law in Modern Society*. New York: Free Press, 1976, p. 54.

In the case of legal authority, obedience is owed to the legally established impersonal order. It extends to the persons exercising authority of office under it only by virtue of the formal legality of their commands and only within the scope of the authority of the office.[14]

Weber contrasts this impersonality with the personal basis of legitimacy in the cases of political orders supported by traditional or charismatic authority.

The effect of the deployment of law as the specific mode for the exercise of political power is to afford some protection to the individual by restraining the state. The individual subject's essential autonomy is recognized by the legal guarantee of a sphere of private personal sovereignty within which his freedom to enter into the legal relationships of his choice sets him up as his own legislator. Respect for this sphere of autonomy entails that although law is a central principle of social and political organization it should be minimal in character, and not converted into a vehicle for projects of social intervention and reconstruction. Here, the rule of law complements economic liberalism in contributing a merely formal framework for social participation enshrining the ideals of equality before the law, freedom under the law, and formal justice, rather than constituting the machinery for the political quest of substantive objectives of redistribution and social justice. The role of the rule of law in legitimating inegalitarian social orders by projecting these ideals has been treated as its central vice in recent critiques.[15]

In the liberal social universe evolving in the early nineteenth century, law had the following significance. The characteristics of freedom, autonomy, and responsibility identified with legal personality had now come to be defined as the essence of human personality itelf and it was therefore fitting that it should be in the general recognition of the capacity to exercise legally embodied rights that expression was to be given to the ideals of humanity in social and political organization. Hence the contemporary liberal critique of the institution of slavery as the denial of the equal humanity of the slave.[16] However, this equalization of legal status was not to be unlimited and there were certain residual categories to whom it did not extend and for whom special legal provision had to be made within the liberal order, namely those deemed not to have attained adulthood and the

[14] M. Weber, *The Theory of Social and Economic Organization*, p. 328.
[15] For a collection of contributions to the debate on the rule of law, see B. Fine (ed.), *Capitalism and the Rule of Law*. London: Hutchinson, 1979.
[16] B. Hindess and P. Hirst, Chapter 3.

mentally disordered, comprising the mentally handicapped and the insane. These categories were subject to partial legal exclusion because of their perception as deficient in the rational self-determination which would qualify them as fully human and capable of exercising legal rights. Their treatment should be distinguished from that of paupers and criminals whose civil and political disqualifications were imposed as a deliberate mark of social disapprobation, as they were held responsible for their own predicament.

In the case of the insane, the reasoning employed to justify special legal treatment can be illustrated by reference to H. M. R. Pope's *A Treatise on the Law and Practice of Lunacy*.[17] In Pope's analysis, it is deduced from the inherent nature of law and of society. Law, defined as a command[18] addressed to a rational being, cannot operate unmodified upon the insane, who are by definition the victims of irrationality. As far as society is concerned, the insane are 'in it but not of it' and special intervention can be justified on grounds of paternalism and social defence. Pope concludes:

Where the conditions are so peculiar, the rules regulating them will be peculiar also. The absence of reason creates in fact an elementary difference in the relations of the individual to the state and the law of the state. Among all the varied circumstances of civil life, there is scarcely one but is affected by it. In the eyes of the law the insane in life and after death stand for a thousand purposes in a class separate and distinct.[19]

---

[17] H. M. R. Pope, *A Treatise on the Law and Practice of Lunacy*, 2nd edn. Ed. J. H. Boone and V de S. Fowke. London: Sweet and Maxwell, 1890.

[18] The employment of this definition reflects the dominance of the Austinian command theory of law and thus the persistence of absolutist notions into the era of the rule of law. Richard Kinsey touches on this phenomenon, which he interprets as the expression of 'the historical tendency towards juridical equality . . . through extremely contradictory forms.' He proceeds: 'Basically this means, so far as English law is concerned, through the archaic and outmoded institutions of the absolutist state, which together with its Hobbesian justifications, have hung over and distorted the contemporary history both of the practice and of the theory of the English law. Hence the domination in English legal thought—especially in the nineteenth century—of notions of command, sanction, the absolute power of the sovereign etc. as typifying legality. Thus we find a continuing tension between liberal aspirations and the design of the nineteenth century's institutional and conceptual heritage.' R. M. Kinsey, 'Marxism and Law: Preliminary Analysis', *British Journal of Law and Society* 5 (1978), p. 221.

[19] Pope, p. 5. A modern expression of this belief in the fundamental exceptionality of the mentally disordered is to be found in Bernard Williams, 'The Idea of Equality', in P. Laslett and W. G. Runciman (eds.), *Philosophy, Politics and Society*, Second Series. Oxford: Blackwell, 1962 at p. 118: 'I omit here, as throughout the discussion, the clinical cases of people who are mad or mentally defective, who always constitute special exceptions to what is in general true of men.'

Socially atomized and powerless, the populations falling under these residual categories were in no position to resist the imposition of legal statuses which subjected them to the control of the family, agencies of the state and, in time, a range of therapeutic professionals. In the course of the nineteenth and twentieth centuries, as the courts and the legislature elaborated a status for the adult sane individual reflecting his postulated freedom, rationality, and responsibility in the capacity to enter into a wide span of legal relations, they unfolded in parallel the modifications in legal status appropriate to the 'peculiar' situation of children and the mentally disordered, refining the rudimentary provisions already present in the law. For example, M'Naghten's case, in 1843, afforded the judges the opportunity to formulate the exact criteria for determining the criminal liability of the insane, and they crystallized the celebrated test that the defendant would be held responsible if he had knowledge of the act's nature and quality and knowledge that it was wrong. An analogous test of knowledge that the act was wrong was evolved in a series of cases in the 1830s and 1840s to establish the criminal liability of children between the ages of eight and fourteen years.[20] In each of these instances a theory of moral responsibility was applied, drawing a distinction between those whose mentality and behaviour could be assimilated to the pure classical model and those in whose case it could not. This contributed to the installation of a neo-classical revisionism as the theoretical orthodoxy of the legal system in its dealings with deviancy.[21]

However, the development of a special legal status for children and the mentally disordered was not simply a question of their accommodation in a scheme of legal order designed to be as far as possible all-encompassing. In the wake of the expansion of industrial capitalism, the early nineteenth century witnessed a profound reorganization of social discipline, central to which was the creation, in 1834, of the New Poor Law, embodying strict principles of economic liberalism summarized in the workhouse test of 'less eligibility'. The mass of the mentally disordered, being recruited from the ranks of the poor and perceived as socially threatening, were caught up in this reorganization. As we shall see, they were extracted from the generality of the deviant and unproductive amongst whom they had been placed

---

[20] Glanville L. Williams, 'The Criminal Responsibility of Children', *Criminal Law Review* (1954), p. 493. He cites the cases of *Owen* (1830) 4 C & P 236; *Manley* (1844) 1 Cox 104 and *Smith* (1845) 9 JP 682.

[21] Taylor *et al.*, Chapter 1.

under the Elizabethan Poor Law as an aspect of the problem of pauperism and vagrancy, and segregated in purpose-built 'asylums' which were rapidly converted into the exclusive domain of the medical profession. This transformation generated new legal structures: regulations for the foundation and operation of the new institutions; supervisory bureaucratic apparatuses concerned with visitation, inspection, licensing, and the scrutiny of documents; a system of legal confinement concerned with the admission, detention, and discharge of patients entailing the applications of relatives or Poor Law officials, medical certificates, and magisterial orders. Within these structures, which arose after all in the transition from a paternalistic pre-industrial social order to the liberal order of early industrial capitalism, the mentally disordered were, paradoxically, situated in a legal dependancy, Castel's tutelary relationship. In formal terms this was reminiscent of the feudal inheritance which liberalism was supposed to have superseded.[22]

These concessions to regimes of paternalism and assumptions of determinism in respect of the mentally disordered and children formed the Achilles' heel of the classical system, the gateway to Thomas Szasz's Therapeutic State. For when, from the late nineteenth century, and especially after 1945, liberal political theory and the rule of law ideal waned as corporatist and collectivist directions in social development gained pace, it was the social and legal treatment of these categories which was most vulnerable to positivistic incursions.[23] Later, we shall see how effective were these tendencies in accentuating the subversion of notions of legal entitlement and responsibility in favour of various styles of discretionary control, a movement culminating in the Mental Health Act 1959 and the Children's and Young Persons' Act 1969.[24] The history, therefore, of legal provision for the mentally disordered since the early nineteenth century has consisted of the construction, within the context of a legal order based upon principles of formal freedom and equality, of a limited status composed of what H. P. Macmillan, Chairman of the Royal Commission on Lunacy and Mental Disorder (1924–6) aptly captured in the phrase 'something more subtle than rights'.[25]

[22] P. Q. Hirst and P. Woolley, *Social Relations and Human Attributes*. London: Tavistock, 1982, p. 178. See generally pp. 93–210.

[23] Unger, pp. 192–203.

[24] A. Morris *et al.*, *Justice for Children*. London: Macmillan, 1980, Chapter 1.

[25] *Royal Commission on Lunacy and Mental Disorder: Minutes of Evidence*, 1926, I, Question 10, 900.

Special Legal Provision for the Mentally Disordered

There are two aspects to the question of special legal provision for the mentally disordered. Firstly, there is the problem of the extent to which evidence of mental disorder should be regarded as restricting the exercise of standard legal capacities or inhibiting the imposition of standard legal liabilities and penalties. Secondly, there is the question of the direct legal regulation of the mentally disordered as a class of social deviants in the form of control, treatment, and the jurisdiction to manage their property and affairs.

The first problem is one of the legal accommodation or integration of the mentally disordered, or moulding general rules to take into account the particular deviations from standard legal personality manifested by a given social category. This is a familiar task for a legal system, arising in relation to other exceptional legal subjects such as infants, drunkards, and corporations. In England the relevant criteria of competency have been evolved largely by the courts in the process of case-law development. This incremental character of their evolution means that in some areas the authorities are incomplete and ambiguous, but broadly, the courts' approach can be defined as particularistic and pragmatic. They have applied different criteria of mental impairment in different legal contexts. Pope's statement is still true that 'a person, medically speaking insane, may be legally sane for one purpose and legally insane for another'.[26]

The law's concern has been with the relevance or influence of mental disorder in relation to the exercise of a particular legal capacity or the commission of a particular legal wrong: the notion of the 'lucid interval', for example, carries legal status. The question has tended to be one of the extent to which, on the facts of the case, the particular individual, despite evidence of mental disorder, is assimilable to the model of the rational legal subject. This assimilative impetus of the legal approach has produced serious tensions with forensic psychiatry, especially in the criminal sphere. Medicine has entertained a wider determinism which would produce a more expansive exemption from legal responsibility, and law's humanism of crediting the individual with self-determination has clashed with medicine's humanism of tolerance for the individual driven by circumstances beyond his control. Historically, lawyers have insisted that medical testimony as to mental disorder bears only evidential status in the courtroom and so may only contribute to and cannot

[26] Pope, p. 6.

itself determine a finding of 'insanity'. As a basis of legal liability 'insanity' is a legal term of art; it has a meaning specific to legal discourse and one which cannot be equated with that which it possesses in an exclusively medical context. This attitude has often offended medical susceptibilities by appearing to impugn the scientific status claimed for psychiatry and to invade medical territory.[27]

The law's approach to problems of civil capacity and liability may be illustrated by reference to the law of contract. A contract rests upon the parties' consent to mutually acceptable terms intended to be legally enforceable, and the question raised by evidence that one of the parties suffers from a mental disorder is whether this should invalidate his consent and release him from the performance of his contractual obligations. The courts have therefore addressed themselves to the creation of a test establishing the degree of disorder which must be present to render the contract voidable at the option of the party under disability. Given the mutual nature of the arrangement, it has been decided that it is insufficient solely to take into account the state of mind of the mentally disordered party himself, as the question of justice to the other contracting party must also be settled. The general rule in English law enshrines the compromise that the contract will be binding unless the party subject to mental disorder and seeking to avoid it can show that by reason of his disability he was rendered unable to appreciate the nature of the transaction into which he was entering and that the other party knew of his incapacity. If both conditions are satisfied, the mentally disordered party can relinquish his obligations.[28] The law's policy is thus not to treat the existence of delusions as conclusive *per se*, but to formulate rules to determine the relevancy of the disability in the context of a given set of legal relations.

In terms of legal provision specifically addressed to the mentally disordered from the point of view of control and treatment, the emphasis historically has been upon prerogative and statutory jurisdiction rather than case law. The applicable criteria of mental disorder have been dependent upon the purpose of legal intervention, and borne different relationships to the medical evidence. Direct legal provision can be considered under three broad heads: powers for the management of patient's property, the provision of

[27] On this theme see R. Smith, *Trial by Medicine*, and Chapter 3.
[28] *Brown* v. *Jodrell* (1827) Mood. & M.105.

60 10 p. 50

control and treatment for the non-criminal mentally disordered, and special arrangements for mentally abnormal offenders.

Jurisdiction conferring powers for the control of patients' property, now contained in Part VII of the Mental Health Act 1983, is the most ancient instance of statutory provision, being medieval in origin and deriving from feudal principles of land tenure. The statute *De Praerogativa Regis* (generally cited as 17 Edward II c. 9 & 10)[29] declares the pre-existing prerogative entitlements of the Crown to the lands of idiots and lunatics. Idiocy or supervening lunacy constituted an interruption in the performance of the services in return for which a tenant's estates were granted under the feudal system. Management of the estates of incapacitated tenants, of which wardship of the lands of infants during the period of their minority was the most common example, was a valuable incident of feudal lordship. The Crown arrogated this privilege to itself in derogation of the original rights of the lesser lords and thereby acquired an investment which was to maintain its value beyond the medieval period, being tied to the rents and profits of the land and not vulnerable to erosion by inflation as in the case of payments in commutation of services. Intervention therefore possessed a fiscal as well as a paternalistic aspect, a fact which attests to the multiplicity of the historical origins of state provision for the mentally disordered. Idiots and lunatics were differently treated. Where the disability of the tenant flowed from idiocy the Crown was entitled to the rents and profits of his estates for the duration of his life, subject to the expense of his maintenance and that of his dependent family. However, lunatics were more favourably treated. Lunacy created a hiatus in the performance of services of unpredictable and possibly short, temporary duration, whereas idiocy was a permanent condition and the minority of an infant a conventional fixed period. Here the excess of income over the expenses of maintenance was not to find its way into the royal coffers but to be held in trust pending the lunatic's recovery or, in the event of his death, applied for the benefit of his soul. It is worthy of note that this earliest special statutory jurisdiction in English law should have differentiated between idiots and lunatics. It was not until the Idiots Act 1886 that the principle of separate statutory arrangements for the mentally handicapped was revived. In time, the jurisdiction over the estates of idiots became

---

[29] This is the citation used by Pope. See M. Donnelly, *Managing the Mind*. London: Tavistock, 1983, p. 16.

assimilated to that exercised in respect of lunatics, but Sir William Blackstone's *Commentaries on the Laws of England* (1765–1770) still recorded the rents and profits of the lands of idiots as one of the sources of state revenue.[30] Also, although the feudal jurisdiction applied exclusively to realty, with the increasing relative importance of personal property as a repository of private wealth, it was extended to embrace personalty.[31]

This prerogative jurisdiction has a convoluted institutional history. Initially delegated to the Exchequer as an aspect of tax collection, it then passed to the Lord Chancellor appropriately enough given its paternalistic basis in the conscience of the Crown and the consideration that the income of the lunatics' estates was held in trust and not for the profit of the Crown. In the Tudor period, the history of the jurisdiction was influenced by the reassertion of royal power under a strong centralized monarchy and the revival of fiscal feudalism, culminating in the notorious Statute of Uses 1535. Henry VIII instituted new Prerogative Courts, including the Court of Wards and Liveries, created in 1539–42, to which the Lord Chancellor's jurisdiction over the estate of lunatics was transferred.[32] These Prerogative Courts became an important site of the constitutional struggle between Crown and Parliament under the Stuart monarchy, and ceased to operate during the Interregnum, being formally abolished at the Restoration.[33] With the fall of the Court of Wards, its jurisdiction over lunatics reverted to the Crown, whence it returned permanently to the Lord Chancellor. Toward the end of the eighteenth century there emerged within the Chancery a Court of Lunacy, the forerunner of the modern Court of Protection. The Court of Protection administers powers under the Mental Health Act 1983 which constitute the contemporary statutory counterpart of the old prerogative jurisdiction. The latter has not been abolished, but has been rendered obsolete because no authority has been entrusted under the sign manual with a mandate to exercise it. The criterion of mental disorder appropriate to invoke the statutory jurisdiction retains elements of the old formulation, requiring the court to be satisfied that there is sufficient medical evidence to establish that 'a

[30] W. Blackstone, *Commentaries on the Laws of England*, 16th edn. Ed. J. T. Coleridge. London: Butterworth, 1825, I, pp. 302–3.

[31] Pope, p. 26.

[32] See G. K. Elton, *The Tudor Revolution in Government*. Cambridge: Cambridge University Press, 1953, pp. 219–23.

[33] See R. Lockyer, *Tudor and Stuart Britain 1471–1714*. London: Longmans, 1964, pp. 255–6, 268, 324.

person is incapable, by reason of mental disorder, of managing and administering his property and affairs', except that under section 98, in cases of emergency it is possible for the court to act without being finally so satisfied.

This jurisdiction is solely and exclusively concerned with furnishing practical machinery to secure patients' property and not with availing the court of control over patients themselves. Historically, however, procedures in Chancery to obtain powers over a patient's estate were linked to the issue of the guardianship of the patient himself, although not to the issue of his admissibility to an asylum, which was a separate question. This link stemmed from the medieval position that the exercise of the prerogative over the lands of idiots and lunatics not only delivered up their property to the sovereign, but also converted them into his wards. At the beginning of the period with which we are principally concerned, the number of Chancery lunatics was small but significant, as in practice this was a procedure particularly employed where it was desired to separate a person of wealth from control of his fortune, although technically it was not so limited: indeed there was a special jurisdiction to deal summarily with 'small' properties of less than £1,000 or £50 per annum, dating from 1845. The basis of the jurisdiction was a finding that a person was 'unsound in mind to a degree rendering him incapable of managing himself or his affairs' and such a person was a 'lunatic so found'. Upon the petition of some person interested or a Lunacy Commissioner, the Lord Chancellor would grant a general commission to determine the sanity of the patient. An inquisition was conducted by a Master in Lunacy, with the observance of full court procedure, in certain cases including a jury. If the requisite degree of insanity was established, then the care of the patient's person was entrusted to a 'committee' (normally an individual, so designated because the patient was committed to him) called 'the committee of the person', and the care of his property was assigned to 'the committee of the estate'. The judicial and public nature of the proceedings meant that they afforded a convenient model for legal and libertarian critics of the more general civil procedures for control of the mentally disordered.

The general provisions of the civil processing of mental disorder which operate independently of the capacity to manage property are much more recent in origin. They derive in the first instance from the law of vagrancy, within which wandering lunatics were first mentioned as a distinct group in a statute of the last year of Queen

Anne.[34] Lunacy legislation as such was initiated by an Act for regulating Madhouses in 1774.[35] Detailed analysis of the history of the civil legislation will be undertaken in later chapters, but a structural outline, and an examination of its early origins are in order here.

In Georgian and Victorian legislation, no attempt was made to provide an authoritative statutory definition of lunacy for purposes of its civil control and treatment. The interpretation of terms such as 'lunatic', 'idiot', 'insane person', or 'person of unsound mind' was left to the officials charged with its implementation: Justices of the Peace, overseers of the poor, parish clergymen, and constables. The assumption at the outset was no doubt that such states were easily recognizable and subject to common-sense consensus definition. However, from early on medical men were assured of a leading role in the official identification of lunacy, in recognition of their specialist concern with its diagnosis and treatment. Indeed, in the case of legislation to regulate private madhouses, from its very inception in 1774 it was the Royal College of Physicians which was given the power to elect Commissioners to licence and inspect these institutions and the proprietors were liable to a £100 fine for admitting a lunatic without the written order of a medical man.[36] Twentieth-century legislation has, however, ventured into the definitional arena, reflecting a concern to rationalize statutory provision, to give expression in law to medico-scientific distinctions, and to differentiate the provision of social control and therapeutic services in sensitivity to the variety of conditions subsumed under broad legislative categories. The encompassing notion of mental disorder has been broken down into a variety of sub-classifications, which have been defined by linking a given type or degree of mental impairment to the ability to function according to some social, moral, or educational standard. The Mental Deficiency Act 1913 pioneered this approach, first of all by syphoning off the mentally defective into a separate statutory category following their re-subsumption under lunacy by the Lunacy Act 1890, and secondly by grading them into idiots, imbeciles, the feeble-minded, and moral defectives.[37] Each of these sub-categories was then further defined; for example, idiots were persons 'so deeply defective in mind as to be unable to guard

---

[34] 12 Anne Stat. 2 c. 23.
[35] 14 Geo. III c. 49.
[36] 14 Geo. III c. 49, section 21.
[37] Mental Deficiency Act 1913, section 1.

against common physical dangers', so specifying in each case a type of inadequacy which furnished a reason for statutory intervention. Section 4 of the Mental Health Act 1959 similarly defined and classified 'mental disorder', the object of the statute being specified to comprise 'mental illness, arrested or incomplete development of mind, psychopathic disorder and any other disorder or disability of mind'. 'Subnormality', 'severe subnormality', and 'psychopathy', corresponding to conditions which formerly fell within the ambit of mental deficiency legislation, were further defined in the Mental Health Act. Section 1(2) and (3) of the Mental Health Act 1983 substitutes for references to subnormality and severe subnormality references to mental impairment and redefines these conditions to narrow the scope of compulsory powers. But the Act follows lunacy and mental treatment legislation in foregoing the attempt to supply an official definition of 'mental illness' as the modern analogue of 'unsoundness of mind' and 'lunacy'. This was in view of the notorious susceptibility of the term, and of its positive counterpart 'mental health', to an infinite range of competing interpretations.

Until the 1930s, care and treatment in mental institutions was provided overwhelmingly on a compulsory basis,[38] so that it was those who were sufficiently wealthy to afford treatment at home for 'nervous diseases' outside the purview of legislation who were able to benefit from voluntary submission to psychiatric treatment. There was, however, a degree of facility for voluntary residence in the asylum, albeit very limited. This commenced in 1853 when the Lunatics Act of 1845 was amended to allow a discharged patient to remain in a licensed house (a private commercial institution receiving lunatics for profit) if he or she desired, with the proviso that the proprietor had to obtain the prior written consent of two or more of the Commissioners or Visiting Justices responsible for licensing the house.[39] Voluntary treatment was limited to the private sector, and it

[38] Certification as of unsound mind did not automatically lead to institutionalization, however. Under section 22 of the Lunacy Act 1890, the Justice could entrust the patient to the care of relatives or friends.

[39] 1853 c. 96, section 6. This opportunity for voluntary admission to licensed houses was extended in 1862 to anyone who had been a patient in *any* asylum, hospital, licensed house, or under care as a single patient within the five years previous to the assent (1862 c. 111, section 18). The Commissioners in Lunacy recognized practice along the same lines in registered hospitals in 1879. The Lunacy Act 1890, section 229 (1)–(6) followed the recommendation of the 1877 Dillwyn Committee that patients should be admissible to licensed houses as voluntary boarders whether or not previously under certificates, and the Lunacy Act 1891, section 20 extended this by inference to registered hospitals.

was not until the Mental Treatment Act 1930 that voluntary admission to a public mental hospital received general legislative authorization.[40] Since the Mental Health Act 1959 the vast majority of patients have been admitted with complete informality.[41] When compulsion was the rule, however, it was not the case that mental disorder *per se* activated coercive powers. Although early legislation sometimes referred to insanity itself as the basis for commitment and sometimes to the patient having to be a proper person to be confined or received,[42] it was settled statutory form by the second half of the nineteenth century that the patient had to be 'a proper person to be detained under care and treatment'. The issue of civil commitment was one of whether the medical evidence established a disorder sufficient to warrant detention in an institution. This is a further instance of the law's purpose-oriented approach to the definition of mental disorder and its preoccupation with degrees of mental impairment. The provisions in Part II of the Mental Health Act 1983 concerned with compulsory admission to hospital or guardianship reaffirm this long-established position by requiring that, for the powers to be invoked, the disorder must be of a nature or degree which warrants, as the case may be, the detention or treatment of the patient in a hospital or reception into guardianship and that this ought to happen in the interests of the patient's own health or safety or for the protection of other persons.[43] Thus, the statutory justification of coercive intervention rests squarely on the alternative supports of paternalism and social defence.

The form of modern compulsory powers over the mentally disordered can be readily traced back to eighteenth-century vagrancy legislation and to eighteenth- and nineteenth-century lunacy legislation. The latter contained separate legal regimes for private and pauper patients. The Parliamentary Select Committee on Lunacy Law reported in 1877 in favour of the unification of these procedures, and this was also a recommendation of the Royal Commission on Lunacy and Mental Disorder in 1926, but it was only with the demise of the Poor Law in 1948 that assimilation was finally achieved. Lunacy legislation in the nineteenth and early twentieth centuries evolved in intimate relationship with the Poor Law. There were many reasons for this: the great majority of patients were technically paupers, many were pauperized by their disorder, the

---

[40] Mental Treatment Act 1930, section 1.
[41] Mental Health Act 1959, section 5.
[43] Mental Health Act 1983, sections 2–4, 7.

officialdom of Poor Law and lunacy structures overlapped, and a substantial proportion of lunatics remained accommodated in general workhouses despite the construction, in the first half of the nineteenth century, of a national infrastructure of purpose-built asylums. An examination of the component elements of the legal procedures affecting admission, detention, and discharge of patients will elucidate these connections and demonstrate formal continuities over a long period.

The Vagrancy Act of 1744[44] was a typical expression of the Whig oligarchy's anxiety to protect landed property against the property-less, and consistent with the political considerations discussed earlier. It begins with the ringing assertion that 'the number of Rogues, Vagabonds, Beggars and other idle and dishonest persons daily increases to the great Scandal, Loss and Annoyance of the Kingdom . . .'. The objects of the statute were an exotic assemblage of 'wanderers abroad' including 'all persons pretending to be Gypsies, or wandering in the Habit or Form of Egyptians, or pretending to have Skyll in Physiognomy, Palmistry or like crafty Science, or pretending to tell fortunes, . . .' and all unauthorized 'Petty Chapmen and Pedlars'. The relevance of the insane to this mischief is clarified by Section 20 which states that 'there are sometimes persons, who by Lunacy, or otherwise, are furiously mad or are so far disordered in their senses that they may be dangerous to be permitted to go abroad'. Two or more Justices of the Peace were authorized to direct a constable, church warden, or overseer of the poor to apprehend such a person and send him 'to be kept safely locked up in some secure place, and if such Justices find it necessary to be there chained' for the period of the lunacy. The section was concerned with the apprehension of wandering lunatics as a species of vagrant, their transmission to a secure place—typically a house of correction, and provided for the payment of their maintenance either out of their property, if any, or if not by their place of settlement. Included in the charge against the person's estate or place of settlement was the cost of 'curing' as well as keeping and maintaining him.[45]

D. J. Mellet makes the point that to the extent that this essentially repressive Whig legislation introduced judicial machinery to mediate the application of control, so the insane acquired rudimentary procedural rights in relation to confinement, linking this process with

[44] 17 Geo. III c. 5.
[45] See K. Jones, *A History of the Mental Health Services*, pp. 25–8.

E. P. Thompson's work on the Black Act and the growth of the rule of law in the eighteenth century.[46] The procedure under the Act of 1744 involving two Justices was retained as the method for civil admission to the new county asylums which local magistrates were empowered to build by the County Asylums Act 1808,[47] and two Justices continued to be used until 1890 for lunatics 'not under proper care and control' in parallel with routine procedures for compulsory admission to an asylum as 'a proper person to be detained under care and treatment' which after 1845 required one Justice only.[48] The modern counterparts of these powers entrusted to overseers of the poor and constables to apprehend the mentally disordered on grounds of neglect or a threat to public order are to be found in sections 135 and 136 of the Mental Health Act 1983. Section 135 authorizes a Justice of the Peace, on the application of a mental welfare officer, to issue a warrant for police entry into premises where there is reasonable cause to suspect there is a person believed to be suffering from mental disorder who is unable to care for himself or is being ill-treated or neglected. Such a person may be removed to a 'place of safety'[49] and detained for three days pending medical assessment and a decision as to his future treatment needs. Section 136 provides a similar power of removal and detention where a person who appears to be suffering from mental disorder and to be in immediate need of care and control is found in a public place by a police officer.

The procedures for commitment other than in these circumstances of crisis, of which there were several, only the basic elements being discussed here, until 1948 differed for pauper (later rate-aided) and private patients. The former were closely associated with the machinery of the Poor Law, while the latter were rather the province of the family, transfer to an asylum being conceived as a contractual delegation of domestic responsibilities. Thus, in the nineteenth century the relieving officer made the application for commitment of

---

[46] D. J. Mellet, 'Society, the State and Mental Illness, 1790–1890: Social, Cultural and Administrative Aspects of the Institutional Care and Control of the Insane in Nineteenth Century England'. University of Cambridge Ph.D thesis, 1978, p. 143.

[47] 48 Geo. III c. 96.

[48] 8 & 9 Vict. c. 126, section 48.

[49] Section 135(6) defines 'a place of safety' as 'residential accommodation provided by a local authority under Part III of the National Health Service Act 1946, or under Part III of the National Assistance Act 1948, a hospital as defined by this Act, a mental nursing home or residential home for mentally disordered persons, or any other suitable place the occupier of which is willing temporarily to receive the patient.'

pauper lunatics, his duties being inherited by the duly authorized officer and then by the mental welfare officer, reflecting the origin of the mental health social worker's role in the processes of the Poor Law. In the private sector, technically, 'any person' could originally sign the order, but the Lunacy Acts Amendment Act 1889 specified that, where possible, that person be a relative. The small number of private patients admitted as such to public asylums were subject to this procedure and not that for pauper lunatics. The fusion of procedures for public and private patients from 1948[50] produced the problem of the respective roles of family and social workers in making the decisions to apply for admission. The Mental Health Act 1959 placed the mental welfare officer under an obligation to consult with the nearest relative before making an application for admission for treatment under section 26 and allowed the nearest relative to block the application. However, section 52 provided that on application to the County Court the nearest relative's functions could be transferred to a replacement if he or she was held to have 'unreasonably' objected. The relative was accorded a parallel power to make application under section 26 which the mental welfare officer could not prevent. The 1983 Act, while upgrading and extending the role of the social worker, basically maintains this balance of responsibilities.

The role of medical certificates in support of the application for admission originated in 1774 in the private sector and in 1815 for pauper lunatics. The Madhouses Act 1774[51] section 21 provided for a £100 fine of the proprietor unless the patient was received under 'an Order, in Writing, under the Hand and Seal of some Physician, Surgeon or Apothecary, that such person is proper to be received into such House or Place as a Lunatick'. In the case of pauper lunatics the first statutory mention of medical certificates is in a statute of 1815,[52] section 8 of which obliged overseers of the poor to return lists of lunatics and idiots within parishes accompanied by certificates from medical practitioners. The medical certificate first became a formal part of the commitment process in 1819.[53] The requirement was gradually rationalized by provisions relating to such matters as complicity between certifying doctors and the need for a specialist acquaintance with psychiatry. For private patients, two

---

[50] See Chapter 8.
[51] 14 Geo. III c. 49.
[52] 55 Geo. III c. 46.
[53] 59 Geo. III c. 127, section 1.

medical recommendations came to be required and for pauper
lunatics one, though in the pauper case there was the additional
requirement of a magisterial order, which was not extended to
private patients until 1889. When the Mental Health Act 1959
abolished the requirement of a Justice's order as the determinant
element in long-term civil commitment, it was provided that two
medical recommendations should be required, as in the case for
private patients before the introduction of the Justice's order. The
elevation of medical recommendations within the commitment
process heightened the question of the respective roles of doctors
and social workers in activating the procedures. We shall see that this
was a matter for interprofessional recrimination in the 1950s.[54] The
1959 Act did safeguard that in the final analysis the mental welfare
officer may, after the necessary consultations, refuse to follow
medical advice to apply for the patient's compulsory admission. The
requirement of Justices' orders for commitment to county asylums
was present from their inception in 1808, but in relation to private
admission the authority to detain was that of the person seeking the
admission of the patient and that person possessed a power of
discharge in addition to those of the Medical Superintendent, the
Lunacy Commissioners, and the Visiting Justices. The order of
a specially constituted 'judicial authority' was added to private
commitment procedures by the Lunacy Acts Amendment Act 1889[55]
as a judicial safeguard of individual liberty. Another figure who
officiated in relation to commitment in the Victorian period was the
clergyman, who was an alternative to the Justice of the Peace in the
commitment of pauper lunatics.[56] His role was abolished as part of
the triumph of legalism in 1889–90, but it is interesting that the
concept was revived in the proposals for a new treatment order short
of full certification as of unsound mind in the Mental Treatment Bill
1923. Originally commitment was indefinite, pending discharge by
the relevant authorities, medical, supervisory, visitorial or private,
but formal periodic review in the form of 'continuation orders' was

[54] See Chapter 9.
[55] Section 2(1).
[56] Philip Bean refers to a Bill drawn up by the Alleged Lunatic's Friend Society in
1847 for transferring lunacy and asylums to the control of the bishops and clergy of
each county. Apparently *The Lancet* (understandably, given the radical background of
its founder, Thomas Wakley) derided this idea of 'giving the bishops a finger in the pie'
as one 'which could scarcely have originated in any other but the brain of a lunatic'.
See P. Bean, *Compulsory Admissions to Mental Hospitals*. Chichester: John Wiley, 1980,
p. 37.

introduced in the late nineteenth century. Long-term commitment orders were supplemented by procedures of emergency admission for both paupers and private patients in the course of the Victorian period, but express admission for observation for an intermediate period under the Mental Health Act was a new legislative concept. Powers of discharge were constructed in terms of a hierarchy of control determined by 'barring certificates': section 72 of the Lunatics Act 1845 empowered the person who signed the order for admission of a private patient to discharge, but section 75 provided that the medical man in charge of the house or the registered medical attendant could block its exercise by certifying the patient 'dangerous and unfit to be at large'. This in turn could be overruled by the Lunacy Commissioners' written consent. The 1959 Mental Health Act's introduction of Mental Health Review Tribunals has rendered discharge rather than admission the key point at which a formal safeguard operates, albeit one subject to the limitations which will be discussed later.

Medical men signing certificates for admission to an asylum had been conceded special statutory protection against suit by the end of the nineteenth century. The 1889 Lunacy Acts Amendment Act section 12 (the Lunacy Act 1890 section 330) provided substantive protection in that no action could be sustained unless bad faith or lack of reasonable care were demonstrated and procedural protection in that the defendant could stay the proceedings by proving the absence of a prima-facie case against him. This derogation from patients' normal rights of access to the courts in respect of wrongful detention is compounded by the substantive inefficacy of Habeas Corpus in this area because of its dependence for success upon lack of proper formal authority for detention.[57]

Detention as a mental patient has specific effects upon civil capacity, thus linking the questions of modification of legal status and special legal provision which have so far received separate treatment. Such matters as court access, which has already been discussed, voting, the possession of a driving licence, liability to censorship of correspondence, and jury service are all affected. It is noteworthy that informal patients are subject to some of the same disabilities. The 1959 Act's censorship of the correspondence of informal patients was justified on the basis of the principle that once admitted,

[57] See the discussion in *X. v. United Kingdom*, application no. 6998/75 (1981) 4 EHRR 181.

discrimination between patients of different legal status was therapeutically undesirable. The position of informally-admitted mental patients was thus assimilated to that of formally-admitted patients and not to equally informally-admitted patients suffering from somatic illness, despite the professed aim of assimilating the general treatment and care of psychiatric disorder to that of physical illness.

Special provision for mentally abnormal offenders can be briefly indicated. They first became the objects of separate legislation in the Criminal Lunatics Act 1800. Although they were initially admitted to county asylums with civil patients without affording special asylum accommodation, the Criminal Lunatics Act 1860 created Broadmoor as an institutional repository specifically available for this category under Home Office control. Under the Mental Deficiency Act 1913 special hospitals were also provided at Moss Side and Rampton for defectives of violent, criminal, or dangerous propensities by the Board of Control. Historically, argument regarding the appropriate legal framework for mentally abnormal offenders and disruptive patients within civil categories has partly hinged upon whether their disposition is conceived in essentially penal or therapeutic terms. The disposition of disruptive patients, clinically defined as suffering from psychopathy or personality disorders, has caused particular problems where their behaviour does not justify maximum security accommodation. Because the 1959 Act accorded ordinary mental hospitals the power to refuse to admit patients, unnecessarily restrictive dispositions may be made necessary. It is in this context that the movement to intermediate Regional Secure Units developed.

We now turn from the general legal context within which the rise and fall of legalism is situated to the institutional structures in relation to which the law has assumed shape.

3 Foundations of the Modern Mental Health System

THE care and treatment of the mentally disordered has undergone many radical changes in the last two hundred years, but it is nonetheless possible to detect certain themes in its development which provide continuity and to identify conflicts and contradictions which have exerted an important influence throughout the period. In major respects, the late eighteenth and early nineteenth century was formative of the modern mental health system, fixing its most fundamental characteristics and establishing the basis for the struggles which were to shape its future. As we have seen in relation to the legal status of the mentally disordered, this period was seminal for modern social thought and practices. Michel Foucault treats the transformation as being so profound as to constitute an epistemological break in the history of Western culture. Geoffrey Pearson defines the nature of this break in the following terms:

At this precise point—not before, and not later—the modern controversies announce themselves. There was crime, deviance and madness before this point, of course, but it is then that men begin to relate to it, and see it, in a different way. Social thought and practice undergo a convulsion, and out of it emerge the institutions of the police, the penal system, psychiatry, education and welfare; and also new conceptions of life, family and work.[1]

This helps to explain the persistence of particular themes in perceptions of deviance and strategies of social control between the second half of the eighteenth century and the second half of the twentieth century, which have only lightly been obscured by terminological revolutions. Mapping these continuities provides us with some important organizing concepts for analysing the relationship of law to the modern mental health system.

The late eighteenth and early nineteenth century period witnessed a gradual shift in the structures of social discipline from the paternalism, localism, and generality which had been their character in pre-industrial England under the government of the landed gentry, toward more mechanistic, centralized, and specialized systems for the

[1] G. Pearson, *The Deviant Imagination*. London: Macmillan, 1975, p. 147.

management of poverty, crime, and madness appropriate to an urbanizing, industrializing society and a rapidly advancing capitalist mode of production which thrived upon rational calculation. For the mentally disordered, the consequent reorganization entailed a dramatic escalation in the rate of their consignment to institutions, their substantial segregation from other classes of the deviant and the destitute, and the emergence of the medical profession as the pre-eminent therapeutic power in the new system of asylums.

The Impact of the Asylum

Institutionalization may be treated as the most important of these changes, in that the other two flowed from it. The experience of confining the mentally disordered in general mixed workhouses, gaols, and houses of correction in the eighteenth century had been unfortunate as they proved disruptive and troublesome, both to the other inmates and the authorities. It is significant in this respect that the Act of 1808 'for the better Care and Maintenance of Lunatics, being Paupers or Criminals in England' which authorized counties to build institutions for the reception of lunatics at public expense incorporated both pauper and criminal lunatics and described the existing practice of their detention in other types of accommodation as 'highly dangerous and inconvenient'.[2] So segregation was not only a manifestation of the concerns of the lunacy reformers of the day, whether Evangelical humanitarians seeking to establish provision specially suited to the needs of the insane or Benthamite utilitarians indulging their passion for classification, marking off the boundary between those who were and those who were not capable of participating in liberal contractual society. It was also a phenomenon generated in 'the depths of confinement itself'.[3] Similarly, the advent of an institutional system designed exclusively for the accommodation of the mentally disordered created the need for professional and bureaucratic apparatuses of management, that is, a site for the development of psychiatry as a specialism of medicine and a domain in which the medical profession could claim the foremost right to control the organization of patients' existence as against others—the magistrates, Poor Law officials, lawyers, and relatives—who also had claims to participate.

[2] 48 Geo. III c. 96. The Criminal Lunatics Act 1860 took the process of classification a stage further by providing for the separate institutionalization of criminal lunatics.
[3] M. P. Foucault, *Madness and Civilization*. New York: Vintage Books, 1973, p. 224; A. T. Scull, *Museums of Madness*. London: Allen Lane, 1979, pp. 41–2.

The process of institutionalization of the mentally disordered was not new: although in the second half of the eighteenth century unknown numbers still languished as 'single lunatics' in cellars and attics, or in mixed institutions as paupers or criminals, specialized institutions did exist. The most famous of these was Bethlem Hospital, founded in 1247 as the Priory of the Order of St Mary of Bethlehem, which had been an institution for the insane since the fourteenth century. Its name became corrupted to 'Bedlam' and by the eighteenth century the term had become synonymous with untamed madness:

> With its shaven-headed, near-naked crew of grinning zanies, melancholy scholars, pentecostal fanatics, and Hogarthian Tom Rakewells whose rakes' progress had ended here, Bedlam was a kind of Spectator Club of uncivilization, pure animality.[4]

What was exceptional about the later eighteenth century was the expansion of the realm of the institution. The Act for the Regulation of Madhouses of 1774 reflected the growth of private commercial institutions.[5] In London and the major cities, where the pressures to institutionalization were greatest, state-sponsored provision was anticipated by the erection of hospitals financed by voluntary public subscription in London (1751), Newcastle upon Tyne (1764), Manchester (1766), York (1777), and Liverpool (1795).[6] The Act of 1808 authorizing county Justices to levy a rate to finance the construction of public asylums marked the first initiative by the

---

[4] R. Porter, 'Being Mad in Georgian England', *History Today* 31 (December 1981), p. 43.

[5] See W. Ll. Parry-Jones, *The Trade in Lunacy*. London: Routledge and Kegan Paul, 1972.

[6] Andrew Scull has argued that it was the dissolution of the ties of the old paternalistic order by the creation of a national market economy and the reorganization of social relationships on the basis of the cash nexus which created the conditions for the movement toward institutionalization rather than the pressures of industrialization and urbanization *per se*. It was changing social relations and not the consequences of technical change which were responsible (*Decarceration* pp. 26–36). In support, he adduces the fact that the earliest county asylums were mainly built in *rural* areas. A problem with this proposition is that surely the erosion of paternalistic structures was at its most advanced in the industrial areas and the cities, so that one would, on Scull's own thesis, still expect institutionalization to have proceeded at a greater pace in an industrial and urban context. The burgeoning of public subscription asylums in major cities in the second half of the eighteenth century and the boarding out of pauper lunatics in private asylums do partially satisfy this expectation. State sponsored capital spending on institutional provision was, however, impeded by the resistance of ratepayers to the various new and costly responsibilities being thrust upon them.

central state to promote special institutional provision for the insane. However, the response at the level of the local state was uneven. Only seventeen asylums had been built by 1842, and there were none in the West Midlands and the North,[7] the majority of authorities having been dissuaded by cost. To remedy this, the Lunatic Asylums Act of 1845[8] made the establishment of asylums mandatory. Such a necessity for the resort to compulsion in the relationship between central Government and local authorities was a feature of the history of early nineteenth century state intervention, another example being the conversion of the discretion to establish county and borough police forces into a duty by the County and Borough Police Act 1856.[9] In the movement toward the institutionalization of the deviant and unproductive, it paralleled the imposition of duties to build workhouses (1834)[10] and prisons (1835).[11] Within these institutions, some modelled explicitly upon Bentham's prototypical Panopticon, the incarcerated populations were subjected to highly structured disciplinary regimes dedicated to the inculcation of principles of orderly behaviour.[12] Once a developed institutional system was available, it could serve as a convenient solution to the difficulties of disposal of a wide range of social misfits, affording a welcome release to poor families with such dependants. The fact that there was a corresponding massive increase in officially recorded insanity suggests that the definition of the term was expanded to enable the asylums to perform this function. Between 1845 and 1890, while the general population rose by 78 per cent, the number of lunatics more than quadrupled.[13] The size of asylums increased from an average of 116 inmates in 1827 to 297 in 1850 and 802 in 1890.[14] This increase was concentrated significantly amongst pauper lunatics: between 1844 and 1890, private patients increased by 101 per cent, but their pauper counterparts were swelled by an enormous 363.7 per cent increase.[15] According to Andrew Scull, 'pauper lunatics were quite definitely recruited from only the poorer

[7] K. Jones, *A History of the Mental Health Services*, pp. 88–9, 114–15; A. T. Scull, *Museums of Madness*, p. 29.

[8] 8 & 9 Vict. c. 126.

[9] On the early British police, see T. Bowden, *Beyond the Limits of the Law*, pp. 215–18.

[10] 4 & 5 Will. IV c. 76.

[11] 5 & 6 Will. IV c. 38. See A. T. Scull, *Decarceration*, pp. 21, 34.

[12] M. Foucault, *Discipline and Punish*. London: Allen Lane, 1977, Part 3, Chapter 3.

[13] A. T. Scull, *Museums of Madness*, p. 223.

[14] V. Skultans, *English Madness*. London: Routledge and Kegan Paul, 1979, p. 122.

[15] A. T. Scull, *Museums of Madness*, p. 233.

segments of the community', although some may have been drawn from the 'respectable' working classes,[16] and it should also be borne in mind that the evidence before the 1877 House of Commons Select Committee on Lunacy Law makes it clear that the high cost of care in private licensed houses led to many members of the middle classes finding themselves confined in public asylums as 'pauper lunatics'. Contemporaries were very disturbed by this apparent increase in insanity, attributing it either to a real surge in the incidence of the phenomenon, brought on by the pressures of advancing civilization, or to artificial factors such as the modern revelation of a previously largely concealed problem.[17]

In qualification of this picture, it needs to be appreciated that the insane poor were not wholly segregated from the mass of paupers. In 1876, in the early stages of the agitation which produced the Lunacy Act 1890, there were 54,407 pauper lunatics, and of these, while 33,719 were accommodated in county and borough asylums, 15,509 were in workhouses and 6,526 were in receipt of outdoor relief.[18] Until 1845, the cheaper cost of building workhouses rather than asylums and maintaining paupers in the former rather than the latter conspired to impede the transfer of the insane to specialized institutions.[19] In the late 1840s, following the conversion of the construction of public asylums into a positive duty, there was a considerable transfer of lunatic inmates from the workhouses to the asylums, but as the latter became filled, they returned a proportion of their chronic population to the workhouses.[20] The distribution of the mentally disordered between asylums and Poor Law institutions was to remain problematic until the Poor Law's abolition.

The asylum has been a constant element in the mental health system. It is true that while custodial institutions, workhouses, prisons, and lunatic asylums, loomed large in the physical and social landscape of Victorian Britain, in the twentieth century there has been a partially successful reaction against the institution, stimulated by perception of the ill effects of institutionalization. However, the critique of the institution is of some antiquity as a feature of British cultural life. Daniel Defoe (1660–1729), whose breadth of interest

[16] Ibid., pp. 241–2.
[17] See *Special Report of the Commissioners in Lunacy to the Lord Chancellor on the Alleged Increase of Insanity*, 1897.
[18] *Thirtieth Report of the Commissioners in Lunacy*, 1876.
[19] R. G. Hodgkinson, 'Provision for Pauper Lunatics, 1834–1871', *Medical History* 10 (1966), pp. 138–54.
[20] V. Skultans, *English Madness*, p. 129.

extended to the treatment of lunatics—he wrote essays calling for the construction of a public asylum for 'fools' or 'naturals'[21] and for public control of private madhouses[22]—was himself a victim of the institution, being held as a debtor in Newgate, and in *Moll Flanders* he took his revenge upon it: 'There are more thieves and rogues made by that prison of Newgate, than by all the clubs and societies of villains in the nation.'[23] The ironic contention of the societal reaction theorists that the apparatuses of social control can in a variety of senses actually generate deviance has a long pedigree. Charles Dickens, who was also personally acquainted with the effects of institutionalization, his father and the rest of his family having been detained in the Marshalsea Debtors' Prison, gave the subject extensive treatment in his novels. Dickens was concerned with the phenomenon of constraint, both psychological and physical: in *Great Expectations*, Miss Havisham had condemned herself to live out the rest of her life in a timeless prison of her own construction, while in *Little Dorrit* (1857) he selected the Marshalsea itself as the centre-piece. Dickens develops an extraordinarily sensitive portrayal of the psychology of institutionalization, which is at its most poignant in the character of William Dorrit, who bears the shame of imprisonment by trading upon his status as 'the Father of the Marshalsea', the object of the supposed great respect of his fellow 'Collegians'.[24]

The perception of the institution as positively harmful to its inmates was applied in the Victorian period to the asylum as well as to the prison. Before the 1877 Select Committee, certain witnesses took the view that the characteristic functioning of asylum life itself bred mental disorder. Mr. Ramsay, one of the members of the Committee, asked Sir James Coxe, a Medical Commissioner of the Scottish Board of Lunacy: 'I presume I may assume that a patient may be so far irritated by confinement in an asylum, that the mental disease would be aggravated by his confinement there?' To which the reply was 'Yes, I have no doubt that there are a good many cases that are hurt by being placed in asylums.'[25] Dr Joseph Mortimer Granville, who in the

---

[21] D. Defoe, *Essay upon Projects*. London, 1697. Reprinted Menston, Scolar Press, 1969, pp. 178–84.

[22] In R. Hunter and I. Macalpine, *Three Hundred Years of Psychiatry 1535–1860*. London: Oxford University Press, 1963, pp. 266–7.

[23] Quoted in M. Foot, *Debts of Honour*. London: Picador, 1980, p. 165.

[24] C. Dickens, *Little Dorrit*. Harmondsworth: Penguin, 1967. See especially pp. 273–4.

[25] *Report from the House of Commons Select Committee on Lunacy Law*, Minutes of Evidence, Question and Answer 2, 104.

same year headed *The Lancet's* inquiry into 'The Care and Cure of the Insane', referred to the 'dementia' into which fresh cases were liable to drift in the absence of individual treatment and when associated with large numbers under a common regime.[26] This Victorian recognition of the pathological potential of the asylum foreshadows that to be elaborated in Russell Barton's *Institutional Neurosis*.[27] This anti-institutional sensibility called forth, both in the nineteenth and the twentieth centuries, movements in favour of decarceration. Mortimer Granville, before the 1877 Select Committee, claimed that one-third of the patients in asylums could safely be released[28] and Dr Charles Alexander Lockhart Robertson, former Superintendent of the Sussex County Asylum and one of the Lord Chancellor's Visitors in Lunacy, called for the boarding out of chronic patients on the grounds that they would be happier outside the confines of the asylum. Unlike their twentieth-century counterparts, however, the Victorian decarcerators were not even partially successful in converting the state to non-institutional strategies of social management.[29]

Disciplinary institutions, as houses of destitution, criminality, and madness, became stigmatized, partly because of their authoritarian, detentionary, and penal aspects, and partly because of the anti-social reputation of their populations. In popular consciousness, insanity was still perceived as 'part of a gothic landscape of doom and terror, synonymous with bestiality' forming 'a configuration of which confinement (was) a necessary part'.[30] Despite the formal supersession of the medieval demonological characterization of madness by the conception of mental disease, outside 'enlightened' and official circles the latter lost its status of scientific neutrality by popular classification as a contagion. In 1887, a medical writer distinguishing specialist and popular views of insanity observed as follows:

For the general public it is fully established that one becomes a lunatic himself who listens to the ravings of others, and that it is sufficient to be shut up in an asylum to completely lose one's reason. Altogether opposed to this is the opinion of specialists. . . . Many facts, including the apparent immunity of doctors and attendants, in spite of being constantly thrown upon (the insane) seem to favour a negative reply.[31]

[26] Ibid., Answer 8, 846.
[27] R. W. Barton, *Institutional Neurosis*. Bristol: John Wright, 1959.
[28] *Report from the Select Committee on Lunacy Law*, Minutes of Evidence, Answer 8, 890.
[29] A. T. Scull, *Decarceration*, Chapter 7.
[30] V. Skultans, *English Madness*, p. 17.
[31] D. Hack Tuke, review of an article by Dr Ball in *L'Encéphale. Journal des Maladies Mentales et Nerveuses, Journal of Mental Science* 33 (1887–8), p. 140.

Under these conditions, moral panics regarding the dangers of sane people being locked up in asylums could readily be generated, especially in periods of therapeutic pessimism, as in the late nineteenth century, when the custodial functions of the lunacy system were dominant. It was in response to agitation inspired by this concern that the 1859 and 1877 House of Commons Select Committees were established. A surge of popular fear that unscrupulous doctors and lunacy administrators were locking up people whose reason was still intact took place in the 1920s, precipitating the appointment of the Royal Commission on Lunacy and Mental Disorder (1924–6). On each occasion, however, the official inquiry negatived allegations of endemic abuse and failed to concede radical demands for further legal safeguards.

Popular concern has not solely been concentrated upon the fate of the sane, however. The argument has been about the legitimate boundaries of medical coercion as much as about the fear of insanity per se, thus matching the twin origins of asylum stigma noted above. It is sometimes difficult to disentangle, when one examines the lunacy reform campaigns of the 1880s and 1920s, whether the main fear was that the sane should through mistake or conspiracy suffer mixture with the insane, or that the medical concept of insanity should expand to embrace mere eccentricity. Peter McCandless has in fact characterized nineteenth-century lunacy reform campaigns aiming at greater public control of private madhouses and more extensive judicial involvement in processes of commitment as involved in a dispute as to where the line demarcating sanity from insanity should be drawn and thus resisting the further psychiatric conversion of non-conformity and 'immorality' into illness.[32]

Prominent in the campaigns to strengthen legal safeguards of civil liberty throughout the period have been societies formed by ex-patients and their sympathizers, which have engaged in vocal and often sensational agitation. In 1845, John Perceval, son of the assassinated Prime Minister, Spencer Perceval, and author of Perceval's Narrative (1838),[33] an account of his own experiences in a private madhouse, founded the Alleged Lunatic's Friend Society 'for

[32] P. McCandless, 'Liberty and Lunacy: the Victorians and Wrongful Confinement', Journal of Social History 5 (1978), p. 381. This article furnishes some extremely interesting historical detail regarding the individual causes célèbres of the lunacy reformers of the period. For alienists' tendencies to correlate insanity with vice see V. Skultans, English Madness, Chapter 5.

[33] G. Bateson (ed.) Perceval's Narrative: a patient's account of his psychosis 1830–2. London: Hogarth Press, 1962.

the protection of the British Subject from unjust confinement on the grounds of mental derangement and the redress of persons so confined'.[34] The activities of this Association were in part responsible for the appointment in 1859 of a House of Commons Select Committee to investigate the lunacy system and determine whether scandalous complaints of abuse were justified. The 1877 Committee received evidence from Louisa Lowe, Secretary of the Lunacy Law Reform Association, founded in 1871,[35] and from its offshoot, the Lunacy Law Amendment Society, formed in 1876.[36] The Macmillan Commission on Lunacy and Mental Disorder (1924–6) allocated substantial time to the evidence of Robert Montgomery Birch Parker, Chairman of the National Society for Lunacy Reform, founded in 1920,[37] and in the period preceding the Mental Health Act 1959, two MPs, Donald Johnson and Norman Dodds, the former of whom was an ex-mental patient, launched a similar campaign for the better protection of patients' liberties.[38] Popular fears for the 'liberty of the subject' were also fuelled by sensational press revelations of abuses, and, in the Victorian period particularly, by novels recounting experiences of the unjustly confined, notably Henry Cockton's *Valentine Vox* (1840)[39] and Charles Reade's *Hard Cash* (1863).[40]

These societies and campaigns consistently failed to make any real impact upon the legislative process. There were a number of general reasons for this. One was the fact that the hostile views of ex-patients toward their former curators were liable to be discounted as the residual effects of mental illness. Secondly, ex-patients who felt sufficiently strongly to combat the existing system on the basis of their personal experiences were often so incensed at the treatment they had received at the hands of what they perceived as a medical and bureaucratic autocracy whose unresponsiveness to the resistance of 'deluded' patients was impenetrable, that they were prone to intemperate attacks which tended to confirm their misguidedness in the eyes of officialdom. Thirdly, the demands of these societies were

---

[34] *Report of the House of Commons Select Committee on Lunatics*, 1860, p. 214.

[35] *Report from the House of Commons Select Committee on Lunacy Law*, Minutes of Evidence, see especially Questions and Answers 5630–4.

[36] Ibid.: James Billington, Questions and Answers 6,899–7,022; 7,042–7,191.

[37] *Report of the Royal Commission on Lunacy and Mental Disorder: Minutes of Evidence*, 1926, I, Questions and Answers 10,346 *et seq*. Mr Parker was a non-practising barrister and claimed 1,000 members for his society.

[38] *The Times*, 18 May 1957.

[39] H. Cockton, *The Life and Adventures of Valentine Vox the Ventriloquist*. London: Robert Tyas, 1840.

[40] C. Reade, *Hard Cash*. London: Sampson Low, Son, & Marston, 1863.

often unclear. Were they opposed to the conceptualization and treatment of insanity as a *medical* condition? Did they accept this, but object to *coercive* psychiatry? Did they in fact wish the treatment of mental illness to be more assimilated to that of physical illness or less? The answers to these questions were not always clear, with the result that they tended to articulate a generalized suspicion and sense of grievance rather than to base their case upon systematic analysis of the deficiencies of the system and how they could be remedied. It could be argued that what they lacked was anything comparable to the corpus of critical Anti-Psychiatric literature which so undermined the dominant logic of psychiatry in the 1960s and the 1970s. To the extent that MIND (National Association for Mental Health) can be said to have inherited the mantle of these earlier societies for lunacy reform, its contribution to the success of legalism in the early 1980s in part reflects the contemporary intellectual defensiveness of orthodox medical psychiatry.

The Medical and Bureaucratic Management of the Asylum System

The new asylum system being established in the early nineteenth century furnished the main *institutional* basis for the development of psychiatry as the exclusive province of a branch of the medical profession, and provided the rationale for special apparatuses of bureaucratic supervision and control. The deepening involvement of doctors in the treatment of the insane in the course of the nineteenth century has been characterized by Thomas Szasz[41] and Andrew Scull,[42] among others, as an instance of medical imperialism, an example of the medical profession striving to establish hegemonic control over wider areas of the community's experience. Scull seems to draw on two main theoretical perspectives within the sociology of the professions in his analysis of the rise of the psychiatric profession. Following Freidson,[43] who identifies in autonomy the core characteristic of professional status, he portrays medical men occupied in the treatment of the insane as engaged in a vigorous struggle to fight off the challenges of rival therapists such as the Moral Managers and to repel interference by laymen, especially the local magistrates, who until 1889 were the managers of the public asylums. Implicitly, he also seems to be influenced by, or to share elements in, the perspective of Margaret Larson, who counterposes to the function-

41 See T. S. Szasz, *The Manufacture of Madness*. London: Paladin, 1972.
42 See A. T. Scull, *Decarceration* and *Museums of Madness*.
43 E. Freidson, *Profession of Medicine*. New York: Dodd, Mead, 1970.

alist view of professions arising to fulfil objective social needs a concept of 'professionalization as the process by which producers of special services sought to constitute *and control* a market for their expertise'.[44] This approach accentuates the active role of professions in creating, shaping, and controlling markets for their services, and presents them as aggressively expansionist.

On this basis we would expect the medical profession, and especially psychiatric practitioners, to have been united against increasing legal formalities and restraints on treatment of the insane and consistently to have resisted the extension of the lay magistrate's role in the processes of admission to an asylum. This is the impression given by David Ewins, who seems to accept the view that the profession's legal demands have rested upon a strategy of medical expansionism, at least in the case of the professional élite.[45] Thus, doctors appear in the role of a powerful pressure group whose demands regarding the relaxation of legal controls have been met because they have been in harmony with the broad objectives of the state. We shall see that this view tends to overvalue the part played by the medical profession in this process relative to that of the state. Emphasis on medical expansionism can even lead to an apolitical account of the medicalization of insanity in which doctors become 'the villains of the piece'. It is important to stress that doctors not only possess rights and powers conferred upon them by the state as members of an ancient and powerful professional calling, but also have obligations as servants of the state's interest in controlling the liberties of mental patients and channelling their treatment and rehabilitation in accordance with the state's demands.

A useful key to comprehension of attitudes within the medical profession to legal aspects of their involvement with the insane is to be found in the work of Michel Foucault. In interpreting the reaction of doctors from the early nineteenth century to their situation in the relatively new social construct of the asylum, Foucault stresses the essentially moral authority and techniques they employed to regulate the conduct of their patients. Foucault defines this moral authority of the doctor as founded upon:

Family-child relations, centred on the theme of paternal authority; Transgression-Punishment relations, centred on the theme of immediate justice;

---

[44] M. S. Larson, *The Rise of Professionalism*. Berkeley: University of California Press, 1977, p. xvi.
[45] D. Ewins, 'The Origins of the Compulsory Commitment Provisions of the Mental Health Act 1959', University of Sheffield MA thesis, 1974, p. 57.

Madness-Disorder relations, centred on the theme of social and moral order.[46]

The power of asylum doctors was, then, at root, a moral power:

> But very soon the meaning of this moral practice escaped the physician, to the very extent that he enclosed his knowledge in the norms of positivism . . . psychiatry would become a medicine of a particular style: those most eager to discover the origin of madness in organic causes or in hereditary dispositions would not be able to avoid this style. They would be all the more unable to avoid it in that this particular style—bringing into play increasingly obscure moral powers—would originally be a sort of bad conscience; they would increasingly confine themselves in positivism, the more they felt their practice slipping out of it.[47]

This analysis recognizes that the medical profession's annexation of the care and treatment of the insane was not one which brought with it professional aggrandisement and social enhancement so much as a host of ambiguities, contradictions, and problems. On the one hand, doctors naturally wished to justify their claims to exclusive competence in treating the insane by the application of medical paradigms and by projecting themselves as healers. On the other hand, they were engaged in practices of regulating and attempting to rehabilitate a wide range of social deviants. In particular, their 'patients' were under legal detention in their charge, and the authorization of that detention incorporated an element of medical recommendation. Asylum doctors and general practitioners, through the responsibility of certification, were thus placed in the position of casting themselves in the role of healers when they were also vested by the state with the role of gaolers.

How was coercion to be integrated in and reconciled with the ideology of medical practice as a benevolent, healing enterprise at the service of its clients? As far as legal regulation was concerned there were really two alternative strategies, the one cautious and conservative, the second more ambitious and radical. The medical profession could leave decisions affecting patients' liberty in the hands of legal or lay authorities and in that way distance themselves from the operation of the apparatuses of coercion. Alternatively, they could bid for control of compulsory powers themselves, and by ousting the authoritarian figure of the magistrate and eliminating

[46] M. P. Foucault, *Madness and Civilization*, p. 274.
[47] Ibid., pp. 274–5.

formalistic procedure, attempt to portray their use as an integral part of the therapeutic process, drawing upon the analogy with somatic illness where the patient is unconscious and unable to consent to treatment.

Historically, attitudes to these competing legal strategies have varied both within the medical profession at large and within the ranks of its psychiatric branch, and the strategy predominantly favoured has varied *inter alia* with expectations as to the political feasibility of demands for the relaxation of legal restraints. Looking beyond their significance within the medical profession, one can detect in these views traces of broader ideological positions. The conservative strategy possesses an affinity with classical liberalism in its restrictive conception of professional authority, in which the professional expert inhabits the narrowly prescribed province of the technician. Here, the professional role is defined essentially as that of consultant. Professional skill should be at the service of the client on request, but where there exists a danger that specialists' competence might be abused in such a way as to threaten the liberty of those whom they purport to serve, as might be the case with psychiatrists or civil servants, it is considered imperative that their activities be subjected to restraints incorporating a lay element in order to safeguard individual freedom. It is this conception of professional authority which is expressed in Thomas Szasz's notion of 'contractual psychiatry', which he idealizes as the goal of political individualism.[48]

This may be contrasted with the more ambitious conception of professional authority which meshes with state interventionism and legitimizes the radical strategy toward medicalizing the doctor's psychiatric function. In this conception, professional expertise must be mobilized by the state to advance the solution of social problems. In order to be able to operate effectively, professional experts must be less hampered by controls and especially by lay regulation, laymen being by definition ill-equipped to judge the decisions and actions of professionals. Interventionism therefore encourages professional expansionism, but this is not universally welcomed by professionals themselves, sections of whom may shy away from the concomitant responsibility and the impact upon relationships with their clients. When, in 1959, there was finally a radical reduction in legal restrictions upon the medical practice of psychiatry, and magisterial control of civil commitment was abolished, many doctors were

[48] See, for example, *The Manufacture of Madness*, pp. 129, 264–5.

anxious precisely because of its consequences in terms of the transfer of coercive powers and the adverse change this might effect in doctor-patient relationships.[49] The recognition of the use of coercion in this context as essentially a therapeutic question answerable only by the relevant experts thus did not meet with the unanimous approval of its beneficiaries.

The process of medical colonization of psychiatry was indeed a complex one. It certainly did not flow from the scientific mastery of insanity by medical men. The scientific status of medical knowledge regarding insanity in the early nineteenth century, as in relation to most other conditions, was very primitive and unsystematized. Until the Medical Registration Act 1858, there was as yet no basis for a unitary medical profession. Although their hold was being relaxed as the ascendant market system eroded traditional guild control,[50] medical practice was still divided into three separate professional orders ranked in correspondence with social class. These were the physicians, providing medical services for the rich and usually themselves drawn from the upper classes, the middle-class surgeons, and the relatively humble lower middle-class apothecaries. Certain medical men from all three of these orders were engaged in the private madhouse trade in the eighteenth century, and it was from this base that they were able to bid for a monopoly of the care and treatment of the insane against their clerical and lay rivals. Institutionalization and classification posited a need for the development of a psychiatric profession which, it can be argued, doctors were peculiarly fitted to fulfil. In Scull's persuasive analysis their advantages included the claimed possession of 'cure-alls' which could easily be advertised as effective against insanity, public recognition of their development of these efficacious 'remedies', and the amenability of medical knowledge and treatment to presentation in a scientific milieu appropriate to an age in which thought was becoming increasingly rationalized and secularized.[51]

The development of a medical monopoly was initially hampered, however, by the temporary popularity of a therapeutic method which did not require recognized medical skills. This was moral treatment, developed both in theory and practice by the Tuke family at 'The Retreat', the Quaker asylum near York, from the last years of the

---

[49] See Chapter 9.

[50] N. Parry and J. Parry, *The Rise of the Medical Profession*. London: Croom Helm, 1976, p. 104.

[51] A. T. Scull, *Museums of Madness*, pp. 127–8.

eighteenth century. Much has been written on this novel therapeutic philosophy because its emphasis on humane treatment and optimistic, curative orientation represented a decisive rejection of the eighteenth-century conception of insanity as a species of bestiality,[52] responsive only to crude physical confinement and restraint. Moral treatment rested on the belief that orderly behaviour could be cultivated in the insane by a communication with their remaining humanity through the operation of a calculated system of rewards and deprivations. In other words, appropriate environmental conditions could catalyse recovery. The advocates of moral treatment expressly denied the efficacy of medical treatments, but their nonmedical practices in the end failed to generate an occupational group of lay therapists with the capacity to rival the medical profession. The theory of moral treatment was not a sound basis for the advancement of claims to expertise because it emphasized common skills in human relations, and it omitted to develop a sufficiently distinct theoretical base, remaining reliant upon the medical language of illness, treatment, and cure.[53] Without effective rivals, doctors were able, by such means as the profession of specialized learning regarding insanity elaborated in medical treatises, plausibly to claim exclusive competence to treat and care for the insane. Statutory requirements for medical visitation and superintendence of asylums dating from the 1828 Madhouses Act[54] legally embodied the newly acquired medical monopoly. While the somatic view of insanity as an organic disorder remained the main prop for medical claims, the public credence gained by moral treatment even enabled medical men to claim that those moral practices of their own which were not yet sufficiently disguised in positivism were a legitimate part of the therapeutic armoury. In the increasingly crowded public asylums, however, moral treatment could only really be said to exist in the bastardized form of routine carrot-and-stick management.

Before the middle of the century, the asylum doctors had organized themselves and were furnished with regular journals to foster psychiatric knowledge and to provide a forum for exchanges and debates, so that a sense of professional community, identity, and interest could be generated. In 1841, the Association of Medical Officers of Asylums and Hospitals was founded. This became the Medico-Psychological Association in 1865 and acquired the title

[52] See M. P. Foucault, *Madness and Civilization*, pp. 65–84.
[53] A. T. Scull, *Museums of Madness*, pp. 141–5.
[54] 9 Geo. IV c. 41.

Royal Medico-Psychological Association in 1925, eventually becoming the Royal College of Psychiatrists. The organization's journal, the *Asylum Journal*, was founded by John Charles Bucknill of the Devon County Asylum in 1853, its title changing to the *Asylum Journal of Mental Science* in 1854, to the *Journal of Mental Science* in 1859, and to the *British Journal of Psychiatry* in 1962. An earlier psychiatric journal was the *Journal of Psychological Medicine and Mental Pathology*, established in 1848. Within the psychiatric branch of the medical profession there were, as in the profession as a whole, different sectors with to some extent different interests and perspectives based upon gradations of status and different working environments. There were those who were members of the medical staff of large county asylums, largely concerned with the care of chronic patients, working in enclosed institutions, and absorbed in administration and estate management as well as, or perhaps rather than, medicine. There were, on the other hand, the stars of the profession like Bucknill, Lockhart Robertson, and Granville, who were able to sustain private practices. There was the division between Medical Superintendents of public asylums and medical proprietors of licensed houses and between asylum treatment and the domiciliary treatment of the propertied for 'nervous disorders'. These overlapping divisions ensured that there was no guaranteed unity in the psychiatric ranks, especially on the controversial issues of statutory reform. Less still was unity between 'alienists' and the rest of the medical profession assured. Medical treatment of the insane was of low status within the profession, the psychiatrists suffering from vicarious stigma and the custodial rather than curative orientation of their work. We shall see that there was considerable bad feeling on the part of psychiatric practitioners towards their colleagues in general practice for lack of solidarity on the issue of resisting further legal restraints in the period leading up to the Lunacy Act 1890.[55]

Turning from internal to external conflict, we have seen that the medical ascendancy was purchased at the expense of the moral managers. The psychological approach to the treatment of insanity was inherited in the twentieth century by psychiatric social workers and by clinical psychologists and in the 1960s and 1970s disillusion with the medical paradigms applied by the majority of psychiatrists was to be translated into a renewal of interest in psychological analysis and techniques. At different periods, therefore, in the

[55] See Chapter 4.

medical profession's history as the dominant therapeutic power in the care and treatment of the insane, it has been forced to negotiate territorial challenges from rival groups of therapists purveying alternative concepts and techniques. Asylum doctors also had initially to establish their autonomy in the administration of asylums. Public asylums were built by committees of magistrates who, until the Local Government Act of 1888, which introduced an elective system, constituted the machinery of local government. Visiting Committees of local Justices were the managers of the asylums and responsible for the selection, employment, and the dismissal of medical staff. Although they could have clung to detailed control over the running of the asylums the historical progression was toward administrative delegation to Medical Superintendents.[56] In their associated capacity as arbiters of civil commitment, routinely deciding who was and who was not a fit person to be maintained at public expense as a pauper lunatic, they were again in a position which enabled them to determine the practical limits of medical discretion. It was in relation to this question that the medical profession became engaged in its most bitter external conflict in the civil sphere of its psychiatric practice—not with magistrates themselves but with the judiciary. As Smith makes clear in the criminal context, conflict between medical and legal discourses, because of their differential conceptual order, could not be resolved by synthesis, but only by power.[57] This is equally true in the civil sphere, where the main argument in the late nineteenth century was about whether private commitment should be essentially determined by doctors or by a judicial authority. The stock psychiatric position was that the question 'Who is so insane as to require confinement?' should be interpreted medically: 'Who is too ill to be permitted normal liberties?' The stock legal position was that it should be interpreted as a question of social defence to be determined judicially: 'Whose behaviour, on account of insanity, constitutes a public danger requiring his detention?' The claims of the medical profession to be able to determine questions affecting individual liberty could be seen as threatening to displace the traditional trial model for the ascription of guilt, with which lawyers were intimately familiar, by a therapeutic model for the diagnosis of illness. From a legal point of view this could be perceived as placing decision-making power over vital questions of civil liberty in the

[56] See A. T. Scull, *Museums of Madness*, pp. 162–3, 164–85.
[57] R. Smith, *Trial by Medicine*, p. 40.

hands of experts guided by esoteric knowledge rather than judicial authorities whose reasoning notionally incorporated commonly accepted behavioural standards.

Again, this discursive collision could only be resolved politically and as we shall see, it was the élite of the legal profession who, in the late nineteenth century, drove their side of the argument on to the statute book under the momentum of their superior political power. Similarly, I shall argue that the later triumph of medical discourse and the corresponding decline of legalism in civil aspects of legislation for the mentally ill owed much to a radical reorientation in the political philosophy of the British state.

Turning from the professional territories that were staked out within the developing lunacy system in the nineteenth century to the bureaucratic structure which it generated, we find that there emerged a specialized new administrative and supervisory institution which, although its membership contained elements from both the medical and the legal professions that were by definition potentially antagonistic, was able to develop its own independent interests and policies and played an important part in the conflicts over the direction of Lunacy legislation. This was the Lunacy Commission, the origins of which are traceable to 1774 and which, having been translated into the Board of Control in 1913, survived until the administrative reorganization achieved by the Mental Health Act 1959.

The Act for regulating Madhouses of 1774[58] set up supervisory machinery to check the unbridled expansion of the pioneering private commercial sector without proper controls to protect patients from abuse, either of their liberty or their persons. A Commission was established with authority in the Metropolitan area ('within the cities of London and Westminster and within seven miles of the same, and within the County of Middlesex'), the Commissioners, five in number, to be elected annually by the President and Fellows of the Royal College of Physicians and to perform functions of licensing,[59] visitation[60] and reporting.[61] This Commission was initially temporary but was granted permanent status in 1786. In the provinces the 1774 Act furnished Justices of the Peace with comparable powers. The delegation of control over the composition

[58] 14 Geo. III c. 49.
[59] 14 Geo. III c. 49, section 2.
[60] 14 Geo. III c. 49, section 14.
[61] 14 Geo. III c. 49, section 15.

of the Metropolitan Commissioners to the Royal College of Physicians was an early mark of the state's recognition of medical claims to dominate the care and treatment of the insane, but as concern about the problems of maltreatment and wrongful incarceration escalated and the Commission was vested with more effective and wider powers, the state assumed a more direct interest in its membership. The Madhouses Act 1828[62] reconstituted the Metropolitan Commissioners, increasing their number to fifteen and providing that they should be appointed by and responsible to the Home Secretary. The minimum number of medical practitioners and the number in fact appointed to the Commission in that year was five.[63] In 1832 the legal interest in monitoring detention of the insane was accommodated by the introduction of a statutory requirement that at least two of the Commissioners should be barristers and their transfer from the orbit of the Home Secretary to that of the Lord Chancellor.[64] In 1842, by an Act to operate for an initial period of three years,[65] the Commissioners were given national responsibility and their charge was extended to all types of asylums, including public subscription hospitals. Again the number of Commissioners was increased, and minima of medical and legal membership specified.[66] Finally, in 1845, a full-time, salaried, permanent national Lunacy Commission was installed, with a catchment that extended to lunatics in gaols and workhouses as well as those in asylums, and 'single lunatics'. The Commission was composed of medical, legal, and unpaid lay members, with a lay chairman, to be elected by the other members. The first and greatest Chairman was Lord Ashley, later the 7th Earl of Shaftesbury (1801–1885), who held the position throughout the forty years until his death. Despite the centralization and rationalization represented by this climax of administrative reform, the overall position remained complex: the Commissioners were made partly responsible to the Lord Chancellor and partly to the Home Office;

[62] 9 Geo. IV c. 41. The aristocracy were keen to preserve the private sanctity of the madhouse to avoid scandals and repeated attempts to increase statutory control by leaders of the humanitarian reform movement were blocked in the House of Lords. A Bill pressed by Charles Watkin Williams Wynn in 1819 was rejected on the ground that it trespassed on the province of Medical Superintendents, the Lord Chancellor, Lord Eldon, remarking that 'there could not be a more false humanity than an over humanity with regard to persons afflicted with insanity': 40 *Parliamentary Debates*, col. 1345 (24 June 1819).

[63] K. Jones, *A History of the Mental Health Services*, p. 109.

[64] 2 & 3 Will. IV c. 107.

[65] 5 & 6 Vict. c. 87.

[66] 5 & 6 Vict. c. 87, section 2.

they shared control over pauper lunatics in workhouses with the Poor Law authorities; duties of licensing and visiting provincial private madhouses remained with local Justices, who managed county asylums and were responsible to the Home Secretary, and, further, there was a separate body of Chancery Visitors, responsible to the Lord Chancellor, for Chancery lunatics.

The creation of a permanent national Lunacy Commission was the product of a convergence between the interventionist strand in Benthamism and Evangelical humanitarianism. In the early nineteenth century, these were the two main ideological components of lunacy reform. Benthamites like Sir Samuel Romilly and Sir George Onesiphorus Paul, a magistrate and High Sheriff of Gloucester who was also a prison reformer, made common cause with Evangelicals, amongst whom Ashley, an aristocratic conservative paternalist, became pre-eminent in the field, to fight for public purpose-built asylums and a Lunacy Commission with effective powers. In the pursuit of these objectives the former were primarily motivated by a concern for the efficient and rational organization of provision for the insane which was the concomitant of emergent early industrial capitalism whilst the latter were inspired by a moralism which criticized the social evils attendant upon the new order in terms of the paternalism of that which was being replaced. It was this ironic fusion which established paternalistic interventionism as the predominant character of the Lunacy Commission. It may be seen as a part of the so-called English Revolution in Government[67] whereby in the early to mid-nineteenth century machinery of state intervention progressively expanded in response to the identification and attempted amelioration of a number of social problems, this machinery often taking the form of central supervisory bodies such as the Factory Inspectorate (1833) or the General Board of Health (1848), which represented a compromise between the impetus to central intervention and resistant traditions of local autonomy.[68] The essentially protective definition of the Commission's task justified the entrenchment of a legal element in its composition, and the Commission's heavily bureaucratic and routinized practices led it to

[67] See in particular, O. MacDonagh, 'The Nineteenth Century Revolution in Government: A Reappraisal', *Historical Journal* 1 (1958), pp. 52–67; H. Parris, 'The Nineteenth Century Revolution in Government: A Reappraisal Reappraised', *Historical Journal* 3 (1960), pp. 28–32; W. L. Burn, *The Age of Equipoise*. London: Allen and Unwin, 1964; W. C. Lubenow, *The Politics of Government Growth*. Newton Abbot: David and Charles, 1971.

[68] D. J. Mellet, p. 150.

acquire a legalistic rule-bound image. However, Shaftesburyite paternalism and interventionism militated against these legalistic tendencies converting the Commission into an ally of the legal profession and the lunacy system's other libertarian critics in the late part of the nineteenth century. The Commissioners and later the Board of Control became very much a part of the lunacy establish-ment and were pilloried as such by its detractors, even acquiring amongst the working classes something of the infamy of 'the workhouse Bastilles' and the '"blue butchers" of the police'.[69] They stood by the adequacy of existing safeguards and took the lead from the psychiatric professionals amongst their number in prioritizing early treatment over legal checks on commitment. They resisted the legalism of the Lunacy Act 1890, entering fully into the political manœuvrings which prefigured the measure. The Commission continued after 1890 to oppose the legalism of the Act and its successor, the Board of Control, took several initiatives to reverse the legislative trend, which culminated successfully in the Mental Treatment Act 1930. In 1959, the demise of the Board of Control reflected the belief of its own Commissioners that the very existence of specialized administrative machinery to protect the liberties of individual patients (its other responsibilities having been ceded to the Ministry of Health) was unhealthily reminiscent of an earlier legalistic era. The specialist bureaucracy was therefore an important element in the politics of the decline of legalism in civil legislation for the mentally ill, although not a determinant one: the Lunacy Commis-sioners were unsuccessful in placing their stamp upon legislation in the 1890s because the time was politically inappropriate, but successful in the 1920s because the political climate had significantly changed.[70] The advent of the Mental Health Act Commission under the Mental Health Act 1983 establishes a (similarly) specialized supervisory body which is likely to exert an independent influence upon the future of legal safeguards.

[69] E. C. Midwinter, *Victorian Social Reform*. London: Longmans, 1968, p. 28.
[70] See Chapter 5.

4 The Lunacy Act 1890: Lunacy, Liberty, and the Rule of Law

THE Lunacy Act 1890, Kathleen Jones's 'triumph of legalism', remained in force exercising a pervasive influence over the mental health services for a period of nearly seventy years. It is impossible to appreciate the extent of the revolution in legislative provision accomplished by twentieth-century legislation without an understanding of the Lunacy Act's custodialism, therapeutic pessimism, and intricate legalism. From the standpoint of the reformers of the 1950s it was a monument to formalistic and myopic intervention by the legal profession in affairs which it had not yet admitted to be beyond its competence. From the standpoint of the new legalism of the 1970s, condemnation of its preoccupation with the security of middle-class eccentrics and the somewhat primitive and naïve quality of the safeguards is offset by admiration for its glimmering comprehension of the wider libertarian dimensions of the problem, its general accentuation of legal rights and remedies being seen as philosophically preferable to the Mental Health Act's antipathy to law as a medium for the regulation of the relationship between the mental health system and its clients.

Therapeutic Pessimism and Moral Panic

The first half of the nineteenth century had been a period of therapeutic optimism, expressed in the popularity of Moral Treatment, the Non-Restraint movement pioneered by John Conolly at the Hanwell Asylum in Middlesex, and the curative expectations reposited in the new asylums. The two Acts of 1845,[1] laboured for with great determination by Lord Ashley, constituted a major victory for those who had striven to secure effective legislative protection of the insane from exploitation, abuse, and inhumane treatment. However, the achievement of a permanent national Lunacy Commission and mandatory rather than permissive legislation for the construction of public asylums was to represent a high-water mark, as far as the nineteenth century was concerned, in legal intervention on behalf of the insane. Benthamite and Evangelical reformism gave way in the

---
[1] 8 & 9 Vict. c. 100, c. 126.

second half of the century to a new kind of reform movement. Kathleen Jones characterizes this reversal as follows:

Ashley and his small group of parliamentary reformers had done their work only too well. They had aroused public indignation in order to press for legal control over the private madhouses. By the 1845 Act they obtained it . . . but public opinion was now fully aroused, and would not be quieted . . . public indignation was not directed at the conditions under which the genuine 'lunatic' lived [and] the phrase 'lunacy reform' came to connote the protection of the sane against conditions which were considered suitable for the insane. This was a connotation with which Shaftesbury and his colleagues were totally out of sympathy. The Commissioners, previously the spearhead of reform, were now forced into a defensive position, and a great deal of obloquy was heaped upon them.[2]

How was it that Shaftesburyite reform came so rapidly to be denigrated as a species of repression? We have seen that institutionalization bred anti-institutionalism. Popular sentiment could be roused by sympathy for those who were ill cared for, but also for those who were wrongly or unnecessarily subjected to the disciplines of the institution. It would seem that as the institutional lunacy system became established in the course of the nineteenth century, popular consciousness of the vulnerability to abuse at its hands of the sane, and particularly those who were in lay terms merely 'eccentric', gained ground. Perceived as the most vulnerable were the wealthy. They were likely to be consigned to licensed houses, whose proprietors had a financial interest in their continued retention, and they had more ready access to the Press, the Courts, and those with political power as channels through which to generate public concern and campaign for greater legal protection. Agitation thus centred on two demands: the abolition or severe restriction of private licensed houses and the extension of the requirement of the order of a magistrate for detention as a lunatic from pauper to private cases, as a protection of 'the liberty of the subject' and a check on medical opinion. The latter won official endorsement as early as 1860 when the 1859–60 Select Committee adopted a proposal to this effect made by the Secretary of the Alleged Lunatic's Friend Society.

The ability of a philosophy of legalism to imprint itself upon legislation at this stage can be explained firstly in terms of the general political context and secondly in terms of the state of psychiatry. The dominant political ethic of individualism and formal liberty pro-

---

[2] K. Jones, *A History of the Mental Health Services*, p. 154.

claimed that sane adult citizens, as rational individuals with free will, were entitled to the legal protection of their civil freedoms. Neither the state nor any concentration of private power was to be above the law. When lunacy reform was designed to protect the insane it was naturally paternalistic in character and accorded discretions to the medical profession because insanity deprived the sufferer of the characteristics which attracted legal rights. Once, however, attention passed to the sane, discussion of lunacy reform began to centre on the principle of the universality of the rule of law. It was thus able to serve lawyers in their own conflict with the medical profession. The redefinition of lunacy reform was therefore both in harmony with a dominant political ideology and able to benefit from the support of a very powerful professional grouping.

The political basis of the Lunacy Act 1890 can be located more precisely, for this was the era of the Diceyist reaction against the perceived onward march of collectivist tendencies within the British state. Albert Venn Dicey (1835–1922) belonged to the Whig constitutionalist and pro-Union camp of the Liberal Party. Conservative and pessimistic, he was nostalgic for the age of high liberalism, before working-class enfranchisement and the growth of social legislation began to transform the face of British politics.[3] *The Law of the Constitution*, published in 1885, popularized the concept of 'the Rule of Law', which he defined as possessing three aspects, the first of which was the 'absolute supremacy or predominance of regular law as opposed to the influence of arbitrary power' excluding 'the existence of arbitrariness, of prerogative, or even of wide discretionary authority on the part of the government'.[4] The debate unleashed about the erosion of 'the Rule of Law' by collectivist legislation which vested bureaucratic and expert powers with excessive discretion provided a fertile environment for critics of lunacy law to press for the legalistic restraint of the '"unlimited despotism" of the alienists' practice'.[5] In a context where the rule of law was perceived to be everywhere under threat and it 'was being constantly emphasized that freedoms were fragile and easily eroded',[6] the senior legal establish-

---

[3] On Dicey, see R. A. Cosgrove, *The Rule of Law: Albert Venn Dicey, Victorian Jurist.* London: Macmillan, 1980, especially pp. 69–79, 123. See also R. B. Stevens, *Law and Politics.* University of North Carolina Press, 1978, pp. 225–7.

[4] A. V. Dicey, *The Law of the Constitution,* 10th edn. London: Macmillan, 1959, pp. 202–3.

[5] P. Miller, 'The Territory of the Psychiatrist', p. 91.

[6] P. Bean, *Compulsory Admissions to Mental Hospitals.* Chichester: John Wiley, 1980, p. 34.

ment took up the theme and did not desist until new legal safeguards were assured. The successful redefinition of lunacy reform could be seen as a symbolic reassertion of the rule of law in an epoch when classical liberal principles were perceived by their adherents to be under siege. The man who placed himself at the helm of the campaign to reform the lunacy laws was Hardinge Stanley Giffard, first Earl of Halsbury (1823–1921), the remarkably determined reactionary whose anti-trade union judgements helped to provoke the Trade Disputes Act 1906 and who led the 'ditchers', hardline opponents of the reform of the House of Lords in the Liberal budget crisis of 1909. An ardent believer in the rule of law and an unmovable opponent of 'collectivist' legislation, he was strategically placed, as Lord Chancellor in Salisbury's Conservative administrations from 1885, to champion the cause. For him there was no room for specialist decision-making in the process of commitment. The issue was essentially that raised in a criminal trial:

... every person accused of lunacy should, if he wished, have the right to demand that he should be brought before a judicial tribunal ... [I cannot understand] why a magistrate should not be as competent to decide the question with as judicial a mind as a medical man.[7]

Contemporaneously, the asylum system itself and psychiatric theory developed in such a way as to encourage demands for greater legal protection of the sane. We have seen how asylums increased enormously in size in the course of the century, encouraging the routinization of asylum life and an apathetic custodial attitude on the part of their superintendents. The cures which asylums had been built to deliver failed to materialize: the proportion of 'recoveries' to direct admissions was given as 36.9 per cent for all lunatics in care in 1873. It reached 41.99 per cent in 1885 and was 36.87 per cent in 1898.[8] As J. B. Tuke lamented in 1889,

Although they have had proper machinery placed at their command, asylum physicians have failed to stay the progress of the disease by the exercise of their art, and have but partially succeeded in bringing their specialty within the pale of medical science.[9]

This manifest failure bred a pervasive therapeutic pessimism, a conception of insanity as intractably rooted in the individual's

[7] *Parliamentary Debates* 311, cols. 137–8 (21 February 1887).
[8] *Fifty-third Report of the Commissioners in Lunacy*, 1899, pp. 86–7. These figures of course provide only a broad indication of perceived medical performance.
[9] J. B. Tuke, 'Lunatics as Patients not Prisoners', *The Nineteenth Century* 25 (1889), p. 596.

84 The Lunacy Act 1890

constitution which Skultans terms 'the tyranny of organization' and which is documented in the writings on insanity of Henry Maudsley, arch-proponent of genetic explanations of insanity, and Furneaux Jordan.[10]

The failure of the asylums to fulfil their early curative promise encouraged their perception as essentially custodial institutions which should be legally regulated as akin to prisons rather than hospitals, a belief lent substance by their isolated geographical situation[11] and fortress-like appearance. As Castel argues with reference to French psychiatry, the professional victory of medical men in establishing a regime for the treatment of insanity centred upon the asylum, over which they exercised exclusive control, had been in a sense too perfect. Being a patient, in the great majority of cases, meant being committed to an asylum and the population requiring psychiatric care had become typified by the 'indigent, exhibiting spectacular pathological behaviours, dangerous or incurable'.[12]

In the transition from small institutions, where the possibility of individual treatment and cure was realistic, to massive asylums where there was necessarily a strong emphasis on the orderly management of inmates, 'treatment' tended to become a question of restraint. The widespread employment of mechanical restraint had been condemned as one of the harshest features of the unreformed conditions of the insane. Other forms of restraint were therefore evolved, including chemical restraint, the administration of pacifying drugs. It was recognized that this had deteriorating effects on the patients and at its Annual Meeting in 1884, Dr H. Rayner, President of the Medico-Psychological Association, declared himself pleased to be able to say, in his review of treatment prospects, that 'chemical coercion' was dying out, a hope not particularly borne out by later historical experience.[13] Other established therapeutic strategies with restraint potential continued to develop in these years. One of these was a strong movement in favour of employment, not only

[10] See generally V. Skultans, *Madness and Morals*. London: Routledge and Kegan Paul, 1975. For its influence on attitudes to lunacy law see *The Lancet* (1889) 1, p. 796.
[11] That isolation was not originally inspired simply by the desire to segregate but possessed some therapeutic logic is indicated by the 1808 Act's injunction to the Visiting Justices in situating new public asylums to 'fix upon an airy and healthy situation': 48 Geo. III, c. 96, section 16.
[12] P. Miller, 'The Territory of the Psychiatrist', p. 89.
[13] H. Rayner, *Journal of Mental Science* 30 (1884–5), pp. 337–53 at p. 348. A twentieth-century example of 'chemical restraint' was croton oil, in use until about 1930: see Chapter 5.

agricultural, but also industrial. Its restraint value is indicated in a paper delivered by Dr Yellowlees on 'The Employment of the Insane' to the 1883 Annual Meeting of the British Medical Association, in which he 'advocated the discriminate occupation of lunatics in some well-selected form of industrial work as tending to promote recovery, or in less favourable cases as counteracting the tendency to mischievous excitement.'[14]

Another technique was dietary restraint. There was an upsurge of the temperance ethic in these years and a debate was conducted as to whether beer should be withdrawn from the patients' diet. A number of features regarded as innovative and progressive were under discussion or subject to experimental introduction at this time, however. Doctors urged early treatment in which they expressed confidence as a means to a much higher level of recoveries. It was argued by some members of the medical profession, most notably by Dr Bucknill, that only in cases of danger to the public should legal coercion be employed, so that compulsory admission should become the exception rather than a normal precondition of treatment.[15] There were advocates of decarceration, such as Dr Charles Lockhart Robertson and Dr J. Mortimer Granville. Boarding out was a frequent practice and there was the recognition of a need for 'half-way houses': Dr James Chrichton Browne was able to say that a number of county asylums and one or two registered hospitals had convalescent homes. An 'open-door system of management'[16] was increasingly adopted, at the Fife and Kinross Asylum for example. Summarizing the evidence on this point the 1877 Select Committee Report states that

The Committee were told that the system of unlocked doors, the liberty of walking alone in, and in many cases outside, the grounds, and the almost uncontrolled admission of visitors have the best effect and . . . were being extended throughout the three kingdoms.[17]

There was a system of probationary release, the need for after-care was emphasized (the Mental After-Care Association was launched in 1879), the facility for certain patients to live in the community by day and sleep in the asylum by night was recommended,[18] the separation

[14] *Journal of Mental Science* 29 (1883–4), p. 451.
[15] J. C. Bucknill, *The Care of the Insane and their Legal Control.* London: Macmillan, 1880, p. 38.
[16] Ibid., p. xix.
[17] *Report from the Select Committee on Lunacy Law,* p. 4.
[18] *Report from the Select Committee on Lunacy Law,* Minutes of Evidence, Answer 8,906: Dr J. Mortimer Granville.

of different classifications of patients in different blocks was practised,[19] and the probationary hospital, outdoor departments, and preventive treatment were also under debate.

The House of Commons Select Committee on the Operation of the Lunacy Law, 1877

The evidence to this Select Committee appointed to inquire into the Lunacy Law 'so far as regards the security afforded by it against Violations of Personal Liberty', affords a fascinating overview of the entire lunacy system, both in theory and practice, as it operated in the late nineteenth century. The witnesses included Lunacy Commissioners, proprietors of licensed houses, Poor Law officials, medical men specializing in insanity, and solicitors. Although Scotland and Ireland had separate legislation as they do now, evidence relating to their experience was provided for comparative purposes. In fact, there was intense interest in the design of the Scottish lunacy system, which had escaped the waves of agitation which produced more restrictive legislation during this period in many countries including the United States, France, Holland, and New Zealand.[20]

The Scottish lunacy system, based on the Lunatics Act 1857, incorporated a number of distinctive features which endeared it to the advocates of legalism. Patients could not be confined without the order of the sheriff, supported by two medical certificates; all categories of patient were subject to the same legal regime, and there was no restriction of voluntary admission, as in England and Wales, to those under care within the previous five years. There were no special restrictions on private houses run for profit, but in fact these occupied a very minor position in the Scottish system, accounting for a mere 15 per cent of private patients. Most private patients in Scotland were in Royal Chartered Asylums.

The interpretation of these provisions as a model for legalistic revision of the English system seems, however, to have been somewhat misplaced. The sheriff's role appears usually to have been administrative rather than judicial in practice: he did not personally

[19] Answer 693: James Wilkes, a medical Commissioner in Lunacy.

[20] Dr Bucknill collected detailed information concerning the lunacy laws in a number of American states which was summarized by D. Hack Tuke and presented to the Committee as 'An Abstract of American Lunacy Laws'. See *Report from the Select Committee on Lunacy Law*, Minutes of Evidence, Appendix 6. In 1885, Earl Granville circulated a letter to British ambassadors for reports on lunacy law in their countries, the information being published in a Blue Book. See *The Lancet* (1885) 1, pp. 573–4.

examine patients but checked that the certificates of insanity had been accurately completed. This was precisely the function performed by the Lunacy Commissioners, who were sent copies of admission documents for inspection. Furthermore, medical control over admissions could be extended 'by stealth' through invoking the emergency certificate, which required only one medical recommendation, in cases of convenience as well as in genuine emergencies.[21] General satisfaction in Scotland probably flowed less from the allegedly legalistic philosophy of the system than from effective operation of the regulatory and supervisory machinery. In Scotland the sheriff knew the certifying doctors personally and there was a very much higher ratio of Commissioners to patients (1 : 4,400 as compared with 1 : 10,000 in England).[22] The very small role played by licensed houses and greater community-orientation, voluntarism, and more liberal treatment limited the scope for suspicion of irregular practices. The alienists' counter-claims that it really provided evidence in favour of placing the lunacy system on a more strictly medical basis seem to have been correct.[23] In the sphere of criminal lunacy, in contrast to the medically-contested English M'Naghten Rules, the defence of diminished responsibility was already partly recognized,[24] involving the greater legal recognition of medical claims. Nevertheless, the legalistic reforms of the Lunacy Act 1890 were explicitly projected as an elaboration of Scottish procedures.[25]

The Select Committee regarded itself as primarily concerned with the legal safeguards provided against improper detention in licensed houses. Stephen Cave, questioning Charles Spencer Perceval, the Secretary to the Lunacy Commissioners, and the first witness, thought that the state of legal provision for the protection of the pauper patient in a public asylum was only marginally relevant:

There are a few questions about pauper lunatics which scarcely come within our order of reference, except that cases have been mentioned of undue interference with liberty with regard even to pauper patients, so that I think we ought not entirely to pass it over.[26]

This preoccupation with the private sector—in fact, with that part

[21] *Report from the Select Committee on Lunacy Law*, Minutes of Evidence, Answer 9,882: Dr Arthur Mitchell, a medical member of the Scottish Lunacy Commissioners.
[22] Ibid., Answer 10,109.
[23] See the correspondence of John Batty Tuke with *The Lancet* (1886) 1, p. 1046.
[24] R. Smith, *Trial by Medicine*, p. 84.
[25] See, for example, *Justice of the Peace* 53 (1889), p. 707.
[26] *Report from the Select Committee on Lunacy Law*, Minutes of Evidence, Question 364.

of it run for profit, the licensed houses—of course reflected the distribution of public agitation.[27] The private licensed houses were the usual places to which prosperous families sent members who were considered insane, a few patients paying as much as £5,000 per annum to be so accommodated. They were not within the financial reach of the lower middle classes.[28] The absence of accommodation for the insane of the lower middle classes led the Committee, as they heard more and more evidence, to show an increasing interest in the state of the law in relation to public asylums and workhouses, for they became aware that the pauper class by no means accounted for the whole lunatic population of public institutions. It was clear that insanity pauperized the lower middle classes, because they could not afford the private care available and had to be admitted to county and borough asylums, and even to workhouses.

The main institutions catering for the lower middle classes were the registered hospitals. Of these, Bethlem and St Luke's were the most notable. These two hospitals admitted 'curable' cases only, however, and discharged each patient after twelve months whether recovered or not. For those in the Cornwall area, the County asylum at Bodmin had a separate block for private patients built by subscription, which set charges at a lower level than licensed houses. The destination of many lower middle-class patients was still, however, the pauper lunatic asylum, via the workhouse. No total figure was submitted in evidence for patients in this position, but the evidence suggests that it was more than was generally supposed. Dr James Chrichton Browne stated to the Committee that he had had constantly under his care in a pauper asylum 'governesses, clergymen, medical men, officers in the army, and cultivated people of various grades'.[29]

[27] There was a reluctance logically to extend concern to single patients, despite the allegation that the single patient business was more profitable than the licensed houses. Lord Shaftesbury stated in his evidence that the keeping of single patients was much more profitable than the running of a licensed house, although of course there were fewer of them than patients in licensed houses: Answer 11,540.

[28] According to the evidence of J. H. Henry, a General Inspector with the Local Government Board, the minimum weekly charge in 1877 was 15s. per week (Answer 3,562). This compared with a cost to the parish of 10s. to keep a pauper patient. Lord Shaftesbury and many other witnesses lamented the absence of accommodation for the lower middle classes as one of the most glaring defects in contemporary provision for lunacy in England and Wales.

[29] Answer 1,253. See also the evidence of Dr Richard Adams, Medical Superintendent of the Bodmin Asylum at Answer 7,943. James Chrichton Browne (1840–1938) was a Lord Chancellor's Visitor from 1875 to 1922.

In the public asylums these patients were not legally entitled to superior treatment. However, some superintendents apparently extended favoured treatment to those from social classes nearer to their own: Dr Maury Deas, Superintendent of the County Asylum at Macclesfield, said in his evidence that he allowed his private patients and pauper patients 'of a better class' separate bedrooms, the right to wear their own clothes and their own table for meals.[30]

Once the Committee's attention had been drawn away from the threat posed to liberty by licensed houses and the incarceration of private patients without magisterial order, and it became concerned with more general aspects of the lunacy system, it eventually produced a Report reflective of the views of the Lunacy Commissioners and the Medico-Psychological Association. As we shall see, the evidence of critics of the lunacy laws largely failed to impress and the Report thus reproduced an official version of knowledge, laying itself open to charges of 'whitewash'.

The essence of the Committee's conclusion was that although further safeguards might beneficially be introduced into law, the system basically worked well because most of those responsible for its operation were honest: 'assuming that the strongest cases against the present system were brought before them, allegations of *mala fides* or of serious abuses were not substantiated.'[31] They recommended, however, that all patients, whether propertied or not, private or pauper, whether in lunatic wards of workhouses, or in hospitals or asylums, should henceforth be subject to the same legal regime. A procedure for emergency certification should be introduced, requir-

---

[30] Answers 7,792–5. Robert Castel describes a similar social hierarchy within the public asylums in France, 5,067 out of 40,804 inmates escaping the common regime in 1874. See P. Miller, 'The Territory of the Psychiatrist', p. 90. As to how non-pauper patients could legally be admitted to pauper asylums, the explanations advanced were as follows. According to Dr James Chrichton Browne, a pauper being a person wholly *or partly* maintained by the rates, the statute could be complied with by the patient's paying nine shillings and sixpence and the Board of Guardians the remaining sixpence. The retention of the sixpence to be paid out of the rates was also necessary for the Guardians to qualify for the four shillings government grant, introduced in 1874, for each patient received into an asylum, to divert lunatics from the workhouses. Patients pauperized *in fact* by the incapacity following insanity could be paid for by their relatives, who were under a legal obligation to support them. That non-paupers were also detained in workhouses is clear from the evidence of Mr William White Parkinson, Master of the workhouse at Bermondsey, among others, who states that the practice was to make their relatives pay for them. The issue of non-paupers being confined as paupers was, in fact, highlighted by evidence on the case of Mrs Petschler who, though allegedly of independent means, was detained in a public asylum against her will.

[31] *Report from the Select Committee on Lunacy Law*, p. 1.

ing one medical certificate and authorizing detention for a period of three days. In other cases, two medical certificates were to be required and the order was to be signed by the nearest relative or 'some responsible person who could be called to account', instead of any person connected with the patient, as in the existing system. The Committee considered that the statements required by the certificates ought to be more precise and, as well as reports after two and seven days, there ought to be monthly reports, a proposal strongly recommended by Lord Shaftesbury in his evidence. Terminability of certificates—at that time they continued in force indefinitely unless the patient was discharged—was to be introduced to promote the individualization of patients, now that most asylums were so large, by forcing the Medical Superintendent periodically to make a definite decision whether the patient was to be further detained. A special report was to be required annually.

Having earlier in their report followed medical opinion by attaching the greatest importance to early treatment, they appended to the exposition of this proposed regime the statement that they did 'not attach special importance to the order emanating from a magistrate, such as the Sheriff in Scotland, or a Justice of the Peace in England, as this intervention has been shown in many cases to be ministerial'.[32] Later they also rejected the abolition of licensed houses: while not approving private care in principle they thought that, until there was sufficient accommodation for all classes in public institutions, a need for licensed houses for the upper and middle classes would continue to exist, and urged that 'legislative facilities should be afforded by enlargement of the powers of magistrates, or otherwise, for the extension of' alternative public provision.[33] Thus they clearly rejected the two most prominent causes of the existing system's critics. For the protection of liberty, they placed greatest emphasis on 'frequent and careful visitation of all places in which a lunatic is confined, with full power placed in the hands of the Commissioners to order his discharge, and, in the more general adoption of the system of probationary release'.[34] They also explicitly demonstrated a concern for the insane as well as for the sane improperly confined: some of the early treatment medical men placed such great hopes in could surely be carried out at home, and patients no longer dangerous to themselves or others and not likely

[32] Ibid., p. 3.
[33] Ibid., p. 4.
[34] Ibid., p. 3.

to benefit further from asylum treatment ought to be released, preferably into some 'half-way' environment. Finally, they added their approval to liberal tendencies in asylum management like the open-door system and 'the absence of restraint, the occupation and amusement which may be said to be the universal characteristics of the system in this country at the present day'.[35]

The Lunacy Acts Amendment Act 1889 eventually followed these recommendations in some respects, but not in others: terminability of certificates for all classes of patient was introduced by section 30 and monthly reports by section 29(1). Section 45 required a medical certificate for each exercise of mechanical restraint, section 46 gave patients greater rights of correspondence, and it was provided by section 38 that any person could have a patient examined by two medical practitioners and subsequently discharged with the consent of the Commissioners.

Specific provisions were made in respect of pauper patients: under section 20 the Justice signing a summary reception order for the removal of a patient to a public asylum had to state that the patient was a pauper in receipt of relief or in such circumstances as to require relief for his proper care and maintenance. This was presumably designed to bring an end to the practice of non-paupers being confined as paupers in public asylums, and was complemented by the provision under section 67 of a power for county and borough authorities to provide separate accommodation for private patients. The alternative of the joint order of the clergyman and relieving officer was abolished. Under section 21(3) it became necessary to obtain a Justice's order and two medical certificates to confine a person as a lunatic in a workhouse for more than fourteen days.

However, most of the Act was devoted to the protection of private patients and the twin objectives of the advocates of legalism which had been rejected by the Select Committee in 1878 were its most important provisions: under section 2(1) the order of a judicial authority (defined as a County Court judge, Stipendiary or Metropolitan Police Magistrate or a Justice of the Peace specially appointed as provided by the Act) became necessary in all private cases except when there was an emergency (when an urgency order supported by only one medical certificate was appropriate) or the person was a lunatic so found by inquisition. A further protection, in section 3(5), was that, except in the case of an urgency order, one of the doctors had 'whenever practicable' to be 'the usual medical attendant'. Also, the petition for the order had, if possible, to be presented by the husband or wife or another relative. The second objective, the abolition of private asylums, was partly conceded by section 56 in that no further licences were to be issued. The powers of the Commissioners were extended to enable them to enter charitable and religious institutions and places where patients were retained without payment, the former provision being designed to pacify 'zealous Protestants' who asserted 'that in Romish and Anglican convents insane nuns are kept locked up, as Mr Rochester kept his first wife'.[36]

Similar Bills had been introduced several times previously by the indefatigable Thomas Dillwyn and then by successive Lord Chancellors, but they had always failed to reach the statute book, not by defeat in Parliament, but through becoming dropped orders. There had been a Bill introduced by Lord Selborne in 1885, another by Lord Herschell in 1886, and a further two by Lord Halsbury in 1887 and 1888. In these Bills the requirement of a judicial order in private cases was a constant and they were all substantially similar. Lord Selborne had originally introduced the controversial provision into the 1885 Bill after consultation with the Home Office, which endorsed the hard-line view that:

Incarceration in a lunatic asylum is virtually an imprisonment and an imprisonment of a very serious character. Such an imprisonment ought not to be directed except by a responsible judicial officer in sworn evidence given orally, and with the opportunity for the friends of the alleged lunatic to cross-examine such evidence and to be heard in opposition to it.[37]

The provisions of the Act, passed in July 1889, did not come into effect until 1 May 1890, when incorporated in the consolidating statute, the Lunacy Act 1890, while section 12, which protected doctors issuing certificates of insanity, came into force immediately.

It is perhaps at first sight surprising that the objectives of the libertarian agitators should have attained legislative recognition only a decade or so after the proceedings of the Select Committee which had launched such an exhaustive investigation into the lunacy system

[36] T. Raleigh, 'The Lunacy Laws', *Law Quarterly Review* I (1885), p. 157.
[37] Memorandum of 27 January 1885 on Lunacy Acts Amendment Bill 1885 submitted to the Home Secretary, Sir William Harcourt, this passage marginally marked 'I entirely concur': Public Record Office, State Papers, Lord Chancellor's Office, 1/64.

without uncovering substantial evidence to support their claims. However, the complexity and diversity of the evidence of the Committee as a whole, combined with the brevity and scant reasoning of the Report itself, provided a context for continued animated debate and widespread dissatisfaction. Dr Bucknill recorded in 1880 that 'the subject was not even shelved . . . the inevitable result being that the feeling of the public has since become more uneasy and distrustful than ever before',[38] while the conditions for a succession of moral panics remained unchanged. If it had been intended to do so the production of an official report with an appearance of complacency was unlikely to stem the tide of agitation. The remainder of this chapter will be devoted to a discussion of the respective roles of the various forces and organizations concerned in the struggle for and against the ascendancy of legalism.

The Lunacy Law Reform Societies

In the last quarter of the nineteenth century, three societies were prominent: the Lunacy Law Reform Association, the Lunacy Law Amendment Society, and the National Association for the Defence of Personal Rights. These organizations attracted ex-patients who believed themselves to have been wronged and fulfilled a representative function in respect of individual cases, although their prime role was to propagandize for reform. In this task of fuelling public alarm they were no doubt aided by the contemporary growth in literacy and increasing availability of cheap magazines and newspapers.[39] They shared a commitment to legalism in lunacy legislation, and campaigned for radical reform of the law.

James Billington, interviewed by the Select Committee of 1877 as Secretary of the Lunacy Law Amendment Society, enumerated the proposals of his society as follows: the abolition of private asylums; the right of every person alleged to be insane to be brought before a magistrate in open court, or have the power to demand a jury; the right to full information in respect of this allegation and to call witnesses to refute it; the display of notices, setting forth patients' rights of correspondence and access to a solicitor, in the principal rooms of asylums; the opening of private asylums to inspection and freer access for patients' friends, and the creation of non-specialist

---

[38] J. C. Bucknill, p. ix.
[39] P. McCandless, 'Liberty and Lunacy: the Victorians and Wrongful Confinement', *Journal of Social History* 5 (1978), p. 366.

(medical *or legal*) visiting committees with power to place patients in probationary asylums.[40] Louisa Lowe, Secretary of the Lunacy Law Reform Association, was also interviewed by the Select Committee, although in her personal capacity as a former patient with grievances.[41] She demanded the clear legal definition of coercible insanity; the removal of the requirement of the Lunacy Commissioners' permission for prosecutions under the Lunacy laws; trial by jury before admission in all except emergency cases (in which a magistrate should have the power to sign an order on depositions made before him on oath); and the discharge of patients by a public authority or on their own application. The National Association for the Defence of Personal Rights, meanwhile, demanded the absolute right of every supposed lunatic to trial by jury, with the utmost possible publicity, that deprivations of liberty should only follow the commission of what would be regarded in a state of sanity as a legal offence, and that safety, not treatment, should be the criterion of commitment.

As would be expected, given the concentration of concern upon the private sector and the financial burden of pressure-group activity, the social composition of these societies seems to have been largely middle class. James Billington, describing himself as 'of no profession' claimed that the committee of his society was recruited from 'Gentlemen of position in the City'.[42] Similarly, Alfred Aspland, surgeon and magistrate, described a committee formed in Manchester after a scandal concerning the confinement of Mrs Petschler, a photographer, at the instigation of her sister, as

one of the most influential committees that has ever been formed in Manchester, consisting of the mayor, the town clerk, the chairman of quarter sessions, the stipendiary magistrate, and a number of others, barristers, and the chief bankers in the place, a large committee of the most influential kind.[43]

We may remember in this context that the original Alleged Lunatic's

[40] *Report from the Select Committee on Lunacy Law*, Minutes of Evidence, Questions and Answers 6,899–907,1022, 7,042–191.
[41] In an unsuccessful action for assault and false imprisonment against the proprietor of Brislington House, a licensed house near Bristol, Louisa Lowe reargued her own case before the House of Lords, 'taking all the points open to an experienced counsel'. See *Justice of the Peace* 51 (1887), pp. 458, 657; *Lowe* v. *Fox* [1885] QBD 667 (CA); [1887] App. Cas. 206 (HL).
[42] *Report from the Select Committee on Lunacy Law*, Minutes of Evidence, Answer 6,903.
[43] Ibid., Answer 4,556.

Friend Society was itself founded by a son of the assassinated Prime Minister, Spencer Perceval, and that at the time of the 1859 Select Committee investigation of lunacy provision its chairman was Admiral Saumarez, 'a member of a well-known Guernsey family' possessing 'a distinguished naval record'.[44] To some extent, this impression of respectability was doubtless exaggerated: they were obviously in danger of being dismissed as 'cranks' or imperfectly recovered lunatics sporting imagined grievances, an insecurity which shows in the decision in 1876 of certain members of the Lunacy Law Reform Association, in existence since 1871, to break away and form the alternative Lunacy Law Amendment Society. This did not reflect a policy disagreement, but arose from the fear that Louisa Lowe's association with spiritualism might confuse the public and damage the cause of lunacy law reform.

The tenor of the campaigns mounted by such elements in the 1870s and the 1880s was characterized by the paranoia and the melodrama calculated to create the phenomenon of moral panic. Frustrated by the structured invisibility of injustice, the lack of hard evidence that the lunacy system posed any serious or widespread threat to liberty produced by the invalidating effects of the attribution of insanity, and the general bureaucratic rectitude of psychiatric practices, they tended to be driven to a sensationalism which negated their credibility. This was also true of later campaigns, notably that consisting of a series of celebrated court actions initiated in 1884 with the support of the Lunacy Law Reform Association by Mrs Georgiana Weldon, described by Kathleen Jones as 'an extremely eccentric lady of considerable means and some social position',[45] relating to the circumstances of her attempted incarceration as a lunatic by her husband.

In the result, the new breed of lunacy reformers failed to sustain their case. James Billington, for example, before the 1877 Select Committee, was unable to produce anything more than hearsay evidence in support of his extreme assertions against the lunacy system and was humiliated by the members of the Committee on this ground. On their own the lunacy law reform societies were unsuccessful in influencing official bodies or achieving real political

[44] K. Jones, *A History of the Mental Health Services*, p. 159.
[45] Ibid., p. 168. Kathleen Jones records that she was a confederate of Louisa Lowe and a fellow spiritualist. Apparently she believed that the spirit of her deceased mother had taken up residence in her pet rabbit.

impact. It was only when their views were seriously pressed by the legal profession that legislative change was finally effected.

The Legal Profession

The legal profession provided a much more powerful and effective channel for libertarian pressure than the lunacy law reform societies, and was instrumental in achieving legislative change. It was an established and influential power-centre, with an inclination to resist any medical encroachment upon areas traditionally defined as a judicial province. Concern for the formal protection of individual liberty was a fundamental component of the prevailing legal ideology. Those who felt themselves aggrieved at the hands of the lunacy system understandably looked to the courts for protection and redress, so that the issues were dramatized in a legal context. This tended to embroil the judiciary in the question of lunacy law reform, as in the cases of *Weldon v. Winslow* and *Weldon v. Semple*, in which Baron Huddleston and Hawkins, J, respectively were moved to urge more effective safeguards.[46]

Nevertheless, the state of the civil law of lunacy was not of any direct interest to lawyers. There was no medical threat to deprive them of areas of decision-making which they then controlled, and it was envisaged under the various Lunacy Acts Amendment Bills that much of the workload arising from the new requirement of a judicial order for private admissions would anyway fall to lay magistrates. In spite of this, members of the legal profession made violent attacks on the lunacy laws and the role of the medical profession in their operation. The Earl of Milltown, a barrister, who introduced a motion in 1884 after the Weldon affair condemning these laws which drew from Lord Selborne a promise to introduce reforms, described them as 'positively startling' and a 'damning blot' on the statute book.[47] Baron Huddleston, the trial judge in *Weldon v. Winslow*, delivered the following memorable attack upon the procedures of private certification:

---

[46] For the Weldon cases see *The Times* from 6 December 1883 to 4 July 1886. Dr Lyttelton Forbes Winslow was an eminent forensic alienist, the son of Dr Forbes Benignus Winslow (1810–74) who was a President of the Medico-Psychological Association. It was damaging for the profession to have one of its élite subjected to adverse publicity in this way, as in the 1920s, when the most celebrated litigation of this type concerned Dr C. Hubert Bond, a former President of the Medico-Psychological Association.

[47] *Parliamentary Debates* 287, cols. 1269–70 (5 May 1884).

It is somewhat startling—it is positively shocking—that if a pauper, or as Mrs Weldon put it, a crossing-sweeper should sign an order, and another crossing-sweeper should make a statement, and then that two medical men, who had never had a day's practice in their lives, should for a small sum of money grant their certificates, a person may be lodged in a private lunatic asylum, and that this order, and the statement, and these certificates are a perfect answer to any action.[48]

Lord Halsbury, the Lord Chancellor, in discussion of the 1887 Bill in Committee in the House of Lords, stressed 'the necessity there was for them to resist the desire of the Medical Profession to have the certifying of lunatics entirely in their hands' and went on to refer to 'the examination which medical men were supposed—he used the word deliberately—to make, before signing a certificate for (a lunatic's) removal'.[49] These remarks were highly provocative to the medical profession and did not fail to draw fire in the editorials of its journals.

One source of so great an antagonism was to be found in the parallel conflict in the criminal sphere which concerned the extent to which those committing criminal acts should be held responsible when insane. In criminal trials, alienists confronted judges face to face and insisted that the normal legal penalties should not be applied. Broadly, criminal lunacy was for lawyers a question of legal responsibility and for doctors a medical question of pathology. Most lawyers were hostile to amendment of the M'Naghten Rules to allow more weight to be given to medical evidence as to the presence and effects of mental disease, although some judges, notably Barons Bramwell and Huddleston,[50] were more incredulous of the claimed scientific status of psychiatric evidence than others. The jurist Sir James Fitzjames Stephen (1829–94) was exceptional in his sympathy with the alienists' contention that recognition should be given to the effect of mental disease upon the criminal's ability, despite the presence of knowledge and moral comprehension, to control his own actions. Stephen, impressed by Indian law and administration as a

[48] *Standard*, 19 March 1884. See K. Jones, p. 170.
[49] *Parliamentary Debates* 311, cols. 137–8 (21 February 1887).
[50] In the course of a trial at the Winchester Assizes in November 1886 he 'animadverted upon the evidence of medical men, and he thought it proper to assert that they usurped the functions of a jury in getting into the witness-box to show their knowledge and ventilate their own fancies and theories without being able to give the reasons on which they based their conclusions.' See *Journal of Mental Science* 32 (1886–7), p. 527.

legal member of Council there, attempted to apply the lessons of his experience by drafting a criminal code which included a wider degree of recognition of insanity as an exculpatory condition, but this proposal was rejected by the Royal Commission on Indictable Offences in 1879.[51]

It is noteworthy that the same lawyers who were most vocal in attacking civil procedures of certification were also to the fore in resisting attempts to weaken judicial control of the determination of criminal responsibility. In 1885 there was acute controversy concerning the administration of the Insane Prisoners Act 1840, which gave the Home Secretary the power to transfer an untried prisoner to an asylum, in practice avoiding trial, on the basis of a certificate of insanity signed by two Justices and two doctors. Judicial criticism of this practice culminated in a sharp attack on the Home Office by Baron Huddleston in Marshall's case, where a charged murderer escaped trial by transfer to Broadmoor on what appeared to be the order of one of the Home Secretary's officials rather than the Minister himself. The Earl of Milltown put down a question in the House of Lords upon the matter, but was apparently satisfied by the Home Secretary that nothing had been amiss. The result of this conflict between executive discretion and informal medical determination of the disposition of offenders on the one hand, and established trial procedure on the other, was that the Home Secretary issued a Standing Order to medical officers of prisons embodying the policy that untried prisoners should only be removed on grounds of insanity in exceptional cases.[52]

Medical ambitions to overturn judge-made law and put in its place the medical profession's own formulation, and to ease out the jury—so much more susceptible to judicial influence than the doctors, who had the advantage of professional status—from aspects of the determination of guilt and innocence was a much more serious threat to the legal profession than any medical claim to monopolize the control of admissions to asylums. The emotive impact of this more vital line of medico-legal confrontation reverberated in civil law areas which did not have the potency independently to account for the actual degree of interprofessional antagonism. Civil commitment was an area in which psychiatric power could be woundingly curtailed

---

[51] On Stephen, see J. A. Colaiaco, *James Fitzjames Stephen and the Crisis of Victorian Thought*. London: Macmillan, 1983.

[52] See R. Smith, *Trial by Medicine*, pp. 21–2; N. Walker, *Crime and Insanity in England* Vol. 1. Edinburgh: Edinburgh University Press, 1968, pp. 228–9.

and the banner of the rule of law unfurled in a gesture of symbolic rather than immediate instrumental significance to lawyers.

A number of factors favoured the success of pressure from the legal profession for new legislation. It was a much older and better established profession than its medical rival: doctors had only achieved a cohesion of professional identity and organization from the time of the passing of the Medical Registration Act of 1858. In the person of the Lord Chancellor there was an eminent lawyer within the Government to espouse the causes of the legal profession, while there was no comparable medical figure to counteract pressure at that level. In fact it was a succession of Lord Chancellors—Selborne in 1885, Herschell in 1886, and Halsbury in 1887, 1888, and 1889—who were responsible for the introduction of the series of Lunacy Acts Amendment Bills.[53] They were all personally committed to this legislation and were no doubt active in pressing for it to be given a higher priority by the Governments of the day. This was certainly true in the case of Lord Halsbury, who stated in the House of Lords early in 1889 that he would continue to press for its enactment which he said should have taken place long ago and by now be bearing valuable results, and that he would leave to others the job of neglecting it.[54] Kathleen Jones emphasizes the contribution of Lord Selborne as Lord Chancellor to the campaign for Lunacy Law reform, describing him as 'the leader of the movement for tightening up the legal procedure'.[55] However, there is evidence to suggest that each successive Lord Chancellor was more determined to force legislation through, that Selborne was a late convert to this point of view, and that after he left the Chancellorship his Parliamentary role was to urge caution on his more robust successors. Supporting an amendment of Lord Halsbury's Bill in 1887, he proclaimed that to proceed in the case of a lunatic 'as if he were accused of a crime, . . . would be a departure from the whole principle of the law and practice of lunacy'.[56]

Unsurprisingly, the legal profession appears to have been more straightforwardly concerned than the lunacy law reform societies with the plight of the person, by any reasonable definition sane, who was locked up for dishonest reasons. Its sustained assault upon the

[53] On Lords Herschell and Halsbury see R. F. V. Heuston, *The Lives of the Lord Chancellors 1885–1940*. Oxford: Clarendon Press, 1964.
[54] *Parliamentary Debates* 333, col. 253 (25 February 1889).
[55] K. Jones, p. 170.
[56] *Parliamentary Debates* 311, col. 135 (21 February 1887).

assumptions of the early nineteenth-century lunacy reformers was resisted as a reactionary campaign which would do great harm to the insane as such, and we shall now turn to an examination of the sources of that resistance.

The Reaction of Lord Shaftesbury and the Lunacy Commissioners

Lord Shaftesbury, honorary Chairman of the Lunacy Commission at this time, was the most eminent and widely respected of those who defended the existing legislation, maintaining that it provided substantially adequate safeguards against improper detention, and condemning the proposals for reform as restricting the medical profession in providing effective treatment. He was an unshakeable believer in the vital necessity of early treatment if insanity was to be cured, and so the proposal which most provoked him was the magistrate clause. Before the Select Committee of 1859, he had given evidence against private asylums, particularly in support of the allegation that the profit-motive of the proprietors led them to keep patients confined after they had recovered. However, by 1877, he thought that standards in these asylums had improved a great deal, and withdrew his demand for their abolition, claiming that there were some very good institutions in the private sector, the closure of which would be a great loss. But those in favour of reform attempted to enlist previous statements made by Lord Shaftesbury against the continuance of private asylums in their support, and it was claimed by Lord Herschell in the Commons in 1886 that he had died convinced that proprietary houses ought to be abolished.[57]

Shaftesbury was accused of over-complacency by the reformers. Having seen the radical transformation of the lunacy system achieved, with a great personal contribution, over a period of fifty years, he naturally evaluated the present with reference to a very grim and also very distant past. Because direct physical restraint, abuse, and neglect were much less evident, and the management of the insane subjected to an unprecedented degree of legal regulation, he had a tendency to be dismissive of the complaints of critics of the system.

When, in 1885, Lord Selborne published his proposals for new legislation and included the requirement of a judicial order in private cases, Lord Shaftesbury pleaded with him not to proceed with what he regarded as a tragically retrogressive measure. Selborne put this

[57] *Parliamentary Debates* 304, col. 240 (30 March 1886).

point of view to other members of the Government and to the judges, but they refused to capitulate on this fundamental principle. Shaftesbury's reaction was to resign his Chairmanship of the Lunacy Commission. In his letter of resignation, he listed his reasons for opposition to the magistrate clause.[58] Firstly, the publicity implicated in magisterial intervention would deter friends and relatives from bringing the patient forward for treatment until the time when effective treatment could be given had passed. He stressed here that early treatment was 'almost the only hope of cure'. Another consequence of such publicity would be a vast increase in clandestine confinement. Thirdly, many patients, though really insane, would be lodged with medical men and clergymen under pretence of nervous disorders of various kinds. More patients would be consigned to asylums abroad, which would entail neglect by their families. Finally, he claimed that it would discredit the medical profession if even eminent medical men could find their opinion as to a person's insanity overridden by that of a magistrate, and that the issue of a magistrate's order would confer immunity from legal action upon doctors signing certificates.

Thus, Shaftesbury's contention was that the introduction of the magistrate's order in private cases would undermine the whole fabric of the lunacy system, that it would have exactly the opposite of the effect intended: instead of rendering legal control more stringent, it would lead to the withdrawal of patients from areas in which they were subject to regulation into those in which they were not, and those responsible for improper confinement would no longer be legally accountable.[59]

The pressure of Lord Shaftesbury was continued by the other Commissioners after his death. It is not surprising that in this they should have shared his views, for although equally medical and legal in composition and appointed precisely in order to function as the watchdogs of the system, maintaining an independent and critical

---

[58] This was printed in *British Medical Journal* (1885), p. 752. Shaftesbury returned after the Bill fell: see D. J. Mellet, 'Society, the State and Mental Illness, 1790–1890', p. 177.

[59] It might be asked why the magistrate's order that was already required in pauper cases was perfectly acceptable, while that proposed for private cases was expected to have disastrous consequences. The argument was that the attitude of families of the poor to the confinement of insane members was quite different from that of the rich. Instead of doing everything to avoid publicity, the family of a pauper lunatic was at an early stage forced by the economic burden of a member who was incapacitated from work by suspected insanity and needed supervision to seek to place him in public care.

perspective, by the 1880s they had become integrated and identified with the system, as they were hopelessly overworked, and relied heavily on the medical superintendents for information when carrying out inspections, thereby failing to present a public image of defenders of freedom, vigorously seeking out abuses. In fact their approach was one of great caution in investigating all allegations of impropriety, and they secured very few prosecutions, claiming in answer to criticism that patients were loath to come forward and testify.

At a time of intense public disquiet, when literature was widely circulating describing the horrific proportions of injustice within the lunacy system, the efforts of the Commissioners suggested positive collaboration with the proprietors of asylums and the medical superintendents in suppressing the evidence. One of the chief calls of the reformers was for prosecution for breach of the Lunacy Acts to be thrown open to the public and not left in the hands of the Commissioners. An editorial of *The Lancet* indicates the kind of venomous antagonism felt towards the Commissioners. Whilst editorials normally protested that only the system was at fault, sometimes personal attacks were launched:

the pretended supervision exercised by the Commissioners in Lunacy is a farce, a technical travesty of protection, nothing better, and, on the whole, tending to increase the peril of evil by throwing a false glamour of security over the lunacy laws.[60]

A subsequent editorial is even more scathing:

Too much, however, is left to the Commissioners who are assumed to be immaculate, whereas it should be borne in mind by the Legislature that the need for reform has to a large extent arisen out of the careless and perfunctory manner in which the Commissioners have hitherto discharged their duties. If the Commission had not largely been composed of men trained in the evil ways of the asylum system, and very little in earnest for the interests of the insane, the laws already in existence would have sufficed for the protection both of the sane and of the insane.[61]

The Commissioners were therefore very much on the defensive: they were a part of the existing lunacy system that was under attack and were identified as such. Their pressure against new legislation did not have the desired impact, for they were seen as speaking in

[60] *The Lancet* (1884) 2, p. 198.
[61] *The Lancet* (1885) 1, p. 669.

self-defence rather than as independent observers. They were never reconciled to the enactment of the Lunacy Acts Amendment Bill, commencing their report of 1890 by registering their continued rejection of its approach and provisions and regretting its success after a long campaign of opposition on their part.[62]

The Medical Profession

We have seen that medical attitudes toward legal coercion in psychiatry have varied, some sections of the medical profession adopting a conservative legal strategy of medicalizing the doctor's role by ceding control of the machinery of coercion to judicial authorities, others a radical strategy of doing so by claiming control of coercion themselves and legitimating its use on therapeutic grounds. There is evidence of the former approach, sympathetic to greater legal intervention and antagonistic to commercial asylums, both in the wider profession and amongst alienists themselves in the late nineteenth century. Under the editorship of James Wakley *The Lancet* developed an editorial position which deplored the discredit which had been visited upon the medical profession by the annexation of functions which were non-medical or conflicted with doctors' ethical responsibilities, notably involvement in the certification of insanity, in which social and legal disabilities were imposed on patients, and the acceptance of patients for profit in licensed houses. The first gave rise to numerous court actions against certifying doctors and the second had allowed a state of public alarm to develop over how far the therapeutic judgement of medical men might be warped by their having a substantial pecuniary interest in diagnosing patients insane or retaining them when recovered. The remedy for this state of affairs was seen in legislation to render detention of the insane a clear lay responsibility and to abolish commercially-operated asylums.

The following extract from a *Lancet* editorial of 1885 provides the clearest summary of the reasoning behind a leading medical journal's adoption of positions we tend to associate with lawyers and patients' self-help societies:

So long as mental disease is looked upon and treated as something apart from the subject of general medicine, and while special *legal* powers are demanded 'for the protection of doctors', or 'for the safety of society and the

---

[62] *Forty-fourth Report of the Commissioners in Lunacy*, 1890.

insane', there must be dissatisfaction, insecurity and scandal. In truth, medical men ought to have no more to do with the legal and social disabilities of the mentally diseased than they have with the moral character, the financial position or the educational attainments of their patients. If the profession were true to itself, it would cut the Gordian knot of all this difficulty by refusing to give or sign any document having a legal bearing or capable of being used in a court of justice, except it be to protect the insane from the legal consequences of responsibility for wrong-doing in their madness. We repeat the affirmation that no single power is needed by physicians engaged in the medical treatment of the insane which the *common law* does not give every citizen.[63]

In its application to certification this position to some extent reflected the uncomfortable position of general practitioners signing certificates. Any doctor could sign a certificate of insanity, but only a fraction of the medical profession had anything more than general knowledge and perhaps experience of previous certification upon which to base a judgement, because psychiatric training was not a necessary part of the education of all doctors. Also, psychiatry tended to be avoided: the stigma of insanity attached somewhat to those who devoted their lives to its medical treatment, so that asylum doctors were regarded as inferior within the profession, and often were.

Medical ignorance of insanity led to caution in certifying,[64] as did the fear of legal actions by aggrieved patients which became increasingly real in the 1880s. Many doctors probably did not wish to be involved in certification:[65] it was possible for them to rationalize their role by saying that their intervention was not as an expert but as a respected member of the public, that as the decision whether to confine a person was a social rather than a medical one, psychiatric expertise was inessential, and indeed that their lack of expertise was itself a safeguard against unnecessary detention.[66]

It was this current of feeling that *The Lancet* was able to tap in drawing support for its policy. Many doctors at best thought that a Justice's order in private cases might serve them as a protection against 'vexatious' legal actions. As to why *The Lancet* in particular should have articulated this attitude, we need to look at the journal's traditions. It was founded in 1823 by Thomas Wakley (1795–1862), a

[63] *The Lancet* (1885) 1, p. 258.
[64] See *Report from the Select Committee on Lunacy Law*, Minutes of Evidence, Answer 1,598: J. Chrichton Browne.
[65] Answer 3,754: Henry Maudsley.
[66] Answer 7,475: Dr Blandford.

radical who championed the democratization of the medical profession and was an enemy of medical élitism, oligarchy, and nepotism. It would seem that concern for the position of the ordinary medical practitioner and that the profession's therapeutic *raison d'être* should not be clouded by expansionism explain *The Lancet's* position on lunacy legislation. In the 1950s the Medical Practitioners' Union was another anti-establishment medical organ which opposed medical dominance of commitment procedures. On the other hand, the founder of the journal had also been a critic of lawyers. As Coroner for West Middlesex he pressed the view that medical rather than legal qualifications should be necessary for coronership. Whatever the reasons for *The Lancet's* position, after the death of James Wakley in 1886, under the joint editorship of Thomas Wakley Senior (1821–1907) and Thomas Wakley Junior (1851–1909), a more cautious approach was adopted, and in 1889 there was a change of editorial policy against the Lunacy Acts Amendment Bill when the committee of the Royal College of Physicians reported in opposition to its major provisions. It became clear that the medical profession was by now largely opposed to the legislation and that if editorial policy persisted in supporting it (and, indeed, criticizing it for its moderation), the journal could no longer claim to be 'the voice of the medical profession'.[67]

The sentiments of *The Lancet* were echoed in the writings of John Charles Bucknill, a leading alienist who had been Medical Superintendent of the Devon County Asylum and was the first editor of the *Asylum Journal*, forerunner of the Medico-Psychological Association's current mouthpiece, the *Journal of Mental Science*. In a compendium of articles originally published anonymously in the *British Medical Journal* he argued vigorously for uniform magisterial control of commitment, determining the need for detention on a judicial basis with the help of medical opinion in the form of evidence:

Medical opinion must still, no doubt, be the main reason for detention, though considerations of public safety which are not medical may buttress it;

---

[67] *The Lancet* (1889) 1, pp. 992–4. The editorial policy of the *British Medical Journal* fluctuated on the question of the magistrate, but was against proprietary madhouses. Reflecting the preoccupations of general practitioners, support for the extension of the magistrate's role in commitment tended to be in terms of legal protection for certifying doctors. See *British Medical Journal* (1885) 1, p. 949.

but for the welfare of the patients, the liberties of the people, and the dignity of the profession, it must be conceded that the disinterested or delusive sanction now afforded by the order of detention must be supported by something of more authority.[68]

That his support for this position was informed by a consciousness of the contradiction in the doctor's role as both healer and gaoler is indicated by his statement that:

... it is improbable that any legislation will interfere with the legitimate work of the true physician. Rather it is likely to reinstate him in his right sphere of dignity and usefulness if he should have wandered from it by becoming the keeper instead of the curer of diseased persons.[69]

Bucknill also pressed hard for the replacement of commercial licensed houses by the state provision of special institutions reserved for the insane of the middle and upper classes.

Andrew Scull describes Bucknill as a leading figure in the field who had thereby managed to work outside the asylum system as a private practitioner. Alienists of that status

... realized that their professional autonomy was compromised by the obvious lack of application of the medical model in the huge custodial institutions of the period ... it was they who sought, almost desperately, to assert that all aspects of the treatment of insanity were a medical province, and that asylum doctors should therefore be immune from interference by unqualified laymen.[70]

What is interesting here is that Bucknill sought to improve the image of psychiatry as a truly medical domain precisely by the consolidation and expansion of lay interference in the form of lay control of commitment.

Bucknill's writings also preached the moral superiority of professionalism to mere engagement in trade, instancing the competition of professional and entrepreneurial ideals in the Victorian age.[71] This is particularly apparent in Bucknill's aggressive onslaught against medical proprietors of private madhouses:

It is in their character of custodians, and in their association with capitalists

---

[68] J. C. Bucknill, pp. 34–5.
[69] Ibid., p. vii.
[70] A. T. Scull, *Museums of Madness*, pp. 177–8.
[71] H. Perkin, *The Origins of Modern English Society 1780–1880*. London: Routledge and Kegan Paul, 1969.

and speculators in the business of confining and detaining the inmates of these institutions against their will, that physicians engaged in the treatment of the insane must expect to be criticized by their professional brethren....[72]

On the whole, however, doctors engaged in the treatment of the insane strongly resisted the threat of proposed reforms to impose greater legal restraints on their professional activities and to restrict licensed houses. While sharing *The Lancet's* theoretical adherence to the concept of the asylum as a genuine hospital, far from concluding that legislation was needed to reduce medical powers over the insane, they claimed that only medical expertise could correctly determine such questions as whether a person was insane and whether he was in need of asylum treatment. They opposed the proposed legislation in principle as an assault on their profession by ignorant lawyers and an ignorant public. Their main argument against extending the judicial order to private cases was that it would impede the early treatment so crucial to prospects of cure. Some were initially prepared to countenance greater judicial involvement in commitment to the extent that this might shield certifying doctors from legal actions for wrongful detention,[73] but there was little evidence of support for this as a means of enhancing the medical image of psychiatry by distancing doctors from the machinery of coercion. This perspective is more evident in the 1920s and the 1950s when the abolition of the magistrate's involvement rather than an extension of his role was at issue. It is suggested that the asylum doctors were less uneasy about taking responsibility for powers of detention when it was a question of defending the status quo than they were at a later stage in professional development when the issue was the expansion of these responsibilities. As far as their defence of the proprietors of licensed houses is concerned, it is noteworthy that the Medico-Psychological Association itself contained a strong contingent of private asylum proprietors.

The policy of *The Lancet* provoked bitter responses from the psychiatric wing of the profession, who were afraid of being deserted by their colleagues at this critical time if the medical press joined the lay press in clamouring for stringent new laws. In a letter of 29

[72] J. C. Bucknill, p.vii.
[73] For example, Dr Yellowlees and Dr Hack Tuke at a meeting of the Medico-Psychological Association on 8 May 1885. See *Journal of Mental Science* 31 (1885–6), p. 278.

September 1884, H. J. Manning wrote to the editor of *The Lancet:* 'You, sir, have favoured us in your journal of late with many disquisitions upon lunacy law and practice, most of them, let me assure you, galling beyond measure to those gentlemen who are engaged in this speciality'.[74]

Alienists, aware of the ambiguity of their role, yearned to be recognized by the rest of the medical profession as an integral part of it. They, too, wanted the asylum to be transformed into a hospital, in order to reassure them that they really were engaged in a legitimately medical enterprise. In a letter to *The Lancet* of 24 January 1885 headed 'Lunacy Law Reform' Thomas Smith Clouston (1840–1915) of the Royal Edinburgh Asylum wrote that his section of the profession

. . . feel deeply the apparent want of sympathy with them exhibited by some portions of the medical press. I also believe they will be greatly disappointed if the arrangements of the future for the treatment of mental disease do not tend to make them a more integral part of the profession than they are at present.[75]

The argument that the judicial order in private cases should be accepted by the medical profession as providing security against litigation became less tempting as it transpired that protection could be afforded by placing direct constraints upon legal action.[76] For example, defendants could be given the opportunity to stay the proceedings by proving there was no prima-facie case for *mala fides* or lack of reasonable care on the certifying doctor's part before a High Court Judge, and this was in fact introduced in 1889 by section 12 of the Lunacy Acts Amendment Act. At the time this seemed to afford an important measure of protection for doctors as it would save them the trouble, expense and loss of custom from defending 'vexatious' actions.[77] In the light of this alternative method of

[74]   *The Lancet* (1884) 2, p. 615.

[75]   *The Lancet* (1885) 2, pp. 176–7. Sir Thomas Smith Clouston was an eminent figure in the psychiatric profession, at various times during his life being Physician Superintendent of the Royal Asylum, Edinburgh, Medical Superintendent of the Cumberland and West Morland Asylum, President of the Medico-Psychological Association, Editor of the *Journal of Mental Science* and President of the Royal College of Physicians, Edinburgh.

[76]   For evidence to this effect, see *Journal of Mental Science* 31 (1885–6), p. 208 *et seq.*

[77]   By the 1920s, however, doctors had found this provision inadequate and were arguing, in the light of conflicting legal *dicta* on the question, that the interposition of the justice in the commitment procedure should give them witness status, so that they would only be liable for *mala fides*.

protecting the interests of certifying doctors, the medical profession as a whole had no interest in defending the provision for the Justice's order except as a gesture to the public or to bolster the profession's image. It was therefore more susceptible to asylum doctors' arguments regarding the damaging effect of the requirement of judicial intervention upon the rate of patients being brought forward for treatment. This helps to explain the apparent unity of the profession behind psychiatrists in opposing the Bill by 1889.

The doctors' anger at being subjected to legal retaliation after certification was at its height in the period when the series of Lunacy Acts Amendment Bills were being introduced. They demanded legislation to secure adequate protection against harassment by ex-patients, at the same time as lawyers and the public were clamouring for more stringent provisions in the lunacy law for the protection of the sane. It is tempting to see the inclusion in ultimate legislation of provisions to fulfil both purposes as a trade off or compromise whereby the medical profession were willing to accept greater legal intervention in order to achieve better protection against court actions. However, the medical profession became more united against legal controls in the late 1880s and it would seem that the state only conceded protection reluctantly, in recognition of doctors' power to disrupt the lunacy system to demonstrate a grievance. Disruptive action was confined to the issue of exacting protection for doctors in the certification process, but it was effective in creating considerable difficulty. From 1884, goaded on by *The Lancet* and the *British Medical Journal*, many doctors went on a certification 'strike', refusing to lay themselves open to financially and professionally ruinous court actions.

This strike seems to have been widely supported and was attacked by certain members of the medical profession who thought it unethical: George H. Savage, Medical Superintendent at Bethlem Hospital, addressing the Metropolitan Counties Branch of the British Medical Association in March 1885, said:

the medical profession is likely to do injury to itself by joining a form of trades union which has as its object not signing lunacy certificates. It is not a dignified course to take, and is one which is likely to injure the patients, to injure society and do no good to anyone.[78]

It was claimed that the strike was producing an alarming increase

---

[78] *British Medical Journal* (1885) 1, p. 692 *et seq.*

in the rate of suicide as without medical certificates there was no way in which patients could be got into asylums.[79] Nevertheless it continued, and was used as a direct threat to extort adequate protection: a deputation of the Medico-Psychological Association in its address to the Chief Secretary of the Lord Chancellor on 20 April 1885 included the statement that 'The Bill might be greatly hampered in its operation by an extensive refusal of the profession to accept the risks and penalties which might be incurred.'[80]

Medical pressure was exerted on the Government through the Parliamentary Committees of the Medico-Psychological Association and the British Medical Association and through the Royal College of Physicians. The Medico-Psychological Association also urged its members to

impress most earnestly upon members of the House of Commons with whom they were acquainted that insanity is a symptom of disease and that the primary aim and object of all legislation in regard to it should be the care and proper treatment of those suffering from it.[81]

The Medico-Psychological Association sent deputations to the Lord Chancellor to express its opposition to almost every Bill. The Royal College of Physicians sent a deputation before the 1889 Bill to Henry Matthews, the Home Secretary, to express 'the widespread disapproval of the Bill as a whole which prevailed very generally in the profession, and more particularly among those entrusted with the curative treatment of the insane.'[82]

The effect of this counter-pressure on the substance of the Bill does not seem to have been very great. The Medico-Psychological Association was well satisfied in 1885 with the concessions made by Lord Selborne,[83] and in 1886 was pleased that licensed houses were not to be entirely abolished, but that a monopoly was to be created in the hands of current licence-holders, all vested interests being respected. This limitation in the Bill may also however have been produced by a recognition on the Government's part of the strong practical factor of the difficulty of finding places for the patients whose asylums it was desired to close in accommodation of the standard they were used to, and not only by pressure from the

---

[79] *The Lancet* (1884) 2, pp. 570–1.
[80] *Journal of Mental Science* 31 (1885–6), p. 210.
[81] Id.
[82] *The Lancet* (1889) 2, pp. 33–4.
[83] *Journal of Mental Science* 31 (1885–6), p. 210 *et seq.*

medical side. Lord Halsbury was less flexible however and the Medico-Psychological Association found him less amenable to its pressure, although there was an important concession on the taking in of single patients by doctors.[84]

The medical profession was thus forced to reconcile itself to a new legislative philosophy based upon suspicious legalistic restraint of its activities in relation to the care and treatment of the insane. It was only in the very different social and political climate of the 1920s that its engagement in the psychiatric enterprise regained legislative endorsement by the state and the frontiers of legal intervention could be rolled back. However, the twin pillars of the 1890 reform were not the simple victories for individual liberty that they might appear. The restriction of licences for commercial madhouses constituted another example of interventionism in the name of individualism, in that it purported to dim the nightmare of the sane person unwarrantedly incarcerated with the mad by closer regulation of the private market in lunacy. Meanwhile, in effect, the judicialization of private commitment procedure was not such a serious incursion upon medical prerogative. Rather, it encircled medical judgement within a stockade of legitimatory legal formality, and doctors had also secured a new measure of insulation from suit. Nevertheless, the dedication of Lord Halsbury did not bring agitation for more safeguards to an end, neither did the defensive device of the procedural bar close off the option of litigation as a means of satisfaction for aggrieved patients. By the 1920s, the medical profession was again to be beleagured, but this time the legislature was anxious to rescue and restore it.

[84] The Medico-Psychological Association Parliamentary Committee throughout opposed restrictions on medical men in particular taking in single patients. Originally the practice was to be abolished altogether, but the final solution was that a maximum of two patients could be taken in subject to the sanction of the Commissioners in Lunacy. See 'The New Lunacy Act', *Journal of Mental Science* 35 (1889), p. 396.

5 The Mental Treatment Act 1930: I Psychiatric and Political Context

IF the Lunacy Act 1890 embodied 'the triumph of legalism', its successor, the Mental Treatment Act 1930, while not substituting an entire new code, fulfilled legalism's strategic rejection. The Act was based upon the Report of the Royal Commission on Lunacy and Mental Disorder, chaired by the Rt. Hon. H. P. Macmillan, which proposed that the premise of civil legislation for the mentally ill should no longer be the control of custodial power over mental patients by the construction of effective safeguards, but the reduction of legal formalities in the interest of the early and successful treatment of psychiatric disorders. The themes of the late nineteenth century had been at the ideological level, the Rule of Law, at the legal procedural level, formalism and compulsion, and at the institutional level, the dominance and centrality of the asylum. The Mental Treatment Act 1930 constituted a sharp break with these themes. Ideologically, the objectives to which it was seen as contributing were Public Health, Mental Hygiene, National Efficiency, and Social Reconstruction. At the level of legal procedure, the drive was toward informalization, dejudicialization, and voluntarism. Institutionally, while the asylum, recently rechristened the mental hospital, retained its basic dominance, there was a new emphasis upon alternative facilities for 'incipient' and 'temporary' mental disorders: clinics, out-patient departments, psychiatric wards in general hospitals, distinct reception centres. Within the asylum itself, it was felt necessary that there should be separate admission units for these cases. In addition, the divorce of public psychiatric services from the Poor Law was stressed. The specific reforms which conveyed these new themes into the law were the extension of voluntary admission to public mental hospitals; the introduction of a new Temporary Order for the treatment of so-called 'non-volitional' patients for up to twelve months without certification and also without judicial intervention; the imposition of new obligations and the conferment of new powers upon local authorities in relation to accommodation for temporary patients, the establishment of out-patient clinics, after-care facilities, and the sponsorship of psychiatric research; the extension of medical immunities from suit, the increased professionalization and expansion of the responsibilties of the Board of Control, and the revision of official terminology to reflect the desired therapeutic rather than custodial image of the lunacy system. What was the theoretical basis of this remarkable reorientation, and what new psychiatric and political context made it possible?

The Theoretical Basis of the Rejection of Legalism

The starting point for an understanding of the radical redirection of legislative provision in the 1920s is furnished by the Macmillan Commission in the second Chapter of its Report entitled 'General Considerations of Policy'.[1] This offers the definitive exposition of the theory underlying the later Act. It is a text of profound importance for the modern history of legislation on mental disorder for it gives eloquent expression to the fundamental changes of principle that were in progress. Kathleen Jones captures this effect in her statement that 'The Report was more than an analysis of the existing situation. It was also a stage in development.'[2]

The Royal Commission's 'General Considerations' commence with the firm statement that 'there is no clear line of demarcation between mental and physical illness':

A mental illness may have physical concomitants: probably it always has, though they may be difficult of detection. A physical illness on the other hand, may have and probably always has, mental concomitants. And there are many cases in which it is a question whether the physical or mental symptoms predominate.[3]

The Commission, therefore, declared itself in favour of what might be termed a 'continuum' theory of disease in which mental and physical disorder could not be radically distinguished. It subscribed to the view that such differences as did exist between them lay at the secondary level of symptoms. Instead of being little more than a metaphor for insanity, as it had been hitherto, the concept of disease should, it followed, be taken seriously as the determining factor in legal and administrative provision. The argument based upon the interrelation of mental and physical disorder tended to be pressed

---

[1] *Report of the Royal Commission on Lunacy and Mental Disorder*, (Cmd. 2700, 1926), pp. 15–24.

[2] K. Jones, *A History of the Mental Health Services*, p. 244.

[3] *Report of the Royal Commission on Lunacy and Mental Disorder*, para. 38.

most forcibly by advocates of reform with reference to the early and temporary cases which were the special object of projected new legislation. Rather than drawing a boundary between physical and mental illness, as was traditionally the case, these should be treated alike as far as possible, the boundary being redrawn so as to fall between illness (physical and mental) and full insanity or lunacy, for which special legal machinery should be reserved. The brief of the Royal Commission itself, after all, distinguished 'lunacy' and 'mental disorder'. This view was expressed with particular clarity by Lord Dawson of Penn, during the debate in the House of Lords on the Mental Treatment Bill which took place in November 1929:

> If you leave what we think of as insanity and come down to mental derangement, you will find that it is constantly side by side with physical derangement. It is often a matter of chance whether a patient who has been ill suffers from a mental complication or a physical complication. There is a close connection; the two are often blended with each other at one stage as distinct from the end result—namely, insanity. The two conditions want to be treated as nearly as possible alike . . . When you come to certified insanity it is another problem . . . That patient is so disabled that . . . he has to join a cloistered class.[4]

Lord Dawson cited cases of typhoid and puerperal fever as examples of mere 'derangement', and pleaded that the Bill, as it did not deal with insanity but mental illness, 'should be kept away from all mention of the machinery of insanity'.[5] This strain of argument aided those who, as we shall see, contended that the Board of Control and the asylums should be excluded from the new legal framework. Although typhoid, malarial, and puerperal cases, with their clear physical origins, were often instanced as targets of new legislation, it is clear that it was also oriented to 'disorders', the symptoms of which amounted to social incapacity or deviance, from 'nervous break-downs' and phobias to the disturbances of adolescence. The aim of the measure was to spread a wider and more effective web of preventive psychiatry in the interests of social order in the belief that this would help to combat such problems as crime, suicide, illegitimacy, destitution, vagrancy, and alcoholism.[6] This was a

[4] *House of Lords Debates* 75, cols. 754–7 (28 November 1929).
[5] Ibid., col. 1102 (10 December 1929).
[6] See *Royal Commission on Lunacy and Mental Disorder: Minutes of Evidence*, 1926, II, Appendix XXV: Memorandum of Evidence of the National Council for Mental Hygiene, pp. 967–8.

controversial political objective and one partly legitimated by founding legal innovation on the solid scientific rock of the proposition that mental and physical illness were inextricable.

Although the Commission recognized that the reason for the time-honoured segregation of the mentally disordered from the physically ill was the specific form of its manifestation—the inability of the patient 'to maintain his social equilibrium'[7]—it decided that the disease conception it had adopted demanded the imposition upon the mental treatment system of principles operating in general medical care. Thus each of its recommendations was designed to promote the assimilation of the treatment of mental disorder to the treatment of somatic illness by minimizing the legal formalities imposed in the past to safeguard the liberty of the subject, but now disfavoured as irrelevant to and obstructive of the healing enterprise. In particular there had to be a redirection of legislative ingenuity from the regulation of detention to the facilitation of prevention and cure: 'The keynote of the past has been detention; the keynote of the future should be prevention and treatment.'[8] Whereas the necessity for a large majority of patients to undergo certification as lunatics, involving the intervention of a magistrate prior to asylum treatment, ensured that 'the disease' was only reached at an advanced and often unresponsive stage, and the general restriction of treatment to those institutionalized in asylums and workhouses frustrated prevention, the introduction of voluntary admission to public asylums and involuntary admission without certification, and the provision of treatment in clinics or reception hospitals would allow treatment at an early, recoverable stage. General medical principles would then have supplanted the outmoded system based on certification which affronted 'the accepted canons of preventive medicine which reign in all other types of institution for the treatment of disease'.[9] The Commission believed that this would make it possible to provide for the treatment of mental illness 'from the very earliest moment of the appearance of its symptoms'.[10] This would entail the organization of services for the treatment of mental disorder as a department of public health, being 'essentially a public health problem to be dealt with on modern public health lines'.[11] The Commission specially

[7] *Report of the Royal Commission on Lunacy and Mental Disorder*, para. 39.
[8] Ibid., para. 42.
[9] Ibid., para. 46.
[10] Id.
[11] Ibid., para. 50.

recommended the establishment of psychiatric clinics, to be modelled on those already developed for the treatment of venereal disease and tuberculosis.[12] Its focus was the public sector and the confrontation of mental illness as a mass problem, in contrast to the private sector preoccupation of the Lunacy Acts Amendment Act, with its identification of patients kept for profit as most at risk of losing their liberty without justifiction.

The greatest difficulty for Macmillan and his colleagues was, of course, in legitimating the continued use of formal compulsion, which was alien to general medicine and threatened to frustrate any attempt to present the mental treatment system as genuinely medical rather than quasi-penal in character. First of all they were able to emphasize the proposed shift toward voluntary treatment. The remaining use of compulsory powers could be justified by analogy with the compulsory restraint of patients carrying infectious disease.[13] Although when certification was a prerequisitie of entry to an asylum it appeared to be an object in itself, once it affected only a proportion of the patient population, it could be seen merely as an incident of treatment.[14]

It is striking that Macmillan's 'General Considerations' only represent a systematic attempt to *apply* the logic of assimilation to various facets of the relationship between law and psychiatry. There is no real explanation of *why* assimilation should be the decisive consideration, and there is little concession to assessing issues on their merits or admitting the pertinence of alternative perspectives. This can be amply illustrated, but one apposite example is the differential attitude of the Commission to the role in the admissions process of the doctor and the Justice respectively. There were a number of parallels between the criticisms made by witnesses before the Commission in relation to the medical profession and magistrates in their handling of commitment. It was argued by critics who were in favour of legalism, such as the National Society for Lunacy Reform, that the underdevelopment of psychiatry as a science limited the extent to which decisions affecting the liberty of the subject could safely be left to doctors. The lay Justices on the other hand were criticized for essential ignorance of the subject, inexperience, and the routine processing of lunacy cases.[15] Each of these criticisms

[12] Ibid., paras. 113, 248.
[13] Ibid., para. 43.
[14] Ibid., para. 46.
[15] Ibid., paras. 82–4.

affected the estimation of the competence of their respective targets to play a responsible and constructive role in the processes of commitment, but the reaction of the Royal Commission was very different in the two cases. The lack of training and experience in psychiatric medicine which handicapped the average medical practitioner was acknowledged but it was concluded: 'when all is said and done, reliance must inevitably be placed at some point on the skill and integrity of the medical man. If confidence is not reposed in the medical profession no system of protection can be devised which will not ultimately break down'.[16]

Of course, the central historical problem concerning the reconciliation of compulsory psychiatric treatment with the liberty of the subject has been precisely *at what point* to vest the medical profession with effective decision-making power: where should medical discretion take over from non-medical authorities acting on a judicial basis? The Commission was determined upon assimilation even though it conceded the shortcomings of psychiatry as a scientific medical discipline.

The lay Justices did not benefit from such 'leniency'. Instead of proposing some system of training which would equip them with greater knowledge[17] or recommending greater specialization of magisterial functions,[18] the Justices' shortcomings were used as justification for proposing more reliance on medical opinion: Justices should take steps to see one or both certifying doctors in doubtful cases,[19] and consult the medical practitioner on the issue of disclosure of the proceedings.[20] In reluctantly advising the retention of judicial involvement in the reformed commitment procedures,

[16] Ibid., para. 47.

[17] Training would anyway no doubt have been designed to integrate the potentially discordant judicial element into the therapeutic and control rationalities otherwise governing admission. The British Medical Association was one source of support for the idea before the Macmillan Commission. On the problems of introducing a system of training, see Sir Robert Walden's response to a question from the Commission on the comparison with coroners and medical aspects of the investigation of sudden death: *Royal Commission on Lunacy and Mental Disorder: Minutes of Evidence*, I, Answer 2159.

[18] The 'judicial authority' for private cases under the Lunacy Act 1890 was supposed to be specially appointed, but the practice had grown up of appointing the whole bench. The legal basis of this was the Lunacy Act 1891, section 24(4) which provided that the appointment of a judicial authority should not be invalidated only because it included all the Justices. The Royal Commission did go so far as to deprecate this practice: see para. 109 of its Report.

[19] *Report of the Royal Commission on Lunacy and Mental Disorder*, para. 86.

[20] Ibid., para. 87.

Macmillan looked forward to the demise of magisterial commitment: 'It may be that ultimately the treatment of mental illness will be so assimilated to the treatment of physical illness that the participation of a magistrate will no longer be considered necessary.'[21] The magistrate's involvement was a prominent element in the existing system which militated against assimilation, and as soon as public opinion would allow it must be dispensed with.

In effect the 'General Considerations of Policy' comprise a shift of 'problematic', defined here by Alan Hunt as being

contained in every statement of a frame of reference or a theoretical proposition; it is more than the statement of a problem or a question in that the selection of a particular focus excludes or relegates other foci and thereby presents a potential solution within itself.[22]

Macmillan's theoretical exposition delineates a field of problems to which future legislation should be addressed, namely the facilitation of early and effective mental treatment, and thus rejects the former 'legal' problematic of protecting the liberties of the sane. Indeed, concern for the rights of the sane appears in a quite different guise:

The rights of the patient must be protected, but so also must the rights of the public, who are entitled to be safeguarded against the presence in their midst of persons of unbalanced mind and dangerous tendencies. To suffer insane members to be at large is to permit an infringement of the liberty of the sane members of the community, who are entitled to go about their business unmolested and in safety. Any properly conceived lunacy code must have regard to the rights of the public in the matter as well as to those of the mentally afflicted, and the public are entitled to protection against the risks attendant on failure to detain those who ought to be detained.[23]

However, the Report delivers no real explanation of why the problematic has changed. It was not only that practical developments in the interval since 1890 had undermined the credibility of the earlier focus. Macmillan did not merely say that legal safeguards were in various respects deficient in operation, but maintained that it was wrong in principle to prioritize them. We must therefore look beyond the Report itself and ask why it was thought acceptable and desirable to dismantle legal formalities in the 1920s when it had not

---

[21]   Ibid., para. 107.
[22]   A. Hunt, 'Perspectives in the Sociology of Law', in P. Carlen (ed.), *The Sociology of Law*. University of Keele, Sociological Review Monograph 23, 1976, p. 22.
[23]   *Report of the Royal Commission on Lunacy and Mental Disorder*, para. 168.

been so earlier. Why was the concept of insanity as a species of illness, long accepted by the establishment of the lunacy system, now seen as necessitating the *legal* assimilation of psychiatric to general medical services? We might note that there is nothing in Macmillan's theoretical reasoning which compels this conclusion outright. It would have been logically compatible with the continuum theory of the relationship between mental and somatic illness to maintain that although they both denoted an underlying pathology, mental symptoms were so different in social significance, bearing in mind Macmillan's own reference to 'social equilibrium', that legal safe-guards against the infringement of liberty must be paramount, at least during psychiatry's 'adolescence'. This possibility was personi-fied in the stance adopted by Viscount Brentford (1865–1932), Minister of Health under Baldwin in 1923 and Home Secretary during the General Strike, who managed to combine a passion for the wonders of preventive psychiatry with a conviction that these should not be pursued at the cost of new threats to liberty. Opening a Conference on Mental Health organized by the National Council for Mental Hygiene and the Tavistock Square Clinic in October 1929 he enthused upon such matters as the prospect of securing 'a more general and enlightened appreciation of the relation of mental disorder and mental deficiency to the everyday conditions of domestic, industrial and social life' and congratulated the Macmillan Commission for broadcasting the message of mental hygiene to the world.[24] But when it came a month later in the House of Lords to Clause 5 of the Mental Treatment Bill and the proposed removal of the judicial safeguard for temporary non-volitional patients, he was adamantly opposed, being dismissed by Kathleen Jones as a mouth-piece of 'emotional opposition'.[25] That the Royal Commission nevertheless employed its reasoning to justify a decisive break with the past, and that the Labour Government of 1929–31 was prepared to follow it in this and even go further in the matter of abolishing magisterial participation in the new commitment procedure, requires explanation in terms of the full medical and political context.

The Psychiatric Context

At the time of the Macmillan Commission there were, in fact, plenty

---

[24] *Report of the Proceedings of a Conference on Mental Health*, National Council for Mental Hygiene and Tavistock Square Clinic, 30 October–2 November 1929, p. 7.
[25] K. Jones, *A History of the Mental Health Services*, p. 247.

of grounds for continued therapeutic pessimism, fostering a custodial image of the psychiatric function, and arguing for the retention of a restrictive legal framework. There had been no dramatic improvement in the recovery rates achieved by mental institutions to create a more promising climate for the reception of psychiatrists' demands for liberation from legal strictures. The annual rate of recoveries to direct admissions for public mental hospitals was 34.3 per cent in 1924, much as it was in the 1880s, although registered hospitals and licensed houses traditionally tended to produce higher rates.[26] Of course, the figures themselves were highly problematical to interpret. The Commission itself recognized this, commenting on the difficulties presented by variations in the standard of 'recovery' applied by different Medical Superintendents and the remarkable variations between institutions, with Portsmouth reporting 25 per cent and Norfolk 45 per cent.[27] The statistics were also affected by conditions quite independent of medical success, as they were during the First World War, when asylums were overcrowded as a result of several institutions being turned over to other functions. Only the most urgent cases were admitted, so that recovery rates were depressed by the over-representation of chronic cases in the population upon which they were calculated. The existence of a large proportion of insitutionalized patients medically regarded as irrecoverable could be represented in the figures by expressing recoveries as a percentage solely calculated in relation to the 'recoverable' population. Leicester Mental Hospital was able to provide the Commission with a rate of 57.9 per cent on this basis, but this method of computation was not seized upon as a more reliable indicator of medical progress. It was also the case that readmission rates could be high: in 1924 the figure for London was 29.8 per cent and the rate was 19.8 per cent nationally.[28] It could not be said in refutation of this evidence of persistent custodialism that mass cures were being achieved in established institutions other than the asylum.

[26] The Board of Control explained the apparently better performance of these institutions by 'such factors as discretion to refuse private patients as unsuitable, ability on the part of their friends to have them home immediately on an apparent but only temporary recovery, and perhaps the greater use by public mental hospitals of "trial" before full discharge, which enables lapses within the period of trial to be dealt with without the necessity of a fresh order': see *Annual Report of the Board of Control for the Year 1921*, p. 11.

[27] *Report of the Royal Commission on Lunacy and Mental Disorder*, para. 165.

[28] *Royal Commission on Lunacy and Mental Disorder: Minutes of Evidence*, I, Answer 5,018: Mr Keene; see also *Annual Report of the Board of Control for the Year 1924*.

Many pauper patients were detained in Poor Law Institutions prior to certification, and some recovered in a short period, avoiding transfer to an asylum, but it was agreed on all sides that treatment facilities in these institutions were inferior or non-existent,[29] and so it must be concluded that such recoveries were largely spontaneous.

As yet, there was limited intensive psychiatric treatment in the asylums, either in terms of physical treatments developed specifically for use in psychiatry or in terms of psychotherapy. There was a considerable reliance upon general medical care, routine custodial management, and the imposition of disciplinary regimes which included a substantial element of deterrent punishment—a crude rendition of moral treatment.[30] The thoroughgoing moralism of psychiatrists' evaluations of their patients and accounts of treatment in their evidence to the Macmillan Commission is patent. The Commission itself was very mindful of the need for maintaining order in the asylum, lending its support to the infantilization of the patients and to disciplinary methods of normalization. Earl Russell invoked the analogy of the school, and saw as one of the dangers of legalism that it might convert the patients 'into people who are hunting for rules and regulations and trying to catch out those in charge for having broken this or that regulation'.[31] The National Society for Lunacy Reform had been campaigning against the use of the purgative croton oil as a punishment, claiming that 'as in modern warfare, chemical violence is taking the place of physical violence'.[32] Whilst the Commission came down in favour of the careful monitoring of the administration of croton oil, it also expressed itself as broadly for disciplinary punishment, as long as it was reformative or deterrent rather than retributive, approving the much criticized practice of relegating 'refractory' patients to wards for 'the less well conducted': 'The inculcation of discipline and correction of bad behaviour must be part of the treatment of certain forms of mental disorder in which the patient's cure depends on re-education towards the acquirement of self-discipline and good behaviour'.[33]

The Commission decided to recommend that disciplinary relegation should continue to be administered by the medical man in

[29] See *Annual Report of the Board of Control for the Year 1921*, p. 75.
[30] *Report of the Royal Commission on Lunacy and Mental Disorder*, para. 214.
[31] *Royal Commission on Lunacy and Mental Disorder: Minutes of Evidence*, I, Question 11,641; see also the Chairman at Question 11,606.
[32] *Report of the National Society for Lunacy Reform*, 1926, p. 6.
[33] *Report of the Royal Commission on Lunacy and Mental Disorder*, para. 214.

charge, rather than the Visiting Committee, so that it should remain a part of 'treatment'.[34] The Commission was clearly conscious of the need to maintain boundaries between distinct orders of discipline lest the special efficacy of each be undermined.

A typical description of treatment was provided in the evidence of Dr F. E. Edwards, Medical Superintendent of a private asylum, Camberwell House:

The amount of actual definite treatment from day to day is not very great. Drug treatment in many cases is unnecessary. Take the ordinary routine; a patient is admitted in the ordinary way, put to bed and examined by a doctor. Then within two or three days, if it seems desirable, blood is taken and we get the pathological report; the dentist visits and examines the teeth. It is just the routine of a general hospital in every way, and a certain percentage of patients are very much better without any drugs at all.[35]

As appears from Dr Edwards' description, psychiatrists were now emphasizing the relative lack of specific new psychiatric treatments as a positive factor confirming their links with general medicine.[36] Specific treatments in use included institutionalization itself, as involving the removal of patients from pathogenic home environments, the therapeutic influence of the organization of the asylum (later to be systematized into the concept of 'administrative therapy'), treatment for physical ailments (including dental sepsis, then being investigated as a source of mental disorder), bed rest, detoxication, occupational therapy,[37] psychotherapy, Freudian psychoanalysis, glandular therapy, electrical treatment, hydrotherapy, and hypnosis. There was nothing here that was revolutionary in its impact. However, there had been one definite breakthrough in the conclusive demonstration of the link between general paresis and syphilis. The link had been proposed as early as 1857 by Esmarch and Jessen, and was quite generally accepted by the early twentieth century. However, it was in 1913 that the syphilitic basis of the condition was

[34] Id.

[35] *Royal Commission on Lunacy and Mental Disorder: Minutes of Evidence*, I, Answer 6,454. See also the evidence of J. Francis Dixon, Medical Superintendent of the City Hospital, Humberstone, Leicester at Question 3,831 *et seq.*, and of Dr Henry Yellowlees, Superintendent of The Retreat at Question 5,670 *et seq.*

[36] See for example, ibid., I, Answer 4,360: evidence of Dr H. Devine, Medical Superintendent of the Borough Mental Hospital, Portsmouth.

[37] Feminists will be interested to learn that in this respect 'for women the laundry, the needlework room and the kitchen provide a measure of domestic occupation . . .', although the Commission did recommend for them more out-of-doors occupations in farms and gardens, and more handicraft workshops for both sexes.

confirmed by the isolation of the syphilitic organism in paretic brains. General paresis provided a clear precedent for establishing organic aetiologies for other mental illnesses and in 1918 was found to be tractable to a physical treatment, the Wagner Jauregg method, which involved malarial inoculation. It therefore strengthened the case for closer links with general medicine.[38] By 1919, general paresis itself was in decline relative to other classifications of mental disease, largely as a consequence of the success of public health measures for the prevention and control of syphilis, which were themselves to be adduced as one of the models for the reorganization of services addressed to problems of mental disorder.

Advances in the development of curatively efficacious physical treatments would have helped to 'clinch' the medical view of insanity[39] but the physical treatments that were to have the most impact in the twentieth century—psychosurgery, insulin treatment, electroconvulsive therapy, and, argued to have been the most transformative of all, tranquillizing drugs—post-dated the revolution in official perspective upon the law. Macmillan recognized that there had been no watershed in the development of therapeutic technology. But it was the law itself which took the blame for the disappointing results so far produced.[40] The state of the law was seen to inhibit preventive intervention and impede medical research, imposing upon the medical profession the burden of a disproportionately irrecoverable clientele.

Two lines of reorientation may be accounted as having infected the Commission with optimism as to the prospects for psychiatry if legal bonds were soon loosened. Firstly, the medical profession had persisted in its determination to medicalize the forms and settings of the psychiatric specialty: the asylum, as we saw above, was to be penetrated more and more by the routines of the hospital. Even though there were difficulties of access to incipient and temporary cases the profession congratulated itself that 'patients are treated in a very much more intelligent and humane way than they were,[41] and it was claimed that 'the greatest revolution of all, and that which has

[38] See G. Rosen, *Madness in Society*. London: Routledge and Kegan Paul, 1968, pp. 348–58; V. Skultans, *English Madness*. London: Routledge and Kegan Paul, 1979, pp. 136–8.
[39] D. Ewins, 'The Origins of the Compulsory Commitment Provisions of the Mental Health Act 1959', p. 35.
[40] *Report of the Royal Commission on Lunacy and Mental Disorder*, para. 46.
[41] See *Royal Commission on Lunacy and Mental Disorder: Minutes of Evidence*, I, Answer 7,658.

done most to turn the madhouse into a mental hospital, has been in regard to the care and treatment of the chronic and especially the chronic turbulent cases'.[42] Changes in the terminology utilized by the profession itself—'mental disorder' rather than 'lunacy', 'hospitals' rather than 'asylums'—had become well established in the interval since 1890.[43] Secondly, in the treatment of 'nervous disorders' in the private sector or when under exceptional dispensations psychiatrists were granted access to early cases in the public sector (for example at the Maudsley Hospital, established by the London County Council under special legislative authority in 1915, or during the First World War in the treatment of 'shell-shock'), they were successful in associating themselves with disorders involving merely temporary incapacity and therefore with the notions of recoverability and cure. The concentration of the psychiatric gaze upon early treatment and the emphasis of prevention (a distraction from and an alternative to treatment in the absence of a major therapeutic breakthrough) was part of a profound internal reorganization in psychiatry itself which challenged existing legal parameters.

The period separating 1890 and 1930 witnessed the transition to the 'modern age' of psychiatry following the late nineteenth-century decomposition of its classical or 'golden' age. David Ingleby defines the characteristics of the modern age as including the following:

... with the base of asylum practice securely established, medical authority is extended *beyond* the asylum population; 'mental illness' overlaps insanity, to cover deviations not severe enough to call for incarceration. New categories of pathology are devised, notably the concept of 'neurosis'. New sites of intervention are established in which psychiatry can attack pathology at its very roots—family life, industry and the school system—and new specialities are developed, some relatively autonomous from the medical profession, but all based on the medical model and most under the ultimate jurisdiction of the psychiatrist. Clinical and educational psychology, psychoanalysis, criminology and social work all participate in this expansion, which starts in earnest in the first two decades of the twentieth century.[44]

This was an international movement within psychiatry. Writing in a French context, Robert Castel identifies in the emergence of preventive psychiatry a displacement of moral treatment beyond the asylum, creating the scope for:

[42] *Journal of Mental Science* 72 (1926), p. 600.
[43] See P. Bean, *Compulsory Admissions to Mental Hospitals*, p. 39.
[44] D. Ingleby, 'Mental Health and Social Order', p. 161.

... a veritable 'moralization of the masses', a formidable extension of the medical intervention and a profound transformation of the modality of its exercise. Within this development the doctor was no longer to be the exclusive operator but would come rather to participate within the ensemble of those professionals placed in a position within the social hierarchy from where they would be able to exert a political action toward the masses, a form of preventive psychiatry. ... an indefinite field of interventions was opened up, a strategy ... which broke firmly with the classical psychiatric tradition based as it was on the privileged site of the asylum.[45]

Similarly, Jacques Donzelot observes that:

mental illness was no longer a spectacular exception that must be isolated and eventually treated, but a phenomenon that was always latent, necessitating early detection and a prophylactic intervention embracing all the causes in the social body which favoured the mechanisms of degenerescence: to wit, miserable living conditions and intoxications such as alcohol, to which the poor population were exposed. Thus ... the psychiatrist yearned to leave the asylum in order to become the agent of a project of social regeneration.[46]

The modern age of psychiatry developed most rapidly in the United States, because the American scene had not been subject to the same dominance of the public asylum in the nineteenth century,[47] and the more advanced developments there exerted a direct influence upon Britain via the international Mental Hygiene and Child Guidance movements. This process of reorientation will now be traced in more detail in the domestic context.

From the inception of the Lunacy Act 1890 psychiatrists were resolved to break the deadlock of which it was a part, although they had to be politically cautious in relation to the sensitive topic of 'the liberty of the subject' even in the 1920s. In October 1895, Sir James Chrichton Browne, in his Presidential Address to the Medical Society of London, sketched a vision of a mental hospital of the future which was later to be partly actualized in the creation of the Maudsley Hospital:

For my own part my hopes are centred in the establishment in or near London of one or more, not asylums, but genuine hospitals for mental

[45] P. Miller, 'The Territory of the Psychiatrist', pp. 92–3. This is Miller's rendition of Castel's account.
[46] J. Donzelot, *The Policing of Families*. London: Hutchinson, 1979, p. 128. The psychiatrists' yearnings did not remain unrequited, as their services were in demand as adjuncts of military and educational discipline.
[47] See P. Miller, 'Psychiatry—the Renegotiation of a Territory', p. 99.

disease. These hospitals would be organized like ordinary general hospitals, would have a staff of visiting and assistant physicians, and of consulting surgeons, and specialists in diseases of the eye and ear and in those peculiar to women, and of resident medical officers and clinical clerks. Attached to them there would be an out-patients' department and a school of medical psychology with laboratories and museums, in which systematic investigation, teaching and demonstration would be carried on. A few such hospitals—not merely 'monasteries for the mad' or convenient shoots for human rubbish but real mental hospitals—would exercise a salutory and invigorating effect on the medico-psychological specialty and bring it back into closer correspondence with the medical profession as a whole.[48]

The definitive psychiatric blueprint for a new service was unveiled by Dr C. Hubert Bond, a medical Commissioner of the Board of Control, in his Presidential Address to the Annual Meeting of the Medico-Psychological Association in July 1921, entitled 'The Position of Psychological Medicine in Medical and Allied Services'.[49] This entailed a complex scheme in which treatment facilities would range from domiciliary treatment by general practitioners, through out-patient treatment and in-patient treatment at new clinics, to treatment in mental hospitals. There would be a finely graded progression from domicile to total institution and from informal to certified status. The logic informing the model service was prevention through the promotion of mental hygiene, and the early treatment of mental disorder. Thus the role of the general practitioner in family surveillance:

It is my strong conviction that the general practitioner could, under suitable arrangements, be of the greatest possible service to the cause of psychological medicine. It is he alone who, while in attendance on one member of the family, has the opportunity of observing with a trained eye other members regarded as bodily and mentally sound, but in whom he, however, recognizes interesting traits and temperamental peculiarities. Were he encouraged to be systematic in such observations and to adopt some method of recording them, they would be of inestimable value in collecting reliable data for that which in our work might well be called the 'research magnificent'—in other words, a knowledge of the prolegomena and earliest stages of mental disorder. Whether in 'nativity, chance or death', it is he more than anyone else—not even excepting the priest—whose profession brings him into the

---

[48] J. Crichton Browne, First Maudsley Lecture, *Journal of Mental Science* 66 (1920), p. 202.
[49] *Journal of Mental Science* 67 (1921), p. 404.

most intimate and confidential and social life of the people, both communally and in the family.[50]

This role would, of course, convert general practitioners into a data collection service for psychiatry and forge one of many projected new connections between the practice of general and psychiatric medicine. Bond was also an enthusiast for the vogue concept of the psychiatric in-patient clinic, to be associated with the general hospital and dealing with voluntary and non-volitional cases, not simply as a site for early treatment, but as a centre for teaching and research, integrating psychological medicine more fully into the medical curriculum and enhancing its status as a discipline. Hence the particular emphasis on establishing clinics at teaching hospitals.[51] The demand for clinics threatened the diversion of curable cases from the asylum and its consequent degeneration into a virtual prison with a medical facade that would appear increasingly cosmetic. Some of those who urged the adoption of the clinic, including Dr Bond,[52] issued disclaimers of this intention. Others, like Colonel Goodall, one of the Medico-Psychological Association's witnesses before Macmillan, were content to allow the reconversion of the aspiring mental hospital into an asylum as part of a strategy for psychiatric desegregation. Dr Henry Yellowlees, Medical Superintendent of The Retreat, also in evidence, stated his prophetic belief that whereas the contemporary issue was whether to exclude early and temporary cases from the asylum, the question of the future would be the removal of the chronic incurables.[53] However, while it was his expectation that the need to decarcerate chronics would arise in order to purify the asylum as an active hospital concerned with treatable cases, the policy movement in the era of the Mental Health Act 1959 was to be towards squeezing the mental hospital between an accentuation of provision for acute cases in general facilities and the discharge of 'harmless chronics' into the community.

Psychiatry was not to advance into the social body as an isolated profession, but did so in unequal alliance with other emergent disciplines concerned with social regulation and the positive promotion of social efficiency and welfare, notably psychology and social

[50] Ibid., pp. 422–3.

[51] For elaboration of his views on clinics and other aspects of psychiatric education, see 'The Need for Schools of Psychiatry', *Journal of Mental Science* 66 (1920), p. 10 *et seq.*

[52] Ibid., p. 13.

[53] *Royal Commission on Lunacy and Mental Disorder: Minutes of Evidence*, I, Answer 5,719.

work. The psychiatric pervasion of society by means of the subordination and incorporation of potentially rival professional perspectives and methods during this period is admirable testimony to the effectiveness of its tendencies to absorption. While the organic model remained central, psychiatry was able to thrive by embracing diverse schools, taking on board psychotherapy in the early twentieth century[54] as it had moral treatment in the early nineteenth century. Within an eclectic psychiatry, the ultimate role of the psychiatrist would be that of 'master-detective',[55] able to undertake diagnosis and prescribe treatment on the basis of multiple medical and social scientific perspectives, the overlord of a cluster of psycho-social subdisciplines.

One important overarching organization within which psychiatry coalesced with other professions and interests concerned with the problem of mental disorder was the Mental Hygiene Movement.[56] George Rosen describes the origins of this movement as follows:

At the turn of the century, Americans were confronted by the inescapable fact that poverty, disease, vice and suffering were large-scale urban phenomena, and there was a growing feeling that these were symptoms of a more deep-seated social malaise. The discontent and disorder which plagued England, America, Germany and other countries gave rise to a stream of dissenting opinion, which was manifested concretely in various programmes of reform . . .[57]

This movement for social welfare formed around programmes for intervention in the living conditions of the working class, with a view to removing the causes of physical and moral degeneracy. The Mental Hygiene Movement was a characteristic expression of this tendency, campaigning for a vigorous injection of social work and preventive psychiatry. Interestingly, the American progenitor of what was to become an internationally organized movement for unleashing psychiatry *inter alia* by relaxing legal safeguards, started life much in the manner of the transient patients' organizations which had been a

[54] On the subordination of psychologists to doctors in clinics, see N. Rose, *The Psychological Complex*. London: Routledge and Kegan Paul, 1985, Chapter 8.

[55] G. Baruch and A. Treacher, 'Towards a Critical History of the Psychiatric Profession', in D. Ingleby (ed.), *Critical Psychiatry*. Harmonsdworth: Penguin, 1981, p. 123.

[56] I am indebted to Nikolas Rose for impressing upon me the importance of the Mental Hygiene movement, which has tended to be neglected in earlier accounts of the build-up to the Act, both published and unpublished.

[57] G. Rosen, p. 271.

thorn in the flesh of the psychiatric profession from its earliest years with their clamour for more law and more constitutional liberty. The Mental Hygiene Movement, dating from 1908, was the creation of Clifford Beers, an ex-patient whose account of his experiences, *The Man That Found Himself*, made a great public impact and who worked to improve conditions in asylums. Attracting the support of leading psychologists and the US Public Health Service, however, it became an organizational focus for the reforming impetus described above. Beer's National Committee for Mental Hygiene received the favourable attention both of the state, alerted to the value of psychology by the war, and of private industry.[58]

The English branch of the movement, the National Council for Mental Hygiene, was founded in 1922. It brought together under its umbrella psychiatrists, psychologists, doctors and social workers and defined the potential vehicles of its principles in extremely wide terms:

... the maintenance of a sound mind and the prevention of mental inefficiency is now of interest to sociological bodies ordinarily serving such diverse interests as medicine and nursing, moral and social welfare, teachers and education, infancy and maternity, Boy Scouts and Girl Guides, social hygiene, health and cleanliness, women's leagues and employment bodies, child guidance, hospital almoners, infant mortality, penal reform, sanitation, industrial psychology, Y.M.C.A., etc.—in fact every form of social service. They can now all meet helpfully and sympathetically, however different their specific aims and objects are, on a common platform, namely that of Mental Hygiene.[59]

The National Council addressed not the problem of existing advanced mental disorder, but early treatment, preventive intervention, and the positive promotion of mental health: the healthy as well as the sick were its proper concern, and the participation within it of the psychiatric profession was part of the process of its emergence from the asylum to 'survey the field of human relations in general',[60] from industrial disputes to sex education.

The National Council for Mental Hygiene gave evidence to Macmillan, its contribution providing something of an opposite pole

[58] See J. Kovel, 'The American Mental Health Industry', in D. Ingleby (ed.), *Critical Psychiatry*, pp. 78–9.

[59] *Report of the Proceedings of a Conference on Mental Health*, 30 October–2 November 1929, p. 3.

[60] C. Macfie Campbell, *Destiny and Disease in Mental Disorders*. New York: W. W. Norton, 1935, pp. 33–4, quoted in G. Rosen, p. 283.

to that of the National Society for Lunacy Reform in its preoccupation with facilitating the extension of psychiatric collaboration in
projects of intensified social management rather than with the
procedural protection of civil liberty by inhibiting psychiatry. Its
proposals, which emphasized the treatment of cases of neurosis, and
voluntary and non-volitional cases otherwise certifiable, at voluntary
general hospitals or in special institutions separate from the mental
hospital, were much in line with the consensus before the Commission and were somewhat dismissively described by the Chairman in
oral solicitation of supplementary views from the organization's
representatives as merely 'reinforcing views which have already been
urged upon us'.[61] However, the influence of the Council upon the
Macmillan Commission should not be underestimated. The membership of the two bodies overlapped, and the language of the
Commission's 'General Consideration of Policy' was closely aligned
with that of the Council's Memorandum of Evidence. Sir Maurice
Craig, the 'virtual parent'[62] of the organization in England, and its
Chairman from 1928–35, gave evidence as an individual, and J. R.
Lord, one of the witnesses of the Medico-Psychological Association,
was its Secretary. Although the National Council for Mental Hygiene
was vague on legal specifics, its ideology provided an advanced and
clear expression of the anti-legalist direction that the Commission
decided to espouse.

Within the preventive strategy, special importance became attached to the disorders of childhood and adolescence, as intervention
at these stages could, it was believed, avoid mental disorder in
adulthood.[63] In this connection, it is noteworthy that section 1(2) of
the Mental Treatment Act 1930 provided for the 'voluntary'
treatment of under-sixteens without certification on the application
of parent or guardian. The Child Guidance movement which took
shape around this problem again advanced most rapidly in the
United States. Child Guidance clinics, pioneered by William Healy in
his work at the Chicago Juvenile Psychopathic Institute, commencing
in 1909, were founded upon the co-operation of psychiatrists,
psychologists, and social workers. The proliferation of Child Guidance in America was sponsored and co-ordinated by the Commonwealth Fund and the National Committee for Mental Hygiene, and it

[61] *Royal Commission on Lunacy and Mental Disorder: Minutes of Evidence*, II, Question
17,288.
[62] See his obituary in *Mental Hygiene*, 1935.
[63] See N. Rose, *The Psychological Complex*, p. 163.

was through contacts between an English magistrate, Mrs St Loe Strachey and representatives of the former that a fledgling movement became organized in Britain, the Child Guidance Council being established in 1927. The earliest Child Guidance clinics, the first of which was actually opened by the Jewish Board of Guardians in East London in 1926, were also the product of voluntary initiative, although in the 1930s local education authorities were increasingly involved.[64] The Child Guidance clinic was a key site for the development of the new profession of psychiatric social work, the origin of which lay in the growth of after-care work with discharged lunatics from the 1870s. The first psychiatric social workers were trained in America under the auspices of the Commonwealth Fund and the first British training course was set up at the London School of Economics in 1929, the same year that the Association of Psychiatric Social Workers was formed.

The social and professional desegregation of psychiatry by its fullest participation in these preventive developments in part depended upon its legal desegregation. As Andrew Treacher and Geoffrey Baruch have observed, this was only finally achieved with the passage of the Mental Health Act 1959 and the 'de-designation' of mental hospitals, having the effect that *any* hospital could admit mental patients provided it had suitable facilities for care and treatment.[65] But the recommendations of the Macmillan Commission and even more so the provisions of the Mental Treatment Act moved decisively in this direction. The question which must now be asked is why Commission and Government were prepared to encourage rather than impede the reorientation of psychiatry and specifically at the expense of legal safeguards. Just as psychiatry had undergone an important change since 1890, so had there been a transformation in the dominant conception of the proper responsibilities and frontiers of the state. This gives an explanation of the fresh political receptivity to psychiatric aspirations. There had emerged a new field of 'social politics', to which the quest for Mental Hygiene was integral, being itself part of a stocktaking of 'political, social and spiritual values'.[66]

[64] See N. Timms, *Psychiatric Social Work in Great Britain 1939–1962*. London: Routledge and Kegan Paul, 1964, pp. 17–21, 90–1.

[65] G. Baruch and A. Treacher, 'Towards a Critical History of the Psychiatric Profession', p. 132.

[66] J. R. Lord, 'American Psychiatry and its Practical Bearings on the Application of Recent Local Government and Mental Treatment Legislation', *Journal of Mental Science* 76 (1930), p. 456.

The Political Context

The revolt against legalism signalled by the Macmillan Report could be explained at a very general level as an effect of the progressive rationalization and secularization of society, encouraging greater popular faith to be placed in medical judgment and allowing legal restrictions upon psychiatric practice to be lifted. This could be linked to a parallel movement in the nineteenth and twentieth centuries toward the more humane and enlightened treatment of misfits and deviants, which might be invoked to explain the increasing importance as a consideration in the design of legislation of destigmatization of the recipients of psychiatric treatment and the institutions in which it was administered. From this point of view, the Lunacy Act 1890, 'the triumph of legalism', would have to be dismissed as an aberration in legislative development. That this is so indicates the explanatory inadequacy of such a perspective, which recalls the Whig theory of history in its assumption of inevitable progress, and creates an insensitivity to the historical ebb and flow of legalism in legislative provision for the mentally disordered: after all, in the 1970s and 1980s legalism has again been in vogue. A much more specific explanation can be furnished by locating the Mental Treatment Act in the politics of reform which characterized the late nineteenth and early twentieth-century period. At this time not only was there a proliferation and reorientation of the disciplines, the psychiatric ramifications of which have just been described, but also a redefinition of the liberties which served to accommodate it. In facilitating psychiatric treatment by dismantling legal barriers, the Mental Treatment Act marked a transition from formal to therapeutic liberalism, from the primacy of abstract political liberty to the primacy of a concrete, substantive, socially defined liberty, which had to be positively created by expert intervention lubricated by informal, flexible, discretionary procedures. The redefinition of liberalism was part of a transformation in political ideology and social welfare strategy as a whole which carried major implications for the role of law in mediating control and the provision of services. Whereas in the early and mid-Victorian period, an incremental patchwork of social intervention had coexisted with the ideological dominance of classical liberal principles, from the 1880s philosophies which positively valued intervention became progressively more influential. A central object of reforming attention was the deterrent Poor Law, restrictively concerned with destitution, which managed the consequences of social disorganization without tackling its root causes or promoting positive welfare. This new impetus was not confined to the formal apparatuses of the state: it took place in the body of society and voluntary organizations were important in anticipating and shaping later public intervention. Public and private agencies were functionally interrelated and the personnel of the different sectors overlapped. It was this new sensibility which created the political matrix within which 'mental health' could be constructed as a legislative object and the preoccupation with legalism could come to be disdained for its abstraction, inefficiency and anachronism.[67]

The Lunacy Act 1890 had been very much the counterpart of the ideology of the liberal state, not only in its emphasis of formal liberty and the rule of law, but also in its narrow circumscription of the population properly subject to intervention. It fitted into a system within which intervention was directed to the control of specific problem populations—the destitute the criminal, the mad—within the limits imposed by an overriding concern to minimize the burden on rates and taxes. Given this priority of economy, assistance was provided on the basis of a classificatory principle in that entitlement to relief was contingent upon qualification for an official status of public dependency such as pauperism or pauper lunacy. This was a 'total status' in that, once it applied, citizenship itself was modified and the state assumed a responsibility for and interest in every aspect of the recipient's existence.[68] In such a system, importance naturally attached to correct criteria of classification, such as the test of less eligibility under the new Poor Law, and to the machinery of classification, such as the process of certification as a pauper lunatic. By contrast, the Mental Treatment Act 1930 reflected a movement toward the Therapeutic State, whose very *raison d'être* is positive intervention, extending beyond the limited categories of the deprived and the deviant, who merit special provision even within

---

[67] In Scottish legislation, it is notable that formal legal safeguards have retained a greater presence than in England. Formal safeguards in Scotland functioned within a system traditionally far less reliant upon compulsory commitment and private profit-making asylums and attractive of considerably more general public confidence. They were thus less open to be derided by welfare reformers as seriously detrimental to the effective treatment of mental disorder or to be championed by libertarians as essential to liberty when the anti-legalistic political climate of the early twentieth century arrived. They do not seem to have achieved the contentious status of their counterparts in English legislation.

[68] T. H. Marshall, *Social Policy in the Twentieth Century*. London: Hutchinson, 1970, pp. 19–20.

liberal order, to the population as a whole.[69] The new Act embodied an acceptance that state agencies could be legitimately engaged in the promotion of prevention and cure in the solution of social problems, being charged with the mission of reshaping the habits of the citizen to correct unacceptable behaviour. It was part of a long process of displacing the classificatory basis of state aid with a functional organization of welfare services designed to satisfy particular needs and freely available on request rather than arising from the possession of a demeaning dependent status. This was a transition which involved dismantling classficatory barriers to the receipt of services in the interests of easier expert access to the phenomena of social distress, that is, the relaxation of legal restrictions and the circumvention of judical commitment procedures.

The rejection of legalism in the latter Act reflects the changing valuation of law in the movement away from liberal order and toward therapeutic interventionism. A number of trends are typically associated historically with movements in this direction. From being principally concerned with the protection of 'the liberty of the subject' against potentially oppressive state apparatuses, law becomes the channel for state intervention, taking on a facilitative rather than an inhibitory function. This changes the forms of law so that legislative provisions increasingly empower, or vest officials with discretion, rather than imposing set rules to be followed, and decision-making by agencies of the state emphasizes policy considerations pertinent to the individual case at the expense of formal equality, liberty, and justice. This individualization of justice undermines fixed notions of rights and duties, giving priority to substantive issues of social policy rather than the formal ideals of the rule of law. The result is a 'withering away' of law, and the transmission of decision-making functions, which in a liberal state would be entrusted to judicial functionaries, to administrative and social welfare agencies whose expertise is in these substantive areas of policy rather than in the internal formal logic of the rules and principles of the law. The whole apparatus of the law—judges, juries, penal codes, police—is put at risk and subjected to erosion in the context of a transition from liberal to interventionist state forms.[70]

[69] See T. S. Szasz, *Law, Liberty and Psychiatry*, pp. 212–22 and N. Kittrie, *The Right to be Different*. London: John Hopkins Press, 1973.

[70] E. B. Pashukanis, advocating in 1924 the abolition of the legal form as one of the aims of the Soviet Revolution called in aid the fact that 'Even progressive bourgeois criminology has become convinced that the prevention of crime may properly be

The purely formal level of liberty and equality expressed in the rule of law is subjected to attack as inadequate and the equivalent substantive ideals are pursued at its expense.[71] However, in the move towards egalitarianism, a role for the law may be found in the entrenchment of positive rights to minimum welfare services exercisable against the state.[72]

The Mental Treatment Act incorporated another associated development corrosive of legalism: the decline of moralism in social provision for the criminal, the deviant and the poor. Increasingly, the utilitarian view of society as the aggregate of its composite individuals, the majority of whom were assumed to be rational and autonomous, was giving way to conceptions of social forces as independent and possessing their own effectivity. Phenomena previously considered in individual terms were translated into social products: worklessness became converted from a problem of individual shiftlessness into the impersonal social condition of 'unemployment'.[73] A whole space of 'the social' was opened up: voluntary philanthropic effort came to be conceived as 'social work' rather than charity.[74] The criminal, the deviant, the destitute were able to be seen rather as victims of determining social pressures than as culpable moral failures. Stigmatization was therefore inappropriate: so, for example, the Poor Law Institutions Order of 1913 completely omitted the terms 'workhouse' and 'pauper'. The Mental Treatment Act's relabelling of asylums and pauper lunatics was similarly intentioned. The natural successor to moralistic conceptions of social phenomena was the imagery of health and disease: thus, for the Webbs, unemployment was 'a disease of modern industry'.[75] This general invocation of the language of medicine and medical metaphor must be taken in itself to have assisted the ascendancy of medical definitions of the problems associated with mental disorder.

viewed as a medical-educational problem. To solve this problem, jurists, with their "evidence", their codes, their concepts of "guilt" and of "full or diminished responsibility", or their fine distinctions between complicity, aiding and abetting, instigation and so on, are entirely superfluous.' See *Law and Marxism*, p. 64.

[71] See R. H. Tawney, *Equality*, 5th edn. London: Unwin Books, 1964, pp. 164–73.

[72] T. H. Marshall discusses the importance of minimum legal, social, and political rights, for example the enfranchisement of paupers in 1918, in the legitimation of capitalist social order in the era of mass democracy: See *Citizenship and Social Class*. Cambridge: Cambridge University Press, 1950.

[73] See J. Harris, *Unemployment and Politics*. Oxford: Clarendon Press, 1972, p. 4.

[74] See generally, K. Woodroffe, *From Charity to Social Work in England and the United States*. London: Routledge and Kegan Paul, 1962.

[75] B. Webb and S. Webb, *English Poor Law History*, p. 631.

Determinist discourse may only have thinly disguised moral judgments and harsh discriminatory practices, but it was nevertheless in
conflict with the voluntaristic assumptions and penal connotations of
law and helped to create an alien environment for legalism.

The point of political consensus had shifted so that it became
possible to achieve legislation which pursued mental hygiene *at the
expense of* legal safeguards earlier regarded as sacrosant. 'Mental
illness' was defined as one of a range of social problems to be
eradicated by effective public action, medical men being enlisted as
agents of strategies of prevention and cure. The medical profession's
engagement in psychiatry attracted not suspicion but ready state
support and its yearnings to be liberated from confinement with the
mad in the depths of 'asylumdom'[76] met with affirmation. There were
many affinities between the ascendant philosophies of interventionism which left their imprint on the state and the dominant ethic of
Western medicine: they shared a therapeutic rationale, a deterministic
analysis of individual *malaise* and belief in scientific methods and
technologies. The political conjuncture favoured psychiatric optimism to the extent that the functions of law in relation to provision
for the mentally disordered were radically rethought and libertarian
qualms swept aside. Legislation was no longer to be addressed to the
protection of the sane, who were full juridical subjects, but to
facilitating the treatment of the mentally ill, the objects of tutelage. It
was no longer to focus upon the private sector, where the wealthy
might be deprived of their liberty in order to extract profit, but to the
public sector, as a framework for the specialist scientific treatment of
one particular cause of poverty and social inefficiency: for there was
now a reinvigorated emphasis upon classification and segmentation
of the unfit based upon the discovery of 'the great heterogeneity of
the company of paupers'.[77]

The reason for this reconstitution of the political consensus was
that a number of factors conspired in the period around the turn of
the century to fracture the confidence which had been enjoyed by the
propertied classes through the earlier part of the Victorian age and
to undermine cherished liberal assumptions. It is true that the
Victorian period was hardly an age of pure individualism: as we have
seen, the original creation of the Lunacy Commission and state
funding for the erection of asylums were themselves part of the

[76] D. J. Mellet coins this term for the institutional system established in the Victorian
period in 'Society, the State and Mental Illness'.
[77] T. H. Marshall, *Social Policy in the Twentieth Century*, p. 41.

nineteenth-century 'Revolution in Government', whereby the business of government became more centralized and professionalized and its methods more rational and scientific. The interventionist face of Benthamism and the Disraelian, 'One Nation' tradition, with its emphasis upon paternalism and consensus, were instances of more systematic rationales for the practice of intervention in the early and middle decades of the reign of Queen Victoria.[78] However, the career of Edwin Chadwick, the epitome of the Victorian civil servant cum social reformer and pioneer of public health, illustrates the conflicts to which government growth within a culture heavily infused with the precepts of *laissez-faire* could give rise: in 1854 he was driven from his position as Chairman of the Board of Health as part of a Tory reaction against state controls which actually brought about the abolition of the Board itself in 1858, although in the 1860s there was a countermovement to reinstate the machinery of intervention.[79] By the 1880s the pace of intervention had quickened to the extent that Individualism versus Collectivism became central to political debate,[80] as Dicey and his contemporaries of a like persuasion perceived England's prided constitutionalist tradition to be under threat. It has been argued above that 'the triumph of legalism' in 1889–80 could itself be interpreted as a symbolic reassertion of the rule of law in the face of the challenge of this creeping collectivism.

A convergence of unsettling factors, including the extension of the franchise to sections of the working class, developments in labour and trade union organization, the theoretical and political revival of Socialism, and an intensified awareness of the extent of social distress amongst the working class, set against a background of domestic economic *malaise* and the emergence of the United States, Germany and Japan as powerful foreign competitors, was combining to undermine the ideological hegemony of *laissez-faire*. These pressures culminated in an ideological crisis which can be described as 'an exercise in self-criticism conducted within "the ruling classes"'.[81] In

[78] On the general issue of state intervention in Victorian Britain see A. J. Taylor, *Laissez-faire and State Intervention in Nineteenth Century Britain*. London: Macmillan, 1972. On Disraelian social reform see P. Smith, *Disraelian Conservatism and Social Reform*. London: Routledge and Kegan Paul, 1967.
[79] See H. Perkin, *The Origins of Modern English Society*, p. 330.
[80] See S. Collini, *Liberalism and Sociology*. Cambridge: Cambridge University Press, 1979, Chapter 1.
[81] G. R. Searle, *The Quest for National Efficiency*. Oxford: Basil Blackwell, 1971, p. 81. Searle uses the phrase specifically with reference to the character of the ideology of National Efficiency, but it is applied here to the wider ideological reorganization which was underway.

the two decades preceding the First World War there reigned a remarkable flux in political ideas in which a range of new or developing ideologies, some progressive, some conservative in aspect, grappled with the social and political deficiencies of liberalism which were being thrown into relief by relative economic decline and by the political destabilization consequent upon the growing power of the organized labour movement. The dominant strands in this web of ideologies were Fabian Socialism, the New Liberalism, Social Imperialism, National Efficiency, and Eugenics. The later ideologies of Social Reconstruction and Mental Hygiene which impacted more immediately upon the reform of lunacy legislation were to share several similar assumptions. All of these contemplated, though in differing styles and degrees, a renewed emphasis upon positive social interventionism. Stephen Yeo has characterized this vogue for collectivism amongst the dominant social classes as an instance of ideological imperialism:

What was going on . . . during the late nineteenth and early twentieth centuries was a scramble for Socialism—as imperialistic as the contemporary scramble for Africa. There was an attempt, partly successful, to de-class the idea of Socialism or to nationalize it, to suggest loudly and often that it was a 'good thing' . . . but not attached to working class interests or associations.[82]

It was in the period from the late 1890s, in fact, that social politics can be said to have become established as a central field of reforming activity. The emphasis shifted perceptibly from electoral reform, as in the traditional Liberalism of 'Peace, Retrenchment and Reform', to social reform. The quality of intervention was changing too, for we can detect a transition from the episodic, pragmatic approach to social reform characteristic of the nineteenth century towards a strategic approach in which its achievement was perceived as central to the construction of a stable, consensual politico-economic order. The main site of this transition was the wave of social reform enacted by the radical Liberal administrations of Campbell-Bannerman and Asquith between 1906 and 1914. In many respects they stand at the crossroads between the particularistic Victorian tradition of social intervention and the linking of social reform to modification of the economic order which was to be the basis of the Welfare State.

[82] S. Yeo, 'Working-class Association, Private Capital, Welfare and the State', in N. Parry, M. Rustin, and C. Satyamurti (eds.), *Social Work, Welfare and the State*. London: Edward Arnold, 1979, p. 67.

One obvious element in the political configuration which produced this substantial shift to interventionist reformism was working-class enfranchisement. The Representation of the People Acts of 1867 and 1884 extended the franchise into the urban and rural manual working class, and the democratizing effect was accentuated by a redistribution of seats in 1885, but the vote was subject to restrictive property qualifications which ensured that 40 per cent of adult males were still excluded. Universal male franchise was only secured in 1918, when the vote was also extended to women over 30 for the first time. It is thus clear that the beneficiaries of electoral reform by the late nineteenth century were the 'respectable' working class and it is noteworthy that it was to this section of the labouring population that some of the key reforms of the early twentieth century were explicitly directed, as we shall see. However it is important not to slip into an electoral determinism based upon the *post hoc, propter hoc* fallacy.[83] Whilst Sidney Webb detected an inevitability in the progress from political to social reform, defining collectivism as the economic obverse of democracy, there were and are strong traditions within the British working-class electorate of conservatism and deference, reinforced by a nationalism and chauvinism deriving from its experience as the working class of a European imperialist power. There is also a well-established working class fear of the 'police' aspects of social interventionism. In the mid-Victorian period there had been working-class hostility to the bureaucratic expansionism of Edwin Chadwick,[84] and there were manifestations of a suspicious, anti-statist response to the social reforms of the late nineteenth, early twentieth-century period, well articulated in *Seems So! a working-class view of politics*[85], written by three Devonshire fishermen and published in 1911. Stephen Yeo, examining the role of the Friendly Societies, the organized expression of working-class collective self-help, as an institutional outlet for these feelings, records the following expressive response of Brother Radley, the Grand High Chief Ranger of the Foresters, to an offer of government subsidy for pensions in 1891:

[it is] a mess of pottage which does not exist in reality . . . . Care must be

[83] See J. R. Hay, *The Origins of the Liberal Welfare Reforms 1906–14*. London: Macmillan, 1975, p. 25.

[84] B. Jordan, *Freedom and the Welfare State*. London: Routledge and Kegan Paul, 1976, p. 183.

[85] S. Reynolds and B. and T. Woolley, London: Macmillan, 1911.

taken that the rising generations are not enticed by bribes drawn from the pockets of those who esteem their freedom or forced by legislative compulsion to exchange the stimulating atmosphere of independence and work for an enervating mechanical obedience to state management and control—the certain sequel of state subsidy.[86]

Diffuse grass-roots sentiments must, however, be distinguished from the positions adopted in this period by the organized labour movement, both the industrial and political wings of which were in formative stages of their development, reflecting the increasing homogeneity of the working class. Within the trades unions, the late 1880s witnessed the birth of the New Unionism, which entailed the increasing unionization of unskilled labour and challenged the conservative craft hegemony which had prevailed since the defeat of Chartism in the late 1840s. It was the newer and less skilled unions who supported the Independent Labour Party, founded in 1893, and who were most enthusiastic for the TUC's initiative in 1900 to join with the Co-operative movement and the Socialist Societies to found the Labour Representation Committee, which in 1906 became the Labour Party.[87] Working-class representation in Parliament had been the central focus of labour politics back into the early nineteenth century, but the significance of the creation of the Labour Party was that it was designed to serve as an exclusive and independent vehicle for the representation of working-class interests. The advent of the Labour Party added a new dimension to Conservative–Liberal electoral competition and in the longer term opened up the prospect of a major realignment based upon working-class desertion of the traditional ruling class parties. The intervention of the Labour Party did not, however, provide an unmitigated impetus to the adoption of measures of social reform by its electoral rivals. It was from the beginning a coalition in which wholesale interventionist Fabians like the Webbs participated with conservatively-minded trade unionists who defined the party's role in narrow 'Labourist' terms, that is to say, campaigning for greater legal protection for trade unions, as in the struggle for the Trade Disputes Act 1906, and for particular,

---

[86] S. Yeo, p. 52, quoted from J. H. Treble, 'The Attitude of the Friendly Societies Towards the Movement in Great Britain for State Pensions', *International Review of Social History* 15 (1970), p. 266.

[87] See H. Pelling, *A Short History of the Labour Party*, 5th edn. London: Macmillan, 1976, Chapter 1; D. Coates, *The Labour Party and the Struggle for Socialism*. Cambridge: Cambridge University Press, 1975, Chapter 2; R. Miliband, *Parliamentary Socialism*. London: Merlin Press, 1972, Chapter 1.

limited measures of social reform. Although it is true that Labour MP's joined with Radical Liberals in pressing for the 1906–14 Government to adopt measures to deal with worsening unemployment and other social evils, and that Labour was to the left of Progressive Liberalism in the breadth of its advocacy of nationalization, it did not adopt a Socialist Constitution (*Labour and the New Social Order*, of which Sidney Webb was the author) until 1918. Even then, of course, it retained its commitment to a gradualist, Parliamentary, Socialist strategy, which was strongly reasserted in the late 1920s when the left-wing challenge mounted by the ILP was successfully rebuffed by the Parliamentary and union leadership.[88]

The ascent of organized labour coincided with a prolonged phase of economic retardation which did much to depress the High Victorian optimism and confidence which accompanied prosperity and growth in the third quarter of the nineteenth century. Economic historians have rejected the specific characterization of this as 'The Great Depression', precisely located in the span of years from 1873–96,[89] but contemporaries were certainly aware of an anxiety-provoking turn in national economic fortunes, and it was at this time that Britain's commanding international lead as a great industrial and imperial power began to be eroded by the advance of foreign competitors.

An intensified awareness of the dimensions of social distress also served to undermine complacency regarding the capacity of the existing virtues of political economy to secure the basis for social stability and efficiency.

It is not of course that the propertied classes had previously been virtually unaware of the social conditions which prevailed amongst the labouring population. One factor that was conducive to ignorance was that the layers of social stratification were reproduced in the physical organization of the Victorian city. Writing of Manchester in 1839, the Reverend R. Parkinson observed that 'The separation between the different classes, and the consequent ignorance of each other's habits and customs, are far more complete than in any other country of the older nations of Europe, or the agricultural parts of our own kingdom'.[90]

[88] R. Miliband, pp. 157–8; R. E. Dowse, *Left in the Centre: the I.L.P. 1893–1940*, London. Longmans: 1966, Chapter 11.

[89] See, for example, S. B. Saul, *The Myth of the Great Depression 1873–1896*. London: Macmillan, 1969.

[90] Quoted in A. Briggs, *Victorian Cities*. London: Pelican, 1968, p. 114.

However, this was mitigated by the availability of graphic accounts of 'the lower orders' in literature, from the quasi-Gothic fiction of Charles Dickens's *Oliver Twist* to the aspirant sociology of Henry Mayhew's *London Labour and the London Poor*, first published in 1851 and reissued with an additional fourth volume in 1862, 'a vast, shapeless, repetitive and indescribably rich description of the lives of almost every kind of urban underdog'.[91] Similarly, in an age of limited public welfare provision, the middle classes were to some extent acquainted with the proportions of social squalor through engagement in voluntary charitable activities. The contribution of the social surveys of the period[92]—in particular Charles Booth's *Life and Labour of the People . . . of London* (1888–1903), B. Seebohm Rowntree's *Poverty: A Study of Town Life* (1901) and the Reports of the Interdepartmental Committee on Physical Deterioration (1904) and the Departmental Committee on Vagrancy (1903)—was not therefore so much to precipitate a 'rediscovery of poverty' as to apply social scientific techniques with a view to quantifying social problems more reliably than hitherto. The traditional interpretation of the role of these social statistical interventions as an element in the erosion of *laissez-faire* is that they helped to invalidate the prevalent judgemental middle-class view of poverty as a mark of individual moral failing and to direct attention instead to the environmental conditions which continually reproduced poverty and how they could be improved by the assumption of greater public responsibility. However, recent accounts have emphasized the likely impact of these findings, given the attitude of their readership. Whilst they provided major evidence of the urgent need for social reform, they may also be interpreted as having confirmed the social pessimism of its conservative opponents.[93] Furthermore, a key component of the Victorian middle-class conception of the social space beneath it was the division between the 'respectable' labouring classes and 'the dangerous classes', a residuum of the feckless, the malcontent, and the delinquent, a division conveyed perhaps in Mayhew's bifurcation of London Labour and the London Poor. The individualist variant of Social Darwinism, which portrayed the lowest social strata as failures in the competitive

[91] K. Chesney, *The Victorian Underworld*. Harmondsworth: Penguin, 1970, p. 28.

[92] See M. Cullen, *The Statistical Movement in Early Victorian Britain*. Brighton: Harvester Press, 1975 for the origins of the social survey movement.

[93] Booth was highly moralistic in his literary treatment of the urban poor: see J. Brown, 'Charles Booth and Labour Colonies 1889–1905' *Economic History Review* 21 (1968), p. 349; 'Social Judgements and Social Policy', *Economic History Review* 24 (1971), p. 106.

struggle which provided the dynamic of social evolution, and the Eugenics movement, which campaigned for measures of coercive segregation and in the case of some of its supporters, of sterilization amongst 'the unfit' of 'the submerged tenth', offered apparently scientific substantiations of this distinction.

The abiding fear of the middle class was the conversion of the 'respectable' labouring population to social revolution. The physical-force wing of Chartism provided some relatively recent historical basis for the fear of class violence, which was sharply reinforced in 1886 (and also in the autumn of 1887) when a demonstration of the unemployed in the wealthy heart of the Metropolis spilled over into violence and 'all forms of property were assailed, all signs of wealth and privilege were attacked'.[94] The logic of this perspective of moral discrimination, in the light of increasing documentation of the depth and urgency of social distress, was to extend and humanize public provision for the 'deserving' by building up services outside the Poor Law, whilst reinforcing repressive treatment of the rest. Although some were much less moralistic in their analysis and proposals than others—we can, for example, contrast the heavily individualistic philosophy traditionally associated with the Charity Organization Society with the environmental social reform championed by the Webbs—even the latter did not break with the moral conceptualization of social problems.[95] The Liberal reforms of 1906–14 were pervaded by the distinction between worthy and unworthy categories of the poor. Under the National Insurance Act 1911, dismissed workers lost their right to unemployment benefit, and the Old Age Pensions Act 1908 excluded those who 'had habitually failed to work according to (their) ability, opportunity and need for the maintenance and benefit of (themselves) and those dependent upon them'; all those imprisoned without option of fine during their period in gaol and for ten years after their release, and (until the end of 1910) all those in receipt of non-medical poor relief.[96] The tendency was therefore toward the contraction of the sphere of moralism rather than its elimination, and it is of course the case that elements of moral discrimination have survived into the modern welfare state at

[94] G. Stedman-Jones, *Outcast London.* Oxford: Clarendon Press, 1971, pp. 291–2; see also, G. Pearson, *The Deviant Imagination.* London: Macmillan, 1975, Chapter 6.

[95] See H. V. Emy, *Liberals, Radicals and Social Politics 1892–1914.* Cambridge: Cambridge University Press, 1973, p. 158.

[96] J. Brown 'Social Control and the Modernization of Social Policy 1890–1929', in P. Thane (ed.), *The Origins of British Social Policy.* London: Croom Helm, 1978, p. 130. See also P. Thane's Introduction at p. 15.

many different levels, for example in the stigmatization and harassment of social security claimants. Nevertheless, the wide dissemination of surveys anatomizing poverty must be credited with making some contribution, along with pressure from working-class organizations, to growing recognition of the objective factors in its causation and the conversion of 'the social question' into a political priority.

Ideologies of Social Reform in the Early Twentieth Century

In terms of the impact of this changing context upon the development of political ideas, the most immediately productive consequence was the historic shift within British Liberalism from classical or Gladstonian Liberalism to Progressive Liberalism, or the New Liberalism. The New Liberalism was directly influential in producing and shaping the Liberal social reforms of 1906–14 and thus contributed to the foundations of the Welfare State.

Recent historians of the New Liberalism tend to stress its intellectual independence, and continuity with the liberal philosophic tradition. It did not simply reflect the conceptual penetration of Liberalism by Socialism as the Liberal Party struggled with the emergent Labour Party to retain working-class support. Rather, the philosophical redefinition of Liberalism by Leonard Hobhouse (1864–1929), Graham Wallas (1858–1932), J. A. Hobson (1858–1940) and others, and the transformation of its political practice by those who implemented major measures of social reform, notably Lloyd George and Churchill, should be seen as a peculiarly Liberal response to the shifting complexion of politics. Michael Freeden terms it 'the adaptation of the Liberal *Weltanschauung* to the intellectual and material environment of the Victorian *fin de siècle*'.[97]

The particular impact of the more general ideological crisis upon Liberalism was mediated in part by changes in the composition of the Liberal Party. There was a continued drain of business support from the Liberals to the Conservatives, combined with an influx of political activists drawn from the professional and administrative classes to the Liberal Party. It was the latter who were in the vanguard in pressing for the party to commit itself to social reform. They represented a new Social Radicalism, which was in the process of displacing traditional Radicalism as the political philosophy of the Liberal Left. Old-style Radicalism was a politics whose reference points had

[97] M. Freeden, *The New Liberalism*. Oxford: Clarendon Press, 1978, p. 24.

basically been established in the struggle between the middle class and the landed aristocracy. It was anti-landlord, pro-electoral and institutional reform, ultra-individualist and preoccupied with a range of particular issues which reflected its roots in Nonconformism, such as disestablishment and temperance. A classic exemplar of this traditional Radicalism was Josiah Wedgwood (1872–1943), a Liberal and later a Labour MP, to whose politics we shall have cause to return in the context of his individualist critique and attempted Parliamentary sabotage of the Mental Deficiency Bills of 1912 and 1913, and the Mental Treatment Bill of 1929. Social Radicalism represented part of the process of modernizing Britain's political party system to take account of the shifting centre of class conflict from capital versus land to labour versus capital. The Conservative Party was increasingly a party of business interests rather than of landowners, reflecting the changing basis of the ruling class, whilst the rise of the Labour Party expressed the growing homogeneity and strength of the working class. The Liberal Party's attempt to evolve a non-Socialist and distinctively liberal politics of social reform, and the conflict of loyalties this produced between its working-class and middle-class electorates, reflected the party's struggle to come to terms with these changing class orientations. Many Progressive Liberals saw Liberalism as in a state of crisis and the need for the party to adjust to the new lines of battle as urgent, Hobson describing it as in 'an awkward position between two very active and energetically moving grindstones, the upper grindstone of plutocratic imperialism, and the nether grindstone of social democracy'.[98]

It was the particular project of the New Liberalism to try to reconcile the essential Liberal devotion to individual freedom and a state limited by the rule of law, with a new perception of social interdependence and the need for principles of social reciprocity and collective responsibility to order political priorities. Progressive tendencies within Liberalism were not at one with Fabian Socialism, but rather an interconnected outgrowth of the same political conjuncture. Progressive Liberals and Fabians shared specific policy commitments, for example, in 1909 both were pressing the Government to introduce labour exchanges and wages boards. The former were indeed 'Socialists' in the weak sense in which the term was used

---

[98] Liberalism, of course, historically failed to develop a sustained progressive alternative to Labour. In its attempts to do so it drove away business support, but failed to hold the working class. See G. Dangerfield, *The Strange Death of Liberal England*. London: Paladin, 1970. (First published in 1935.)

in the period to connote advocacy of a significant extension of the state's responsibilties toward the social question.[99] But New Liberals were philosophically antipathetic to the authoritarianism and bureaucratism of Fabian strategies of social reform. The New Liberalism was more wary in its interventionism and rested on the perception of a continued need to respect the individual and the law in any revised order of social and political relations. An 'eagerness for government to assume both the responsibility for directing the course of social development and the role of mediator in ensuring a balance between the respective interests of society and the individual' produced a tension in the New Liberals' political philosophy which placed them between the avowed collectivists on the one hand and Radical individualists, conservative economic liberals, and Whig constitutionalists on the other; this allowed scope for the survival of a qualified legalism in their philosophy of social legislation.[100] However, it must be stressed that their position was not simply an unstable compromise between two opposed theories of the role of the state. It was rather a manifestation peculiar to this particular historical epoch of a significant tradition in British social reform which favours a collectivism of organic rather than state-imposed change, places a premium upon consensus, and preserves a space for individuality and the individual basis of society despite its disillusion with Victorian individualism.[101]

Fabian Socialism was another emergent influence in the development of social welfare. 'Fabianism' has of course come to be equated with gradualism, and the Fabian Society, founded in 1884, at least after its break with the Social Democratic Federation in 1886, was committed to a reformist rather than a revolutionary strategy for Socialist change. The Fabians, although 'Socialists', did not define themselves as the intellectual vanguard of the workers' movement. Despite their indebtedness to Marx, the organic conception of society which they espoused led them to oppose the objective of workers' control as an instance of the socially unacceptable assertion of sectional interests: thus Guild Socialism was condemned as 'trade sectionalism', and the Webbs wrote that 'Trade Unionism must be judged not by its results in improving the position of a particular section of workmen, but by its results in permanently raising the

[99]   As in the liberally-quoted statement by Sir William Harcourt, Chancellor of the Exchequer in the Liberal Government of 1892–5, that 'We are all Socialists now.'
[100]   H. V. Emy, p. 168.
[101]   Ibid., p. xiii; M. Freeden, pp. 29, 79 *et seq.*

efficiency of the nation as a whole'.[102] The emergence of the Fabians was part of a significant revival of Socialism as a political ideology and as an organized influence within the Labour movement which also produced the Marxist Social Democratic Federation led by Hyndman, the Socialist League, and the Independent Labour Party. It was against these other tendencies, as is the way with the sectarian Left, that the Fabians defined their political positions and carved a distinctive niche in the configuration of British labour politics. The Fabian Society was able to accommodate an impressive variety of intellectual and personal temperaments, including of course Sidney Webb (1859–1947), Beatrice Webb (1858–1943), H. G. Wells (1886–1946)[103] and George Bernard Shaw (1856–1950). It also encompassed different Socialist influences, as, for example, in the case of Robert Blatchford (1851–1943), who joined in 1890 and became President of the Manchester Fabian Society. As well as being the editor of *The Clarion*, the Socialist Weekly, founded in 1891, he was the author of *Merrie England* (1893), considered a major contribution to the popularization of Socialist ideas, which was influenced by the romantic brand of Socialism associated with William Morris and provided a stark contrast to the mundane administrative Socialism of the Webbs. However, broad distinguishing themes of Fabianism can be identified in a preoccupation with institutional reform and bureaucratic initiative (at the level of the local as well as the central state, Joseph Chamberlain's Municipal Socialism winning Fabian approval) and in an environmental approach to the solution of social problems with the emphasis being placed upon what the Webbs called a 'preventive and curative', that is, a positive and interventionist, role being assumed by state agencies.

It is true that some Fabians, including Sidney Webb and H. G. Wells, demonstrated sympathy for Eugenics, but the common ground here was a concern about deterioration of the race and optimism as to the possibilities of rational rather than natural selection: Fabians opposed the hereditarian arguments being used by conservatives to foster pessimism about the value of environmental social reform. The pre-eminence of Sidney and Beatrice Webb in Fabian counsels and their role in the production and propagation of the Minority report of the Royal Commission on the Poor Law

---

[102] Quoted in H. V. Emy, p. 277.
[103] Wells resigned, however, in 1908 and attacked the Webbs in *The New Machiavelli*.

justifies a close examination of their particular interpretation of Fabian principles. As intellectual descendants of Bentham, they shared not only his preoccupation with practical planning, scientific administration, and bureaucratic structure, reflected in their collaboration with like-thinking members of the administrative élite like Robert Morant, but also the Benthamite elevation of institutional reform of the status of a faith, a civil religion.[104] This was symbolized at a personal level in their exchange of rings inscribed '*pro bono publico*', and expressed in the indefatigable energy which they devoted to research, political and historical writing, campaigning, lobbying, and specific projects, notably the foundation of the London School of Economics and Political Science in 1895.[105] The Webbs' political thought and allegiances naturally altered over time: in the Edwardian period they diverted their efforts away from the independent organizations of labour towards established political and administrative structures, employing the technique of 'permeation' to promote the adoption of favoured policies. As Beatrice observed: 'It is a tiresome fact that to get things done in what one considers the best way, entails so much—to speak plainly—of intrigue.'[106] After the Liberal Government's rejection of the Minority Report of the Royal Commission on the Poor Laws in 1909, a vigorous campaign in support of its proposals signalled their return to the mainstream of the labour movement. In their *Constitution for a Socialist Commonwealth of Great Britain* they made certain concessions to Guild Socialism but ultimately in *Soviet Communism: A New Civilization* (1935) their admiration for a Socialism of bureaucratic rationality asserted itself to such an extent that they became apologists for Stalinism.[107]

Returning to the turn of the century period, their enthusiasm for the social potentialities of the state as collective economic planner and solvent of social pathology encouraged them to advocate many of the elements in a National Efficiency or Social Imperialist position. In

---

[104] On this aspect of Benthamism, see H. Perkin, p. 287.

[105] See L. E. Wickham Legg and E. T. Williams, *Dictionary of National Biography 1941–50*. London: Oxford University Press, 1959, pp. 935–40.

[106] Quoted in P. F. Clarke, *Liberals and Social Democrats*. Cambridge: Cambridge University Press, 1978 at p. 86. The Fabians took their responsibilities of permeating governmental structures very seriously: Bernard Shaw immersed himself in the deliberation of local government matters as a St Pancras Vestryman from 1893.

[107] This must be seen however in the context of the more general political polarization of the 1930s when many intellectuals saw themselves as faced with a stark choice between Soviet Communism and Italian or German Fascism as the solution to deep capitalist crisis.

the divide over the Boer War which split the Fabian Society, the Webbs inclined to the majority imperialist camp on the ground that the war favoured an increase in domestic state intervention. In the interests of efficiency they nurtured the cult of the expert: 'We wish to introduce into politics the professional expert—to extend the sphere of government by adding to its enormous advantages of wholesale and compulsory management, the advantage of the most skilled entrepreneur.'[108] The expert was clearly not to be hampered in the rational pursuit of socially desirable objectives by too much regard for traditional legal and democratic safeguards. The Minority Report of the Royal Commission on the Poor Law, for example, incorporated authoritarian and repressive proposals for processing the poor, including detention colonies for the recalcitrant voluntary unemployed organized along lines of quasi-military discipline.[109] In Geoffrey Searle's view, 'The Webbs in effect wanted to broaden the concept of what constituted a public nuisance until it embraced all forms of destitution, then the appropriate preventive action could be taken.'[110]

The emergence of a British Social Imperialism, of which the most concrete evidence was the political prominence of the theme of National Efficiency, was a further element in the kaleidoscopic ideological response to the combination of circumstances which had fractured Victorian security and prosperity. Efficiency became the watchword of those in all parties who blamed the old regime of political liberalism and administrative generalism and amateurism for Britain's economic and social problems. A leading exponent was Joseph Chamberlain, whose programme of Tariff Reform and Imperial Preference involved financing social reform through protectionism, thus buttressing imperialism by investing in national unity.[111] Other supporters included the autocratic Conservative, Sir Alfred Milner, Liberal Imperialists such as Roseberry and Haldane, leading Fabians such as the Webbs, Wells, and Shaw, and even, in the period 1905–8, the celebrated architect of labour exchange and Welfare State, William Beveridge.[112] Its natural detractors were

[108] Quoted in P. F. Clarke, p. 44.
[109] *Report of the Royal Commission on the Poor Laws and Relief of Distress*, Minority, (Cd. 4499, 1909), pp. 1206–8.
[110] G. R. Searle, *The Quest for National Efficiency*, p. 241.
[111] E. Halévy, *A History of the English People in the Nineteenth Century V: Imperialism and the Rise of Labour 1895–1905*, 2nd edn. London: Ernest Benn, 1929, pp. 23–4.
[112] See J. Harris, *William Beveridge: A Biography*. Oxford: Clarendon Press, 1977, Chapter 5.

Gladstonian Liberals, ultra-individualist Radicals, Whig constitution-alists, and traditionalist Conservatives. Searle defines the tendency as follows:

If one were to sum up its meaning in a single sentence, one might describe the 'National Efficiency' ideology as an attempt to discredit the habits, beliefs, and institutions that put the British at a handicap in their competition with foreigners and to commend instead a social organization that more closely followed the German model.[113]

The autocratic political systems of Germany and Japan were credited with the progress made by those countries in the league table of international powers, with the implication that Britain's liberal democratic political culture was a luxury that could no longer be afforded without substantial modification in an era of intensified international competition which had eroded her hegemony. The Bismarckian model of social and political reconstruction in particular offered the prospect of pre-empting Socialism and fortifying Britain's status as a world power.

The ideology of National Efficiency certainly had a place in the Liberal Government's conception of social reform. Winston Church-ill's letter to Asquith of December 1908 is often quoted to this effect:

There is a tremendous policy in Social Organization. The need is urgent and the moment ripe. Germany with a harder climate and a far less accumulated wealth has managed to establish basic conditions for her people. She is organized not only for war but for peace. Thrust a big slice of Bismarckian-ism over the whole underside of our industrial system and await the consequences whatever they may be with a good conscience.[114]

The German model of state insurance influenced the Liberal Government's National Insurance legislation. Lloyd George's visit to Germany in 1908 helped to persuade him towards a more extensive health insurance scheme,[115] and the merits of the issue were often discussed in terms of the desirability or otherwise of importing Germanic principles of social organization.[116] One particular aspect of National Insurance which has been attributed to German influence was the Court of Referees, established to deal with disputes

---

[113] G. R. Searle, *The Quest for National Efficiency*, p. 54.
[114] D. Fraser, *The Evolution of the British Welfare State*. London: Macmillan, 1973, p. 152.
[115] J. R. Hay, p. 56.
[116] M. Freeden, *The New Liberalism*, pp. 231–2.

in relation to unemployment, which resembled the German tribunal system. These tribunals were composed of a chairman appointed by the Board of Trade, a member from an employers' panel, and a member from an employees' panel,[117] a tripartite model of adjudication indicative of the corporatist direction of state development under the Liberal Government.[118]

Finally, we reach Eugenics, which will be treated in relation to the Mental Deficiency Act 1913 and the reforming legislation of the 1906–14 Liberal Government.

Liberal Social Reform and the Mental Deficiency Act 1913

The Liberal Government of 1906–14 enacted a wave of reforming measures, transforming social welfare and constituting a political watershed which helps to explain the very different character of the two instances of legislation relating to mental illness, the Lunacy Act 1890 and the Mental Treatment Act 1930, which it divided. Unlike the Labour Party in 1945, however, the Liberals did not win office on a programme of wide-ranging social reform, although a substantial number of individual Liberal candidates did so commit themselves. Neither was victory used at first as a mandate for prioritizing reformist social policies. It was only from 1908 that the social question became central, when traditional Liberal issues, such as education and temperance, were exhausted, and electoral popularity was on the wane, providing an opportunity for pressure from Social Radicals and the Labour Party to be exerted effectively.[119] The individual reforms which reached the statute book reflected in differing degrees the prevailing ideological currents just discussed: concern for national efficiency, Fabian influence, and of course, the redefinition of Liberalism itself in a new political era.

The Mental Deficiency Act 1913 embodied a dramatic intensification of intervention in respect of particular categories of the mentally disordered, a sector especially vulnerable to deep interventionism and the associated erosion of concern for 'the liberty of the subject', at a time when traditional liberal values were on the defensive even in

[117] See A. H. Manchester, *A Modern Legal History of England and Wales 1750–1950*. London: Butterworth, 1980, pp. 153–4.
[118] See K. Middlemas, *Politics in Industrial Society*. London: Deutsch, 1979.
[119] See H. V. Emy, pp. 175–6.

relation to the sane adult.[120] It followed the policy of the Idiots Act[121] in providing a distinct legal regime for the mentally defective. The next major legislation dealing with the mentally ill, the Mental Treatment Act 1930, was to be the first to cater exclusively for that species of mental disorder, so sustaining the policy of separate legislation. The Mental Deficiency Act was strikingly coercive in emphasis and philosophically a recoil from legalism in so far as legislation for mental defect was concerned. Although it resembled the later Mental Treatment Act's focus on 'early' cases and temporary and mild disorders in its concern to extend the catchment of institutional psychiatry, it did not at all seek to achieve this by a similar emphasis upon voluntarism and the minimization of stigma. Instead, the main purpose of the Act was to extend compulsory powers to the higher grades of mental defect not previously subject to special legislation. The Act not only applied to the severely

---

[120] Another, and overlapping, category in this position was children. Central to the Liberal Government's children's policy was the Children Act 1908, which modified the operation of the criminal justice system to take into account what were perceived as the special considerations affecting children. The Act provided for separate juvenile courts for young offenders, relaxed the procedures to which they were subject, and abolished imprisonment for children and for young persons except in extreme cases (specified in section 102(3)). These measures accelerated the movement toward the differentiation of young criminals established in the nineteenth century. This process of differentiation represented the partial abandonment of classical liberal principles of formal equality based upon the uniform imposition of a scale of punishments proportionate to crimes in favour of a flexible system of dispositions suited to the needs of paticular categories of offender or to those of individual offenders themselves. Indeed, the Children Act provided for a wide range of dispositions for young offenders, which could be suited to the case in hand, including discharge, fines, probation, and removal from home. This movement may be seen as running in parallel with that which elaborated procedures for the special treatment of mentally abnormal offenders alluded to in earlier chapters. However, its intensification in the first years of the new century was not a process specific to children as a special cateogory whose circumstances required the classical order of criminal justice to submit to a merely limited and exceptional revision. During this period, the criminal justice system as a whole was undergoing a significant reorientation towards a positivistic focus upon the condition of the individual offender and a movement from repression and deterrence towards a therapeutic manipulation which David Garland calls 'the birth of the welfare sanction' (see 'The Birth of the Welfare Sanction', *British Journal of Law and Society* 8 (1981), p. 29). We may note that this penetration of criminal justice by positivistic perspectives had important implications for the civil legal regulation of the mentally ill. We have seen that the penal system provided the model against which advocates of the dominant conservative legalism measured the standard of civil liberty observed by the lunacy system, rejecting the analogy of the general medical system which guided the reasoning of legalism's opponents. They now faced the difficulty that penal practice itself was increasingly permeated by therapeutic rationalities.

[121] This was repealed by the Mental Deficiency Act 1913, section 67.

incapacitaing conditions of idiocy and imbecility, but also to the 'feeble-minded', defined as:

persons in whose case there exists from birth or from an early age mental defectiveness not amounting to imbecility (i.e. incapable of managing themselves or their affairs) yet so pronounced that they require care, supervision and control for their own protection or for the protection of others, or, in the case of children, that they by reason of such defectiveness appear to be permanently incapable of receiving proper benefit from the instruction in secondary schools.[122]

Another new category of mental defect incorporated in the Act was that of 'moral imbecility', the forerunner of the Mental Health Act 1959 category of 'psychopathy', which comprised 'persons who from an early age display some permanent mental defect coupled with strong vicious or criminal propensities on which punishment has had little or no effect'.[123] The overt concern of the legislation to strengthen segregative institutionalized control and quasi-penal preventive detention, indicated by the specification of its clients, is underlined by the definition of the circumstances in which the adult feeble-minded and moral imbeciles became 'subject to be dealt with' under the Act's commitment procedures. These included being an habitual drunkard within the Inebriates Acts 1879–1900, being found guilty of any criminal offence, and being in receipt of poor relief at the time of giving birth to an illegitimate child or being pregnant with such a child.[124] In civil cases, unless the patient was an idiot or imbecile, when a parent or guardian could activate commitment without a judicial order, the order of a judicial authority remained necessary as under the Lunacy Act 1890. Mentally defective offenders were to be dealt with by court orders and those already in institutions could be transferred to mental deficiency hospitals by order of the Home Secretary. However, as the National Council for Civil Liberties stressed in its thoroughgoing critique of the custodial strategy of the Act in written evidence to the Percy Commission (1954–7), some of the safeguards in relation to discharge which prevailed under the Lunacy Act were not incorporated in the new Mental Deficiency legislation. The Board of

[122] The Mental Deficiency Act 1913, section 1(c).
[123] The Mental Deficiency Act 1913, section 1(d).
[124] The Mental Deficiency Act 1913, section 2(1)(b).

Control[125] were given sole power of discharge: there was to be only one hearing at the age of majority when the hospital managers could discharge. There was no power for petitioning relatives to discharge. There were no provisions for a friend or relative to obtain an independent medical inspection of the patient, and the effectiveness of escape as a method of formal discharge was curtailed.[126] The Mental Deficiency Act both extended the scope of detention and made the regime of detention more restrictive. To furnish an adequate institutional framework within which to implement the statutory objectives, the local authority mental deficiency committees which it established were empowered to provide public institutions for mental defectives, and the Board of Control was authorized, subject to the approval of the Home Secretary, to provide institutions for defectives of violent or dangerous propensities.[127]

The Mental Deficiency Act rested upon a perception of mental defect, rather than a generalized moral degeneracy, as being in large part responsible for a whole panoply of social evils: pauperism, criminality, alcoholism, and sexual promiscuity leading to illegitimate births. The Mental Hygiene Movement was similarly to identify mental illness as lying at the root of such diverse social pathologies, but these were complementary rather than competing explanations, possessing a common medico-scientific character. Chronologically, there was a tendency for mental defect and mental illness to alternate as the primary focus of expert attention: mental illness occupied centre-stage in the early inter-war period, with a strong revival of interest in the problem of mental deficiency taking place in the early 1930s, when supporters of Eugenics attributed economic depression to racial degeneration through failure to control the propagation of the unfit.[128] The same figures who proposed Eugenic solutions to the problem of the mental defective were often also advocates of Mental Hygiene, for example Lord Dawson of Penn. The Central Association for the Care of the Mentally Defective, founded in 1914 to assist in the implementation of the provisions of the Mental Deficiency Act 1913, changed its name in 1921 to the Central Association for

[125] The Board of Control, the reconstituted Lunacy Commission, was established by Section 22 of the Mental Deficiency Act 1913: see Chapter 3.
[126] *Royal Commission on the Law relating to Mental Illness and Mental Deficiency: Minutes of Evidence*, p. 793 *et seq.*
[127] Sections 28, 35.
[128] See G. R. Searle, 'Eugenics and Politics in Britain in the 1930s', *Annals of Science* 36 (1979), p. 159.

Mental Welfare to reflect a reorientation of interest towards Mental Hygiene, claiming that it would now be able to 'deal more efficiently with cases of mental instability, incipient cases of insanity and after care . . .'.[129]

The Act was an attempt to reorganize and rationalize apparatuses of control and to stop up gaps in provision which were vexing the various authorities who came into contact with the mentally defective. As in the early nineteenth century, lunacy had been identified as a special problem requiring distinct legislation, authorities, and institutions, so now this happened with mental deficiency. The aim was to address mental deficiency as such, and not in terms only of its symptoms of crime, inebriation, and pauperism. The mentally defective should be relocated from prisons, inebriate reformatories, workhouses, and lunatic asylums (whose hospital facilities were appropriate for the mentally ill) and unified in separate mental deficiency institutions, where continuous rather than merely intermittent and fortuitous (that is, arising from periodic spells in workhouse, prison, or other institutions on other grounds) preventive supervision and control could be expected and any useful training be undertaken. Further, those who languished at large in the community were also to be submitted to legal controls: local authority mental deficiency committees were charged with ascertaining all persons 'subject to be dealt with' in their respective areas,[130] the circumstances for this amounting in effect to a catalogue of the occasions upon which the social inefficiency produced by mental defect attained official visibility. The Radnor Commission, whose report preceded legislation, had calculated that there were some 66,000 feeble-minded requiring further provision beyond supervision who were not already in institutions.[131]

Pressure for legislation to make extended special provision for the mentally defective came from social work organizations, notably the Charity Organization Society and the National Association for the Care of the Feeble-Minded, and from administrative sources: prison authorities, Poor Law authorities, education authorities. An insistent campaign was also launched by the Eugenics movement and in particular by its paramount organization, the Eugenics Education

---

[129] *Annual Report of the Board of Control for the Year 1921*, p. 56.
[130] Mental Deficiency Act 1930, section 30.
[131] *Report of the Royal Commission on the Care and Control of the Feeble Minded* (Cd. 4202, 1908), para. 17.

Society, founded in 1907.[132] It is ironic that this organization was essentially the expression of a conservative middle-class reaction against the Liberal social reforms. The Liberal measures may, of course, themselves be characterized as conservative in motive: Hay, for example, defines them as prompted by the 'desire to retain as much as possible of the existing capitalist economic system, at a time when it was under increasing pressure from within and without'.[133] However, conservative supporters of Eugenics condemned Liberal welfare subsidies as conflicting with their aim of demographic containment of 'unfit' sections of the working class and the lumpenproletariat. Their conservatism was one of imposing segregation and sexual discipline upon the socially pathological in order to reverse a supposed decline in the national stock and promote national efficiency. The Eugenics movement was characteristically Victorian in its cultivation of moral panic about 'the submerged tenth' whose differential effective fertility threatened to pollute and weaken the nation, but it was also a response to the dawning awareness of the social and political inadequacy of Victorian values in its commitment to scientific, rational genetic solutions, and the expansion of state responsibilities in relation to the family and patterns of population growth. It was this rationalistic and interventionist face of Eugenics which enabled the movement to attract some support from New Liberals such as Hobson and Fabians, including Sidney Webb and H. G. Wells, and to render Eugenic-inspired Mental Deficiency legislation compatible with the Liberal Government's philosophy of social reform.[134]

Eugenic thought was much influenced by Darwinism. This link was personified in the circumstance that Sir Francis Galton, the movement's founding pioneer, was Charles Darwin's cousin and that Major Leonard Darwin, elected President of the Eugenics Education Society in 1911, was his son. The variant of Social Darwinism which

[132] On Eugenics generally see G. R. Searle, *Eugenics and Politics in Britain 1900–1914*. Leyden: Noordhoff, 1976.
[133] J. R. Hay, p. 62.
[134] For the historical debate as to whether Eugenics and Fabians shared genuine ideological affinities or Fabians merely opportunistically spoke the language of Eugenics as a fashionable idiom, see D. MacKenzie, 'Eugenics in Britain', *Social Studies of Science* 6 (1976), p. 523; Review Article, *British Journal for the History of Science* 11 (1978), p. 90; 'Karl Pearson and the Professional Middle Classes', *Annals of Science* 36 (1979), p. 138; G. R. Searle, 'Eugenics and Class' in C. Webster (ed.), *Biology, Medicine and Society 1840–1940*. Past and Present Society, Cambridge: Cambridge University Press, 1981, p. 217; M. Freeden, 'Eugenics and Progressive Thought', *Historical Journal* 22 (1979), p. 645.

found expression in Eugenics not only recognized the applicability of the theory of evolution to human social organization and development, but instead of falling prey to a fatalistic hereditarianism maintained that the natural order could be engineered by selective rational intervention to produce significant social amelioration. In order to curtail the propagation of the mentally defective the Society sidestepped the controversies attached to compulsory sterilization by opting for the proposal of compulsory institutional segregation within which disciplining controls could achieve a *de facto* ban on reproduction.

The legislative process which culminated in the passage of the 1913 Act began with the appointment of the Radnor Commission on the Care and Control of the Feeble-Minded in 1904, whose terms of reference were extended to include the insane at the Commission's own request in 1906.[135] The Radnor Commission has been established partly as a response to fears of racial degeneration, and was influenced in its conclusions by its Eugenic medical expert, Dr A. F. Tredgold (1870–1952).[136] The Commission concluded that there were 'numbers of mentally defective persons whose training is neglected, over whom no sufficient control is exercised, and whose wayward and irresponsible lives are productive of crime and misery, of much injury and mischief to themselves and to others, and of much continuous expenditure wasteful to the community' and proposed that 'the mental condition of these persons, and neither their poverty nor their crime, is the real ground of their claim for help from the State.'[137] The Commission's Report, submitted in 1908, supported the strategy which ultimately found statutory expression in the Mental Deficiency Act, in that it advocated a positive policy for the public ascertainment, supervision, and

[135] The original terms of reference were 'to consider the existing methods of dealing with idiots and epileptics, and with imbecile, feeble-minded or defective persons not certified under the Lunacy Laws; and in view of the hardship or danger resulting to such persons and the community from insufficient provision for their care, training and control, to report as to the amendments in the law or other measures which should be adopted in the matter . . .'. The extended terms (granted 2 November 1906) were 'to enquire into the constitution, jurisdiction and working of the Commission in Lunacy and of the other Lunacy Authorities in England and Wales, and into the expediency of amending the same or adopting some other system of supervising the care of lunatics and mental defectives; and to report as to any amendments in the law which should, in our opinion, be adopted.' See *Report of the Royal Commission on the Care and Control of the Feeble-Minded*, p. 1.

[136] See G. R. Searle, *Eugenics and Politics in Britain*, p. 106.

[137] See the account of the origins of the Mental Deficiency Act 1913 in the *Annual Report of the Board of Control for the Year 1917*, pp. 53–5.

detention of the mentally defective. But it envisaged a grand new scheme for legislation, recasting the Lunacy Acts and comprising both lunacy and mental deficiency, which was not enacted. It was less coercive in method, as guardianship and supervision in the community were proposed as a first resort before the invocation of detentionary powers.[138] Legislation was not forthcoming in the immediate term, despite the endorsement of Radnor by both Majority and Minority Reports of the Royal Commission on the Poor Laws in 1909. By 1912, however, there was acute impatience on the part of the Eugenics lobby, and two private members' Bills were introduced to prompt the Government into action. The Government's first Mental Deficiency Bill, presented in 1912, was particularly offensive to Liberal opponents of Eugenics, because it contained proposals for custodial care where it was desirable in the interests of peventing procreation, and for making it a misdemeanor to marry a mental defective. This Bill was successfully sabotaged by its Parliamentary opponents. Although they failed to defeat its successor, it was not by want of effort, and the most provocative and draconian incidents of the earlier Bill were withdrawn in order to facilitate its passage. The Home Secretary, Reginald McKenna, stressed that the Government had 'omitted any reference to what might be regarded as the Eugenic idea'.[139]

The alignments in relation to Mental Deficiency legislation are enlightening as they closely parallel those produced by the Mental Treatment Bill in 1929–30. We may first note the divided and reticent attitude of the medical profession to becoming involved in the coercive machinery of a national Eugenic policy, especially manifest in medical opposition to the notion of medical certificates of fitness for marriage. This recalls the ambiguous position of doctors in relation to medical certificates of insanity where on the one hand they claimed scientific expertise but were also wary of the consequences of legal responsibility and the effects upon doctor-patient relationships of the medical profession's wielding coercive power.[140] Political alignments depended essentially upon the priority of formal liberty in the internal ideological hierarchy of each faction. Eugenists, Fabians, and supporters of National Efficiency could see the sacrifice of

---

[138] Kathleen Jones describes it as having 'steered a sane and sensible course between the Scylla of 'liberty-of-the-subject' agitation, and the Charybdis of eugenic theory'. See *A History of the Mental Health Services*, p. 191.

[139] *House of Commons Debates* 53, col. 220 (28 May 1913).

[140] See G. R. Searle, 'Eugenics and Class', pp. 225–6.

liberties as justified by the prospect of national reinvigoration. Old-style Liberal Radicals, notably Josiah Wedgwood, and traditionalist Conservatives, such as Sir Frederick Banbury and Unionist MP Sir Robert Cecil, were appalled and joined forces in the Parliamentary struggle to disrupt the passage of Mental Deficiency legislation. In Government circles, the inadequacy of existing provision seemed clear in such cases as that of the mentally defective habitual offender, 'continually sentenced and re-sentenced to terms of imprisonment, with intervals of liberty in which he is a nuisance, perhaps a terror to the community and may propagate feeble-minded children . . .'.[141] But libertarian critics were scathing, especially about the Eugenic inspiration behind legislative proposals, Josiah Wedgwood condemning the Government's 1912 Bill as an attempt 'to breed the working classes as though they were cattle'.[142] Wedgwood, as we shall see, was to assume a similar role in relation to the Mental Treatment Bill in 1930 and although again the ultimate opposition was small, both measures had to be steamrollered through by forced closure in the Commons and the Mental Deficiency Bill was also rushed through the Lords as the end of the Session neared. Finally, the issue predictably produced difficult tensions within progressive Liberalism, directly raising as it did the relationship between collective intervention and liberty in the intimate context of reproduction. Churchill was sympathetic to Eugenic arguments, as was Hobson, but *The Nation* was critical. Hobhouse, consistently with his opposition to 'Eugenics, Fabians, "Efficiency" advocates, and all forms of bureaucratic authoritarianism', condemned the 1912 Bill for its abrogation of traditional legal democratic controls over expert discretion, but was more content with the sanitized 1913 version.[143] The New Liberalism's respect for individuality and aspiration to promote social harmony and reciprocity, its ethical concerns, reserved a space for revulsion against the mechanical, efficiency-oriented assumptions of Eugenics and its conservative moralism.[144] On the other hand, the issue provoked a heated debate between some Progressives and traditional Liberal Radicals as to the true meaning of liberty: a contest between the old pursuit of abstract, formal, personal liberty and the new quest for a fully social freedom. Thus, Wedgwood and

[141] Memorandum of 7 January 1911 'The Feeble-Minded: Memorandum as to a Bill of Limited Scope'. Public Record Office, State Papers, Ministry of Health 80/54.
[142] *House of Commons Debates* 39, col. 644 (10 June 1912).
[143] S. Collini, *Liberalism and Sociology*, pp. 140–1.
[144] M. Freeden, *The New Liberalism*, pp. 189–90.

William Pringle, both of whom had opposed the principle of compulsion in the context of National Insurance legislation, saw the Government's mental deficiency policy as an attack upon individualism and the family,[145] only to hear their fellow Liberals redefine liberty itself. Thus, Frederick Cawley, in the debate on the Second Reading of the 1912 Bill, pleaded that

... we should not sacrifice these poor people who are now suffering for an idea of abstract liberty, and we should not deprive them of a restraint which does them no harm in order to let them have the kind of liberty that at present is represented by being in and out of the casual wards, the maternity wards and the prisons.[146]

Even more pointedly, Charles McCurdy lectured Liberal opponents of the 1913 measure as follows, rejecting the suggestion that it should be sacrificed in favour of Welsh Disestablishment and Home Rule:

It is not by building up temples of liberty and by polishing and repolishing political constitutions that the people can grow up to proper manhood and healthy national life. Man does not live by the recasting of liberty alone. In passing, I confess for myself I have but little enthusiasm for these great measures which my honourable friend has mentioned, and why? Because the political enthusiasm which I felt for them in an abounding measure some twenty-five years ago, when I first took an interest in politics, has become a little stale and grey-headed, like myself. The new century has brought new social problems, and it is with one of these problems this Bill makes a courageous effort to deal.[147]

The Government's commitment to increasing special provision for mental defect was underlined by the adoption in 1914 of a companion measure to the Mental Deficiency Act, the Elementary Education (Defective and Epileptic Children) Act. This was the last of a series of Liberal Education Acts[148] augmenting public responsibilities, and obliged local authorities to establish special schools for mentally defective children.

It can be seen from the success of the 'liberty of the subject' lobby

[145] The Act provided for the mentally defective to be detained despite the refusal of parental consent where 'unreasonably withheld'. See section 6(3)(a).

[146] *House of Commons Debates* 41, col. 732 (19 July 1912).

[147] *House of Commons Debates* 53, col. 834 (3 June 1913).

[148] The Education (Provision of Meals) Act 1906 allowed expenditure out of the rates to provide schoolchildren with meals without their parents suffering civil and political disqualifications; the Education (Administrative Provisions) Act 1907 provided for the medical inspection of school children and the Education (Choice of Employment) Act 1910 equipped them with vocational guidance.

in blocking the extravagant illiberalism of the Mental Deficiency Bill of 1912 and the retention of judicial safeguards for commitment of the feeble-minded that there was not yet a sufficiently receptive political context for the reversal of legalism in legislation for the mentally ill. The displacement of the legalistic ethos by the philosophy of therapeutic interventionism in relation to the mentally defective and the comparative coerciveness of the new special legislation was made possible by their perception as a delimited genetically scarred substratum concentrated in the poorest sections of the community. Mental illness, however, although heredity was recognized as a factor, was a random and universal condition. Extended legislative controls here implicated the public as a whole and were perceived as a more serious threat to the liberties of the sane, not being tied to low intelligence or confined to conditions established since birth or infancy. There was needed a prolonged political campaign of public reassurance and a further erosion of classical liberal principles for processing the deviant and unproductive to furnish a conducive political climate. Most directly relevant to the latter was the gathering critique of the deterrent and stigmatizing procedures of the Poor Law, of which the legal and administrative structures of the lunacy system were in so many key respects the psychiatric counterpart.

The Royal Commission on the Poor Laws and Relief of Distress (1905–9)
The Edwardian period witnessed a powerful challenge to the principles of 1834 which still formed the basis of the Poor Law. The Royal Commission on the Poor Laws and Relief of Distress was appointed at the end of 1905 by Balfour's outgoing Conservative administration, its diverse membership incorporating Fabian, Labour, and Charity Organization Society elements. Despite their differing perspectives and the divisive activities of Beatrice Webb, whose behaviour rendered it clear at an early stage that she would produce a Minority Report, the Commission was at least united, when it reported in February 1909, in counselling radical changes in the organization of the machinery for managing poverty, in relation to which the Poor Law remained the only comprehensive provision. Investigation of the problem convinced the Commission that the real issue was how to prevent destitution by intervention at the level of its root causes rather than simply how to reinforce the deterrent efficacy of the Poor Law in a reassertion of rigid principles of less eligibility. In place of deterrence and stigmatization, the time had arrived to

urge an interventionist preventive and curative approach based upon conditional relief. The existing Poor Law was a blunt instrument, designed so that it could only ever provide mere negative relief of destitution which was only the symptom or product of malevolent social conditions, notably invalidity and unemployment, which should be tackled radically by extensions of direct intervention. Well-meaning generosity on behalf of certain Poor Law authorities merely exacerbated the system's structural deficiencies. Indiscriminate unconditional relief amplified social distress by pauperization. The answer was seen to lie in the abolition of the general workhouse and the erection of new administrative structures for the distribution of public assistance equipped to use it as a lever for the reform of personal habits.

Majority and Minority factions within the Commission were agreed on this fundamental reorientation of policy towards destitution, and on certain specific measures, for example, the introduction of labour exchanges and voluntary insurance to deal with unemployment as a cause of poverty. However, they disagreed in philosophic emphasis and in the precise structure of administrative agencies commended as a solution to the inadequacies of the Poor Law system.[149] The Majority, reflecting the conservative influence of the Charity Organization Society, wished to carve out a large role in the future structure for voluntary effort. They listed as one of the main principles of a reformed Poor Law 'that the public administration established for the assistance of the poor should work in co-operation with the local and private charities of the district' and described 'the lack of co-operation between Poor Law and Charity' as one of the leading defects of the existing system.[150] Although they proposed the transfer of Poor Law functions to local authorities, they wished to retain, in the form of new Public Assistance Committees of County and County Borough Councils, a modified form of general destitution authority. These authorities were to remain within the overall control of the Local Government Board. The Majority's temptation to retain a modified destitution authority in their scheme for preventive and curative services reflected their conviction that despite the role of impersonal social factors in the aetiology of destitution, such as seasonal unemployment or certain types of

[149] For comparisons of the Reports see T. H. Marshall, *Social Policy*, pp. 38–44; D. Fraser, pp. 148–9.
[150] *Report of the Royal Commission on the Poor Laws and Relief of Distress*, Majority, pp. 596, 617.

physical disease, there still remained the moral factor, the existence of an objectionable element among the destitute whose condition could only be blamed upon their own anti-social conduct. The Minority did not deny the potency of this moral consideration,[151] but were prepared to proceed on the assumption that social efficiency would best be served by attacking the environmental and structural patterns in the generation of destitution which had been substantiated by social scientific research.

Thus the Minority Report was more radical in its application of an interventionist strategy to institutional reform. It contained recommendations for public assistance to be administered by specialized local authority committees, for example, Poor Law medical services should be transferred to local public health committees and there should be new committees for the mentally defective (as later provided by the Mental Deficiency Act 1913). In contrast to the Majority's proposals these specialized services were to be available regardless of the applicant's financial position and there would be no segregated services for those marked out by their destitution. Further, it was envisaged that the Poor Law division of the Local Government Board would be disbanded and its functions dispersed amongst separate departments responsible for particular aspects of provision for the destitute: in particular, separate Ministries of Health and Labour were recommended. In adopting their approach, the Minority sought to build upon what the Webbs called 'The Framework of Prevention' which had evolved empirically outside the structures of the Poor Law in the course of the nineteenth century in the fields of factory regulation, public health, and education.

A functional approach was favoured by the Minority because it maximized the scope for the application of the appropriate expertise to specific social problems. The Minority proposed as co-ordinator of the various agencies involved a Registrar, whom Leonard Hobhouse described as having 'almost sultanic powers over the lives and liberties of those whose cases are submitted to him'[152]—a telling illustration of the trenchant interventionism which pervades the report.

As a strategy for superseding the Poor Law, the preventive and curative approach, in both its conservative and Fabian varieties, was in the event rejected by Asquith's Liberal Government. Lloyd George

[151] B. Webb and S. Webb, *English Poor Law Policy*. London: Longmans Green, 1910, pp. 304–7.
[152] Quoted in P. F. Clarke: see p. 118 *et seq.*

found the authoritarian and interventionist tenor of the proposals
perturbing and unacceptable and already favoured embarkation
upon the introduction of a system of insurance without dismantling
the surviving structures of the Poor Law. Churchill's position was
reflected in his statement that 'If I had to sum up the future of
democratic politics in a single word I should say "Insurance".'[153] The
Webbs and their sympathizers, while conceding a limited role for
insurance in the field of unemployment, were totally opposed to this
development with regard to sickness. They saw insurance as a
conservative mode of reform which would tragically perpetuate the
Poor Law policy of mere negative unconditional relief. They were
convinced that only the direct intervention of expert social agencies
in the lifestyles of the poor could attain any serious impact upon
levels of destitution in the long term. From their perspective, sickness
led to poverty rather than vice versa: 'It's criminal, to take poor
people's money and use it to insure them; if you take it you should
give it to the Public Health Authority to prevent their being ill
again.'[154]

In the longer term, the broad reorientation of provision for the
poor envisaged by the Royal Commission of 1905–9 was achieved:
The Local Government Act 1929 did replace Boards of Guardians by
County and County Borough Council Public Assistance Committees
and in the major reorganization of welfare services in 1944–8 a
functional rather than a classificatory structure of provision was
adopted as a central principle of the new administrative structures. It
is also true in the case of the Liberal measures themselves, that
although to some extent they reflected a philosophic distaste for the
overt statism, bureaucratism, and authoritarianism of Fabianism, the
machinery of insurance and labour exchanges in particular did effect
an unprecedentedly high level of bureaucratic regulation of the
working class, and Fabian supporters were prominent in the
administrative élites of the new structures. Nevertheless, the adoption of insurance as the key to the solution of the most serious of
Britian's social problems at this juncture did indicate a suitably
modified commitment to individualism, constitutionalism, and the
rule of law, rather than a more directive, bureaucratic, and
mechanical Fabianism in a formative period of the evolution of the
Welfare State.

[153] Quoted in P. F. Clarke at p. 122.
[154] H. Bunbury (ed.), *Lloyd George's Ambulance Wagon*. London: Methuen, 1957,
p. 80.

Both the recommendations of the Royal Commission on the Poor Laws and their fate assist us to understand the politics of the Mental Treatment Act. The lunacy system had evolved during the nineteenth century in interlinked relationship with the Poor Law. Although the asylums were formally separate from the Poor Law system, and vested in the local magistracy and after 1888 in County and County Borough Councils rather than the Boards of Guardians, their inmates were technically paupers. Also, substantial numbers of the insane were still held in Poor Law insitutions. Most importantly, the lunacy system and the Poor Law performed similar functions in relation to similar populations. They had to support, contain, and discipline the deviant and unproductive. The peculiar feature of the clientele of the lunacy system was that their unproductiveness flowed from particular types of deviant aberrant behaviour subsumed under the concept of insanity. Thus, it should not be surprising that the impact of the shift from liberalism to interventionism upon the agenda for Poor Law reform was paralleled by a broadly contemporaneous campaign to 'modernize' the Lunacy system. It was only in the light of major structural change in the state's perception of the problem of poverty as a whole that legislation which dismantled key legal safeguards to prevent infringement of the liberties of the sane could be contemplated.

There were striking resemblances between the recommendations of Macmillan and the Royal Commission on the Poor Laws. The Macmillan Commission, with its emphasis on the importance of the destigmatization of state psychiatric treatment by the hospitalization of asylums and medicalization of admission procedures, together with its proposals for the extrication of public psychiatric services from the Poor Law, and in its relative tenderness to civil liberties, was more in accord with the Majority than with the Fabian Minority faction within the Poor Law Royal Commission.

Macmillan's policy that 'the keynote of the past has been detention; the keynote of the future should be prevention and treatment'[155] corresponded to the Edwardian Poor Law Royal Commission's demand for the replacement of the deterrent Poor Law, with its restrictively conceived role of relieving destitution, by a positively preventive and curative framework of services catering to the broad criterion of need. Just as the Poor Law Royal Commission perceived the deterrent and stigmatizing status of pauper and the conditionality

---

[155] *Report of the Royal Commission on Lunacy and Mental Disorder*, para. 42.

of relief upon actual desititution as impediments to a dynamic assault upon poverty, so Macmillan saw the deterrent and stigmatizing status of certified lunatic and the dependence of treatment upon advanced symptoms of a kind appreciable by a magistrate as the central impediment to major progress toward the prevention and cure of mental illness. Pauperism was an intentionally demeaning status designed to deter any but the most desperate from seeking assistance. It entailed subjection to a moral stigma derived from the assumption firmly embedded in the practices of the Poor Law system that destitution was the fault of failure to compete effectively in the market, taken as an objective measure of individual merit. Assistance was provided in distinct institutions—workhouses, Poor Law infirmaries, and Poor Law schools—which preserved symbolic segregation. While the Majority of the Poor Law Commission deplored the deterrent effects of the stigma of pauperism, and the Minority tended to emphasize the restrictive effects upon what we would now call social welfare agencies of only being able to intervene against poverty once its victims were actually destitute, both were agreed on the necessity of sweeping away pauper status as the basis for initiating a radical preventive and curative social strategy.[156] This was a question of strategic effectiveness rather than humanitarianism.[157] The central problem was the lack of radical access by specialized agencies to the causes of destitution.[158]

The nineteenth-century lunacy system complemented the Poor Law's deterrent and negative form of provision and hence was vulnerable to similar lines of criticism. In the absence of any general entitlement to enter an asylum voluntarily, and given the historical force of political opposition to medically-administered commitment, certification as a person of unsound mind tended to be a precondition of access to psychiatric treatment in an institutional setting.

[156] Apart from the Majority's insistence on the retention of a residual general destitution authority.

[157] See *Report of the Royal Commission on the Poor Laws*, Majority, p. 596; B. Webb and S. Webb, *English Poor Law History*, Chapter V.

[158] On the problem of unconditional relief see Dr J. C. McVail, 'Report . . . on the Methods and Results of the Present System of Administering Indoor and Outdoor Medical Relief', 1907, *Royal Commission on the Poor Laws and Reliefs of Distress: Minutes of Evidence*, Appendix Vol. xiv, pp. 148–9; on the deterrent effect of the stigma of pauperism see *Royal Commission on the Poor Laws and Relief of Distress: Minutes of Evidence*, Appendix Vol. iv, Question 37,927, paras. 12, 29 and 56: evidence of Dr Nathan Raw. The former is quoted by B. Webb and S. Webb, at pp. 513–14 and the latter at p. 515 in *English Poor Law History*.

Although this was not the universal view,[159] its critics claimed that this process was popularly perceived as a quasi-penal labelling ceremony which had become invested with all the stigma of the mysteries and fears surrounding madness. Like pauperism, it officially conferred upon the labelled individual certain stereotypical qualities—in this case not idleness or parasitism, but liability to abnormal and especially to violent behaviour for which there was no obvious rational explanation. This stigma could, of course, have permanent effects on the social standing of its victims even if they were declared 'cured'. Again, the status of certified lunatic paralleled that of pauper in stripping mental patients of essential attributes of citizenship, this time on the ground that by definition they lacked the freedom of will and capacity for rational self-determination which characterizes humanity and entitles to full legal, moral, and political status.

Macmillan challenged the stigma of certification both for its deterrent potency, recommending that it should be a last and not a first resort,[160] and for its restriction of the authority of the medical profession to administer treatment only to 'definite and well-established cases', which contradicted 'all the accepted canons of preventive medicine'.[161] Voluntary treatment and the introduction of the Provisional Treatment Order were proposed as circumventions of certification which would avoid stigmatization, enabling treatment facilities to be presented as medical rather than penal in function, and permitting and encouraging early treatment. This was the Macmillan Commission's strategy for an efficient mental health system.[162]

On a more specific note, the Majority Report of the Royal Commission on the Poor Laws provides interesting parallels with Macmillan in its proposal for an order for the 'detention and

---

[159] For Parliamentary dissension on this see the speeches of Sir Kingsley Wood, *House of Commons Debates* 235, col. 974 (17 February 1930) and that of Ernest Winterton, *House of Commons Debates* 237, col. 2570 (11 April 1930). Some thought that the stigma was associated with involuntary commitment as such rather than with its particular procedural form.

[160] See *Report of the Royal Commission on Lunacy and Mental Disorder*, para. 92: 'The attitude may be irrational, but the existence of this feeling is recognized on all hands, and must be accepted as a cardinal factor in dealing with the situation . . .'.

[161] Ibid., para. 46.

[162] It must be stressed that the Macmillan Report and the Mental Treatment Act 1930, which gave its main proposals statutory force, did not seek the diminution of stigma and the eclipse of certification as a means to restoring the full citizenship of mental patients. On the contrary, as we have seen, section 16 of the Act actually further restricted their right of access to the Courts.

continuous treatment of certain classes of persons receiving or
applying for public assistance'. Compulsion was advocated for the
following conditions: extreme age or extreme youth; *illness or disease
of mind* or body; persistent indulgence in vice or pernicious habits,
instancing unmarried mothers and adults 'repeatedly becoming
chargeable through wilful neglect or misconduct'. The power of
compulsory detention was to be given to the proposed public
assistance authority in order to augment its capacity to deal with its
clients in a 'restorative' manner. One parallel with Macmillan's
justification of compulsion in the specific context of civil commitment of the mentally ill is the employment of the humanitarian
connotations of medical language to legitimate coercive powers:

The term detention is perhaps infelicitous. It is generally associated with the
idea of punishment by imprisonment. Our primary objective in proposing
detention is neither punishment nor imprisonment. We aim at obtaining
opportunities for applying ameliorative treatment to particular individuals
over a continuous period. We desire to substitute for the present period of
incontinuous and inefficacious relief, a continuity of care and treatment . . .
to secure this . . . some powers of control are necessary, but these powers of
control are intended in the vast majority of cases to be curative and
stimulative rather than punitive, nor need they necessarily always be
exercised in an institution.[163]

A second parallel is with Macmillan's decision to retain a magistrate
in the procedures for his recommended Provisional Treatment
Order, in the light of public concern for 'the liberty of the subject.'
The Majority faction considered that the issuing of its Continuous
Treatment Order, described above, ought to be an administrative
matter for the recommended Public Assistance Authority. But
envisaging opposition, given that the order had a maximum duration
of three years, they accepted that Justices of the Peace would have to
issue them.[164] Macmillan was concerned to make a moderate advance
in the light of likely public reaction. Similarly, the Majority of the

[163] *Report of the Royal Commission on the Poor Laws and Relief of Distress*, Majority, p.
635. The Webbs themselves derided the euphemistic quality of the language of this
proposal, but not because they objected in principle to such compulsory powers or to
their being clothed in medical terminology. They wished to use any material available
to discredit the Majority's rival Report, and held to the position that compulsory
powers could not be other than repressive, and moreover politically impossible, in the
context of the retention of a general destitution authority: B. Webb and S. Webb,
English Poor Law Policy, pp. 276, 289–92.
[164] See *Report of the Royal Commission on the Poor Laws*, Majority, p. 635.

Poor Law Royal Commission were not given to the sometimes draconian recommendations of the Fabian Minority, whose enthusiasm overreached any awareness of the likely public response.[165]

Finally, both Commissions took the public health system as a model for advance towards a genuinely preventive and curative approach. The Webbs were fond of contrasting the 'Framework of Repression' represented by the Poor Law with the 'Framework of Prevention' of which public health legislation and services provided the prototype. Similarly, the Macmillan Report recites that 'The problem of insanity is essentially a public health problem to be dealt with on modern health lines.'[166]

Public health medical services which had grown up outside the Poor Law were designed 'to secure the individual and national efficiency which result from the living of a healthy life in healthy surroundings'.[167] Public health services were principally preventative:

the special characteristic of the treatment of disease by the Public Health Authority is, not to wait until the patient is so ill that he is driven to apply either by destitution or by collapse, but positively to search out every case, even in its most incipient state.[168]

The treatment of the immediate suffering of individual patients was therefore incidental to preventive action in the interests of the community as a whole. The Webbs perceived this communal rationale as the essential characteristic of the services and admired its integrative social function: '[the fact that the Public Health Medical service] is rendered in the interests of the community ... actually creates in the recipient an increased feeling of personal obligation and even a new sense of social responsibility.'[169]

The contemporary philosophy of public health was one of moulding the life-habits of the working class to standards of physical and moral conduct generated by the socio-economic system by the implantation of subjective commitment to a reified national interest. To the extent that this was proposed as the model for the mental health services it is interesting to note its implications for the official

---

[165] As Searle observes '... true to the whole ethos of the national efficiency ideology, the Minority Report brutally ignored all susceptibilities.' See G. R. Searle, *The Quest for National Efficiency*, p. 241.

[166] *Report of the Royal Commission on Lunacy and Mental Disorder*, para. 50.

[167] J. McVail, 'Report on ... Medical Relief', p. 154.

[168] B. Webb and S. Webb, *English Poor Law History*, p. 585.

[169] Ibid., p. 587.

conception of voluntary status as a mental patient. It would seem to imply that voluntarism was not to be a realm of freedom in which patients could decide whether to enter or leave hospital according to the balance of their own perceived self-interest. Rather, patients would be expected to appreciate that their psychiatric treatment was administered in the interests of promoting mental hygiene at a collective level and that they were under a social obligation to submit to the therapeutic regime prescribed by the medical expert to suit the requirements of their particular case. This conception of the mental health service as a department of public health defined the role of the doctor in voluntary commitment not as a consultant to whose advice the patient is free to submit or not on the model of a private contractual relationship, but primarily a public agent with an overriding responsibility to eliminate mental disease in the higher interests of social progress.

The Webbs themselves endorsed and approved the preventive orientation of the Macmillan Report and its adoption of the public health model.[170] David Ewins has characterized the Mental Treatment Act as Fabian in political inspiration, being integral to a strategy for perpetuating capitalist socio-economic order by a programme of positive and, where necessary, authoritarian welfare legislation designed to ameliorate social conditions and co-opt the working class.[171] He envisages the key provisions of the Act as a kind of exchange, a social control contract, in which the state confers new legal powers and immunities upon the medical profession in return for their services in the control of the mentally ill as a category encompassing various types of social deviance. However, the Mental Treatment Act's renunciation of legalism was not essentially achieved by naked extensions of the formal coercive powers of the medical profession. Rather, the interventionist strategy was one of seeking to improve the *accessibility* of the problem by restricting, and in the end removing, the barrier of certification, perceived as a deterrent and stigmatizing procedure analogous to pauperization and similarly counter-productive. This is indicated by the introduction of voluntary admission to public mental hospitals as a major reform, and in the reasoning employed to justify the introduction of the Temporary Order for compulsory admission on the basis of medical recommendations without prior judicial sanction. This reasoning stressed the

---

[170] See *English Poor Law History*, pp. 591–2.
[171] D. Ewins, 'The Origins of the Compulsory Commitment Provisions of the Mental Health Act 1959,' pp. 36–43.

need to circumvent the stigma supposedly associated with magisterial involvement so as to promote treatment at an early curative stage. There is no need to dismiss the official prominence of this argument as a mere humanitarian gloss or ideological smokescreen for expanded social control in order to be able to situate the reform in the political reorientation towards interventionism. It reinforces the point that the essential strategy was one of breaking down barriers between the psychiatric profession and the public by transforming the image of the lunacy system into an authentically therapeutic one via the erosion of legalistic safeguards that were perceived as supportive of its quasi-penal, custodial, and therefore feared reputation. The hope was to attract patients by encouraging those under psychiatric stress to submit themselves to treatment, or, if they were unwilling, to encourage their families to deliver them over to hospital authorities at an earlier stage.

The tenor of the legislation was didactic and ideological, expressing the ideal that if a medical rationality of mental disorder could be implanted in its clients, psychiatry could thrive on an informal and co-operative basis. It was not simply an exercise in the promotion of psychiatric efficiency, regardless of consent. The aim was hegemony, not mere domination. In this respect the Act was in the mould of the dominant New Liberal influence in early twentieth-century social welfare legislation, with its deference to the enduring liberalism of the British political tradition and its qualified legalism (the Justice was, after all, retained for unwilling cases), and not an instance of Fabian authoritarianism. It was not only concerned with rationality and efficiency, but illustrates that the shifting boundaries of political debate afforded new channels for the expression of humanitarian and liberal sentiments, which became directed toward remedying the plight of those suffering in default of intervention rather than protecting the objects of intervention from abuse. We may now turn to an examination of the evolution of the legislation and the alignments it produced in the light of this political analysis.

6 The Mental Treatment Act 1930: II Law in Transition

THE enactment of legislation to amend the Lunacy Act 1890 by relaxing legal safeguards in the interests of facilitating therapeutic goals, was achieved as the conclusion to a period of bitter war between two different perceptions of the reality of psychiatric practice. On the one hand there was the official perception, cultivated by most of the psychiatric profession and by the mental health bureaucracy at the Board of Control, that psychiatry was a modern enlightened dynamic therapeutic enterprise, that insanity was an illness of the mind analogous to and often inseparable from somatic illness, and that legal safeguards were largely unnecessary and counterproductive in their stigmatizing quasi-penal connotations. This view articulated well with the more general political impetus toward the expansion of professional and bureaucratic power; the explanation of deviance in deterministic rather than moral or voluntaristic terms, and the destigmatization of public services also evident in the movement toward reform of the Poor Law. If this view, rationalist, modernist, and hopeful toward the potentialities of the rapidly advancing technology and scientific understanding characteristic of the age was to prevail, then it had to do so at the expense of an alternative conviction, supportive of the retention, and indeed the fortification, of legal safeguards—a populist view widespread outside official, professional, and 'enlightened' circles—that psychiatric practice was largely custodial in character, that its medical pretentions were cosmetic, that there was little treatment and frequent punishment, and that stigma arose not from the legalistic nature of formal safeguards of 'the liberty of the subject' but from the condition of madness itself. The champions of this more cynical and alarmist view were the National Society for Lunacy Reform, dissident psychiatrists, and certain MPs, mainly in the Independent Labour Party, whose politics still owed much to old-style Radicalism.

In prosecuting the business of creating an amended legal framework for the operation of psychiatry, the advocates of change had to be wary of public opinion and its vociferous spokesmen and they adopted a politic, graduated approach. It was a characteristic of the proposals of the Board of Control, who had opposed the legalism of the Lunacy Act 1890 from its conception, of the medical profession, and of the 1924–6 Royal Commission, that they adhered to caution. It was as the climax to a drawn-out and carefully plotted process of consulting interested parties, pacifying opponents and preparing public opinion that the Mental Treatment Act 1930 finally reached the statute book.

From Radnor to Macmillan

The Royal Commission on the Care and Control of the Feeble Minded, appointed in 1904 under the Chairmanship of the Earl of Radnor, was the first major official inquiry into the law relating to mental disorder after the Lunacy Act 1890. We have seen that it was primarily concerned with producing new legal arrangements specifically addressed to the problem of mental defectives and that although its Report did incorporate some consideration of the position of the mentally ill, it did not propose any essential departure from the structure of legal safeguards contained in the Lunacy Act. The ensuing passage of the Mental Deficiency Act 1913, establishing separate statutory machinery for the certification and institutionalization of mental defectives, meant that, barring a reversal of the accepted policy of separate provision, the next lunacy reform would for the first time apply exclusively to the mentally ill. However, as the shape of lunacy law had always been determined in the main by developments in relation to the insane rather than the mentally handicapped this was not necessarily of great significance.

The Mental Deficiency Act did not lay a positive duty on local authority mental deficiency committees to secure specialized institutions. Progress toward institutionalization was slow, with only 5,000 of 60,000 ascertained defectives in local authority institutions by 1927.[1] Measures to accommodate criminal and moral defectives were treated as a priority. The Board of Control acquired Moss Side for the purpose of a State Institution for defectives of both sexes with dangerous or violent propensities in 1914, but it was transferred to the War Office as a military hospital for shock cases. Farmfield was rented from the London County Council as an institution for females, and Rampton was opened as a new State Institution for both sexes in 1919. The Board of Control wrestled with the problem of

---

[1] K. Jones, *A History of the Mental Health Services*, p. 213.

whether 'moral imbeciles' were really 'congenital defectives' or 'ordinary criminals', the classic boundary problem of the psychopath.[2] In the aftermath of the war, mental defect was seen as a major source of danger and the acceleration of the Act's implementation as a component of reconstruction.[3] It is significant here that the Geddes Committee refrained from making any reduction in government contribution to local authority expenditure under the Act as this work was regarded as 'essential to the physical and moral health of the nation'.[4]

After 1913, the more coercive philosophy of Mental Deficiency legislation was maintained. Whereas in untutored public opinion the expansion of discretionary professional power in lunacy legislation threatened the liberties of every citizen, the mentally deficient continued to be perceived as a delimited problem class who required extensive control in the public interest. The general political movement toward state interventionism facilitated the subsequent consolidation of the powers of identification and control delivered by the 1913 Act. Interrupted by the First World War, the eugenic campaign revived in the 1920s and early 1930s, stimulated by fears of an increase in the mentally unfit. The Mental Deficiency Act 1927 removed the requirement that the mental defect must have existed 'from birth or from an early age' before the statutory powers could be invoked,[5] in order to bring a larger section of imprisoned criminals within the legislation, and two official committees, the Wood Committee, which reported in 1929,[6] and the Brock Committee which reported in 1934, both proposed further powers of control. The latter was appointed under Laurence Brock, Chairman of the Board of Control, to inquire into the issue of sterilization, and recommended that voluntary sterilization of mental defectives be legalized. This proposal was too controversial to be pursued by Government. Even though sterilization was to be on a 'voluntary' basis, the persistent liberal traditions of the British state which modified the movement to interventionism in the early twentieth century prevailed. Whereas Colonel Wedgwood had been in a minority in his opposition to the Mental Deficiency Act 1927 and the

[2] *Annual Report of the Board of Control for the Year 1921*, p. 51.
[3] *Annual Report of the Board of Control for the Year 1917*, p. 56.
[4] *Annual Report of the Board of Control for the Year 1921*, p. 6.
[5] Mental Deficiency Act 1927, section 1(2).
[6] The Wood Committee was a joint committee of the Board of Education and Board of Control set up in 1924. One of its members was Dr A. F. Tredgold, the prominent eugenist, who had been medical expert to the Radnor Commission.

Mental Treatment Act 1930, the issue of sterilization provoked opposition ranging from the Roman Catholic Church to sections of the labour movement.

In terms of legislative proposals directly concerned with mental illness, a succession of Bills were introduced in the period separating publication of the Report of the Radnor Commission and the appointment of the Macmillan Commission with the aim of facilitating treatment without certification and bestowing legal blessing upon the internal preventive and curative reorientation of psychiatry. Earl Russell brought forward a Voluntary Mental Treatment Bill in 1914 which was given a First Reading in the House of Lords. John Francis Stanley, the 2nd Earl Russell (1865–1931), and brother of Bertrand Russell, was a veritable apostle of professional and bureaucratic expansionism in the sphere of mental health and an extremely active devotee of the principles to be enshrined in the Mental Treatment Act 1930. He was a member of the Macmillan Commission, helping to draft its Report,[7] and was also, at his own request, given the task of steering the consequent Bill through the Upper House. In the gallery of the politics of mental health legislation, Russell provides a counterpoint to the ultra-individualist Nonconformist Radicalism of Colonel Josiah Wedgwood. Like Wedgwood, he was a member of the Labour Party, holding minor office at the Ministry of Transport and the India Office in the 1929–31 Government, but his Socialism was of the Fabian variety. Consistently with the more authoritarian interventionism of the Fabians, Russell regarded the Mental Treatment Bill of 1923, which anticipated the 1930 Act, as merely the thin end of the wedge[8] and in debate on the Bill in the House of Lords he advocated the eugenic sterilization of certain of the insane.[9] At the turn of the century, as a member of the London County Council, he had been Chairman of the Visiting Committee of Hanwell, and felt that he could speak with authority on lunacy matters. He was strikingly contemptuous of popular suspicions of science, bureaucracy, and the state, as the following tirade, delivered in relation to the 1923 Bill, illustrates:

There are few people so ignorant, incredulous and suspicious as the poor on

[7] Memorandum of 18 February 1927 by Peter Barter, a Principal at the Ministry of Health on loan to the Board of Control, who had been Secretary to the Royal Commission: Public Record Office, State Papers, Ministry of Health 51/640, Board of Control File No. 60232/1.

[8] *Transactions of the Medico-Legal Society* XVII (1922–3), p. 209.

[9] *House of Lords Debates* 53, col. 1071 (3 May 1923).

matters of administration and scientific questions; we know perfectly well that they are ready to believe still that hospitals are chiefly used for the purpose of experiment instead of for the purpose of cure and treatment; no doubt they still believe the sort of Charles Reade stories about lunatic asylums, although many have had relations in them, and ought, you would think, to know better . . . .
I do not know that the public every cry out for anything intelligent in these matters, but as far as I can make out from the columns of *Truth*, which is the only source from which one can get an idea of public demands in this matter, they are rather crying out that all asylums should be disbanded and all officials sent to prison. I think however that informed public opinion has asked for this Bill.[10]

The outbreak of the First World War overtook Earl Russell's Bill. The intervention of the war had a double-edged effect. While the process of bringing forward measures to mitigate the rigour of the Lunacy Act 1890 was interrupted and delayed, the war itself generated fresh interest in proposals to informalize civil commitment procedures. There were two important influences in this direction. One was the handling of the problem of shell-shocked military personnel and the efforts to shield them from the stigmas of certification as a lunatic and institutionalization in an asylum. The second was the consonance of proposals to modify the lunacy law with the new ruling ideology at the political level, Social Reconstruction, which demanded that the sharp increases in state intervention to meet the needs of war be sustained into the post-war period as the basis for a radical restructuring of the social edifice.

'Shell-shock' presented a new object for psychiatric treatment and research.[11] Although attempts were made to explain it in organic terms, its appearance provided an important opening for psychological explanations and psychotherapeutic techniques and these became dominant in the treatment of what were accordingly defined as 'war psychoneuroses'.[12] The problem was large-scale, being estimated at 80,000 officers and men throughout the war,[13] and attracted much publicity. So far as law and administration were concerned, this novel classification of psychiatric conditions constituted something of a crisis and compelled the terms of the existing lunacy procedures to be breached. Fighting efficiency required early and flexible facilities

---

[10] *Transactions of the Medico-Legal Society* XVII (1922–3), pp. 209–10.
[11] See P. Bean, *Compulsory Admissions to Mental Hospitals*, p. 40.
[12] See N. Rose, *The Psychological Complex*, pp. 182–3.
[13] Id.

for psychiatric treatment so that the psychological fitness of the manpower affected could rapidly be restored. Furthermore, widespread sympathy was aroused for victims of shell-shock and there was intense concern to protect them from stigma, considered an unfitting reward for patriotic sacrifice. It was found that popular sentiment could be agitated not only in support of sane persons illegitimately incarcerated in asylums, but also in support of those whose acknowledged need for psychiatric treatment arose as a risk incidental to the course of duty. These concerns had conflicting implications for the future of legal safeguards, but they flowed equally from the belief that the machinery of lunacy and the confines of the asylum should be reserved for the unambiguously mad. In the event, the adaptations of legal procedure and the new sites of treatment which were devised for military patients furnished a valuable model and precedent for a new framework for the treatment of the 'mentally ill' as a whole.

In 1915, Sir Cecil Harmsworth, with the support of the Board of Control, introduced into the Commons a Mental Treatment Bill designed to obviate the need for formal certification specifically for 'persons suffering from mental breakdown of recent origin and arising from wounds, shock, etc.' for the duration of the war. This Bill failed to reach the statute book, but even without legislative amendment the Board was able 'with a view to meet the pronounced opposition both in and out of Parliament to the certification of soldiers who during the war suffer from mental breakdown' to set aside 2,000 beds loaned to the Army Council as hospital accommodation for sick and wounded soldiers for the treatment of such cases without certification.[14] Some uncertified cases were treated in special hospitals and military clinics. The Board of Control also formed a scheme to ensure that those soldiers and sailors who were eventually discharged from the services and certified would be classified as private patients on a special service patient list so that they escaped the Poor Law stigma.[15] It was argued in some quarters that institutions completely separate from the asylums should actually be created to accommodate them, but the Board objected, just as it was

[14] Sir E. Marriott Cooke's response (as acting Chairman of the Board of Control for Sir William Patrick Byrne) to the request of the Reconstruction Committee for suggestions concerning measures promoting the conservation and health of the population, 9 February 1917: Public Record Office, State Papers, Ministry of Health 51/687, Board of Control File No. 33387/4.
[15] Id.

later to resist the more general argument for separate institutions under Ministry of Health and local authority control for the categories of voluntary and temporary patients under new mental treatment legislation.[16] Short of institutional segregation, however, the privileged status of service patients was at least given visible social effect within asylum communities by the permission to wear private clothes and the provision of 'distinctive badges'. Service patient status depended upon mental unfitness being certified as 'due to or aggravated by war service during the present war' and was supposed to equate the beneficiaries to private patients. However, whilst sections 72 and 74 of the Lunacy Act 1890 technically applied, authorizing relatives or friends to discharge against medical advice, subject to the Medical Superintendent's barring certificate, the Board of Control encouraged doctors to threaten that any later readmission so necessitated could involve loss of service status with partial loss of pension.[17] Status was not to jeopardize control.

The treatment of shell-shock cases was explicitly adduced by psychiatrists as an argument in support of amending the Lunacy Acts to allow reception of patients without certification in clinics:

In this connection, it will be of interest to recall that in the case of mentally-disordered soldiers the Army authorities arranged, during the war, that they be received into military mental hospitals without any orders or certificates. These men were, in the first instance, not sent to their asylums until the mental disability had lasted for a period of nine months and was deemed incurable: later it was decided that this step should be taken after such an extended period as was necessary to form the opinion that recovery was unlikely. Large numbers of men were received in very early stages of the disease . . . . If these men could be treated thus while in khaki, they could and should be similarly treated as civilians, and under far better medical conditions than in asylums. The war has, in this, as in other instances, been a means of education.[18]

It could, however, be doubted whether psychiatric control without the full detentionary authority of certification would be sufficient in civilian cases, where the supports of military discipline would be absent.[19] Even so, this wartime experience boded well for future psychiatric advance: it demonstrated psychiatry in action beyond the

---

[16] *Annual Report of the Board of Control for the Year 1917*, pp. 23–4.
[17] Ibid., p. 25.
[18] *Journal of Mental Science* 66 (1920), p. 186.
[19] See ibid., p. 341.

asylum, its social utility underlined by association with the highly valued national enterprise of defeating a hostile foreign power. It also identified very specifically, and in relation to a category whose popular heroism could readily be capitalized, the legal and administrative hiatus in facilities for the treatment of 'mental illness' of a temporary and recoverable character perceived as distinct from full insanity. The authorities were placed in the absurd position of having to originate methods of avoiding procedures and institutions provided for the submission of individuals to psychiatric treatment in order that they might receive that treatment without disgrace. Meanwhile the marginalization of the asylum itself in the treatment of shell-shock cases spotlighted recently instituted alternative sites of therapy, the most notable of which was the Maudsley Hospital.

The Maudsley Hospital was initiated in 1907, when Dr Henry Maudsley, one of the most influential figures in psychiatry, provided the London County Council with a benefaction to establish a mental institution which would deal exclusively with early and acute cases, operate an out-patients' clinic, and teach and research on psychiatry as a branch of medicine.[20] The building was completed in 1915 and under the London County Council (parks, etc.) Act of that year special legislative authority was obtained to admit cases on a voluntary basis without certification. For the remainder of the war and into the post-war period the institution was diverted to the treatment of shell-shock cases, in which it played an important part. The Maudsley was conceived as the prototype for a new model mental hospital which would be fully medical in character and organization and integrated with the practice of physical medicine. Nikolas Rose defines its construction and objectives as an instantiation in the realm of mental disease of the new strategy of Neo-Hygienism, in which public health was to be a matter of promoting positive health through preventive surveillance and the positive re-education of families and individuals in sanitary habits.[21] Giving the first Maudsley Lecture in 1920, Sir James Chrichton Browne prophesied that the Maudsley Hospital had 'set an example which will be followed under the more liberal and elastic lunacy law dispensation which is undoubtedly in store for us'.[22] The Macmillan Commission duly obliged by expressing itself to be 'greatly impressed' by the hospital and floated its proposal for voluntary

[20] K. Jones, *A History of the Mental Health Services*, p. 235.
[21] N. Rose, *The Psychological Complex*, pp. 161, 146.
[22] *Journal of Mental Science* 66 (1920), p. 203.

admission as a national extension of the Maudsley system.[23] Another prominent example of a facility engaged in the treatment of shell-shock patients which served as a model around which a new legislative framework could take shape was the out-patient clinic established by Dr Thomas Saxty Good, Medical Superintendent of the Oxford and City Mental Hospital, at the Radcliffe Infirmary in 1918. Expanding successfully serving peacetime uses, attendances in 1929 ran to 3,000.[24] Out-patient clinics attached to general hospitals were seen by the architects of the 1930 legislation as an essential institutional innovation in the prosecution of an effective preventive and curative mental health strategy.

Turning to the second advance produced by the war, Social Reconstruction was significant because it constituted an overarching political strategy at the level of action by the state of which a programme to promote mental hygiene by reducing the legalism of the lunacy laws was a natural component. It was a strategy within which public health occupied a central place and in terms of which a new Ministry of Health was instituted. During the First World War there was a massive expansion of the state built upon the sweeping powers given by the Defence of the Realm Act 1914. Under the pressure of the immediate requirement to organize national resources for military victory, liberal susceptibilities were swept aside. While this 'War Socialism' was accepted by some as an unfortunate necessity, others, notably Lloyd George and his devoted ally, Christopher Addison (1869–1951),[25] supported by interventionists amongst the civil service élite like Sir Robert Morant (1863–1920), welcomed the opportunities for social reorganization and reform, for Social Reconstruction, that the emergency offered.[26] This development represents the high point of the impact of the National Efficiency strand in the emergence of the Welfare State, and it is not surprising that it should have provoked political opposition from similar quarters. Colonel Josiah Wedgwood was one of the spokes-

---

[23] *Report of the Royal Commission on Lunacy and Mental Disorder*, para. 98.

[24] See 'The History and Progress of Littlemore Hospital', *Journal of Mental Science* 76 (1930), p. 611 and *Report of the Proceedings of a Conference on Mental Treatment*, held by the Board of Control with others on the implementation of the Mental Treatment Act, 22 and 23 July 1930, p. 8 *et seq.*

[25] Addison headed two new Ministries which were creations of this intensification of interventionism, as Minister of Reconstruction from 1917–19 and Minister of Health from 1919–21.

[26] See D. Fraser, *The Evolution of the British Welfare State*, pp. 164–6.

men of the Union of Democratic Control which campaigned against wartime state encroachment.[27]

To carry forward the radical social intervention adopted in wartime into conditions of peace and transform exceptional machinery into an accepted and legitimate part of the state apparatus, in 1916 a Cabinet Committee on Reconstruction was established. A second committee of experts was later convened and a Ministry of Reconstruction established in 1917.

The lunacy system was one area of social policy subjected to scrutiny as part of the plans for Social Reconstruction. At the direction of Lloyd George as Prime Minister, in August 1916 the first Reconstruction Committee sought the assistance of several departments, including the Board of Control 'concerning measures which might with advantage be adopted for promoting the conservation and health of the population'.[28] This gave the Board the opportunity to press interventionist measures for which the political climate was now more favourable. Accordingly, in its reply, the Board of Control stressed the importance of improving psychiatric access to incipient and 'recent recoverable' cases, and to mild disorders and nervous illnesses such as phobias and temporary breakdowns under mental stress. It was also emphasized that 'no effort should be spared' in prosecuting preventive measures to combat excessive alcohol consumption, syphilis, and mental stress, which were identified as important causes of insanity. The legal and administrative machinery for the expansion of psychiatric intervention which the Board proposed consisted of recommendations that early treatment should be made available in any institution under the supervision of the Board without certification as in the Bill of 1915; that in-patient and out-patient sections should be established at general hospitals for the diagnosis and treatment of incipient cases, including facilities for psychiatric research where the hospital was attached to a medical school; that the principle of voluntary admission should be extended to public asylums and single care; that after-care services should be more effectively organized, and that special psychiatric qualifications should be made necessary for appointments to higher medical posts in public institutions for the insane, as in the case of Medical Officers

---

[27] H. V. Emy, *Liberals, Radicals and Social Politics*, p. 289.
[28] Letter of 14 August 1916 from Vaughan Nash on behalf of the Reconstruction Committee informing the Board of Control of the Prime Minister's instruction: Public Record Office, State Papers, Ministry of Health 51/687, Board of Control File No. 33387/4.

of Health under the Local Government Act 1888.[29] The Board also demanded greater powers of control over the lunacy system, complaining that their existing powers were visitorial, critical, and advisory rather than executive. To remedy this it was proposed that they should have the same powers in relation to lunatics that they had been given in relation to mental defectives under the Mental Deficiency Act 1913.[30]

The Board of Control thus laid down the main themes of lunacy reform which were eventually to find expression in the Mental Treatment Act: the need for a preventive and curative approach if real progress toward national mental health were to be attained; the need to destigmatize psychiatric services to this end by informalizing commitment procedures; the integration of mental with general medical treatment especially by procuring facilities for psychiatric treatment at or in association with general hospitals;[31] the improvement of after-care; the extension of psychiatric research, and the professionalization and centralization of authority. During 1918, as the war drew to a close, the Board refined these recommendations into the heads of a Bill, which they pressed upon the Home Secretary and Lord Chancellor as an urgent measure, declaring in their next Annual Report, in the politically appropriate language of reconstruction, their belief that 'no proposal affecting the public health is more urgently needed or is more promising of improvement in national efficiency'.[32] The Board was congratulated on its stand in the *Journal of Mental Science* for showing 'a virility which would surprise a former generation of Commissioners' and for its 'bold policy and outspoken utterances of recent years'.[33]

Shortly, however, reconstruction was to be sacrificed to economic restraint and in 1921 its chief exponent, Addison, was dismissed by Lloyd George under Conservative pressure. Momentum was lost. There was no immediate new Mental Treatment Act, nor, despite the Report of the Maclean Committee in 1918, which substantially agreed with the Fabian Minority Report of the Royal Commission on the Poor Laws, was the Poor Law abolished in favour of positive preventive and curative services for the eradication of social distress. One lasting achievement was the creation of a Ministry of Health,

[29] Board of Control's response to the Reconstruction Committee, p. 7.
[30] Ibid., p. 8.
[31] See especially G. Baruch and A. Treacher, *Psychiatry Observed*, Chapter 4.
[32] *Annual Report of the Board of Control for the Year 1918*, p. 4.
[33] *Journal of Mental Science* 66 (1920), p. 289.

and the medical character of mental illness and its official categorization as a department of public health were underlined by the
subsequent transfer of primary accountability for the Board of
Control from the Home Office to the new Ministry. The campaign
for a Ministry of Health was pursued with vigour by Lord Rhondda as
President of the Local Government Board and Dr Addison as
Minister of Reconstruction. Kingsley Wood expressed a common
conviction when he declared that 'If the National Health Problem is
solved the golden masterkey to reconstruction is found',[34] and the
administrative rationalization of health departments and authorities
was seen as crucial if the solution was to be achieved. A Government
Bill to establish a Ministry of Health was announced in March 1918
and introduced by Addison in the following November. The Ministry
was created in 1919.

The Board of Control watched these developments anxiously with
an eye to its own future. The Board was jealous of its existing semi-
independence and declared itself to be satisfied with its relations with
the Home Office,[35] and with the Lord Chancellor, who were the
existing authorities to whom it owed particular responsibilities. The
Board had to decide whether to transfer its affiliation to a new
Ministry of Health or not, and the question was under active
discussion from late 1917. The dilemma was that on the one hand the
Board was committed to advancing the concept of insanity as a
species of disease and its legal, administrative, and therapeutic
assimilation to, and integration with, physical illness, but it also had a
responsibility for 'the liberty of the subject' and was partly legal in
composition. The former consideration suggested that it should
attach itself to the Ministry of Health, while the latter suggested that
the Home Office was the more appropriate location: 'The personal
qualifications still insisted on by the law indicate the intention to
maintain not a Board merely of medical experts but a quasi-judicial
tribunal dealing with the totality of the interests of the insane and the
mentally defective'.[36] Consistently with the movement away from
legalism and the Board's determination to destigmatize the treatment

[34] The *Observer*, 25 November 1917. He was presiding over a meeting of the Faculty
of Insurance, also addressed by Dr Addison.
[35] Letter of 16 July 1918 from Sir E. Marriott Cooke of the Board of Control to S.
W. Harris of the Home Office: Public Record Office, State Papers, Ministry of Health
51/631, File 60193/8/1.
[36] Memorandum of 14 March 1919 by Mr A. H. Trevor, a Legal Commissioner of
the Board of Control: Public Record Office, State Papers, Ministry of Health 51/631,
File 60193/8/1.

of the mentally disordered, the decision was taken to accept transfer to the Ministry of Health. This was effected by the Ministry of Health (Lunacy and Mental Deficiency Transfer of Powers) Order, which was approved by the House of Lords on 28 April 1920 and received the Royal Assent on 17 May. The effect was that the Ministry of Health took over most of the powers of the Home Office in relation to the Board of Control under the Lunacy Acts and the Mental Deficiency Act 1913. Henceforth it was the Minister of Health and not the Home Secretary who answered questions affecting the Board in Parliament.

Before his dismissal, Dr Addison, as the first Minister of Health, was able to introduce into the Commons a measure incorporating elements from the Board of Control's recommendations to the Reconstruction Committee. In August 1920, he presented the Ministry of Health (Miscellaneous Provisions) Bill, Clauses 10 and 11 of which dealt with mental disorder. Clause 10 provided that patients suffering from mental disorder incipient in character and of recent origin might be received in approved institutions and homes without certification. Clause 11 empowered local authorities to maintain institutions for this purpose. The effect of these clauses was strictly limited in scope, amounting merely to an extension of the voluntary boarder system, as the patient's consent in writing was to be a formal precondition of admission for treatment, in addition to two medical recommendations (later amended to one). For this reason it was critically received by the medical profession, being regarded as falling too far short of the proposals in the M.P.A.'s own report on the subject, adopted in 1918.[37] Addison himself was inclined to more radical reform: he voted for an amendment in Standing Committee which would have allowed the nearest relative's consent as a substitute for that of the patient, in effect extending the measure to non-volitionals.[38] However, there was fear of a legal backlash and, as it was, there were several speakers in the Parliamentary debate on the clauses who protested at the reduction in protection of the 'liberty of the subject', the inclusion of private profit-making houses as places of reception under the Bill, and the encroachment upon section 315 of the Lunacy Act, which forbade the reception of certifiable patients

---

[37] This was the report of its English Lunacy Legislation Subcommittee. For a summary of its recommendations, see *The Royal Commission on Lunacy and Mental Disorder: Minutes of Evidence*, Appendix XXIV: Memorandum of Evidence of the Medico-Psychological Association, p. 962.

[38] *Parliamentary Papers*, 1920, vii, p. 701.

for payment or otherwise without the safeguard of certification, and imposed criminal penalties for breach. Another medical criticism came from those who were afraid that the mental hospital would be excluded from the treatment of incipient cases and be assigned an ultra-custodial role within the emergent new institutional arrangements. There was some confusion as to the impact of Clause 10 in relation to the asylums.[39] The medical preference for a self-contained and more promising reform was aided in its realization when the Bill as a whole, having passed the House of Commons, was rejected in the House of Lords at Second Reading by fifty-seven votes to forty-one.

The next Bill to make any substantial progress was the 1923 Mental Treatment Bill, which passed the House of Lords. This was much more in accord with the aspirations of the medical profession. It was in outline similar to the Mental Treatment Bill, which acquired the force of law in 1930 but was less radical, most significantly in relation to the treatment of non-volitional patients without certification. The uncertainty of 1920 as to whether uncertified patients were to be institutionally and administratively segregated from certified patients was resolved by making it clear that voluntary and non-volitional patients would be in the charge of the existing lunacy authorities, including the Board of Control, and that, while there was room for local flexibility in the pattern of treatment facilities, there would be a major role for the existing mental hospitals. The reasons given for this policy position by A. H. Trevor, a Legal Commissioner of the Board of Control, to the Medico-Legal Society, were that members of the new categories would themselves frequently be certifiable and require similar medical facilities, that to appoint a parallel staff within the Ministry of Health alongside the Board of Control would be needless duplication, and that special local authority institutions for the beneficiaries of the new legal provisions were precluded by prevailing financial restraints. Finally, if the alternative course were adopted it was felt that 'the mental hospitals will inevitably tend to be looked upon as mere prisons, and the best medical men and the best nurses will not be attracted to the service'.[40] The decision of course safeguarded the continued involvement of the Board in the new trends of development, to the active prosecution of which, some argued, it had only belatedly been converted. The specific proposals

---

[39] See the letter from Sir Maurice Craig, 16 March 1921, *Journal of Mental Science* 67 (1921), pp. 267–8.

[40] A. H. Trevor, 'The Mental Treatment Bill 1923', *Transactions of the Medico-Legal Society* xvii (1922–3), p. 191.

contained in the Bill were to extend the powers of local authority Visiting Committees in respect of such matters as out-patient treatment and after-care; to reconstitute the Board of Control, reducing the number of Commissioners and easing their workload by allowing statutory responsibilities to be delegated to Inspectors; to provide for the treatment of psychiatric patients in general hospitals; to extend the principle of voluntary admission to public institutions, and to allow non-volitional patients to be treated without certification for up to six months, provided they were likely to benefit from temporary treatment, on the basis of two medical recommendations and a statement of expediency from a Justice of the Peace or Minister of Religion.

The Royal Commission on Lunacy and Mental Disorder 1924–6

It is clear that by 1924, regardless of the party in power, the reform of the lunacy laws was already firmly on the legislative agenda. However, the appointment of a Royal Commission to inquire into the question in that year was precipitated by further controversy about the adequacy of existing legal safeguards against illegal commitment generated by the celebrated case of *Harnett* v. *Bond*.[41] The action had been brought by an ex-patient seeking compensation for eight years' allegedly wrongful detention as a lunatic in various licensed houses. The defendants were not the original certifying doctors, but a Commissioner of the Board of Control and the manager of the original receiving institution, who had co-operated in cutting short a period of leave of absence on the ground that the patient was unfit to be at large. The jury found in Harnett's favour and awarded him no less than £25,000 in damages. The decision was naturally very disturbing of public confidence in the lunacy system, particularly as the jury specifically found a lack of good faith on the part of Dr C Hubert Bond (1870–1945), who was an eminent member of the psychiatric establishment, being both a medical Commissioner of the Board of Control and former President of the Medico-Psychological Association.[42] Furthermore, the trial judge followed the jury's verdict with a call for more legal safeguards in the procedures for civil commitment.

----

[41] [1924] 2 KB 517.
[42] The effect of this, along with a finding of lack of reasonable care on the part of both Dr Bond and the other defendant, Dr Adam, was to prevent their reliance upon the protection afforded by section 330 of the Lunacy Act 1890.

On appeal, the Court found unanimously in favour of the manager of the licensed house, Dr Adam, and in the case of Dr Bond, ordered a new trial to assess damages on the basis that technically his decision was only causally responsible for the illegal detention of the respondent for a period of a few hours. Nevertheless, the public impact of the outcome at first instance had been extraordinary. The *Justice of the Peace* recorded that:

The case of *Harnett* v. *Bond* has probably excited more attention than any civil action for many years past, and it has afforded the popular press unlimited scope for comment more or less ill-informed . . . there has been one particularly deplorable sequel to the trial, viz, the tendency to work up a kind of 'pogrom' against medical men who are associated with the care and treatment of the insane. The wildest charges have been flung about or at least hinted.[43]

This moral panic was reminiscent of that in the 1880s, prior to the Lunacy Acts Amendment Act. It produced a similar medical certification strike and prompted demands for an inquiry into the lunacy laws which was conceded in principle by the Government. After the judgment on appeal had been delivered, the immediate focus for public concern was removed and the press reduced to an 'abashed silence'.[44] But, on 25 July 1924, the Home Secretary, Arthur Henderson, announced the Labour Government's decision to appoint a Royal Commission. This response possessed the capacity not only to placate or reassure public opinion, but also to shift the centre of debate from the question of legal safeguards to that of early treatment, which was the established preoccupation at Government level. This intention was reflected in the Commission's terms of reference, which included an instruction to direct its deliberations to 'the extent to which provision is or should be made for the treatment without certification of persons suffering from mental disorder'.

The Royal Commission's membership was dominated by lawyers and so it is at first sight surprising that its conclusion should have been that the legalism of 1890 ought to be rejected, an apparent paradox to which we shall return in a later section. Its Chairman was the Rt. Hon. Hugh Pattison Macmillan, KC, LLD (1873–1952), later Baron Macmillan. Certainly, in terms of the politics of mental health

---

[43] *Justice of the Peace* 88 (1924), p. 180.
[44] Ibid., p. 332.

legislation, Macmillan, although a lawyer, was well suited to the task of modernizing the legal framework for psychiatric treatment and bringing it into harmony with the changing shape of social provision for the deviant and unproductive. His political philosophy was one of moderate interventionism and therefore in keeping with that of the major social reforms of the early twentieth century. He recognized that a significant transformation in the relationship of state and society had taken place, but was also watchful for the liberties of the individual.[45] Macmillan served as Lord Advocate for Scotland in the 1924 Labour Government but this did not reflect any partisan commitment: indeed, he had once stood as a Unionist Parliamentary candidate. In 1929–31 he chaired the Keynesian Treasury Committee on Finance and Industry[46] and in the 1930s, as a Law Lord, he was associated with Lord Atkin and Lord Wright in resisting Neo-Diceyist pressure for tighter judicial control over the executive, and in the creative development of private law precedents to accommodate changes in social conditions.[47] In the field of mental health legislation, Macmillan's political philosophy led him to oppose the legal formalism of 1890, but also to be careful to propose reforms which were moderate and would be acceptable to public opinion. This is particularly evident in the Commission's recommendation that the new Provisional Treatment Order, designed as an alternative form of commitment to full certification, should retain the participation of a magistrate, as not to do so would be too far in advance of existing public opinion, although he later changed his mind.[48] Macmillan's legal eminence was an important consideration in the legitimation of the movement away from the doctrine of the rule of law in this sphere, being called in aid by Arthur Greenwood, the Minister of Health, to try to persuade Colonel Josiah Wedgwood to

[45] See H. P. Macmillan, *Law and Other Things*. Cambridge: Cambridge University Press, 1938, Chapter 1.

[46] Much of the report was actually written by J. M. Keynes.

[47] B. Abel-Smith and R. B. Stevens, *Lawyers and the Courts*. London: Heinemann, 1967, p. 124.

[48] *Report of the Royal Commission on Lunacy and Mental Disorder*, p. 107. This recommendation was not followed when the Labour Government of 1929–31 designed its Temporary Treatment Order. By 1929–30, Macmillan's position was that public opinion had moved sufficiently far to justify the omission of the magistrate from the procedure, and so he agreed with the Government's decision: see the Memorandum by Peter Barter of the 3 December 1929: Public Record Office, State Papers, Ministry of Health 80/11, 1928–30 March, Mental Treatment Bill, Vol. 1.

abandon his disruptive Parliamentary opposition to the Mental Treatment Bill in 1930.[49]

Other legal members who served on the Commission were Earl Russell, who was professionally qualified as a barrister, but, as we have seen, was unswervingly committed to freeing mental health practitioners from legal restraint; William Jowitt (1885–1957), also a barrister, who became Attorney-General in the 1929–31 Labour Government which passed the Mental Treatment Act, and was Lord Chancellor in the 1945–51 Labour Government; F. D. Mackinnon (1871–1946), again a barrister, who had to resign in the first year of the Commission's work on his appointment as a High Court Judge; Nathaniel Micklem KC; Sir Thomas Hutchison JP, DL, LLD (1866–1925) and Sir Ernest Hiley (1868–1949), a solicitor who was a former Town Clerk of Leicester and Birmingham and had served as a Unionist MP. Even the two medical members also possessed legal qualifications. They were Sir David Drummond (1852–1932), Professor of Medicine at the University of Durham, a specialist in diseases of the brain and the nervous system, who had been President of the British Medical Association in 1921, and Sir Humphrey Rolleston (1862–1944), a man of great eminence within his profession who was President of the Royal Society of Medicine from 1918–22 and of the Royal College of Physicians from 1922–6, and in 1925 became Regius Professor of Physic at Cambridge. It is interesting to note that he was at one time President of the Eugenics Society. There were also two sitting MP's on the Commission. Eustace Percy (1887–1958) was Conservative member for Hastings. He had to resign from the Commission early in its deliberations to take up an appointment as President of the Board of Education, but was afforded a second opportunity to influence the course of the history of mental health legislation when in 1954, as Baron Percy of Newcastle, he was appointed Chairman of the Royal Commission preceding the Mental Health Act 1959. Henry Snell (1865–1944) was Labour member for East Woolwich. Like Earl Russell, although with the very different

[49] Greenwood wrote to Macmillan on 17 April 1930, after receiving a deputation of dissatisfied Labour MP's led by Wedgwood, who were anxious to reinsert the magistrate or at least some comparable lay figure, seeking his co-operation in dissuading the rebels from further disruption: 'Your views, of course came up and I explained that you supported what was in the Bill and had, in fact, discussed it with the Law Lords when the Bill was in the Lords.' Macmillan responded favourably to this request for assistance in persuading Wedgwood: Public Record Office, State Papers, Ministry of Health 80/11; 1928–30 March, Mental Treatment Bill, Vol. 1.

social background of an agricultural labourer and the disadvantage of illegitimacy, Snell was a Socialist, secularist, and Fabian.

The legally-dominated composition of the Royal Commission did not give the psychiatric profession much encouragement that it would recommend in favour of the relaxation of legal safeguards and give a green light to the expansion of psychiatric territory within the fields of early treatment and nervous disorders. Commenting on the Commission's Report in 1926, the *Journal of Mental Science* recalled that 'Few of us . . . were optimistic enough to expect the Commission to recommend a complete tergiversation on this subject as exemplified [in the "General Considerations of Policy"]'. Credit was given to Macmillan for 'the absence of that iron-bound legal conception of lunacy, which is the bane of the English lawyer'.[50] Perhaps they need not have been so pessimistic. The political shift in favour of greater interventionism favoured medical claims to be liberated from the constrictions of legalism. The two leading lawyers on the Commission, Macmillan and Jowitt, were not extreme traditionalists, but willing to serve as law officers in Labour Governments. Earl Russell was an extremist in favour of their cause, and there were no determined advocates of legalism on the Commission, as there had been in the case of the 1877 House of Commons Select Committee, in the persons of Thomas Dillwyn and Stephen Cave. The Commission was dominated by people who were likely to define their function as giving expression to what they perceived as an enlightened consensus linking increased state involvement in the social management of the problem of mental disorder with reasoning based upon the dominant medical view of insanity as analogous to physical disease. Certainly where the objectives of cure and liberty might conflict, Macmillan's guiding light was 'the public interest'.[51] There was no Josiah Wedgwood or Risien Russell[52] to challenge this view from within the Commission or produce a dissident report. The élite of the legal and medical professions shared a devotion to certain recognized rational modes of argument, to an official discourse, with which the very temper of the claims and demands of the critics of the lunacy system—emotional, sensational, rebellious—was in conflict. In taking evidence, the Commission attempted to adopt a position of tolerance toward the more strident critics of the mental health

[50] *Journal of Mental Science* 72 (1926), p. 598.
[51] See *Royal Commission on Lunacy and Mental Disorder: Minutes of Evidence*, II, Question 12,834.
[52] See p. 214 of the present work.

system, in particular the National Society for Lunacy Reform. However, the latter exhausted the Commission's patience by trying to convert the proceedings into something approaching a series of public trials of individual cases of alleged abuse. A statement was issued announcing that henceforth such cases would have to be heard in private. Not only had 'the ordeal of public examination' damaged the mental health of some of the ex-patients brought forward, but 'the procedure adopted had had the result of creating an atmosphere of controversy and recrimination' which could not be allowed to continue.[53] The Commission was therefore clearly intent upon purging its own proceedings of legalism as well as recommending a reaction against legal formalism in the structure of mental health legislation itself. It saw itself as playing an important part in advancing a supposedly enlightened, modern, informed, rationalist conception of mental disorder and its treatment, which could be obscured by the publicity that would inevitably be attracted if its proceedings were to become dominated by sensationalist allegations.

The Royal Commission rejected accusations that the existing system was prey to widespread abuses of liberty. Not one of the specific allegations of wrongful detention was found to be estab- lished. To have failed to unearth even one confirmed instance was such an absolute state of affairs that it must even have unnerved the Commission, but the powerful implication that once a patient was labelled insane and institutionalized there reigned a formidable presumption against his original mental fitness was not registered in its Report. On the subject of ill-treatment, one which 'has provoked more sensational publicity than perhaps any other aspect of lunacy administration'.[54] the Commission came down firmly on the side of the official stance that although there were isolated incidents which might be lessened by administrative reforms, the evidence did not justify a picture of deliberate or systematic abuse of patients by staff. An important consideration adduced in support of this conclusion was that at the time ex-patients who had given evidence had allegedly witnessed instances of ill-usage, they had themselves been in a mentally disordered state and so, whilst their evidence could not be discounted, it had to be treated with some scepticism. The Commis- sion took the view that:

A perusal of the evidence before us . . . will reveal the large number of cases

---

[53] *Royal Commission on Lunacy and Mental Disorder: Minutes of Evidence*, I, p. 531.
[54] *Report of the Royal Commission on Lunacy and Mental Disorder*, para. 209.

in which the witness testified to ill-usage which he had seen meted out to others rather than to anything which he had suffered himself; and in matters of this kind it is impossible to overlook the probability that a patient, who is *ex hypothesi* of disordered mentality, may misinterpret what he sees happening to other persons.[55]

It is ironic that the opposite view—that while mental patients were unreliable in recounting what had happened to themselves, they could be trusted in their testimonies regarding others—had been taken in the proceedings of the 1877 Select Committee.

The Commission went further, however, than simply to endorse the essentials of the status quo, as that Committee had done. Instead it proposed the radical change in the whole philosophy of legal provision examined in the last chapter. In these circumstances, the National Society for Lunacy Reform was forced to console itself with the comment that although the Report 'has been hailed in some quarters as a vindication of the present system, and to the casual reader it may appear so, . . . when critically examined, it is found that drastic changes in every department of lunacy law and administration are recommended.'[56] The problem for the Society was that these recommended changes were based upon confidence in the system and the conviction that certain traditional legal safeguards were largely unnecessary and counterproductive.

The Recommendations of the Royal Commission

The consensus of witnesses in favour of some relaxation of the restrictions on psychiatry embodied in the Lunacy Act 1890 was impressive—even the National Society for Lunacy Reform, despite its legalistic ethos, expressed itself under questioning to be in favour of the BMA's proposal for a Provisional Order, of voluntary admission to public mental hospitals, and of treatment of mental patients in special wards of general hospitals.[57] The Provisional Treatment Order was envisioned as retaining the judicial element, and voluntarism provided a bridge between the libertarians and the medical profession. The Commission sought to reproduce the direction of this consensus in its recommendations, which were

[55] Id.
[56] *Report of the National Society for Lunacy Reform*, 1926, p. 1.
[57] See *Royal Commission on Lunacy and Mental Disorder: Minutes of Evidence*, I, Answers 10,479, 10,500 *et seq.*, 10,601.

similar in character to the strategy of recent Mental Treatment Bills, and which vindicated and invigorated the Board of Control.

The Commission recommended that the Board of Control remain under the auspices of the Ministry of Health, retaining its semi-independent status, but that it be streamlined and given new executive powers. The Commission recognized that much criticism had been directed against the Board but concluded that it was largely ill-informed and that where there were justifiable grounds for dissatisfaction 'the cause is to be found rather in defects in the existing system than in any want of zeal on the part of the members of the Board'.[58] The Commission thought that the new categories of non-certified patient should be subject to the Board of Control: to create separate new machinery for them within the Ministry of Health would be 'unscientific'. It was proposed that the Board of Control should be able to report defaulting local authorities to the Ministry of Health rather than see its advice flouted, and that it should be given detailed rule-making powers over institutions.[59] To improve the Board's ability to cope with its workload it was recommended that a rump of four Commissioners would be stationed in the Metropolis and permanently available to deal with complaints and matters of concern in lunacy administration, whilst fifteen peripatetic Assistant Commissioners would take over duties of visitation.

The Commission also pleased medical practitioners, not only because of its general reaction against legalism, but more specifically by responding to their fears of legal reprisals from aggrieved patients fuelled by the Harnett litigation. Doctors argued that Section 330 of the Lunacy Act 1890 gave them inadequate protection against such actions and were critical of section 315 of the Act which imposed penalties for the treatment of certifiable cases without certification. The Commission was prepared to recommend that public sector voluntary treatment and temporary treatment without certification be legalized, and to suggest that the form of the continuation certificate be amended to allow the retention of patients who would not be certifiable if their case were examined *de novo* by a magistrate.[60] However, the medical profession's demand for full witness status in certification proceedings, with the attendant absolute immunity in the absence of *mala fides*, was found unaccep-

[58] *Report of the Royal Commission on Lunacy and Mental Disorder*, para. 263.
[59] Ibid., para. 265.
[60] Ibid., para. 163.

table. Macmillan made the more limited concession of shifting the onus of proof in the action to stay proceedings against medical practitioners for performing their responsibilities under lunacy legislation, and that the burden upon the plaintiff should be one of establishing 'substantial grounds' rather than simply a prima-facie case.[61]

Macmillan recommended both a reform of the existing procedures of certification and the introduction of procedures for treatment without certification. A uniform procedure was recommended for private and pauper cases.[62] This was designed so that the latter would benefit from a requirement for two medical recommendations and the order of a specifically constituted judicial authority, as for private cases under the Lunacy Act 1890, section 10. The former would gain the advantage of the right to be seen by the Justice, previously only conceded to pauper patients as an automatic incident of certification proceedings. It was also urged that mental treatment be divorced from the Poor Law.[63] As there was still an inadequacy of institutional facilities with a moderate level of fees, many who could in fact afford to reimburse the authorities in whole or in part were forced to resort to public asylums and up to this time were technically pauperized. The so-called 'stigma of pauperism' had thus become firmly attached to these institutions.[64]

Admission as a voluntary patient was to be permitted by written application and without medical recommendation. The Board of Control would provide supervision and voluntary patients should be free to leave at will subject to giving seventy-two hours' notice. It was also suggested that minors should be accepted as 'voluntary' patients without their consent, application being made by the parent or guardian, especially to promote the early treatment of instability in adolescents who 'often prove quite intractable to home discipline' and 'ultimately appear in court as young offenders'.[65] The Commission also proposed a major change in relation to the admission of involuntary patients. They recommended the introduction of a new compulsory procedure, falling short of full certification, to be entitled the Provisional Treatment Order. As we have seen, it was reluctantly concluded that it would be too far in advance of public

[61] Ibid., para. 90.
[62] Ibid., para. 73.
[63] Ibid., para. 75.
[64] Ibid., paras. 73–4.
[65] Ibid., paras. 96, 106.

opinion to dispense with judicial participation in this procedure and so the requirement of a Justice's order for involuntary admission was preserved.[66] The order was to be obtained by a relative, friend, or public official on petition, supported by just one medical recommendation. The significant difference from certification was that the patient would not be designated 'of unsound mind and a fit person to be detained': it would simply be stated that the patient's mental condition made it expedient for his or her own welfare or that of the public that he or she be detained under observation, care, and treatment. The initial order was to authorize detention for a period of one month, subject to renewal for a further maximum period of five months. Renewal would require a second judicial order, based upon medical recommendation that the patient had a reasonable prospect of recovery within that time and that it was expedient that he or she remain under care. This alternative procedure was designed for patients with a prognosis of early recovery in the hope that resort to psychiatric assistance in such cases would be expedited by the availability of a new means of admission free of the stigma of certification as a person of unsound mind.[67] Macmillan's scheme did not contain a specific admission procedure for non-volitional patients. New emergency procedures of seven days, one on the basis of one medical certificate and one on the authority of the relieving officer to replace the three-day provision under the Lunacy Act 1890, section 20, were also recommended.[68]

To some extent the Commission's conclusions legitimated and regularized practices already adopted within the lunacy system. Section 315 of the 1890 Act and the criminal penalties laid down for treating certifiable patients without certification or other legal authority could be circumvented by admitting as voluntary boarders to licensed houses or registered hospitals patients who lacked genuine volition.[69] Further, the Board of Control was becoming more amenable to tacit authorization of the treatment of certifiable patients without certification.[70] The administrators of the lunacy system had also managed to clear paths through the jungle of complex and confusing legislative procedures to treat short-term

[66] Ibid., para. 107.
[67] Id.
[68] Ibid., para. 111.
[69] *Report of the Royal Commission on Lunacy and Mental Disorder*, para. 99. See also the *Royal Commission on Lunacy and Mental Disorder: Minutes of Evidence*, II, Question 15,860 *et seq.*: Professor Robertson.
[70] Ibid., I, Answers 5,749–50: Dr Henry Yellowlees.

patients compulsorily without invoking the certification process.[71] In evidence, the Royal Commission was told that combinations of various powers were being employed in a series to create an 'observation period' in the workhouse which could last for as long as twenty-three days: the relevant provisions were sections 14, 19, 20, 21, and 24 of the 1890 Act, which distributed a mosaic of detentionary powers amongst relieving officers, medical officers of workhouses, and Justices. Indeed, a period of up to sixty days could be accumulated by obtaining the relatives' consent if the patient did not actively resist at the expiry of the period collected under the Lunacy Acts. The Commission considered some of the methods by which this *de facto* observation period was achieved to be of dubious legality, but it is symptomatic of its attitude to legal formality generally that instead of censoring the practitioners of this system of evasion it sought to formalize it by the introduction of the Provisional Treatment Order as a period of observation and treatment to promote a high rate of discharge prior to certification.[72] Invocation of this new procedure would allow patients to be detained for an initial period of one month without resort to the irregular manipulation of statutory powers, and would transfer the location of detention from the workhouse to a clinical setting, as would the assimilation of the emergency procedure for rate-aided patients to that for private patients.

On the subject of discharge, the Commission, consistently with its general position, refused to agree to judicialization, shifting the major responsibility to a Justice of the Peace on the basis that detention itself was ordered by the Justice, as proposed amongst others by the National Society for Lunacy Reform. It actually proposed to reduce the anyway infrequently invoked lay power to discharge, vested in the Visiting Committee of the local authority, by requiring that if this was to be exercised contrary to medical advice, the responsibility should be taken by the whole Committee and not by its representatives who had taken the initiative in a particular case.[73] The Commission's strong preference for medical over legal criteria is well illustrated by its justification of the recommendation that discharge of certified patients should depend not upon recovery

---

[71] See *Report of the Royal Commission on Lunacy and Mental Disorder*, para. 94. See also in the *Minutes of Evidence*, the evidence of Dr E. J. Lidbetter, President of the National Association of Relieving Officers, and of Dr A. L. Baly of Lambeth Infirmary.

[72] See ibid., Question 2739.

[73] *Report of the Royal Commission on Lunacy and Mental Disorder*, paras. 148–9.

merely to the point of non-certifiability, but upon a medically defined restoration of the ability to 'face the world with a reasonable chance of avoiding a further breakdown':

Legally, no doubt, it would be improper to deprive a subject of his liberty merely because it is advantageous to his health, but this is a point at which the legal and medical views must be accommodated in the light of the welfare of the individual and of the public interest. Purely legal criteria are not appropriate in this sphere. We are dealing with a stage in the patient's recovery where the medical issues are most delicately balanced, and we consider that the medical man must be trusted with a reasonable measure of latitude.[74]

To accommodate some of the 'incipient' and mild cases for whom the new categories of admission were designed, the Commission recommended changes in the pattern of institutional provision. Here the objective of the Commission was detachment from the demeaning association of the Poor Law and variegation so that the gateway to treatment was not also a gateway to the stigma of the asylum. The solution of rigidly demarcated institutional sectors exclusively catering for particular *legal* classifications of patient was rejected. The emphasis instead was upon separate accommodation for early cases. Thus, separate admission units in mental hospitals, an obligation upon local authorities to provide reception houses for Provisional Treatment Order and emergency cases separately from general Poor Law institutions, and the creation of residential and out-patient clinics, preferably attached to general hospitals and modelled on venereal disease and tuberculosis services, were all itemized as desiderata of the new mental health regime.[75] Local authorities, it was felt, should also be the beneficiaries of new powers in relation to after-care.

The question of licensed houses was still controversial. On 1 January 1924 there were 130,334 recorded lunatics of whom the great majority, 103,892, were detained under certificate in public asylums; only 3,797 of the remainder were accommodated in licensed houses.[76] The major tendency in the distribution of institutional provision in the interval since the passage of the Lunacy Act 1890 had been the relative decline of the private sector. The decline of the licensed house as an element in this sector had naturally been

[74] Ibid., para. 162.
[75] Ibid., paras. 112–13, 248.
[76] *Annual Report of the Board of Control for the Year 1924.*

hastened by the legal disabilities which had been imposed upon it at the height of legalism, whereby the number of licences was to remain static and annual renewal of each licence became necessary. In 1890 there had been eighty-seven licensed houses, in 1914 this had shrunk to sixty-eight and by 1924 only fifty-five survived. Nevertheless, there was evidence of a continuing demand for these institutions, and the eclipse envisaged by Parliament in 1889 had not occurred. The Royal Commission was irreconcilably divided into two camps on the future of licensed houses. On the one hand there were those who saw proprietorial institutions run for profit as satisfying an expanding public demand and wanted the embargo imposed by the Lunacy Act 1890, section 207 repealed. On the other were those who believed that the conflict of interest and duty involved created such temptations and generated so much public suspicion that this form of provision should be excluded from the system in future. No section of the Commission wanted to retain the arbitrary compromise of 1889. Practical proposals were mapped out for each course which the Government might adopt, but the Commission was not prepared to advise further.[77]

The issue of licensed houses, however, was really a distraction from the main preoccupations of the Commission. It was an aspect of the problem of 'the liberty of the subject' and the security of the sane which had dominated discussion in the late nineteenth century. Macmillan and his colleagues were concerned with what they perceived as the social problem of mental illness itself, and with identifying the essentials of a new model of legal framework which would promote an effective mental treatment system.

The Mental Treatment Act 1930

The lapse of four years between the publication of the Macmillan Report and the enactment of some of its main recommendations is explained by the radicalism and administrative complexity of certain of its proposals, notably the procedural unification of the regimes for private and rate-aided patients and the extrication of the latter from the Poor Law; by the controversiality of moving away from formal legal safeguards or altering the law on licensed houses given the excited state of public opinion, and by the general lack of legislative priority accorded to mental health questions. Despite pressure from

---

[77] *Report of the Royal Commission on Lunacy and Mental Disorder*, para. 242.

Earl Russell, who in late February 1927 put down a Parliamentary motion calling attention to the Royal Commission's Report and asking whether legislation was planned, the 1924–9 Conservative Government did not make time for it. However, the Local Government Act 1929, section 104 did increase the responsibility upon local authorities to provide public health services, defined to include lunacy and mental deficiency services.

With the arrival of the second minority Labour Government, substantial progress was achieved. But it was the relatively modest measure which reorganized the Board of Control, opened up public mental hospitals to voluntary patients, and provided a new temporary treatment order, and which had been gestating within the Board since the First World War, that finally emerged so far as to be submitted to Cabinet. Again, it was Earl Russell who urged a more ambitious measure, assimilating certification procedures for private and rate-aided patients and completing the separation of public psychiatric provision from the machinery and institutions of the Poor Law and the transfer of responsibility for licensed houses outside the Metropolitan area from the Justices to the Board of Control.[78] But comprehensive implementation of Macmillan would have constituted 'a first class Government measure raising some acutely controversial issues'[79] and so the Mental Treatment Bill concentrated upon certain key amendments with a view to 'the maximum' of accomplishment 'with the minimum of controversy'.[80]

The ideological appeal of the measure to Labour, as the most advanced of the major parties in its commitment to social reform and therefore the sanctuary of progressive fugitives from Liberalism such as Addison, can be gauged from the terms in which it was commended to the Home Affairs Committee of the Cabinet by Arthur Greenwood, the new Minister of Health. It was pointed out that the Macmillan Commission had itself been appointed by the last Labour Government, that the Bill would rationalize and modernize mental health administration, complete the extrication of rate-aided patients from the Poor Law, and promote egalitarianism by

[78] Note of a meeting between Arthur Greenwood, Minister of Health, and Earl Russell, 19 July 1929: Public Record Office, State Papers, Ministry of Health 51/568, Board of Control File No. 60160/8.
[79] Peter Barter's Memorandum for the Board of Control on the debate in the House of Lords on Earl Russell's motion: Public Record Office, State Papers, Ministry of Health 51/640, Board of Control File No. 60232/1.
[80] *House of Commons Debates* 235, col. 970 (23 December 1929).

extending voluntarism to 'the poorer classes'.[81] At the same time, the safeguards attendant upon the new procedures for voluntary and temporary treatment, including, for example, the application of all the lunacy law safeguards relating to discharge, had to be stressed to persuade the Government that the reform was politically possible. None the less, the enduring controversiality of the provision enabling temporary treatment without certification is apparent from the fact that it was held in reserve in the early stages of preparation of the Bill for presentation to Parliament on the ground that it would be better to wait until public opinion was prepared for such a procedure without the intervention of a magistrate than to settle for a compromise provision in the short term.[82]

In the course of the development of the Bill out of the Royal Commission's Report, the Board of Control had actively engaged in converting public opinion and attempting to counterbalance virulent attacks upon itself concerning the conduct of the lunacy system generally and any substantial proposed reduction in legal safeguards. In this last respect the active support of Macmillan, as one of the country's foremost lawyers, was valuable, as was that of George Robertson of the Hartwood, Lanark Asylum in promoting English appreciation of the apparently smooth operation of more informal and flexible legal procedures in the Scottish system. In addition, there was the useful influence of the National Council for Mental Hygiene, the Central Association for Mental Welfare, and other centres of 'enlightened' as opposed to 'vulgar' public opinion. But there were three main centres of opposition which had to be confronted: the 'liberty of the subject' critics, led by the National Society for Lunacy Reform and Colonel Josiah Wedgwood, who were never reconciled; the doctors, who were determined to extract greater legal immunity than that recommended by Macmillan, with whom a concordat was eventually arrived at; and the local authorities in the form of the County Councils Association led by Sir William Hodgson, a strident critic of the Board of Control, who were anxious about the imposition of duties to provide new services and whose responsibilities did in the event involve considerable discretion.

---

[81] Arthur Greenwood, Minister of Health, Memorandum to the Home Affairs Committee on the reform of lunacy legislation, November 1929, Public Record Office, State Papers, Ministry of Health 51/568, Board of Control File No. 60160/8.

[82] Letter of 17 April 1929 from Peter Barter to Laurence Brock, Public Record Office, State Papers, Ministry of Health 51/568, Board of Control File No. 60160/8.

Although it was not the 'new complete code' advised by Macmillan, the Bill introduced by Earl Russell in the House of Lords in November 1929 was still a radical measure. It supplemented the old legislation, making available a simple counter-system of new procedures which, as the hoped-for first resort of the authorities, would neutralize it and frustrate its perceived worst ill-effects. The Bill did contain those measures regarded as essential to remodel the lunacy system as a medical service. Looking in detail at its provisions it was entitled a Bill to reorganize the Board of Control, which it did by broadly implementing the recommendations of the Commission on this subject, although the Government was in favour of more control of the Board by the Ministry of Health.[83] Accordingly, unpaid Commissioners were no longer made eligible for appointment,[84] a measure of professionalization which met with some Conservative opposition. The Board of Control was also given powers to make rules respecting the new categories of voluntary and temporary patients.[85] This concentration on the reorganization of the Board as the centre-piece of the Bill was politically inastute, as the Board was the most hated element in the lunacy system in the eyes of its critics, having been described, amongst many other things, according to a regretful Minister of Health, as 'a Star Chamber, a body of mysterious far distant persons . . . whose sole object . . . appeared to be to "put away" . . . the largest possible number of British subjects'.[86]

Although the ideal of uniform procedures for private and rate-aided patients had to be sacrificed, the removal of the pauper stigma had already been partly achieved by other legislation. The Local Government Act 1929, a product of Neville Chamberlain's brand of Conservative social reform, with its emphasis upon administrative rationalization, did not abolish the Poor Law outright, but moved substantially toward the position of the 1905–9 Royal Commission by replacing Boards of Guardians with Public Assistance Committees, abolishing the Poor Rate, and officially dispensing with the term 'pauper'. The Mental Treatment Act built upon this foundation. Under section 18(1) patients receiving rate support were not to be deemed to be in receipt of Poor Relief and deprived of rights or

---

[83] Mental Treatment Act 1930, sections 11–15.
[84] Mental Treatment Act 1930, section 11(7)(i).
[85] Mental Treatment Act 1930, section 15.
[86] *Report of the Proceedings of a Conference on Mental Treatment*, 1930, Address by Arthur Greenwood, Minister of Health, p. 99.

privileges.[87] Section 20 purged Poor Law terminology from the lunacy system, pauper patients being designated 'rate-aided', and section 19(1) provided that rate-aided patients liable to be removed to a workhouse under sections 20, 21, 24, and 25 of the Lunacy Act could be taken instead to a local authority hospital.[88] The chronological coincidence and substantive interrelationship of the Mental Treatment Act and the Local Government Act 1929 underlines the importance for an understanding of the reform of lunacy legislation of its links with the Poor Law and of the political transformation in the late nineteenth and early twentieth century which produced the impetus towards the disavowal of the principles of 1834.

In the case of admissions, the aim was to provide the mass of the people with access to psychiatric treatment 'without the stigma of judicial interference, fear of which often causes unconscious conspiracies of delay by relatives with disastrous results for patients'.[89] Section 1 authorized the voluntary admission to public mental institutions of persons 'desirous of voluntarily submitting [themselves] to treatment for mental illness'. Two formalities, however, were attached to this facility: the patient had to make a written application, and notice of his reception had to be supplied to the Board of Control. Seventy-two hours' notice of self-discharge was required. These provisions were more far-reaching than those in the Earl of Onslow's unsuccessful Mental Treatment Bill of 1923, which had required two medical recommendations for admission as a voluntary patient and stipulated a forty-eight hour period of notice for self-discharge. Section 1(2) incorporated a 'voluntary' form of admission for minors, following the recommendations in the Royal Commission's Report. Under this provision, a person below the age

---

[87] The Representation of the People Act 1918 had already abolished disqualification of those in receipt of Poor Relief from the franchise, and, by section 10(1), the Local Government Act 1929 removed their disqualification from the membership of local authorities. The purpose of the Mental Treatment Act provision was to make clear that rate-aided mental patients were to be exempt from any residual discrimination.

[88] This provision was motivated by the concern that Poor Law infirmaries appropriated by local authorities as public health hospitals under section 5 of the Local Government Act would technically cease to be workhouses and so the accommodation into which such patients could lawfully be received would suffer a reduction. Section 17 facilitated a similar relocation of rate-aided patients by extending to them the urgency order for private patients under section 11 of the 1890 Act.

[89] Peter Barter's memorandum of 3 December 1929 on Clause 5 of the Bill: Public Record Office, State Papers, Ministry of Health 80/11, 1928–30 March, Mental Treatment Bill, Vol. 1.

of sixteen could be detained on the written application of the parent or guardian, which provided the consent enabling the patient to be described as voluntary.

The second major innovation, perceived as central to the Act, was the provision in section 5 for 'Temporary treatment without Certification'. Contrary to the scheme for admission proposed by Macmillan, these procedures applied specifically to a new category of 'non-volitional' patients who, in the words of the section, were 'incapable of expressing [themselves] as willing or unwilling to receive [temporary] treatment'. Also contrary to the Commission's advice was the exclusion of the Justice from the temporary admission process and the substitution of a second medical recommendation. The official justification for this was that the Commission's proposed Provisional Treatment Order was too close to full certification to be of value. The Bill had initially stipulated a maximum of six months' detention as a temporary patient, but during its Parliamentary passage that maximum was extended, subject to certain safeguards, to one year. In dispensing with the Justice, the Act went further than either the Commission or the 1923 Bill. The formulation of the type of patient for whom the order was designed represented an amalgam of two conceptually distinct groups: those who had a prognosis of early recovery and those who were not actively resistant, but none the less unable to consent to treatment. Here the Act was less radical than the Commission's Report, as the Provisional Treatment Order was to apply to resistant cases as well, while the statutory reform reserved the principle that such cases should be certified and invoke the decision of a Justice. The Parliamentary debates reveal real confusion on all sides as to what types of patient were to be considered 'non-volitional', and, as we shall see, once the Bill became law the section was little used, so that in practice voluntary admission became the main alternative to certification.

As well as reforming the admission procedures, the Act imposed new duties and devolved new powers upon local authorities. Section 6(1) imposed a duty to provide accommodation for the reception of temporary patients. Ministers stressed, however, in the light of the financial situation, that most envisaged temporary patients would otherwise be certified or under local authority care anyway, falling within existing duties under the Lunacy Acts and the Local Government Act. They also stressed that Poor Law institutions transferred from Boards of Guardians to local authorities under the Local Government Act would present opportunities to provide separate accommodation for early cases.[90] Although segregation on the basis of legal status was regarded as reactionary,[91] the possibilities of separate treatment for these cases helped to legitimate the measure in the eyes of critics who opposed the Board of Control and the administration of existing mental hospitals. Section 6(3) additionally authorized local authorities to make arrangements for the establishment of out-patient clinics, to engage in after-care, and support research, as the Royal Commission had recommended.

Significantly greater protection against legal actions by aggrieved former mental patients was extended to those responsible for operating the compulsory procedures by section 16 of the Act. The Mental Treatment Act introduced reforms both of procedure and of substance: the mechanism of protection by stay of proceedings was replaced by an obligation upon the plaintiff to obtain leave from the High Court before commencing the action and the standard of proof was raised from reasonable to substantial grounds for the allegation of misconduct. This strengthening of the medical profession's legal position was consistent with the Act's presupposition that the state should place its trust in doctors rather than design legislation on the suspicious assumption that they were likely to make improper use of their powers. Finally, changes were made in official terminology to reflect the desired curative, medical reorientation of the lunacy system: 'asylum' was replaced by 'mental hospital', and 'pauper lunatic' by a 'rate-aided' person or patient 'of unsound mind'.[92]

[90] See Arthur Greenwood, *House of Commons Debates* 237, col. 2554 (11 April 1930).
[91] See Susan Lawrence, *House of Commons Debates* 237, col. 2578 (11 April 1930).
[92] The Mental Treatment Act 1930, Section 20.

7 The Mental Treatment Act 1930: III Medical, Legal, and Political Alignments

The Medical Profession

ONE factor in the reversal of legalism in mental treatment legislation in the 1920s was the increasing prestige and influence of the medical profession. Kathleen Jones contends that after 1845 the movement for further lunacy reform became an affair of unequal pressure groups, the rise of the medical and social work professions accounting for the decline of the legal approach in the early and mid-twentieth century.[1] David Ewins also cites 'the increasing prestige of medicine as a result of scientific developments and increasing professionalization, and the increasing prominence of medical pressure groups' as influential in the reformulation of legislative policy.[2] Certainly the medical profession had gained credit for taming the epidemic disease of smallpox and cholera which had plagued Victorian society and its professional organization as a source of pressure on government had recently been improved in the battle to exact concessions in relation to the National Insurance Act 1911.[3] There was also greater medical unity on the issue of the reform of lunacy legislation in the 1920 than in the 1880s. The psychiatric speciality having won increased credibility with the profession as a whole, there were fewer of the acrimonious exchanges which had punctuated communications between psychiatric and non-psychiatric practitioners in the period before 1890. However, an examination of the content of medical organizations' demands emphasizes the importance of the political context within which they were advanced: the Macmillan Commission and the 1929–31 Labour Government did not defer to the medical profession in recognition of its status so much as move beyond medical demands in key respects in the enthusiastic pursuit of a positive mental health strategy.

[1] K. Jones, *A History of the Mental Health Services*, p. 153.
[2] D. Ewins, p. 36.
[3] See H. Eckstein, *Pressure Group Politics*. London: Allen and Unwin, 1960, and F. Honigsbaum, *The Division in British Medicine*. London: Kogan Page, 1979.

The demands of the MPA and the similar proposals of the BMA to the Macmillan Commission had been framed against a background of pessimism as to what Parliament would countenance in terms of increased medical control of detentionary powers in the face of supposedly hostile public and professional legal opinion. The legal aspect of the psychiatric strategy for desegregation and expansion beyond the asylum in alliance with general medicine and welfare was *not* therefore one of demanding a major transfer to medical men of formal coercive powers (as was to happen in 1959 with the abolition of the magistrates' intervention in commitment), but to press for the maximum informalization of admissions and the derestriction of the conditions and facilities in which psychiatrists were legally permitted to work.

The MPA's position in the 1920s rested essentially upon the recommendations of its Status of British Psychiatry Committee, appointed in 1911, which were reinforced by the Report in 1918 of its English Lunacy Legislation Subcommittee. At the end of the First World War the Association saw an opportunity to redouble its efforts to extend the legal scope for treatment of incipient insanity without certification in the new climate engendered by the public impact of the plight of shell-shock cases,[4] and 'the ferment of reconstruction in the air, particularly as regards questions of health' so that it 'would be ready to direct and support any measures of reform that might be proposed'.[5] The prime demand of the MPA was the establishment of clinics for mental disorders to be associated with general hospitals, universities, and medical schools, and which would provide for the early treatment of mental illness and constitute centres for education and research. Clinics would provide psychiatrists with the outlet for claimed preventive and curative skills which could not be turned to good effect within an antiquated asylum system overloaded with chronic cases and primarily devoted to custodial and control functions. Although its witnesses before the Commission tended to stress the issue of the clinic strongly in their oral evidence, it was a highly controversial one within the Association itself, some taking the view that greater emphasis should be placed upon the hospitalization of the asylum. An editorial in the *Journal of Mental Science* in 1926 characterized the split as follows:

---

[4] *Royal Commission on Lunacy and Mental Disorder: Minutes of Evidence*, II, Answer 16,636.
[5] *Journal of Mental Science* 66 (1920), p. 338.

In the one view, the public mental hospital was to be a back number in regard to the treatment of early and possibly curable cases (a minority view). In the other, the public mental hospital was to undergo more and more hospitalization, both structurally and administratively, and all cases of mental disorder as far as possible were to be admitted there direct, or, if this was not in the majority of cases practicable, through the medium of special receiving houses. In the former view psychiatric departments or special psychiatric institutions attached to voluntary general hospitals and infirmaries, especially such as were teaching schools of medicine, were to receive and deal with all recent and possibly curable cases. There were views within these views, and these two standpoints had many and diverse ramifications. . . . The great majority of members, however, found themselves in agreement with the broad proposals set forth in the Association's *Précis* of Evidence before the Royal Commission, in which most of the contending views were so adjusted as to form a really practical scheme sufficiently plastic as to be applicable in principle to the varying needs of different localities and districts. There still remained, however, some extremists in the two main directions . . . unreconciled and unsatisfied.[6]

This probably understated support for the relegation of the mental hospital as the *Journal's* own editorial policy appears to have been to support the second view described.[7]

The Association did not seek powers of detention in clinics.[8] It had been assumed since 1911 that such an objective was unrealistic without accepting the judicial authority which would be counterproductive.[9] Rather, voluntary and non-volitional cases would simply be 'retained', subject to the qualification that if they wished to leave they would have to give seventy-two hours' notice. Admission would depend upon one medical recommendation and notice of admission would have to be given to the Board of Control within twenty-four hours. The new procedure would authorize six months' stay. As detention was not at stake, judicial involvement was omitted. This proposal for largely informalizing the admission of non-volitional patients was a radical one. The subsequent mental treatment legislation in its final form provided for the detention of non-volitional patients under the new Temporary Treatment Order. It was only with section 5 of the Mental Health Act 1959 that such

[6] *Journal of Mental Science* 72 (1926), pp. 607–8.
[7] *Journal of Mental Science* 67 (1921), pp. 55–6.
[8] Although there was some confusion on this matter amongst the Association's representatives when giving oral evidence to the Royal Commission.
[9] *Royal Commission on Lunacy and Mental Disorder: Minutes of Evidence*, II, Answer 16,757.

patients could be admitted without formal powers of detention being invoked.

On the question of detention itself, however, as already indicated, the MPA's position was a conservative and cautious one. Radicals had pressed for a proposal to abolish magisterial control over commitment to be adopted as part of the recommendations to Macmillan, but were unsuccessful.[10] Pessimism was reinforced by the Atkin Committee's rejection of the Association's proposals for the supersession of the M'Naghten Rules in 1923, the Harnett furore in 1924, and the appointment of a legally-dominated Royal Commission which followed. The MPA conveyed to the Commission the view that 'the authority for detention, discharge and continuation orders should entail the responsibility of some authorized person not acting in a medical capacity'.[11] In oral evidence on the subject of certification its representatives conceded that 'insanity' was a legal and not a medical category and that the role of doctors was to provide the medical evidence upon which a legal decision could be reached:[12] 'We want to get away from the medical man expressing an opinion as to insanity. Our field is to express the fact that (the patient) is suffering from a mental disorder.'[13] The MPA's proposed procedure for commitment to menal hospital short of certification as of unsound mind accompanied by a Justice's order was modest both in terms of duration and the retention of judicial participation. The projected 'Provision Order' specified the patient to be in need of 'temporary care, observation and treatment' and did not actually mention the word 'detention' although this was intended to be its effect. The order was not to be restricted to cases of urgency and was to be valid for an initial three days, after which the authority of a Justice or two members of the Visiting Committee of a public asylum was to be necessary to extend it for a further period of twenty-eight days. This was basically a compulsory observation order, intermediate between emergency procedures and full certification, anticipating section 25 of the Mental Health Act 1959. The Association was actually in favour of strengthening the judicial character of the procedure for admission via certification: the certifying Justice should always be a

[10] Ibid., II, Appendix XXIV: Memorandum of Evidence of the MPA, p. 963.
[11] Ibid., II, p. 962.
[12] The Association had been rebuffed by the Atkin Committee on Insanity and Crime on account of its failure to appreciate this distinction in the criminal sphere: see p. 218 of the present work.
[13] *Royal Commission on Lunacy and Mental Disorder: Minutes of Evidence*, II, Answer 16,910.

specially appointed 'judicial authority', at that time only a requirement in private cases, and he should always see the patient, at that
time only a requirement in pauper cases.

The psychiatrists stressed the principle of voluntary admission
wherever possible. This promoted assimilation to the norms of
general medicine with which they were so anxious to form increasing
links. They obviously felt that a substantial improvement in access to
the various categories of disorders encompassed by the notions of
incipiency and recoverability could be achieved by voluntarism and
the retention of non-volitional cases in psychiatric clinics. The MPA's
position can also be interpreted as representing what has been
described earlier as the conservative legal strategy for medicalizing
the psychiatrist's role: that is, surrendering legal powers over patients
to judicial authorities or the family as a way of emphasizing their
professional healing function and negating their gaoling, control
functions. In the justification of their position, there were explicit
references to the contradiction between the roles of gaoling and
healing and psychiatrists' desire to resolve these by persuading the
legislature to cede their detentionary powers to other agencies. One
of the MPA's witnesses before the Macmillan Commission, Dr Cole,
in answer to the Chairman's question: 'Are you not the best judges of
abnormality?' replied:

We admit that we want to dissociate psychiatry from the position, as it were,
of being a governor of a prison; in other words, we want to state what the
patient is suffering from and treat that, and if it is necessary for the patient to
be detained for that purpose, then we think some person other than the
medical authority ought to step in and say: This person ought to be
detained.[14]

Similarly, the *Journal of Mental Science* in its response to the
publication of the Royal Commission's Report in 1926 called for the
right of discharge of rate-aided patients to be vested in the relatives,
asserting that:

The popular idea, not without basis as the law stands, that the rate-aided
patient is detained solely by the action of the medical officer (or as hinted by
the Commission, possibly by his inaction) would have no foundation, and the
medical officer would be regarded not so much as a doctor gaoler, but a
physician.[15]

[14] Ibid., Answer 16,913.
[15] *Journal of Mental Science* 72 (1926), p. 13.

In keeping with this attitude, the MPA also later supported
Parliamentary moves to increase the safeguards for the 'voluntary'
admission of adolescents where the consent was provided by their
parent or guardian.[16] The adoption of this conservative legal strategy
reflected psychiatrists' political pressimism. They did not yet perceive
a climate in which they could benefit from a political redefinition of
professionalism. State interventionism favoured the expansion of the
domain of scientific professionals with the purported ability to
maximize the rationality and efficiency of decision-making processes,
if necessary at the expense of the preservation of certain traditional
individual liberties. Applied to psychiatry, this involved recognition
of the psychiatrist as the figure possessing the expertise necessary to
decide whether compulsion was in all the circumstances likely to be
conducive to recovery or to the protection of the public. But the
medical profession was sensitive to the popular clamour on behalf of
'the liberty of the subject' and moved more slowly than the
underlying movement in its favour in terms of the changing shape
and functions of the state.

Another consideration which made it in doctors' interests to
distance themselves from formal responsibility for detention was the
pressure of legal actions by aggrieved patients at this time, backed as
they were by the resources of the National Society for Lunacy
Reform, and the surrounding legal uncertainty. There were a
number of judicial decisions in the 1920s with implications for the
legal effect of medical recommendations in commitment proceedings, but they were inconclusive and controversial. The crux of the
matter was whether medical certificates were the cause of detention,
so that the Justice's order was 'mere machinery', or whether the
decision of the Justice constituted a *novus actus interveniens* interrupt-
ing the causal link which was necessary to found an action in tort
for negligence. In *Everett* v. *Griffiths*[17] and *Harnett* v. *Fisher*[18] actions
where wrongful detention was alleged reached the House of Lords
but the issue was not the subject of a direct ruling and judicial *dicta* in
the appellate courts were divergent. Surveying the state of the case
law in *de Freville* v. *Dill*[19] in 1927, McCardie J. concluded against his
own leanings that on balance judicial opinion favoured the view that
the medical certificate was the effective element in the proceedings.

[16] Ibid., p. 590.
[17] [1920] 3 KB 163 (CA); [1921] AC 631 (HL).
[18] [1927] AC 573.
[19] (1927) 43 TLR 702.

To protect themselves, the medical profession campaigned vigorously to be given full witness status in certification proceedings so that they could only be liable in the event of perjury. The Macmillan Commission was not willing to recommend that such an extensive immunity should be granted, but it did propose that when the defendant applied to stay an action under section 330 of the Lunacy Act 1890 the onus of establishing a prima-facie case should be placed on the plaintiff rather than continuing to require the defendant to prove that there was no such case.[20] The Commission was sympathetic to the medical argument on this issue, expressing grave concern at the fear of doctors to certify, and accepting the equation of mental patient and vexatious litigant.[21]

Given its low expectations, the medical profession was taken unawares by the Commission's positive response to its proposals for reform of the lunacy laws. Medical witnesses giving evidence were surprised by its sympathetic and encouraging attitude, as indicated by the following exchange in discussion of the MPA's proposed twenty-eight day Provisional Order:

EARL RUSSELL. I am anxious that you should have more than twenty-eight days. Do you not think that a longer period might be useful, and that more people might escape certification if you took a longer period?
DR COLE. That is so, but what would Parliament say?
DR LORD. I do not think we should raise any objection to the extension of the period. We put that period because it was hopeless for us to ask any more.[22]

When Earl Russell offered the BMA representatives a second twenty-eight day period, the response was: 'We hardly dared suggest such a thing.'[23]

In the event, of course, the Commission recommended a six-month order, and the Mental Treatment Act provided for a maximum of one year's detention without certification. The medical press was infused with pleasure and surprise when it had digested the Commission's Report. The response of the *Journal of Mental Science*

[20] *Report of the Royal Commission on Lunacy and Mental Disorder*, para. 90.
[21] Ibid., para. 54.
[22] *Royal Commission on Lunacy and Mental Disorder: Minutes of Evidence*, II, Question and Answer 16, 927; Answer 16, 930.
[23] Ibid., I, Answer 8,116.

has been recorded above. The *British Medical Journal*, somewhat over-personalizing the responsibility for the tradition of legalism in lunacy legislation, welcomed it as follows:

[The Report] is important chiefly because it may confidently be expected to quicken the shifting of opinion from the fatalistic legal view to the rational and scientific. It was an obsession of the late Lord Halsbury that thousands of sane people were confined under certificates. He used the great influence his position gave him to imbue lunacy law with this idea, but it was an *a priori* view for which he had no adequate body of facts that would stand examination.[24]

Following the publication of the Report, the energies of the medical profession's representative organizations were concentrated upon strengthening the protection from suit which Macmillan had recommended. On the contents of the proposed legislation as a whole they did not have major criticisms, particularly as the Government revived the medical profession's favoured legislative recognition of a non-volitional category which, to their disappointment,[25] Macmillan had omitted. It appears that the profession's leadership appreciated that the Macmillan recommendation to shift the onus of proof represented a substantial concession, but this was not enough to satisfy the mass membership of the professional organizations in the atmosphere of anxiety stimulated by the extended Harnett litigation. The Lunacy Law Commitee of the British Medical Association which reported on the Macmillan proposals concluded that full witness status for certifying doctors should not be pressed, but the representative assembly decided to refer the report to this effect back to the Council with a request to reappoint the Committee. A new Committee was installed with approximately the same composition as that which had reported in favour of a conciliatory position. This Committee attempted to reconcile the demand of the membership with the need to resile on the impolitic claim for witness status by proposing that as a further safeguard medical assessors selected from a panel appointed by Government should sit with the Judge in court or in chambers to assist in the weighing of medical affidavits, aiding him in distinguishing the reputable from the dubious psychiatric opinion.

This suggestion, with Workmen's Compensation and Admiralty

[24] *British Medical Journal* (1926), 2, p. 208.
[25] See *Journal of Mental Science* 72 (1926), pp. 613, 615.

precendents and comparative evidence from Australia adduced in support, was pressed upon the Board of Control and the Ministry of Health without success, as was a proposal to increase the onus on the plaintiff patient based upon the model of the action for malicious prosecution.[26] A deputation to the Minister of Health from the British Medical Association on 15 January 1930 failed to extract a concession on medical assessors. Laurence Brock (1879–1949), who had succeeded Sir Frederick Willis as Chairman of the Board of Control in 1928, took the view that successive proposed amendments to clause 16 advanced by the medical profession failed to improve upon the protection given by the clause as drafted by Macmillan and Jowitt to give effect to the recommendation of the Royal Commission, whilst witness status would never be countenanced by public opinion.[27] Arthur Greenwood, Minister of Health from 1929, was very reluctant to improve medical protection further.[28] Finally, a compromise was reached in acceptance by the Ministry of a proposal based on a draft clause prepared by Stuart Bevan for the BMA and adopted by its Lunacy and Mental Disorder Committee on 27 January 1930, when it met with a strong deputation from what had in 1925 become the Royal Medico-Psychological Association. This increased the onus on the aggrieved patient by requiring that he prove substantial grounds for his allegation *before* commencing the action, in place of the former procedural obstacle that the proceedings, once commenced, might be stayed if the defendant could prove that there was no prima-facie case.[29] Whilst the Ministry was advised that placing the procedural barrier at the very outset and requiring the plaintiff to take the initiative would not appreciably increase the degree of protection in law above the Macmillan level, the view prevailed that the new form of words might have the right psychological effect from the medical point of view in deterring actions, and if it satisfied the doctors there was one less interest to

[26] The Parliamentary links of the professional organizations are illustrated by the tabling of amendments to write these propositions into the Bill, in the first case by Lord Sandhurst and the second in the House of Commons by Sir F. Boyd Merriman.
[27] Letter of 2 January 1930 from Laurence Brock to Alfred Cox, Medical Secretary of the British Medical Association: Public Record Office, State Papers, Ministry of Health 51/568, Board of Control File No. 60160/8.
[28] Note on Minister's position of 4 February 1930: Public Record Office, State Papers, Ministry of Health 80/11, 1928–30 March, Mental Treatment Bill, Vol. 1.
[29] See letter of 31 January 1930 from Alfred Cox to Sir Arthur Robinson of the Ministry of Health: Public Record Office, State Papers, Ministry of Health 51/568, Board of Control File No. 60160/8.

placate and one less issue to provide a focus for time-consuming Parliamentary opposition during a congested Session.[30]

There were some dissentients in the profession from the position that legal protection for certifying doctors should be strengthened and that the reduction in formal legal procedures recommended by Macmillan and implemented by the Mental Treatment Act was desirable. The most prominent of these was Dr Risien Russell, whose status within the profession was virtually that of a heretic. Described by Laurence Brock in internal Board of Control correspondence as a 'clever clinician' but one who had achieved an 'unenviable notoriety' by his willingness to testify against fellow practitioners,[31] Russell had received frequent rebukes for his unorthodox activities. During the First World War, the National Service Ministry apparently ceased to give credence to medical certificates of unfitness for military duty which bore his signature on account of their frequency, and in the case of *Easton* v. *Johnson & Potts*[32] his evidence was expressly criticized by Scrutton. Indeed, it was primarily his readiness to supply affidavits disputing the certificates of insanity supplied by other doctors which inspired the BMA proposal for medical assessors. The availability of psychiatrists prepared to violate the ethic of intra-professional solidarity was helpful to the National Society for Lunacy Reform, with which Russell was associated,[33] in its pursuit of remedies for patients' grievances through the courts, but the legal credibility of their opinions was liable to suffer by the very fact that they were being offered whilst their authors remained in such a contentious minority.[34]

Another well-known 'lunacy reformer' amongst the medical profession in the 1920s was Dr Montagu Lomax. The publication of his book *The Experiences of an Asylum Doctor*,[35] which made serious allegations regarding ill-treatment of patients at the Prestwich

[30] Letter of 24 January 1930 from Laurence Brock to Sir Arthur Robinson: Public Record Office, State Papers, Ministry of Health 51/568, Board of Control File No. 60160/8.

[31] Letter of 30 December 1929 from Laurence Brock to Peter Barter: Public Record Office, State Papers, Ministry of Health 51/568, Board of Control File No. 60160/8.

[32] (1929) 168 LTJ 537.

[33] He was a member of a deputation of the National Society for Lunacy Reform led by Sir John Withers, MP, on 6 December 1929 to the Minister of Health seeking assurances on strengthened legal safeguards and related matters in the Mental Treatment Bill.

[34] *Transactions of the Medico-Legal Society* XVII (1922–3), pp. 204–6.

[35] London: Allen and Unwin, 1921.

Asylum at Manchester, where he had served as a temporary Assistant Medical Officer during the war, prompted much public concern and was followed by the appointment by the Minister of Health in 1922 of a Departmental Committee under Sir Cyril Cobb to hold a public inquiry.[36] He also promoted the publication of a personal account of the experience of a female patient at the hands of the lunacy system.[37] In his evidence to the Macmillan Commission, Lomax portrayed asylum life as stagnant and characterized by systematic rather than merely incidental ill-treatment.[38] He expressed the view that while the sane were not wrongly certified, the uncertifiably insane were[39] and it is symptomatic of his status as a subversive influence that he was actually reproved by the Commission for his tone.[40] The publicity-drawing activities of these marginal dissidents fuelled precisely the kind of controversy which the profession as a whole was keen to avoid, but as it happened, their challenge to medical complacency regarding the operation of the lunacy system did not sabotage the chances of a legislative breakthrough.

The Legal Profession

The most intriguing question raised by the behaviour of the legal profession in relation to the emergence of the Mental Treatment Act is why it abstained from acting as a focus for opposition to a measure which rolled back procedural safeguards designed for the protection of 'the liberty of the subject'. Indeed, those prominent lawyers who were members of the Royal Commission on Lunacy and Mental Disorder were actively engaged in preparing the ground for this development. The élite of the legal profession, moral entrepreneurs

[36] See *Annual Report of the Board of Control for the Year 1921*, p. 6 *et seq.* The Board's previous Annual Report records that a deputation led by Ben Tillett, MP, to forward complaints on behalf of 268 ex-servicemen in the Prestwich Asylum had led to an official visit there by a Legal and a Medical Commissioner of the Board with the Deputy Director General of Medical Services at the Ministry of Pensions on 20 September 1920. They reported favourably to the asylum. In relation to similar complaints regarding two asylums by *Friend*, organ of the Society of Friends, the Board excused some of the deficiencies which it subsequently uncovered on account of the war conditions which had prevailed at the time to which the complaints referred. See *Annual Report of the Board of Control for the Year 1920*, pp. 15–7.
[37] Rachel Grant-Smith, *The Experiences of an Asylum Patient*, ed. M. Lomax. London: Allen and Unwin, 1922. On Lomax generally, see G. Baruch and A. Treacher, *Psychiatry Observed*, pp. 76–7.
[38] *Royal Commission on Lunacy and Mental Disorder: Minutes of Evidence*, II, Answer 12,709.
[39] Ibid., Answer 13,003.
[40] Ibid., Question 12,757.

of legalism in the 1880s, were no longer prepared to provide a powerful voice within the apparatuses of the state in favour of the continued tight restraint of psychiatry. In the legal mind, 'lunacy reform' ceased to form a part of that populist discourse of the liberties of free-born Englishmen in which the late Victorian Lord Chancellors had helped to establish it. The medical profession saw the legal profession as a formidable traditionalist barrier to the advancement of psychiatric aspirations. Yet this barrier did not have to be stormed: it simply collapsed of its own accord.

There was some evidence of a lingering preoccupation with 'the liberty of the subject' in the legal profession's attitude to the state of the lunacy laws in the 1920s. We saw that in *Harnett* v. *Bond*, the trial Judge commented upon the possible need for surer safeguards. In the Court of Appeal, in the same case, Scrutton, LJ, expressed a similar concern:

> If it were a Royal Commission, this case shows that serious consideration should be given to the question whether the judicial inquiry preceding the making of a reception order should be more precise in its procedure by informing the alleged lunatic of the nature of the charges against him and hearing him in defence. Another question also requires more thought, whether the existing system of constant visits and reports affords sufficient safeguard against undue prolongation of detention.[41]

However, he proceeded to qualify this by recognizing that it may be found difficult to improve upon the existing machinery in practice and that the interests of the community as well as the liberty of the individual were at stake. In the earlier case of *Everett* v. *Griffiths*, far from adopting a position hostile to the medical profession, Scrutton had expressed himself in favour of a 'liberal' measure of protection against suit for medical men carrying out their responsibilities under the Lunacy Acts, citing the immunity of Judges in support.[42] It was one ingredient in the common ground between lawyers and doctors, balancing their frequently conflicting perspectives, that as practising professionals they were both vulnerable to the tiresome attentions of the complaining client.[43]

---

[41] [1924] 2 KB 517, 554–5.

[42] [1920] 3 KB 163, 197–8.

[43] There was an interesting exchange between Macmillan and Mr Stewart, a barrister appearing for the National Society for Lunacy Reform, when evidence was being given to the Royal Commission, which reflects this sentiment of inter-professional solidarity:

In general terms, the 1920s appears to have been a period of selective legal accommodation to medical claims. Contemporaneously with the Macmillan Commission's substantial adoption of the psychiatric profession's position on the legal framework for the treatment of the non-criminal mentally ill, the Lord Chancellor's Committee on Insanity and Crime was prepared to move some way toward its position in relation to the insanity plea.[44] The Committee, appointed in 1922, was overwhelmingly legal in membership and chaired by Atkin, LJ. Atkin was something of a bridge-builder between the legal and medical professions. He served as President of the Medico-Legal Society from 1920 until 1927, and his biographer describes it as one of the principal objectives of his Presidency 'to promote a better understanding between the different points of view of the two professions on subjects where their interests touched each other—compensation of workmen for injury, nervous shock in tort, cruelty and other matrimonial offences, and insanity and civil liberty.'[45] He advocated the study of medical jurisprudence as an element in the professional training of both doctors and lawyers.[46] It has been seen that following his elevation to the House of Lords in 1928, Atkin was in the 1930s associated with Macmillan in the relatively creative and progressive development of the judicial role,[47] and in fact the two figures performed parallel functions in shaping the relationship between law and psychiatry in the 1920s in the

Question 9,119 '. . . You say that with your experience of doctors who deal with mental disorder, you think they are not always very reliable in your opinion?' . . .
CHAIRMAN. 'Some people say lawyers are not reliable.'
STEWART. 'Some are, Sir.'
CHAIRMAN. 'And so are some doctors.'

[44] See *Report of the Committee on Insanity and Crime* (Cmd. 2005, 1923). The terms of reference of the Committee were 'to consider what changes, if any, are desirable in the existing law, practice and procedure relating to criminal trials in which the plea of insanity as a defence is raised, and whether any and, if so, what changes should be made in the existing law and practice in respect of cases falling within the powers of section 2(4) of the Criminal Lunatics Act 1884.' It was made clear by subsequent correspondence that the Lord Chancellor, Viscount Birkenhead, did intend the inquiry to have a wide scope, including consideration of possible changes in the M'Naghten Rules. Section 2(4) of the Criminal Lunatics Act concerned the effect of supervening insanity upon the imprisonment and execution of committed prisoners.
[45] G. Lewis, *Lord Atkin*. London: Butterworths, 1983, p. 159.
[46] Id.
[47] See p. 188 of the present work.

criminal and civil spheres respectively, by attempting to attune the law to what they perceived as the enlightened consensus of informed public opinion.

Like the Macmillan Commission, the Atkin Committee was the official response to a 'reactionary' public outcry, this time in favour of hanging and prompted by the Home Secretary's reprieve of Ronald True in the murder case of *R. v. True*.[48] The Committee considered specially prepared reports expressing the views of the British Medical Association (supported by the Central Association for Mental Welfare) and the Medico-Psychological Association and heard evidence in support. Two members of the Board of Control, Dr Bond and Mr Trevor, gave evidence in support of the MPA's proposals, a fact which indicates the close professional-bureaucratic nexus which was operative in the psychiatrists' attempts to influence the medico-legal policy of Government. Both the MPA and the BMA wished to change the basis for determining the criminal responsibility of the mentally disordered, but the former organization's proposals were much more far-reaching. The BMA was prepared to retain the M'Naghten Rules but wanted to add a provision absolving defendants subject to irresistible impulse.[49] The MPA, however, proposed to abolish the existing rules and substitute a new set of questions for the jury, throwing on to the prosecution the burden of proving that the defendant's crime was unrelated to mental disorder as a precondition of his being held responsible.[50] The Committee, adhering to the traditional legal view that criminal responsibility was a distinctively legal conception which could not be determined directly by the presence of a medically recognized condition of mental disorder, objected to the apparent position of the MPA that mental disorder and irresponsibility were coextensive.[51] The Committee felt that much of the medical criticism of the M'Naghten Rules

---

[48] (1922) 16 Cr. App. R. 164. True had killed a prostitute and was convicted and a capital sentence passed despite medical evidence that he acted subject to uncontrollable impulse. The Court of Criminal Appeal dismissed his appeal, but he was reprieved by the Home Secretary because of his mental state. The eventual recommendations of the Atkin Committee would have permitted him to be found 'guilty but insane' at trial without stretching the existing M'Naghten Rules, as the Judge had attempted to do in giving his directions to the jury.

[49] *Report of the Committee on Insanity and Crime*, Appendix D: Memorandum of Evidence of the Council of the British Medical Association, para. II(c).

[50] Ibid., Appendix D: Memorandum of Evidence of the Criminal Responsibility Committee of the Medico-Psychological Association.

[51] Ibid., p. 5.

derived from a failure to appreciate that the legal test of insanity was not intended to rival the modern medical conception but to establish the extent of mental disorder necessary to undermine criminal responsibility:

When once it is appreciated that the question is a legal question, and that the present law is that a person of unsound mind may be criminally responsible, the criticism based upon a supposed clash of legal and medical conceptions disappears. It is not that the law has ignorantly invaded the realm of medicine; but that medicine with perfectly correct motives, enters the realm of law.[52]

The radical propositions of the MPA alarmed the members of the Committee, who thought they would entail the transfer of many inmates of prisons to criminal lunatic asylums and thought that 'the interests of both the administrators of justice and of the liberty of the subject require that so far reaching a change would be adopted only on the ground of some imperative public necessity'.[53]

However, Atkin and his fellow members of the Committee did come down in favour of the more moderate position pressed by the BMA. Even this, considered by Atkin himself to be a moderate step, did not find much favour with a legal profession in which many were still wedded to the M'Naghten view. To the deep-dyed Diceyist, Lord Hewart, the Lord Chief Justice, its recommendations were anathema, embodying as they did 'the fantastic theory of uncontrollable impulse which, if it were to become part of our criminal law, would be merely subversive. It is not yet part of the criminal law and it is to be hoped that the time is far distant when it will be made so.'[54] In this climate, the M'Naghten Rules were able to survive unchanged, but the Atkin Report remains as evidence of a significant degree of liberalization in legal attitudes toward psychiatry.

The 'excessive' claims of the MPA in relation to criminal insanity having been dismissed by the Atkin Committee, and the paramountcy of legal over psychiatric discourse in the criminal trial having thereby been assured, lawyers seem to have been content to make substantial concessions to psychiatric demands in the sphere of civil commitment. Whereas they had a hard professional interest in preserving control of the disposition of offenders and limiting the penetration

[52] Ibid., p. 6.
[53] Ibid., p. 8.
[54] *R. v. Kopsch* (1925) 19 Cr. App. R. 50, 51, quoted in G. Lewis, p. 161.

of the criminal trial by the alien and still suspect psychological determinism to which psychiatrists were so prone, in civil commitment lay Justices, not professionally trained lawyers, in practice constituted the decision-making authority. The space for conflict was therefore ideological rather than territorial, and at this time, as we shall see, conditions did not augur well for a symbolic victory of the judicial over the medical view. Macmillan chose entirely to dissociate the two issues:

I think in this matter the lawyers and the doctors are not involved in their familiar conflict upon the subject of criminal responsibility—fortunately that does not arise here. We are both engaged in the same pursuit, namely, the pursuit of the best system which will enable cases to be dealt with, with the minimum of interference and the maximum of medical benefit.[55]

The main reason why lawyers were in a weak position to argue for the continued primacy of judicial controls in commitment was the strength of evidence that the Justice's intervention was ineffective as a safeguard. The picture which emerges from the evidence of their number who appeared before the Macmillan Commission is that magistrates tended to be intimidated by their certification responsibilities because of their lack of medical expertise and the possible dangers to person and property of an ill-judged decision.[56] They demonstrated deference to medical opinion,[67] were likely to define their role in co-operative administrative rather than scrutinizing judicial terms,[58] and in these circumstances the judicial element was frequently merely routinized.[59] The evidence from magistrates did not detract from the consensus of witnesses in favour of some relaxation of safeguards in the interests of early treatment. Brigadier-General Sir John Barnsley, Deputy Chairman of Birmingham Justices, for example, expressed support for the introduction of a period of observation and treatment without certification and the accommodation of voluntary and non-certified patients in separate

[55] *Royal Commission on Lunacy and Mental Disorder: Minutes of Evidence*, I, Question 7,187.
[56] Colonel P. Broome-Giles, JP, stated that he had only known a Justice go against a doctor on two occasions, in one of which the patient had later badly cut his wife's throat and committed suicide: *Royal Commission on Lunacy and Mental Disorder: Minutes of Evidence*, I, Answer 3,690.
[57] See the evidence of Sir John Barnsley at Answers 2,007–8, and of Sir Robert Walden at Answer 2,364.
[58] See particularly the evidence of Sir Robert Walden.
[59] *Report of the Royal Commission on Lunacy and Mental Disorder*, para. 84.

clinics.[60] It must be remembered that in their capacity as triers and sentencers of criminals, magistrates were directly implicated in the new developments whereby psychiatry was extending itself well beyond the confines of the asylum under the banner of prevention. Magistrates figured as active members of the National Council for Mental Hygiene and the Magistrates Association was involved in the foundation of the Child Guidance movement in the United Kingdom in the late 1920s.[61] Through their responsibilities in juvenile courts and associated activities, magistrates were a part of the complex and expanding web of positive social management within which psychiatrists were playing a key role. A limited de-judicialization of admission to psychiatric facilities could from this magisterial perspective be seen as a contribution to crime prevention rather than an affront to the rule of law. It was also open to lawyers to see it in these terms.

The judicial safeguard was symbolic, a sop to the public, rather than substantive, and it was difficult to establish convincing evidence of abuse. If the legal profession were to have sprung to the defence of legalism in the 1920s, it would have had to recognize the shortcomings of the existing machinery of safeguards and propose a much more stringent set of proceedings. It would also have had to argue in some way that more safeguards were actually needed. This would have aligned the profession with the 'eccentric' National Society for Lunacy Reform and against the remainder of the élite. The issue clearly did not merit such dramatization. It seems that lawyers were prepared to concur in the derestriction of a psychiatry which now sought to present itself as community-oriented, preventive, and curative, rather than custodial and sinister, given the impressive consensus for a relaxation of safeguards, and the extreme rigidity of the Lunacy Act 1890, which did not even allow a public mental hospital to receive voluntary patients. Once Macmillan and Jowitt had adopted this stance, the generality of the profession deferred to their eminent opinions. It represented an opportunity to concede to the medical profession in recognition of its growing power and prestige in a sphere where lawyers lacked a material incentive to resist the rising social and political trend.

The legal profession's 'conversion' should indeed be set in the context of the more general political reaction against legalism in

---

[60] *Royal Commission on Lunacy and Mental Disorder: Minutes of Evidence*, I, Answers 1,827, 1,839, 1,846.
[61] N. Timms, *Psychiatric Social Work in Great Britain*, p. 17.

social legislation. Increasing social interventionism of itself tends to challenge the ideology of the rule of law, threatening to remove important areas of decision-making from lawyers to scientific experts and forcing a reassessment of the character, reasoning, and functions of law. In Britain, however, the subordination of the law in the creation of state machinery for providing social welfare was pronounced because of the particular historical record of the courts as a negative and obstructive element in the workings of early modern social legislation. The Workmen's Compensation Acts of 1897 and 1906 were designed to replace the common law fault-based liability of employers as the main source of compensation for accidental personal injury sustained by their employees at work with a system of strict liability which would be administered on the basis of settlements and the decisions of arbitration tribunals with minimal reference to the courts. Joseph Chamberlain, who was responsible for the 1897 Act, wanted to take the scheme entirely outside the purview of the courts, but this was succesfully resisted by the legal profession.[62] The intended informality of workmen's compensation was in practice undermined when lawyers representing employers' insurance companies trying to resist liability developed legalistic defences which generated intricate new areas of legal learning, particularly around the meaning of the statutory precondition of liability that the injury must arise 'out of and in the course of employment'. As a counterweight, trade unions had to build up large legal departments of their own. Contrary to the original intention, arbitration by the County Courts became the rule rather than the exception and there were a significant number of appeals to the higher courts, so that the scheme became bedevilled by the expense and delay traditionally characteristic of English legal administration.[63] The design of later social legislation was influenced by a determination to avoid a repetition of such legal sabotage. In the case of old age pensions in 1908 the administration of the scheme was placed in the hands of local pensions committees, with an ultimate appeal to the Local Government Board rather than the courts. Similarly, under the National Insurance Act 1911, benefit disputes were referred to specially instituted Courts of Referees, with an appeal to the Insurance Commissioner.

---

[62] B. Abel-Smith and R. Stevens, *Lawyers and the Courts*, p. 115.
[63] See B. Abel-Smith and R. Stevens, pp. 115–7, and P. S. Atiyah, *Accidents, Compensation and the Law*, pp. 360–3.

These precedents for the exclusion of the courts from the machinery of social legislation and the image of the law as self-serving, archaic, and inefficient, upon which they were based, created a situation in which there arose a general political presumption against extensive legal involvement in social legislation and general legal compliance with the injunction to remain at a distance from newly-acquired territories of state intervention. The Mental Treatment Act did not provide for the dispensation of new types of monetary benefit, but in contrast to the Lunacy Acts Amendment Act 1889 its target was essentially the public sector and its object was the provision of new services. It could therefore be perceived by both lawyers and politicians as an instance of social legislation in which field legalism was definitely unwelcome and unacceptable.

In one respect there was actually a revival of militant legalism in the late 1920s. This consisted of the attempt of Lord Hewart in his book *The New Despotism*, published in 1929, to attract support for his Neo-Diceyist position on judicial control of the executive.[64] A Committee on Ministers' Powers (the Donoughmore Committee) was appointed to investigate the question, but its explicit concurrence with some Neo-Diceyist positions did not have a serious impact on the subsequent direction of the British state. This debate did intersect with that surrounding the emergence of the Mental Treatment Act, account being taken of Lord Hewart's book in the internal deliberations at the Board of Control and Ministry of Health[65] and in the Parliamentary debates.[66] However, concern was confined to the specific issue of administrative regulation and the rule-making powers to be accorded to the Board of Control in respect of the new categories of voluntary and temporary patients. It does not appear to have invaded the argument about the priority to be given to formal judicial safeguards in legislation for mental treatment.

The Political Parties

Turning finally to the political divisions produced by the reform of

---

[64] The Rt. Hon. Lord Hewart, LCJ, *The New Despotism*. London: Ernest Benn, 1929. See also R. Jackson, *The Chief: the biography of Gordon Hewart, Lord Chief Justice of England 1922–40*. London: George G. Harrap, 1959.

[65] Memorandum on the first draft of the Mental Treatment Bill prepared by Peter Barter 5 November 1929: Public Record Office, State Papers, Ministry of Health 51/568, Board of Control File No. 60160/8.

[66] Lord Danesfort, *House of Lords Debates* 75, col. 759 *et seq.* (28 November 1929).

the Lunacy Acts in Parliament, its most committed supporters were Earl Russell, presenting the Bill for the Government in the House of Lords, and members of the medical profession in the Conservative Party. Libertarian-inspired opposition was vociferous, but small and fragmentary. In the House of Lords, Viscount Brentford was the champion of 'the liberty of the subject'. In the Commons the theme was taken up by Josiah Wedgwood and a small number of backbenchers on the Labour side, mainly Nonconformists and members of the Independent Labour Party. Liberal Radicals alienated by the leadership's militarism and nationalism in the First World War were attracted by the contrasting pacifism and internationalism of Labour. Their departure was one strand in a tripartite fracture of Liberalism, whereby radicals and progressives gravitated to Labour, while some pro-business Liberals deserted to the Conservatives and the Liberal Party itself, destined not to form the majority party again, soldiered on under the leadership of Lloyd George. Josiah Wedgwood moved to the ILP in April 1919 and entered the Labour Party in the following August. He became a member of the Party's Executive, was Vice-Chairman of the Parliamentary Labour Party from 1921–4, and served as Chancellor of the Duchy of Lancaster in the first Labour Government. His rebellion against the second Labour Government on the Mental Treatment Bill was consistent with his earlier dissent from the position of the Liberal leadership over mental deficiency and Eugenics in 1912–13, but also symptomatic of his unapologetic individualism in struggling against party discipline. Wedgwood's supporters on the issue included James Maxton and Fenner Brockway, and he was accompanied by Brockway and three other Labour members on a deputation to Arthur Greenwood, the Minister of Health, on 17 April 1930, which unsuccessfully demanded the authority of a Justice or minister of religion as an added safeguard in the procedure for the admission of non-volitional patients.

The Mental Treatment Bill was introduced in the confident expectation that it would meet with broad all-party agreement. It did not, after all, touch on the provocative issues of principle which divided Socialists from Conservatives and Liberals. It lent itself to presentation as a reform dictated by supra-political considerations of humanity and scientific progress. Its interventionist assumptions were by 1930 tolerable to both front benches in such a subject area given 'the revolution in thought ... in enlightened public opinion' which had taken place since the Act of 1890.[67]

On the Second Reading, the debate was so serene that Susan Lawrence, Parliamentary Secretary at the Ministry of Health, for the Government, was able to remark that 'It is very seldom that a Bill is received with such general favour',[68] and Dr Vernon Davies, a Conservative, and a member of the medical profession, whose criticism was that the Bill did not move more rapidly toward positions in fact to be reached with the Mental Health Act 1959, described it as having been received with 'a wonderful feeling of unanimity'.[69] However, this accord was soon to evaporate. The Bill's progress was halted by spending eleven days in Standing Committee and provoking an unforseen level of controversy on its Third Reading.[70] Under the pressure of the Government's legislative programme, Arthur Greenwood, as the Minister in charge of the Bill, was driven to the adoption of unpopular procedural tactics in order to guarantee its passage into law within the Parliamentary Session. Although in the course of the Third Reading, Dr Vernon Davies had complained that opposition from the Labour side was being insufficiently aired owing to the activation of the party whips, by the end of the debate his and his colleagues' complaint was that libertarian amendments proposed by Labour's radicals had dominated the discussion at the expense of those sought by Conservative members of the medical profession. The first Conservative amendment (to add two lay members to the Board of Control in a move to combat centralization, strengthening the Board's position as against the Minister, which had some support from its existing professional members) was only called at 2.00 a.m. and the Third Reading taken at 4.00 a.m. Dr Davies protested at '... passing a Bill like this in the early hours of the morning with the minimum of discussion and the maximum of forced closure.'[71] It was his view that the medical profession (now more ambitious and optimistic in the newly receptive political climate) had been deprived of the opportunity to give 'the advice of men who [know] what they are talking about. Honourable Members opposite simply jeer at the medical profession .... The medical profession has been more or less

[67] B. Webb and S. Webb, *English Poor Law History*, p. 549.
[68] *House of Commons Debates* 235, col. 1,065 (17 February 1930).
[69] Ibid., col. 1,068 (17 February 1930).
[70] *House of Commons Debates* 238, col. 1,777 (13 May 1930).
[71] Ibid., col. 1,836 (13 May 1930).

the butt of the party opposite.'[72] The libertarian alarms of Labour's radical wing had struck home.

The effect of the foreshortening of debate may have been to produce a less substantial modification of the nineteenth-century legislation than some of the medical profession's Parliamentary spokesmen may now have thought to be within their grasp.[73] The great consolation was that the Government had conceded a more congenial form of immunity from litigation than that which was originally written into the Bill. As amendments representing fears for 'the liberty of the subject' largely failed to win acceptance, the Mental Treatment Bill was enabled to reach the statute book in a form broadly acceptable to its Government sponsors.

As far as libertarian opposition was concerned, Viscount Brentford's critique was developed in terms of the Bill's authoritarianism and erosion of the rule of law: '... there is distinctly a difference between the disease of insanity, and every other physical disease to which flesh is heir to. That is, of course, the question of the liberty of the subject.'[74] He found influential support in the House for modification of the provision dealing with the 'voluntary' treatment of children and adolescents, important targets of the Bill's preventive objectives. In the provision's original form, a parent or guardian could apply for the 'voluntary' admission of a person aged under eighteen years without the order of a judicial authority or even any kind of medical certificate. The Government was prepared to make concessions and in its final form sixteen and seventeen year olds were exempt and a medical recommendation was required, although a judicial element was not restored. Debate of this facility for parents to submit their children to treatment reveals a sharp conflict of political philosophies. While to Lord Brentford it presented the danger of 'a troublesome child or even an unwanted child' being 'locked up', a risk which the social interest in minimizing mental disorder could not justify, Lord Dawson of Penn regarded as essential the augmentation of parental power in order to combat the anti-social conduct symptomatic of such disorder:

If we were dealing with people of normal mind I would give my support entirely to the young person having the right of decision; but unfortunately

---

[72] Ibid., col. 1,837 (13 May 1930).
[73] See the speech of Vernon Davies on Second Reading, *House of Commons Debates* 235, cols. 1,069–70 (17 February 1930).
[74] *House of Lords Debates* 75, col. 741 (28 November 1929).

... there is a great proneness for these mental disorders, which may so easily develop into insanity properly so-called, to arise at these ages of sixteen and eighteen; and the very existence of these disorders, slight as they may be at that stage, makes these young people very difficult.... They are, in a sense, anti-social ... and ... it is desirable to put a little more power in the hands of the parents for this type of ailment.[75]

Brentford also attacked Clause 5, the provision for temporary treatment of non-volitional patients without magisterial intervention, identifying it as the main item in the Bill,[76] but his plea for the reintroduction of a judicial element in some form[77] went unheeded.

Earl Russell's response to Viscount Brentford's critique of the Bill's 'authoritarian' presuppositions was threefold: to accuse him of wishing to deny to the poor facilities already available to the rich,[78] thus portraying him as essentially reactionary; to characterize preoccupation with the rule of law in this sphere as deference to abstract theory without relevance to the realities of psychiatric practice;[79] and to plead with him to abandon penal for therapeutic language: 'detention may be a necessary part of it, but that is not the part on which we wish to insist'.[80]

The focus of opposition to the Bill by Labour Radicals in the Commons was its extension of the powers of the medical profession and the Board of Control. This was perceived as authoritarian and detrimental to working-class liberties in particular. It is interesting that whilst supporters saw the Bill as 'a great charter for the poor of this country',[81] its detractors could see it as especially dangerous from the point of view of the poor. From an interventionist perspective it offered equality of opportunity in the sense of access to mental treatment without stigma which the rich could gain by being treated in their own homes without certification.[82] From a libertarian position it was precisely the poor who were least equipped in terms of education, access to legal advice and assistance, and influence in the community to resist the decisions of the medico-bureaucratic machine.

[75] Ibid., col. 1,056 (10 December 1929).
[76] Ibid., col. 1,075 (10 December 1929).
[77] Ibid., col. 1,078 (10 December 1929).
[78] Ibid., col. 1,082 (10 December 1929).
[79] Ibid., col. 1,085 (10 December 1929).
[80] Ibid., col. 1,083 (10 December 1929).
[81] Dr Morris Jones, *House of Commons Debates* 238, col. 1,838 (13 May 1930).
[82] *House of Lords Debates* 75, col. 1,082 (10 December 1929).

Labour critics of the Bill who expressed concern for 'the liberty of the subject' were also prominent in voicing the widely shared concern, in and outside Parliament, that the new categories of patient should be removed entirely from the supervision of the Board of Control and be treated in separate new institutions run as part of local authority social services and linked to general medicine. This theme encompassed both some enthusiasts for mental hygiene and those who saw the existing machinery with which the Bill had become entangled as authoritarian and remote from democratic control. Some very emotive verbal onslaughts were launched upon the Board of Control. John Warburton Beckett pilloried members of the Board for their 'lies, their malevolence, their libellous statements and their maliciousness' and accused them of being 'permeated by the very worst type of charity organization mentality'.[83] Josiah Wedgwood claimed that if the Board was left in the Bill then the reason for the new categories of patient being submitted to treatment '. . . will be less and less the desire or the possibility of cure, but the fact that this is in the interests of the public and the family. It is the worst way of dealing with these temporarily afflicted people.'[84] Its detractors were adamant that the involvement of the Board of Control would ensure that voluntary and temporary patients became the victims of stigma and hopelessness, but an amendment to leave the Board out of the Bill was defeated by 205 votes to 18. The asylums were similarly lambasted. The change of nomenclature to 'mental hospitals' was derided as cosmetic and their character impugned by drawing attention to recent increases in the rate of suicides amongst patients.[85] Accordingly, Labour dissidents pressed an amendment to the effect that only certifiable patients should be admitted to a public mental hospital on a voluntary basis. The proposer, Ernest Winterton, and Colonel Wedgwood also stressed the difficulties of establishing meaningful voluntarism in cases of mental disorder whatever type of institution was at issue.[86] The best supported amendment proposed from this section of the House, attracting substantial backing from Conservatives, was designed to make it impossible for voluntary patients to be transferred to temporary status once

[83] *House of Commons Debates* 237, col. 2,561 (11 April 1930). J. W. Beckett was a Labour MP from 1924 to 1931 and then successively joined the ILP and the British Union of Fascists. He was imprisoned during the war under the Defence of the Realm Act.

[84] Ibid., col. 2,547 (11 April 1930).

[85] J. Kinley, ibid., col. 2,540 (11 April 1930).

[86] Ibid., cols. 2,569–70, 2,546 (11 April 1930).

admitted. It was argued that this would both safeguard voluntarism and strengthen the confidence of potential voluntary patients to come forward. In the event, the amendment was lost by 241 votes to 106.[87]

As for the distribution of libertarian anxiety between the sane and the mentally ill, the usual ambiguities can be observed. Whilst Wedgwood declared that he had been 'inspired by the terror of people who are not lunatics getting locked up in lunatic asylums'[88] and employed the rhetoric of protecting 'the liberty of the subject' from 'this new tyranny of the bureaucratic expert',[89] at times he and his sympathizers seemed to be concerned with the rights of patients themselves.[90]

An interesting ideological split on the Conservative side was provoked by an Opposition initiative in Commons Committee to widen the Bill to include provision for the increased regulation of private licensed houses, a matter which we have seen had been omitted in order to avoid a controversy which might threaten the achievement of any reform at all. A new Clause to require an audit of the accounts of licensed houses was proposed by Conservative leaders, and accepted by the Government on the assumption that with agreement across the front benches in the Commons earlier fears of far-reaching damage by extending the scope of the Bill were unfounded. However, the idea was met with hostility by Conservative Peers led by Lord Halsbury (son of the Lord Chancellor responsible for the Lunacy Act) who regarded such state economic regulation of the private sector as 'socialism of the deepest dye'. The House of Lords proposed deletion of the Clause, and as it was not anyway a Government initiative, it was quietly dropped.[91]

The Mental Treatment Bill thus passed into law a limited reform, but one which reflected a profound shift in the approach of the state to the philosophy and organization of the mental health services. Libertarian opposition, exposed as incapable of stanching the flow in this direction, was branded as stubbornly anti-progressive and so the way was open for further success in combating late nineteenth-century legalism.

[87] *House of Commons Debates* 238, col. 1,758 (13 May 1930).
[88] *House of Commons Debates* 237, col. 2,589 (11 April 1930).
[89] Ibid., col. 2,598 (11 April 1930).
[90] J. W. Beckett, *House of Commons Debates* 238, col. 1,776 (13 May 1930).
[91] See Memorandum of 15 May 1930: Public Record Office, State Papers, Ministry of Health 80/12, 1930 February—May Mental Treatment Bill Vol. 2.

8 The Mental Health Act 1959: I Mental Disorder in the Era of the Welfare State

THE critical legislative turning-point against the legalism of lunacy legislation has now been located in the Mental Treatment Act 1930 and explained in terms of the movement towards a substantially more interventionist state in the early twentieth century which was most sharply advanced by the Liberal social welfare reforms of 1906–14. In keeping with this analysis, the Mental Health Act 1959 should be seen as achieving the more radical implementation of an interventionist strategy toward mental disorder as a social problem, although one still tempered by the survival of strains of liberal individualism within a new post-Second World War reformist consensus. Although not enacted until 1959, the Mental Health Act logically belongs to the clutch of measures carried into law by the 1945–51 Labour Government, which finally abolished the Poor Law and replaced the ramshackle welfare structures which had been erected to supplement it by the far more comprehensive, rationally organized, and freely available services of the Welfare State. The Mental Health Act's informalization of procedure in the interests of destigmatization and a more expansive and pervasive system of state psychiatry may be seen as very much the mental health counterpart of the National Health Service Act 1946, the National Insurance Act 1946, and the National Assistance Act 1948. Just as these enactments were designed to complete the construction of a national minimum of social, physical, and economic well-being, accessible to all without the degradation of pauperism, so the Mental Health Act was an attempt to provide a legal framework for the achievement of national psychological well-being without consigning the recipients of care and treatment to the correspondingly stigmatizing status of certified lunatic. It was the anachronism and discordancy of Victorian lunacy legislation within the new structure of welfare services which directed early attention to its more thoroughgoing reform and we shall see that the Mental Health Act was conceived as an integral part of the architecture of the Welfare State. The continuity of mental health policy after the Mental Treatment Act 1930 was dependant upon a sustained bipartisan commitment to a moderate interventionism within which the rule of law was subordinated to the pursuit of directionist social welfare objectives. However, the political contingency of anti-legalism was obscured in the 1950s by the dominance of a consensual reformist optimism that society was becoming more humane and civilized and that this progressive social enlightenment would foster unilinear development in social policy.

Anti-Legalism and the Mental Health Act 1959

The Mental Health Act 1959 was presented as a reaction against and negation of the Lunacy Act 1890, the late Victorian assumptions of which had only partially been ousted by the amending Mental Treatment Act in 1930. The Mental Health Act injected into mental health law a contrary set of assumptions drawing upon the logic of the view of insanity as analogous to physical disease and upon a reorientation from the Victorian institutionally-centred system to 'Community Care'. The libertarian and legalistic tendencies of the Lunacy Act were reversed, and expert discretion, the autocratic possibilities of which had alarmed the authors of its procedures, was allowed much freer rein at the expense of formal mechanisms incorporating legal and lay control of decision-making processes.

This is at its most evident in the reform of the procedures for civil admission. By section 5 of the 1959 Act voluntary admission was completely informalized, it being provided that nothing in the Act should be construed as preventing a patient in need of psychiatric treatment from admission to or continued residence in a mental institution 'without any application, order, or direction rendering him liable to be detained'. The informalization of voluntary admission was part of a general reorganization of admission procedures. The Mental Health Act introduced a new division, that between formal and informal admission, to replace the pre-existing basic divide between compulsory and voluntary methods of admission. The Mental Health Act allowed non-volitional patients to be admitted altogether informally, authorizing their reception, rather than detention, as had been urged by the psychiatric profession prior to the 1930 Act. Formal procedures were to be reserved for residual resistant categories of patient, which amounted to about one-fifth of admissions in the event.[1]

---

[1] See K. Jones, *A History of the Mental Health Services*, Appendix 1, p. 360.

The main formal procedures for civil commitment introduced by the Mental Health Act were those for admission for treatment under section 26, admission for observation under section 25, and emergency admission for observation under section 29. The most radical reform which they entailed from the point of view of the reaction against legalism was that in the case of admission for treatment, rendering the patient liable to detention for a maximum period of one year in the first instance (the functional equivalent of certification as of unsound mind under the Lunacy Acts), the role of the magistrate in the decision-making process was altogether abolished. The Lunacy Act had extended the intervention of the Justice from the Poor Law to the private sector, and although in the former sphere its origins were administrative rather than owing to any great concern for the liberties of the poor, in 1890 this element in the commitment process was positively designed as a judicial safeguard, as confirmed by the courts, at least for private patients, in *Hodson* v. *Pare* in 1899.[2] Thus medical opinion was not to be conclusive and had to be sufficient to convince a lay authority. The Mental Health Act, however, removed this requirement that the decision to commit should ultimately be in lay hands. Judicial intervention prior to commitment was dispensed with, and essential decision-making power was transferred to medical practitioners. The two medical recommendations in support of an application for treatment under section 26 of the Act were now to pass directly to the hospital managers. There was, however, the proviso that whereas certification proceedings had culminated in an order on the receiving hospital to accept the patient, under the Mental Health Act hospitals were to be able to refuse admission, as an application merely authorized detention.[3]

---

[2] [1899] 1 QB 455. It was decided by the Court of Appeal that a Justice of the Peace or other judicial authority (this being a private case) to whom an application was made under the Lunacy Act 1890 for an order for the reception and detention of a lunatic was acting judicially, so that defamatory statements made in the course of the proceedings attracted absolute privilege. However, subsequently, in *Newman* v. *Foster* (1916–17) 115 LT Reps. (KB) 871, it was held that Justices sitting as a judicial authority to hear an application regarding the liability of the father of a defective over the age of majority to contribute to her maintenance under the Mental Deficiency Act 1913 were acting in an administrative capacity so that a case could not be stated for the opinion of the High Court under the Summary Jurisdiction Acts. The question of the nature of the commitment proceedings under the Lunacy Acts also arose in relation to the liability of medical men in tort for the signing of certificates of insanity as to whether the intervention of the justice amounted to a *novus actus interveniens*, breaking the chain of causation: See Chapter 7.

The movement towards medical domination of admissions was reflected also in the abolition of the power of the local authority duly authorized officer, forerunner of the mental welfare officer, to detain a patient for up to three days in the case of urgency on his own initiative.[4] The Royal Commission on the Law Relating to Mental Illness and Mental Deficiency had similarly recommended that the powers of the police to detain a person suffering from mental disorder found in a public place should be restricted to their normal powers of arrest, but in the event this was not followed.[5]

The removal of prior magisterial sanction was balanced at the point of discharge by the introduction of a system of Mental Health Review Tribunals with jurisdiction to review the application of compulsory powers subsequent to admission. This afforded an avenue of discharge additional to the powers of the responsible medical officer, hospital managers, and nearest relative under section 47 of the Act. However, in a multitude of respects the structure, procedures, and remit of Mental Health Review Tribunals represented a significant departure from traditional legalism and the judicial model for determining the need for detention. First of all, application to a tribunal was restricted in the civil context to patients admitted for treatment under section 26 of the Act, or received into guardianship on a similar basis in accordance with the provisions of section 33. The facility was not extended to those admitted for observation for a maximum of 28 days under section 25, or, more understandably on practical grounds, to those subject to compulsory powers for up to three days under section 29, section 30(2), section 135, or section 136 of the Act. Secondly, application to a Mental Health Review Tribunal was not to be an appeal procedure in the ordinarily accepted legal sense. Section 123(1) of the Mental Health Act

---

[3] See Lunacy Act 1890, section 16 and Form 12, and Mental Health Act 1959, section 31. This ability to refuse patients operates also in a criminal context where it has proved highly disruptive. Mentally disturbed offenders not requiring the security of a special hospital have of necessity been accommodated in prison in the absence of a special NHS hospital willing to receive them. An important influence here has been the refusal of the Confederation of Health Service Employees to accept what they regard as hazardous patients into non-secure accommodation, exposing nurses to physical danger. See L. O. Gostin, *A Human Condition*. London: MIND (National Association for Mental Health), 1975–77, ii, pp. 48–51.

[4] This power was exercised under section 20 of the Lunacy Act 1890.

[5] *Report of the Royal Commission on the Law Relating to Mental Illness and Mental Deficiency*, para. 412; Mental Health Act 1959, section 136.

234 The Mental Health Act 1959 I

provided that it was the duty of the tribunal, in arriving at its decision as to whether the patient should be discharged, to consider his mental fitness for release at the time of the hearing and not to judge the merits of the original decision to activate compulsory powers. Thirdly, whereas application to a magistrate before commitment was an automatic procedure which took place independently of the patient's desire to take advantage of it, application to a Mental Health Review Tribunal under the Mental Health Act 1959 was at the option of the patient and so depended upon his positive determination to challenge the opinion of the hospital authorities as to his unfitness for release. This militated against the cases of patients who were rendered passive by the particular nature of their mental disorder or by medication ever coming before a tribunal for review.[6] Fourthly, the composition of the tribunal with review jurisdiction itself incorporated a medical element. Section 3(3) of the Mental Health Act 1959 laid down that Mental Health Review Tribunals must consist of a minimum of three members and Paragraph 4 of the First Schedule that there must be at least one medical member, one legal member, and one lay member. Paragraph 2 did however require that there must be a legal chairman. Finally, the procedural framework of tribunal proceedings set out in the Mental Health Review Tribunal Rules 1960 established by the Lord Chancellor's Department pursuant to section 124 of the Act was particularly flexible and informal in character when compared with ordinary court procedures, allowing for example, the admission of hearsay evidence,[7] this in spite of the fact that these were the only such tribunals in the English legal system with the authority to discharge an individual from powers of detention. Further, Mental Health Review Tribunals were directly locked into the traditional court structure only to the extent of the availability of reference to the High Court on points of law.[8]

The reaction against legalism is demonstrated more broadly by other major reforms introduced by the Mental Health Act 1959. The Board of Control, which continued to enjoy a separate existence after the reorganization associated with the introduction of the National Health Service in 1948 as the supervisory authority concerned with the protection of individual patient's rights, was

---

[6] L. Gostin, *A Human Condition*, i, pp. 68–9.
[7] The Mental Health Review Tribunal Rules, 1960, S.I. No. 1139, Rule 14(2).
[8] Mental Health Act 1959, section 124(5).

abolished.[9] The Board's public reputation had been one of intimate association with the old regime of detailed legal control of mental health administration, despite its own record of resistance to legalism following the lead of Lord Shaftesbury, who, as Chairman of its antecedent, the Lunacy Commission, had fought a fierce rearguard action against the introduction of further legal safeguards into lunacy legislation in the period before his death in 1885. The Board in fact actually welcomed its own demise. Its departure also brought to a close the system of central scrutiny of admission documents, a task assumed by the Lunacy Commission in the mid-nineteenth century which had survived in spite of its laboriousness in circumstances of chronic understaffing, and its purely technical quality as a check against wrongful admission, in that impeccable documentation might easily mask a reality of flagrant impropriety. The Mental Health Act's de-designation of mental hospitals, whereby, theoretically, any institution could admit psychiatric patients provided it possessed suitable facilities for care and treatment, and the Act's endorsement of the concept of Community Care, also undermined legalism, by shifting the focus of psychiatric provision from segregated, claustrophobic institutions, of which carefully monitored legal controls were a natural corollary, towards alternative, less formal treatment facilities. We shall now look at how these developments related to the creation of the Welfare State.

Toward the Welfare State

In the inter-war period no government made a systematic attempt to reorganize the structures of social welfare. The Conservatives were the dominant party of Government: they exercised the decisive influence within the Coalition under Lloyd George which held on to power in the 'Coupon Election' of 1918, forcing the abandonment of Social Reconstruction in the interests of financial restraint; provided majority government as a single party in 1922–3 and 1924–9, and were predominant in the National Governments returned with huge overall majorities in the General Elections of 1931 and 1935. Lloyd George aspired to develop a convincing non-socialist politics of social reform in the early 1920s, in effect to revive and extend the New Liberalism, but his hopes of 'fusion' between his Liberal supporters and sections of the Conservatives in a new party to carry this into effect were defeated. The Labour Party held office twice during the

[9] Mental Health Act 1959, section 2.

inter-war period—in 1924 and in 1929–31—but each time as a minority government and under compliant and cautious right-wing leadership: that the 1924 Government hardly discussed the reform of the Poor Law despite its long standing commitment to abolition is a measure of the limitations of pre-War Labour Government.[10]

That Conservatism was politically dominant in the inter-war period did not preclude social reform. At the least the threat of social revolution, posed by mass unemployment and underlined by the Bolshevik success in Russia in 1917, provided a powerful incentive for those committed to the existing social order to shore it up by extending the state's responsibility for the effects of financial and industrial crisis upon working-class living standards. Indeed, unemployment insurance was repeatedly overhauled to meet the rising toll of those out of work in the 1920s and 1930s.[11] But the response was unsystematic. The devastation was ridden out without resort to drastic changes in strategic direction, whether state capitalist or Keynesian. The most influential custodian of social policy during the period was Neville Chamberlain, who was Minister of Health from 1924–9. Chamberlain's perspective upon social reform was the narrow one of administrative rationalization. We have seen that he introduced the Local Government Act 1929, which modified the Poor Law. In this he was not inspired by the vision of an opportunity for constructing apparatuses of preventive social intervention, rather he sought, in the light of a general recognition that the Poor Law was discredited, to improve administrative efficiency, conceiving it as a reform of the structure of local government and taxation.[12] Thus, in substance, the impact upon the principles of the system was modest. While the functions of the Boards of Guardians were transferred to local authority Public Assistance Committees, the latter's responsibilities were still general, instead of being parcelled out to specialist committees so that the barriers between Poor Law and non-Poor Law provision could be broken down. In 1939, despite the alternative sources of protection that had been developing over previous decades, one million people were still at least in part dependent upon

[10] B. B. Gilbert, *British Social Policy 1914–1939*. London: Batsford, 1970, p. 210. See also D. Coates, *The Labour Party and the Struggle for Socialism*. Cambridge: Cambridge University Press, 1975.

[11] See the Unemployment Insurance Act 1920, the Unemployment Insurance Act 1921, the Unemployment Insurance (No. 2) Act 1921, the Unemployed Workers' Dependants (Temporary Provision) Act 1921, the Unemployment Act 1934.

[12] B. B. Gilbert, *British Social Policy*, p. 211.

the Poor Law. Conservative social reform was thus reactive, incremental, and minimal. None the less, Bentley Gilbert concludes that

... by the coming of the Second World War, a consensus on social responsibility had appeared ... the British State had committed itself to the maintenance of all its citizens according to need as a matter of right without any concurrent political disability.[13]

The problem, however, was that the political history of the inter-war period had ensured that there was no co-ordinated legislative and administrative framework expressly designed to give effect to this revolutionary political development, nor was it given explicit principled recognition by government. Its machinery was 'an edifice which had been built, shambling and rickety, without an architect'.[14]

The intervention of the Second World War provided the opportunity for the formulation of means to translate this *de facto* into a *de jure* national minimum. As in the case of the First World War, massive extensions of state power were authorized to organize the war effort and again 'War Socialism' legitimated interventionism, stimulating innovative plans for social reconstruction based upon the greater deployment of state responsibility in times of future peace. The most celebrated blueprint for a new infrastructure of social and economic regulation was the *Report of the Committee on Social Insurance and Allied Services*,[15] which was appointed by the Wartime Coalition in June 1941 precisely in order to inquire into the anomalies produced by the unsystematic development of British social security. The author and sole signatory of the Report was William Beveridge (1879–1963), the other members of the Committee, who were permanent civil servants, having been downgraded to advisers and assessors to reduce the official imprint of what was clearly to be a radical and wide-ranging document of social reform.[16] Beveridge proposed a comprehensive system of social insurance guaranteeing minimum subsistence levels of income, co-ordinated by a new Ministry of Social Security; the adoption of policies of full employment apparently based upon state control of production rather than Keynesian policies of demand management, to which he was, however,

[13] Ibid., p. 308.
[14] Id.
[15] (Cmd. 640, 1942).
[16] J. Harris, *William Beveridge*, p. 388.

converted in 1943;[17] a free national health service, and family allowances. This network of reforms promised a new post-war social democratic order, but one which would be built upon ideological assumptions and structural characteristics that were well-established in British social reform. Beveridge himself was concerned about the problems of how to reconcile the collective effort to eradicate great social problems with the preservation of essential individual freedoms. That he was prepared to advocate major extensions of state planning in the early 1940s can be explained in terms of the reassuring practical experience of extensive interventionism in the war period,[18] and he later embraced Keynesianism, which offered the prospect of achieving full employment without massive state economic controls. The retention of insurance as the central method of social security provision was the legacy of the New Liberalism, originally adopted as an explicit alternative to the draconian social controls espoused by the Webbs. Beveridge's proposals thus represented a greater degree of collectivism, but of a type which was in keeping with Britain's traditions of social reform in compromising significantly with liberal individualism.

The Beveridge Report met with an unusually enthusiastic popular reception and indeed generated a degree of public expectation of radical social reform which sections of the Government found politically unrealistic and embarrassing. A version for compulsory discussion amongst the troops, distributed by the Army Bureau of Current Affairs with the aim of fortifying military morale, was withdrawn, and the Report itself and the widespread knowledge of its attempted suppression contributed to the radicalization of a returning army perhaps more politicized than any since the seventeenth century. The Labour Party's first overall majority in the General Election of 1945 may be attributed to this army radicalism, and to Labour's successful projection of itself as the party of social reform:

The reaction manifest in the election of 1945 against Chamberlain's party was to a large extent founded upon the belief that the Conservatives could not be trusted any longer with the stewardship of social reform.[19]

Labour's programme of nationalizing basic industries, central

[17] Ibid., pp. 429–30.
[18] Ibid., p. 440; see also V. George and P. Wilding, *Ideology and Social Welfare*. London: Routledge and Kegan Paul, 1976, Chapter 3.
[19] B. B. Gilbert, *British Social Policy*, p. 196.

planning of the private sector, and a comprehensive system of health and welfare services, free at the point of use, unencumbered by stigmatizing disqualifications, and financed out of insurance contributions and more steeply progressive taxation, promised the avoidance of a return to the pre-war economic, social, and industrial conditions associated with unreconstructed Toryism. Together with the Coalition Government's Family Allowances Act 1945, Labour's National Insurance (Industrial Injuries) Act, National Health Service Act, National Insurance Act, and National Assistance Act implemented the main outlines of the plan for comprehensive social responsibility for individual misfortune set out by Beveridge in 1942.[20]

The Labour Government's reorganization of the health and welfare services, together with the taking into public ownership of the 'commanding heights' of the economy, state regulation of private economic activity, and the reform of taxation, were hailed by its supporters as methods for effecting a qualitative transformation in social relations and promoting a new material prosperity, which would constitute the displacement of capitalism through peaceful Parliamentary means. But millenial expectations were not realized. The Labour Party's rejection of syndicalism and belief in the effectiveness of the mechanical transfer of private assets into public

[20] The Industrial Injuries measure made workmen's compensation part of the state national insurance system financed by equal contributions from employers, workmen, and the state. Claims disputes were to be settled by reference to Ministry of National Insurance officials, with rights of appeal to an administrative tribunal and ultimately to a state Commissioner, a structure which consolidated the Welfare State's anti-legalism. The main National Insurance measure compulsorily insured the whole adult population for unemployment benefit, sickness benefit, maternity benefit, retirement pension, widow's benefit, guardian's allowance, and death grant. It achieved administrative simplification by consolidating different types of insurance contributions and centralized the administration of payments, excluding not only the commercial insurance companies, but also the friendly societies. The National Health Service Act sought to provide free medical treatment, including hospital and general practitioner services, ophthalmic, and dental services, financed out of general taxation and insurance contributions—a particularly ambitious socialization of medicine which provoked fierce resistance from the medical profession who feared becoming salaried state employees, but the ultimate impact of which was modified by the retention of a private sector. Local authority hospitals were vested in the Ministry of Health and, as we shall see, mental health services were integrated administratively with general health services. Finally, the National Assistance Act secured a national minimum for those who were not entitled to claim under the national insurance provisions. It abolished the remnants of the Poor Law, including the workhouse, and gave local authorities extended powers to provide social welfare services on a functional rather than a stigmatizing classificatory basis, in accordance with particular individual needs rather than general status.

ownership ensured that the working-class perception of the changes was of a shift in the composition of management toward the state and trade union bureaucracy rather than a democratization of industrial and social decision-making. Many of Labour's key measures would probably have been enacted in some form by the Conservatives had they won office in 1945. They too would have had to respond to the undeniable popular enthusiasm for social reform at the end of the Second World War. The progressive Education Act 1944 and the Family Allowances Act 1945 were themselves introduced by the Conservative-led War Coalition. It is notable that the 1951–55 Conservative Government, although it had provided robust opposition to its predecessor, notably in joining with the doctors in attacking basic principles of the proposed National Health Service, did not attempt to reverse the major legislative achievements of the immediate post-war period, except in that the Iron and Steel industry, the one example of the extension of public ownership into a profit-making area of private industry, was denationalized. Naturally there were differences of emphasis, especially in the greater pace of de-control favoured by the Conservatives, but their essential strategy was one of accommodation and the occupation of new ground within an emergent political consensus in favour of welfare capitalism at home and intensified anti-communism in foreign policy.

The general reasons for the creation of the Welfare State included those which have been discussed in relation to the Liberal social reforms early in the century which prefigured it: the growth of mass democracy, the rise of the Labour Party, the strength of the trade unions, and the State's interest in national efficiency, with the inter-war industry and financial crisis underlining the deficiencies of economic reliance upon unrestrained market forces and the need for more comprehensively protective social services. As the structure of new welfare provisions to a large extent systematized, or built upon foundations that were already in existence, the Welfare State bore the marks of diverse ideologies: Conservative paternalism, Social Liberalism, and Fabian collectivism. Although presented as a stage in the gradual transition to Socialism, it was compatible with the operation of a predominantly capitalist economy and while it embodied a significant increase in interventionism and in collective responsibility rather than individual self-help, it was designed to promote a new basis for social consensus rather than to assert sectional working-class interests.

The bipartisan consensus which formed around the mixed eco-

nomy, the welfare state, more permissive legislation in areas of
personal morality, and commitment to the Western alliance in the
1950s, was founded in economic prosperity and social optimism.
There was a convergence of the Conservative and Labour parties,
epitomized in the term 'Butskellism' which coupled the name of R. A.
Butler, Chancellor of the Exchequer in the new 1951 Conservative
Government, with that of his Labour predecessor, Hugh Gaitskell.
Gaitskell's Labour revisionism and Butler's progressive Conservatism
permitted distinct continuities in economic policy. The Conservatives
were able to retain the Keynesian elements in Labour's post-war
economics, whilst throwing overboard the reliance upon planning
and physical controls, attributable to New Fabian influence in the
1930s,[21] with which they had been combined—a shift of direction
already, in fact, initiated by Labour at the end of the 1940s. Political
consensus was not purchased without a struggle, however: throughout the 1950s the Labour Party was wracked by conflict between the
Gaitskellites and the Bevanite Clause IV fundamentalists who were
determined that the changes wrought in 1945–51 should be a phase
in the transition to socialism rather than providing a political
destination in themselves. Nevertheless, the degree of consensus in
social policy in favour of a social interventionism softened by a
substantial reliance upon informal methods of control and a
diminished but significant retention of the legal protection of
individual liberty, was large, and furnished the political basis for the
impressive measure of agreement which supported the Mental
Health Act 1959.

The Consequences of the Mental Treatment Act 1930 and the National Health Service Act 1946

The Mental Treatment Act's strategy for circumventing the admission procedures of the Lunacy Act met with only partial success. The
section 5 procedure for temporary treatment of non-volitional
patients, intended as the main alternative to certification, was

---

[21] On the origins of Labour's post-war economic ethos, see B. Pimlott, *Hugh Dalton*.
London: Jonathan Cape, 1985, pp. 394–6. Several influential socialist intellectuals
were impressed by evidence of the success of planned production in the Soviet Union,
which they gleaned on visits sponsored by G. D. H. Cole's New Fabian Research
Bureau. See H. Dalton, *Practical Socialism for Britain*. London: Routledge, 1935; B. F.
Wootton, *Plan or No Plan*. London: Gollancz, 1934.

surprisingly little used after 1930[22] and in practice it was in greater use in licensed houses and registered hospitals rather than equalizing the access of rate-aided patients to stigma-free care, as intended.[23] The theory had been that in the maximum of one year during which patients could be kept in hospital with temporary status, most would recover and thus permanently avoid certification, which could then be reserved for those who actively objected to admission. However, this did not occur in practice. The paucity of temporary patients was such that Dr Edward Mapother was able to compare the duty under section 6 of the Mental Treatment Act to provide accommodation for their reception to 'a strict obligation to provide for the maintenance of the snakes of Ireland'.[24] The reasons typically advanced for the failure of the temporary procedure were its restriction to the somewhat uncertain category of 'non-volitional' patients and the simpler and cheaper character of the Lunacy Act procedures.[25] The persistence of traditional certification, involving a judicial agency, as the main method of compulsory admission after 1930 demonstrated the need for more radical legal surgery than that applied by the Mental Treatment Act. It appeared that some procedure akin to that for temporary treatment would have to be adopted as a positive substitute for certification rather than merely as an optional alternative, and that this would have to be applicable to all patients and not just those capable of being designated non-volitional. It could be argued in support of this that the usage of the temporary procedures albeit limited, for a period of over twenty years, indicated that it was now in principle acceptable to admit patients to mental hospital, in the absence of consent, without prior judicial sanction.[26]

If the temporary procedure had made little headway, the introduction of voluntary admission to public mental hospitals had been a

[22] Temporary patients accounted for 5.4% of admissions in 1938, 3.4% in 1947, and only 1.8% in 1952. See *Royal Commission on the Law Relating to Mental Illness and Mental Deficiency: Minutes of Evidence*, Appendix C: Evidence of the Ministry of Health and Board of Control.

[23] See *Journal of Mental Science* 81 (1935), p. 239.

[24] E. Mapother, 'Mental Treatment under Modern Regulations', *Mental Hygiene* (1935), pp. 133–4.

[25] See, for example, *Royal Commission on the Law Relating to Mental Illness and Mental Deficiency: Minutes of Evidence*, p. 270: Written Memorandum of the Royal Medico-Psychological Association, para. 31. See also *Annual Report of the Board of Control for the Year 1931*, pp. 3–4.

[26] *Royal Commission on the Law Relating to Mental Illness and Mental Deficiency: Minutes of Evidence*, p. 270: Written Memorandum of the Royal Medico-Psychological Association, para. 32.

notable success, as had the proliferation of out-patient clinics. The expectation in deliberations prior to 1930 had been that the new temporary procedure would play the primary role in furnishing an alternative to certification. In fact, by 1952, 68.5 per cent of admissions were voluntary and in the case of some hospitals the figure was in excess of 90 per cent.[27] By 1957, the Percy Commission was able to record a figure of 75 per cent nationally.[28] Although these figures mask regional variations, and differences of practice and policy in individual areas, they indicate a considerable change, with important implications. It is true that 70 per cent of the population of mental hospitals remained certified, but this reflected the accelerating turnover of patients: between 1938 and 1952 admissions increased by 120 per cent (from 30,000 to 66,000) and discharges by 160 per cent (from 20,000 to 52,000).[29]

This victory in terms of the scale on which voluntary admission was operating demonstrated that voluntarism was not only a desirable ideal but a wholly practical proposition. What had historically been an almost automatic reliance upon formal coercion to populate the nation's mental hospitals was now clearly at an end. This is not to say that voluntary patients were immune from subtle informal constraints upon their notional freedom to leave hospital at will. The one legal restriction, however, was the requirement of seventy-two hours' notice, written into the Mental Treatment Act provisions, and there was some doubt as to whether this gave the hospital authorities power actually to detain for the length of that period.[30] The problem with voluntary status from a therapeutic perspective was the degree of formality which still attached to it as a legacy of the nineteenth-century preoccupation with safeguards. As every voluntary patient had to be capable of signing an application for admission, this limited the range of those who could be accepted into hospital without becoming subject to some formal compulsory procedure. Furthermore, as we have seen, if volition was deemed to have been lost for a continuous period of twenty-eight days, then the patient had either to be transferred to temporary status or certified, if he was to remain

---

[27] Ibid., Appendix C: Evidence of the Ministry of Health and Board of Control. See also W. Rees Thomas, 'The Unwilling Patient', *The Lancet* (1952) 2, p. 972.

[28] *Report of the Royal Commission on the Law Relating to Mental Illness and Mental Deficiency*, para. 221.

[29] *Royal Commission on the Law relating to Mental Illness and Mental Deficiency: Minutes of Evidence*, Question 5: Ministry of Health and Board of Control.

[30] Ibid., Answer 5,438: British Medical Association.

in hospital.[31] Legal authority was dependent upon consent and there was no 'doctrine of the continuing will' enabling the initial consent to be taken as authorizing restraint and treatments during subsequent periods of non-volition.

This created difficulties for medical authorities anxious to avoid certifying their patients, especially in relation to cases of senility. If a patient were unable to give a valid signature for the purpose of application for voluntary admission, and were also suffering from some irrecoverable condition so as to produce ineligibility for temporary status, then even though they might not be positively resistant or hostile, certification would have to be imposed to retain them in hospital. In these circumstances, certification remained, as it had been for the generality of cases prior to 1930, a precondition of long-term hospitalization, in spite of the fact that powers of detention might not be actively desired by the medical authorities. The logical solution to this problem, and one frequently canvassed in the course of evidence to the Percy Commission,[32] was the complete informalization of status for the majority of patients so that both voluntary and non-volitional cases could be admitted without resort to the compulsory procedures. It is noteworthy that it was a general humanitarian criticism of the unreformed legal structure of mental hospital admissions that it had led to the certification of the old and senile, thus subjecting them and their families to unnecessary disgrace.[33]

The effect of the rapid and sustained expansion of voluntary status combined with the increasingly temporary nature of mental hospital residence, attributed to the impact of new physical treatments,[34] was to render much more realistic the claim that the psychiatric services were essentially medical rather than penal in character. As the image of these services was assimilated to a health service, so the legalism of the Lunacy Act 1890 seemed more and more out of place. The success of the principle of voluntarism lent credence to the view that staff and patients were engaged in a common enterprise and united by the search for effective treatments and ultimate cure. Approxima-

[31] The Mental Treatment Act 1930, section 2(3).

[32] *Royal Commission on the Law Relating to Mental Illness and Mental Deficiency: Minutes of Evidence*, p. 269: Written Memorandum of the Royal Medico-Psychological Association, para. 28.

[33] *Report of the Royal Commission on the Law Relating to Mental Illness and Mental Deficiency*, paras. 319–20.

[34] See for example, V. Norris, 'The Mental Hospital Service and its Future Needs: A Statistical Appraisal', *The Lancet* (1952) 2, p. 1172.

tion to the model of the health services required that patients put their faith not in the formal and negative type of protection afforded by a screen of legal rights, but in the paternalistic sympathy and ethical reliability of the medical and paramedical professions. The rise of voluntarism thus hastened a shift in the basis of mental health legislation from formal control to informal trust.

The National Health Service Act 1946, which came into effect in 1948, generated further pressure towards a complete legislative overhaul. Although the failure altogether to repeal the Lunacy Act 1890 ensured that the mental health services were subject after 1948 to an anomalous legal framework, they were administratively integrated with the rest of the health services for the first time. Public mental hospitals were vested in the Minister of Health and their regulation was subjected to the same structure of Regional Hospital Boards and local Hospital Management Committees as other medical institutions in the public sector. Although the Board of Control continued to function, some of its powers were transferred to the Minister of Health.[35] The intention was that the Minister should have comprehensive responsibility for the supervision of National Health Service hospitals and local authority services and for the accrediting of institutions performing similar functions outside the National Health Service.[36] As far as the mental health services were concerned, this meant that the Board of Control had to lose its executive functions in respect of what had until 1948 been local authority mental hospitals, and registering private institutions. It was left with those duties under Lunacy, Mental Treatment, and Mental Deficiency legislation relating to the protection of individual patients from the point of view of 'the liberty of the subject', such as monitoring the operation of the compulsory procedures and the visitation and inspection of mental institutions. Until its voluntary liquidation in 1959, therefore, the Board of Control was the repository of limited and special functions redolent of nineteenth-century preoccupations, while the administrative operation of the mental health services was largely transferred to the ordinary machinery of the National Health Service. The role of the National Health Service Act in regulating the mental health services was thus carved out at the expense of older special legislation.

---

[35] The National Health Service Act 1946, section 49.
[36] *Report of the Royal Commission on the Law Relating to Mental Illness and Mental Deficiency*, para. 106.

The continued presence of the Board of Control, with its legalistic ethos, served as a reminder that the mental health services were not wholly subject to the same modes of regulation and control as the rest of the National Health Service. Its retention of powers of inspection of National Health Service hospitals, which, as we shall see, caused problems for the Ministry of Health, diluted the principle of administrative integration. Furthermore, the persistence of the practice of designating mental institutions for the reception of patients under the Lunacy and Mental Treatment Acts and the retention of certification, detracted from the general reorientation of the health and welfare services from classificatory to functional criteria of division. It is contentious whether that degree of administrative unification which did take place really made a significant contribution to transforming their internal atmosphere and external image. Kenneth Robinson, a Labour MP and future Minister of Health, who was a prominent advocate of the reform of mental health legislation in the 1950s, has stressed the impact upon the practice of the mental health services of being swept into the medical mainstream organizationally and structurally, with the Regional Hospital Boards bringing new standards and attitudes to bear.[37] Kathleen Jones, while pointing out the administrative difficulties, refers to its 'manifest advantages' in terms of the promotion of parity of esteem between the psychiatric services and other branches of medicine, the unification of the treatment of mind and body, and of the psychoses and neuroses, and the reduction of the stigma.[38] However, Tom Butler has recently argued that the belief that the reforms of 1946–8 created an integrated service is 'illusory and unfounded' and that mental health remained characterized by professional and social isolation.[39] To the extent that it is legitimate to maintain that administrative integration did have an effect, it must be taken to have highlighted those aspects of the operation of psychiatric medicine which were inconsistent with the modes of thought and practice characteristic of medicine generally, and thus to make yet more inevitable greater measures of legislative harmonization with the legal and administrative structure of the health and welfare services as a whole.

[37] Interview with the author, 2 April 1977. Kenneth Robinson was himself a member of the North West Metropolitan Regional Hospital Board in the early 1950s.
[38] K. Jones, *A History of the Mental Health Services*, p. 275.
[39] See T. Butler, *Mental Health, Social Policy and the Law*. London: Macmillan, 1985, pp. 125–7.

One functional division stressed in the National Health Service Act was that between hospital and welfare services. The latter were to be in the hands of new local health authorities who were empowered by section 28 of the Act to make provision for the prevention of illness and the care and after-care of patients. The principle of integration was respected here in that the section applied to all types of illness and patients and not just the psychiatric sphere. In creating the legal basis for the local authority provision of preventive services and residential alternatives to hospital, section 28 represented an advance on the provisions of the Mental Treatment Act, which only referred to after-care facilities and out-patients clinics.[40] Although permissive, the provision incorporated a ministerial power to mandate local authorities to take action by order.[41] Local health authorities had alternative powers to provide for the mentally ill under the National Assistance Act 1948, sections 21 and 29. These were directed to the establishment of social rather than more medically-oriented services for persons suffering from some permanent handicap or chronic disability.[42] Confusion as to the division of responsibilities for provision of facilities 'in the community' between mental hospitals and local health authorities, and the permissive nature of local authority responsibilities, were factors leading to considerable local variations in the quantity and quality of services.[43] The paucity of services in certain areas was another consideration which played a part in generating demands for further legislative reform.[44]

In terms of provisions directed specifically towards revision of the legal framework of the mental health services, the most important innovation of the National Health Service Act was the abolition of legal distinctions between private and rate-aided patients.[45] Henceforth, all admission and discharge procedures were to be available to all patients, with the result that rate-aided patients could take advantage of the normal method of discharge for private patients—discharge by the 'appropriate' relative, subject to the possible

[40] The Mental Treatment Act 1930, section 6(3).
[41] In 1959, this ministerial power was used as a method of expediting the provision of Community Care facilities without waiting for the Mental Health Act to come into force.
[42] *Report of the Royal Commission on the Law Relating to Mental Illness and Mental Deficiency*, para. 707.
[43] Ibid., para. 596.
[44] See, for example, *House of Commons Debates*, Standing Committees, 1958–9, IV, cols. 141–3, (19 February 1959).
[45] National Health Service Act 1946, section 50.

248 The Mental Health Act 1959 I

imposition of a 'barring certificate' from the Medical Superintendent stating that the patient was dangerous and unfit to be at large.[46] The assimilation of the legal position of private and publicly assisted patients, so often recommended, reflected the principle of equality of status in the reception of services inherent in the post-War reorganization of social provision. The effect of this measure was to improve the formal legal position of rate-aided patients. However, as Larry Gostin has argued, in criticism of a similar discharge provision in the Mental Health Act 1959,[47] it cannot be assumed in practice that the capacity of a relative to intervene on a patient's behalf will be a reliable safeguard against unjustified detention. Its effectiveness will inevitably vary with the dynamics of the family situation. Rather than providing a substantial injection of libertarianism, this new right seems to have served further to liberalize the image of the mental health services and to confirm their medical character without seriously interfering with the power of the medical profession to make effective decisions on therapeutic grounds. Thus, the Society of Mental Welfare officers were able to observe as follows in their evidence to the Percy Commission:

The new right of discharge by the appropriate relative (or the fact that it exists) has been of the greatest value in establishing confidence in the mental hospitals. Previously many people vaguely but fully believed that the mental hospitals retained patients beyond the recognized period for some unknown and somewhat sinister purpose of their own. The new provision has either dispelled this belief or assured those still holding it that the matter is now within their control.[48]

In the case of what the Society referred to as 'ill-informed, mentally unbalanced or subnormal, perverted or ill-intentioned relatives'[49] the medical authorities held the barring certificate in reserve. However, the occurrence of certain problem cases does seem to have convinced them that its scope needed to be clarified or

---

[46] The Lunacy Act 1890, sections 72, 74. The Medical Superintendent's barring certificate could be overruled, on the relative's appeal, by the Hospital Management Committee, or failing that, by the Board of Control.

[47] The Mental Health Act 1959, section 47(2)(b). See L. Gostin, *A Human Condition*, i, pp. 43–4.

[48] *Royal Commission on the Law Relating to Mental Illness and Mental Deficiency: Minutes of Evidence*, p. 199: Written Memorandum of the Society of Mental Welfare Officers, para. 17.

[49] Ibid., p. 198: Written Memorandum of the Society of Mental Welfare Officers, para. 18.

extended to provide greater opportunity to override 'difficult' relatives.[50] Such criticism from the professions evidences a desire to modify this extension of patients' formal rights to improve professional control over times of discharge and periods of stay in hospital.

In practice, existing legal procedures were circumvented or even misused, with the tacit approval of the Board of Control, in order to achieve greater procedural informality and flexibility. Under the Lunacy and Mental Treatment Acts certifiable patients could only be treated in designated or approved hospitals, or places (which after the National Health Service Act 1946 could include mental hospitals)[51] designated for the reception of emergency cases under the Lunacy Act 1890, section 20. In the 1950s, certain hospitals were de-designated, and other institutional facilities outside the Acts were proliferating. These included special units in general hospitals, special neurosis hospitals, and 'long-stay psychiatric annexes'.[52] In these institutions, patients could be treated completely informally, and there was no power to detain. It was illegal to receive certifiable 'persons of unsound mind' without observing the procedures laid down in the Lunacy and Mental Treatment Acts. Nevertheless, such patients were being treated in non-designated psychiatric units in general hospitals with the knowledge of the Board of Control.[53] Experimentation with complete informality in relation to voluntary patients was also taking place on the basis of arrangements of dubious legality. It was widely felt by hospital authorities that the formalities accompanying voluntary admission under the Mental Treatment Act were deterring patients from entering hospital of their own accord when they were experiencing the early signs of mental breakdown. So it became the practice to declare a physically detached part of the hospital a separate institution not subject to special legislation and therefore able to receive patients without

[50] The Royal Medico-Psychological Association wanted to see the wording of the barring certificate revised to make clear that it included cases where the patient was dangerous to himself but not to others, to increase their control over suicidal cases: see Ibid., p. 275, Written Memorandum of the Royal Medico-Psychological Association, para. 63. The relative's power of discharge under section 72 was not always used against medical advice, however. See Answer 5200: Association of Psychiatric Social Workers.

[51] For comment on this development, see ibid., Answer 1673: Royal Medico-Psychological Association.

[52] See *Report of the Royal Commission on the Law Relating to Mental Illness and Mental Deficiency*, paras. 224–5.

[53] *Royal Commission on the Law Relating to Mental Illness and Mental Deficiency: Minutes of Evidence*, Answer 1599: Royal Medico-Psychological Association.

formality. Where the separate unit contained facilities which formal patients in the main hospital needed to use, legal difficulties were created. They had to be let out on trial to visit the informal section.

These tendencies represented an officially sanctioned movement towards informality of admission for voluntary and non-volitional patients which demanded either legal prohibition or accommodation, and which in the event was legalized by section 5 of the Mental Health Act 1959. Similarly, as in the period prior to the Macmillan Commission, the procedures of the Lunacy Act were manipulated to provide a *de facto* period of compulsory observation. Sections 20 and 21 of the Act were used for this purpose despite their technical restriction to emergency cases. As the Society of Mental Welfare Officers put it to the Percy Commission, this was 'a rather back-door method legally'.[54] Again, the Mental Health Act 1959, by providing an official twenty-eight day observation period separate from the procedures for emergency admission,[55] legalized and clothed with appropriate regulative machinery a practice already developed informally by the authorities responsible for administering the mental health services.

The Growth of the Welfare State and the Origins of the Mental Health Act 1959

Recalling that the post-war reorganization of health and welfare services had depended upon the inauguration of a new functional division which broke with the concept of derogatory categorization and labelling, the Royal Commission on the Law relating to Mental Illness and Mental Deficiency, when it reported in 1957, drew attention to the outdated persistence of this in the mental health services through the certification of the mentally ill, the ascertainment of the mentally deficient, and the specialized supervisory role of the Board of Control.[56] As the Royal Commission Report records:

. . . although those who administer the mental health services look on their work as a social service comparable with other branches of medicine or social welfare, the administrative procedures which the law requires them to use reflect an attitude towards the patients these services are designed to help

---

[54] Ibid., Answer 1124.
[55] Mental Health Act 1959, sections 25 and 29.
[56] *Report of the Royal Commission on the Law Relating to Mental Illness and Mental Deficiency*, para. 590.

which is quite different from the attitude which underlies our other social services today.[57]

From 1946 or so, there was a natural assumption of the need for new legislation. After the National Assistance Act had finally disposed of the Poor Law, it was considered impossible to continue indefinitely with the 1890 Act still in force.[58] Indeed, the reason given why a major overhaul of legislation for the mentally ill was not undertaken in the late 1940s contemporaneously with these other measures was the administrative technicality of the task at a time when the Government was labouring under a heavy legislative programme. While recognizing the need for legislative reform, it was felt that administrative integration of the mental health services with other health services was the most that could immediately be achieved.[59]

It was therefore clear to the architects of the Welfare State that their reorganization of health and welfare services had major implications for the mental health field. It was also clear to those responsible for the passage of the Mental Health Act that they were engaged in the work of completing an unfinished edifice. Thus Professor R. M. Jackson, a legal member of the 1954–57 Royal Commission, was able to observe, at a National Association for Mental Health Conference convened in London in March 1958 to consider the findings and recommendations of the Commission, that:

... all the present legislation is far too much rooted in the past. I think to appreciate it all one has to see how it is linked with the old Poor Law, the older idea that the proper course is to shut people away in special institutions, the conception of defined status, the status of a person is perhaps the most important thing in the whole layout. . . . The job as I see it of this last Royal Commission was essentially to see what had to be done to fit the provisions about mental disorder into the whole setting of the Welfare State . . . . I do not think today that we want to see persons with mental disorder labelled as such in any way, given their own special services

[57] Ibid., para. 72.

[58] 'Between the Appointed Day of the National Health Service Act and the passing of the Mental Health Act is a period of a little over eleven years. As far as the mental health services are concerned, the two pieces of legislation are complementary. The period between them thus has an unusually transitional character.' K. Jones, *A History of the Mental Health Services*, p. 283.

[59] See the statement of Aneurin Bevan, Minister of Health, on the Second Reading of the National Health Service Bill: *House of Commons Debates* 422, col. 45 (30 April 1946).

exclusively, however good the services are, at the price of being excluded
from the general social services . . . .[60]

Professor Jackson regarded this integrative impetus of the Commission's proposals, on which the Mental Health Act was later largely
based, as a feature which distinguished it from the Mental Treatment
Act 1930, which he saw as having a rather narrower emphasis upon
the assimilation of physical and psychiatric medicine.[61]

R. A. Butler, then Home Secretary, adopted a similar interpretation of the significance of the expected reform of mental health law,
addressing the same conference:

I feel that such legislation would fit into the mood of the moment. We seem
to have reached a new stage in our country's attitude to social reform.
During the last decade we have established a comprehensive service of
insurance relief to those who are disabled, sick, unemployed or otherwise in
need of help. At the same time we have added substantially to an already
imposing stock of houses with the result that our welfare state/social services
are at once the envy of the world and the despair of rigid economists.[62]

The relationship between the creation of a new legal and administrative framework for the treatment of the mentally ill and the
consummation of the Welfare State was expressed rather differently
in the course of the House of Commons debate on the Third Reading
of the Mental Health Bill by Mr Brian Parkin, MP. Describing the
measure as a 'massive addition to the Welfare State' he went on to
declare that:

. . . not only does it give encouragement to all those engaged in the medical
profession who are experts on the subject, but in a far wider sphere it will
give encouragement to social workers, schoolmasters, religious leaders, and
all those who have felt there was something missing in the structure of the
Welfare State, some point at which one had to drop a case or problem in
despair, some feeling that it is the last resort when it gets into the hands of
psychiatrists or mental hospitals . . . . We have now reached a stage where the
mental health service will be on equal terms with the rest of the social
services. It leads us to the problem of co-ordinating welfare work between
one social service and another.[63]

[60] The National Association for Mental Health, *Report of the Royal Commission on the
Law Relating to Mental Illness and Mental Deficiency: Implications for Local Authorities and
the General Public*, Proceedings of a Conference held at Church House, 6 and 7 March 1958,
p. 27.
[61] Id.
[62] Ibid., p. 7.
[63] *House of Commons Debates* 605, col. 447 (6 May 1959).

The advent of the Welfare State and changing medical and administrative practice within the mental health services generated the need for a new legal code for the treatment of the mentally ill. However, the scale and complexity of the task of reform was daunting, and this conspired with the low political interest of mental health issues to delay any official review of the legislation in force. When the announcement of a Royal Commission did materialize, in the form of a statement to the House of Commons by Sir Winston Churchill, the Prime Minister, on 22 October 1953,[64] it actually came as something of a surprise to those parties interested in reform[65] and so an initiative at this particular historical juncture requires explanation.

Libertarian Criticism of the Mental Deficiency Laws

In the early 1950s a sense of urgency was supplied by a spate of legal actions seeking the release from mental deficiency institutions mainly of 'high grade' adolescent inmates on grounds of unwarranted detention. The patients in these actions were mostly represented by John Platts-Mills, QC, and some, such as that of Janet Pritchard, which caused much concern in the Summer of 1953,[66] were handled

[64] *House of Commons Debates* 518, cols. 2153–6 (22 October 1953).
[65] This was attested by Alexander Walk of the Royal College of Psychiatrists in an interview with the author on 28 April 1977 and by Kenneth Robinson in a similar interview on 2 April 1977. The phrase 'out of the blue' was used to describe the announcement.
[66] See *The Times*, 21 July–5 August 1953. In *Mental Health, Social Policy and the Law*, Tom Butler attaches great importance to the case of 'the Shropshire girl' (see *House of Common Debates* 518, Written Answers, cols. 282–7 (22 October 1953)) in precipitating the establishment of a Royal Commission. This was a case which turned on disagreements as to whether the patient should be placed in a mental hospital, mental deficiency institution, classifying school, or approved school, and he argues that it was legal uncertainty rather than a scandal regarding 'the liberty of the subject' which was central to the establishment of the Royal Commission. However, at the time, the latter consideration was one of the main foci of public concern about the case, which was one of a series that had created disquiet. It was the case of Janet Pritchard that those who had followed the events at the time have cited as playing the main role. Tom Butler speculates that 'the Shropshire girl' and Janet Pritchard were one and the same (pp. 187–7), but they were not. The former was aged 14, had three previous convictions for theft, was in breach of a probation order, and was sent by Church Stretton Juvenile Bench to an approved school, from which she was sent on an urgency order under the Lunacy Act 1890 to Hollymoor Mental Hospital, Birmingham. As a result of diagnostic uncertainty and difficulties in arranging transfer to a mental deficiency hospital she remained there for several months before finally being sent to a classifying school for observation and assessment. While she was in hospital, her parents had become dissatisfied with the treatment of her case and had eventually sought her return home. Janet Pritchard was aged 20, and had been detained at St

by the National Council for Civil Liberties, which had begun to campaign vigorously for the reform of the law. The National Council for Civil Liberties first took up the issue in 1947 and claimed to have uncovered a serious problem regarding 'the liberty of the subject'. In 1950, a National Conference was held to review the Council's mental deficiency work, to which the Board of Control and Ministry of Health declined to send observers, an indication of their continuing disapproval of any accentuation of the civil libertarian perspective on mental health practices. The outcome of the conference was a call for a public inquiry into the operation of the mental deficiency laws. The National Council for Civil Liberties' campaign generated considerable publicity both in the medical and lay press and their case was further projected by the publication in 1951 of a report entitled 'Fifty Thousand Outside the Law'.

The legal dimension of the campaign was very successful, and culminated in 1956 in the famous case of Kathleen Rutty, who was found to have been illegally detained under section 15(1) of the Mentally Deficiency Act 1913 as being 'neglected, abandoned, without visible means of support, or cruelly treated' when she was actually working in a hospital as a resident domestic worker in the care of Essex County Council.[67] As a result of this decision, over

Lawrence's Hospital, Caterham under the Mental Deficiency Act, having been ordered there after pleading guilty to the theft of a coat. Her mother sought to quash a recommendation of the Visiting Justices to the Board of Control in favour of her continued detention, on the ground that her legal representative had been refused audience, but this was held not to be a determination of a tribunal in respect of which *certiorari* would lie (see *R.* v. *Statutory Visitors to St. Lawrence's Hospital, Caterham, ex parte Pritchard, The Times*, 22 July 1953). The Board of Control accepted the Visitors' recommendation, but an application for her release on licence was quickly agreed on the basis that the patient had originally pleaded guilty without appreciating, not being legally represented, the difference between stealing and borrowing in the belief of permission and with intent to return. Both cases were mentioned by *The Times* on October 23 1953, reporting the establishment of the Commission and observing that individual cases would not be addressed. It is likely that the Home Secretary's statement on the Shropshire case that it illustrated the need for the Royal Commission was an attempt to deflect anxious MPs from their demands for an inquiry into the disputed handling of that particular case. Keith Joseph and Norman Dodds, who later attributed the setting up of the Commission to the Pritchard case, without mentioning the Shropshire one, may possibly have confused the two as the latter girl was not named.

[67] *R.* v. *Board of Control and others, ex parte Rutty* [1956] 2 W.L.R. 822. The question was decided on a successful habeas corpus application to the Divisional Court of the Queen's Bench Division. See *The Times*, 7 and 22 February 1956. For other cases on the issue see *The Times*, 28 November 1956, 12 and 16 February 1957.

5,000 similar cases were declared illegally detained, and hundreds were released, the rest remaining in mental deficiency institutions for lack of alternative accommodation.[68] Like the discovery of tranquillizers, the Rutty case was a major development which took place in the course of the Percy Commission and influenced its deliberations.

The publicity surrounding the coercive machinery of the Mental Deficiency laws generated a ground swell of criticism, and calls for more effective safeguards against unjustified deprivations of liberty were increasingly audible. For example, in July 1951 the Labour Minister of Health, Mr Hilary Marquand, was asked whether he would review the working of the Mental Deficiency Acts and amend them in order to provide stricter safeguards against wrongful certification and detention, and he replied that 'the possibility of amending the Acts is receiving active attention'.[69] Pressure to amend the Mental Deficiency Acts, in order to improve the safeguards, naturally raised the question of overhauling the Lunacy Acts as well, as these were already on the agenda for modernization. Although mental subnormality was a socially and clinically distinct condition from mental illness, its sufferers could be perceived in the context of the philosophy of the Welfare State as sharing with the mentally ill the burdens of formal coercion, stigmatization, and institutionalization. Thus, in 1953 the Conservative Minister of Health, Ian Macleod, after dealing with a question from Lt.-Col. Marcus Lipton, MP, arising from the Pritchard case, under the Mental Deficiency Act 1913, was asked by Kenneth Robinson, who was to take the initiative in Parliament early in 1954 by calling the first general debate on mental health since 1930, whether he was aware that in many other respects this 'forty-year-old Act [was] out-of-line with up-to-date medical thinking', and whether he could hold out any hope of amending legislation in the next session. The Minister replied that he was very conscious that it was important to revise and consolidate 'the Mental Acts' as soon as possible.[70]

The announcement of the establishment of a Royal Commission to inquire into the law relating to mental illness and mental deficiency in 1953, as we shall see, was not the culmination of a campaign of sustained pressure by the medical profession or any other interested professional party. It was appointed in the context of growing concern about the operation of the mental deficiency laws. *The Times*,

[68] See *The Times*, 24 March 1958.
[69] *House of Commons Debates* 491, Written Answers, col. 181 (31 July 1951).
[70] *House of Commons Debates* 518, col. 1508 (30 July 1953).

commenting on the appointment of Lord Percy to lead the
Commission in January 1954, chose to juxtapose the two issues of the
long-term inevitability of legislative change following the setting up
of the National Health Service, and the impact upon public opinion
of litigation concerning the liberty of the subject in relation to mental
deficiency legislation.[71] Norman Dodds, MP, a libertarian opponent
of aspects of the Mental Health Bill in 1959, also linked the role of
these two concerns in the debate on the Report of the Percy
Commission in 1957:

... in 1953 much of the impetus which resulted in the setting up of the Royal
Commission was the result of the case of Janet Pritchard, and one only needs
to look at Hansard after the summer of 1953 to see that there were about 40
Questions on the Order Paper about that case.
It is true that the Royal Commission was set up because of the antiquity of
the existing mental illness and mental deficiency regulations, and because of
the contrast between the spirit which has permeated this legislation and that
of other social service legislation. It is also a fact that much impetus was given
to it by the Press and others who were dissatisfied with what was going on.[72]

In view of the fact that the new legislation which ultimately
emerged predictably reduced the emphasis upon formal legal
safeguards it may seem ironic that concern for the 'liberty of the
subject' played a part in its promulgation. However, it has to be
remembered that previous libertarian campaigns had precipitated
enquiries into the state of the lunacy laws with comparable results,
most critically in 1924. Furthermore, although the 1959 Act
abolished certain prominent safeguards, such as the involvement of
the magistrate in compulsory admissions, which were the legacy of
Victorian legislation, it simultaneously confirmed the movement away
from reliance upon formal coercion which had characterized the
period since 1930. This tendency was particularly evident in relation
to the mentally subnormal, for the Mental Health Act reversed the
heavy reliance of the Mental Deficiency Acts 1913–38 upon
compulsory procedure as a preliminary to institutionalization,[73] and
it was towards the operation of these Acts rather than the Lunacy and

[71] *The Times*, 18 January 1954.
[72] *House of Commons Debates* 573, cols. 155–6 (8 July 1957).
[73] For a systematic and historically documented critique of the coercive assumptions
of the Mental Deficiency laws see *Royal Commission on the Law Relating to Mental Illness
and Mental Deficiency: Minutes of Evidence*, p. 793: Written Memorandum of the
National Council for Civil Liberties.

Mental Treatment Acts that libertarian criticism in the 1950s was directed. This switch to voluntarism and informality enabled supporters of the Mental Health Act to acclaim it as a liberalizing measure. The definition of liberalism they employed was of course very different from the liberalism of safeguards championed by the libertarians. But it created sufficient ambiguity to convince them that on the whole it represented an advance on earlier legislation. To some extent, therefore, the Mental Health Act was welcomed by critics of the Mental Deficiency Acts as a positive response to their pressurizing activities in the Press, the courts, and Parliament in the early 1950s.[74]

One question which remains is why criticism of the ineffectiveness of safeguards was concentrated so heavily on the operation of the mental deficiency rather than the lunacy laws. It is clear from the evidence to the Percy Commission that there were many interested organizations who in the abstract strongly supported the retention of magisterial involvement in compulsory admissions procedure and other safeguards of 'the liberty of the subject' for the benefit of the mentally ill. They also believed that these safeguards had performed a significant role in deterring abuses. But they did not bring forward evidence of malpractices as the basis for arguments in favour of stricter safeguards. The Royal Commission itself received surprisingly few—only sixty—individual complaints, and found not a single one of these to be justified.[75] There was no organization in the early 1950s specifically concerned with mobilizing patients and ex-patients as a force to exert influence on the shape of the law, such as the National Society for Lunacy Reform in the 1920s, and other similar groups in the 1870s and 1880s. The National Council for Civil Liberties only gave evidence on the need to reform the laws relating to mental deficiency and it may be that they had not received the type or quantity of complaints from mentally ill patients to justify advancing proposals on the subject of the law relating to mental illness.[76] The Mental Treatment Act was far less coercive than the Mental Deficiency Acts. In the previous three decades the incidence of compulsion, and the average length of stay in hospital had been in

---

[74] See Chapter 9 of the present work for an analysis of the ambiguous welcome given to the Mental Health Bill by Parliamentary civil libertarian critics of the old Mental Deficiency Laws.

[75] See *Report of the Royal Commission on the Law Relating to Mental Illness and Mental Deficiency*, para. 256.

[76] This was the view of Alexander Walk in interview, 28 April 1977.

decline, and more liberal therapeutic regimes and less restrictive treatment facilities than the old-style asylum were in the ascendant. These conditions favoured a lower level of complaints alleging unlawful detention. It required a political reorientation as radical as that of the 1960s, with its demystification of the bureaucracies and professions administering the Welfare State and its profound rejection of socially incapacitating labels such as 'mental illness', to create the conditions for the regeneration of a libertarian perspective on mental health practices.

The Role of Therapeutic Developments

Some commentators have attached importance to the role of the development of physical treatments within psychiatry, with apparent curative effectiveness, in persuading the state to grant doctors greater legal authority over mental patients. It has been argued that the appearance of these treatments added credibility to the presentation of psychiatric disorder as a species of illness by according doctors a positive therapeutic role and enhanced their social control capability, encouraging the State to grant them greater legal powers.[77] It must be conceded that whether or not the physical treatments developed after 1930 possessed genuine curative potency and whether or not they contributed significantly to declining periods of hospital stay and levels of hospital population, it was certainly the conventional wisdom that they did so.[78] One must therefore assess the contribution of the development of 'cures' as an element in the context within which the Royal Commission was appointed and conducted its proceedings.

Before the 1950s, the major therapeutic innovations were insulin coma therapy (in decline by the late 1940s), electroconvulsive therapy and leucotomy. D. H. Clark vividly recalls their impact, describing first the position prior to their introduction:

. . . the doctor in the mental hospital was in a dilemma. He found himself working in a place where many patients did not get better; he had to endorse many things—such as straight-jackets, padded cells, forced feeding—which he did not like and which conflicted with his picture of himself as a beneficent healer; yet he could see no other alternative. The repugnant ward rituals were deeply established and entrenched . . . .
The first break into this static world came with the physical treatments—

---

[77] See D. Ewins, pp. 22–3, 32, 35–6.
[78] See the discussion in G. Baruch and A. Treacher, *Psychiatry Observed*, pp. 10–11.

insulin coma therapy in the mid 1930's, convulsion therapy, first with cardiazol, and then with electricity, in the early 1940's. These treatments made a tremendous change in the atmosphere of the hospitals. The doctors, the nurses, and the attendants could all feel they were really *doing* something; many patients made dramatic recoveries from years of withdrawal . . .[79]

We have here a classic statement of the contradiction between the roles of gaoler and healer in the position of the doctor, and then the presentation of the new physical treatments as a solution. This solution was not only for internal consumption but could be publicized in order to improve psychiatry's social standing.[80]

The most important breakthrough, however, was the advent of tranquillizers in the early 1950s, ushering in what Kathleen Jones describes as a pharmacological revolution.[81] The main new drug introduced at this time was Chlorpromazine, developed by a French pharmaceutical company, Rhone Poulenc, in late 1950, marketed in England as Largactil, and available in English mental hospitals by the spring of 1954.[82] Chlorpromazine was widely praised on the basis that its tranquillizing effect relaxed rather than sedated patients, so enabling other therapeutic techniques to be operated and the interal regime of the mental hospital to be liberalized. Also, of course, it provided more convincing evidence than any previous specific treatment for the doctors' claim that psychiatry was an unassailably medical discipline. Andrew Scull concedes this in incisive Anti-Psychiatric vein as follows:

At the very least, one must acknowledge that in this period they were given a new modality which enabled them to engage in a more passable imitation of conventional medical practice. In place of acting as glorified administrators of huge custodial warehouses, and instead of relying on crude empirical devices like shock therapy and even cruder surgical techniques like lobotomy to provide themselves with an all too transparent medical figleaf, psychiatrists in public mental hospitals could now engage in the prescription and

---

[79] D. H. Clark, *Administrative Therapy*. London: Tavistock, 1964, pp. 4–5.

[80] It must be stressed that Clark was not a devotee of physical treatment and proceeded to explain the 'effectiveness' of insulin coma therapy in terms of the social significance of the treatment process. Clark's concept of administrative therapy emphasized the potential of the organization of the hospital community as a therapeutic agency.

[81] K. Jones, *A History of the Mental Health Services*, p. 291.

[82] See generally, Judith P. Swazey, *A Study of Therapeutic Innovation*. Cambridge, Mass.: M.I.T. Press, 1974.

administration of the classic symbolic accoutrement of the modern medicine man—drugs.[83]

Pharmacological innovation was also given credit for the spread of early discharge policies and declining levels of hospital population, which became increasingly marked toward the end of the decade.[84] Scull, along with Geoffrey Baruch and Andrew Treacher, is dismissive of the grandiose claims made on behalf of the psychotropic drugs as an agency of fundamental change in the history of the mental health services. These authors challenge the statistical evidence for the argument that pharmacological developments were the main factor in producing a declining hospital population in the 1950s, pointing to indications of already established trends in this direction.[85] They stress the dangers of technological determinism, and the social as well as the clinical nature of discharge decisions. While Baruch and Treacher have the general aim of discrediting the applicability of 'the medical model', by which they mean assumptions derived from organic medicine, to the treatment of the mentally disordered, Scull's thesis is to lay responsibility for decarceration firmly with right-wing politicians intent upon economizing on welfare services in an attempt to deal with the fiscal crisis of the state. He maintains that the shift to Community Care in Britain from the late 1950s was neither a natural corollary of the introduction of new chemotherapies, nor a response to the sociological critique of the mental hospital as total institution,[86] but a strategy for averting an escalating crisis of overcrowding and underfinancing stemming from the need to invest on a massive scale to replenish and modernize the nation's decaying stock of nineteenth-century mental hospitals. The economic determinism of this argument has recently been modified to take account of the contention of Peter Sedgwick and others that decarceration preceded the fiscal crisis proper and that comparative analysis indicates there is no automatic relationship between the two.[87]

[83] A. T. Scull, Decarceration, p. 79.

[84] For statistical data on this trend see G. C. Tooth and Eileen M. Brooke, 'Trends in the Mental Hospital Population', The Lancet (1961), 1, pp. 710–13.

[85] A. T. Scull, Decarceration, p. 82 et seq.; G. Baruch and A. Treacher, Psychiatry Observed, p. 49 et seq.

[86] Two of the most influential negative analyses of the mental hospital were E. Goffman's Asylums (building on a paper given in Washington at the Symposium on Preventive and Social Psychiatry in April 1957) and Russell Barton's psychiatric critique, Institutional Neurosis. Bristol: John Wright, 1959.

[87] See A. T. Scull, Decarceration, 2nd edn., 'Afterword: 1983', p. 171 et seq. See also P. Sedgwick, Psycho Politics, pp. 202–3.

The adoption of a strategy of Community Care meant that the process of dismantling formal procedural safeguards, pioneered by the Mental Treatment Act 1930, was radically advanced by the Mental Health Act within a very different general context. The earlier Act sought to reduce the formalities surrounding mental treatment as part of a process of assimilating psychiatric to general medical care, and was designed primarily to deal with early and temporary cases. The Mental Health Act was not only concerned with assimilation, but with effecting the reduction of formalities as an element in a broader strategy of desegregating the mentally disordered, including the chronic section of the hospital population, and reintegrating them in the community literally as well as in terms of formal status. The de-emphasis of the mental hospital and procedural informalization were not independent and disconnected developments. The latter contributed to the dissolution of the barriers which separated off the institution from the community, and it oiled the wheels of a system within which sites of therapy had become more differentiated.

The new conviction that the mental hospital should henceforth be at the periphery of mental health provision represented, given that it had been the bedrock of the social response to mental disorder since the early nineteenth century, a profound change of approach. The development of welfare payments and services non-dependent upon institutionalization,[88] and the belief that the new drugs permitted treatment to be administered by a range of professional personnel in a variety of non-segregated settings,[89] were preconditions of this solution. Politically it enjoyed a broad appeal, reinforcing the consensus which greeted the Mental Health Act as a whole. Decarceration was highly compatible with the ideological themes of the Welfare State in terms of its emphasis of the effect of social environment and the need to treat the disadvantaged with paternalistic tolerance. But it also possessed an independent attraction to the Conservative Right, which was the faction least likely to be swayed by these sentiments. A policy of decarceration promised economies in public spending at a time when there was a pronounced tendency amongst such Conservatives to attribute Britain's economic instability to excessive expenditure, especially on welfare measures. This monetarist credo was the inspiration of the Chancellorship of Peter

[88] P. Sedgwick, *Psycho Politics*, pp. 203–5.
[89] See N. Rose, 'Psychiatry: the Discipline of Mental Health' in P. Miller and N. Rose (eds.), *The Power of Psychiatry*. Cambridge: Policy Press, 1986.

Thorneycroft in 1957–8. When Harold Macmillan removed him from this office, one of those to resign in sympathy on the principle of containing public spending was Enoch Powell. In 1961, as Minister of Health, it was Powell who was to announce a radical new phase of the policy of relegating the mental hospital in his famous inaugural speech to the National Association for Mental Health, when he challenged the apparent impregnability of the asylums: 'isolated, majestic, impervious, brooded over by the gigantic water-tower and chimney combined rising unmistakable and daunting out of the countryside'. Apart from the financial dimension, decarceration also held an allure for the Right to the extent that it would create pressures to a privatization of responsibility for the mentally disordered rather than the creation of new community-based welfare services, and thus accord with conservative ideals of self-reliance and the importance of the family.

If technological determinism fails to provide an adequate explanation for decarceration, it also fails to account for the informalization of commitment procedure and other enhancements of medical discretion achieved by the Mental Health Act 1959. The political context within which new treatments emerge must be regarded as crucial in determining their effect upon the priority accorded to formal legal safeguards for mental patients by those with state power. In a political climate highly sensitive to the maintenance of individual liberties, the view of insanity as illness may have won increasing recognition without the social, legal, and moral issues raised by the use of coercion being confidently assigned to medical determination, as recommended in 1957 and adopted in 1959. In this period, it tended to be assumed that the conversion of custodial asylums to centres of active hospital treatment virtually eliminated the need for legal safeguards other than as a concession to public opinion and the rule of law as a tradition, and to provide an outlet for the irrational complaints of so-called paranoid patients. Again, from a political perspective harbouring suspicion of the potential authoritarianism of psychiatry, it would equally have been possible for new treatments to be seen as presenting new dangers against which safeguards should be erected. The involuntary or merely formally volitional administration of such treatments could have been regarded as a form of coercive behaviour modification requiring careful legal monitoring, as has indeed happened with the passage of the Mental Health Act 1983. The designation of liberty itself rather than the traditional responsibilities of diagnosis, prognosis, care, treatment, and cure as a medical question, waited upon political developments and in particular a redefinition of liberalism from the formal concept of civil liberty for the sane to the substantive or social concept of freedom of access to therapeutic services for the mentally ill. The redefinition of freedom was a feature of political change in early to mid-century.

Pharmacological developments were not the only important change to affect the mental health services in the prelude to the Mental Health Act. This was a period of 'therapeutic flux', of many and varied experimental developments within psychiatric medicine. Many tendencies in the organization of psychiatry in the post-war period were developments from earlier practice, but in combination, and when implemented on a significant scale, they constituted a discernible and, to many in the field, an inspiring movement away from the therapeutically limiting resources of the traditional mental hospital, providing the organizational foundations for the adoption of Community Care. These developments included the open-door policy, industrial therapy, the shift system, with one set of patients using accommodation by day and another by night, out-patient clinics, day hospitals, hostels, therapeutic social clubs, psychiatric units in general hospitals, growing social work involvement in local authority mental health services, and the therapeutic community system. This last was most associated with Dr Maxwell Jones of Belmont Hospital, who established such a system for the treatment of psychopaths and gave evidence on his experience to the Percy Commission. The concept of the therapeutic community was that social environment was a critical factor in the cultivation of recovery and that the hospital community had to be carefully structured in such a way as to promote cure. The hierarchical, disciplinarian, and segregative nature of the traditional asylum was regarded as the positive antithesis of a truly therapeutic environment which would encourage participation, democracy, and personal responsibility within a co-operative framework.[90] The concept of the therapeutic community therefore entailed a sociological critique of the established mental hospital structure and, implicitly, of the social values dominant beyond its boundaries. Psychiatrists who were practitioners of or sympathetic to this perspective, such as Dr D. H. Clark and Dr R. N. Rapoport came to be identified as a distinct school of Social Psychiatry.[91] The political basis of Social Psychiatry lay in anti-Fascism

---

[90] See, for example, R. N. Rapoport, *Community as Doctor*. London: Tavistock, 1961.
[91] M. Jones, *Social Psychiatry*. London: Tavistock, 1952.

and a democratic communalist response to totalitarian values
deriving from the experience of the Second World War: therapeutic
community techniques were initially employed in the rehabilitation of
disturbed soldiers during and after the war and were then translated
to civilian settings.[92] Social reconstruction was therefore not only a
political impulse which impacted on mental health through the
reorganization of health and welfare services, but one which
operated within the mental hospital itself as a challenge to its
traditionally authoritarian principles of organization. The application of radical democratic values in the resocialization of psychiatric
patients by the most advanced disciples of Social Psychiatry was to
cultivate a critique of the relationship of orthodox psychiatry to the
political order and contribute to the genesis of Anti-Psychiatry.

The radical reappraisal of the role of the mental hospital coexisted
with the persistence of the trend in the early part of the century
toward the expansion of the population of 'the psychiatrized', with
greater concentration upon the treatment of neurosis and the
positive promotion of variously defined states of mental health.[93]
Psychiatry's acquisition of associations with the ideal of scientifically
generating social harmony, with progressive experimentation in the
egalitarian structuring of human relationships, and with the development of advanced new forms of organization for the administration
of therapy, attuned well with the aspirations embodied in the Welfare
State and a self-conscious New Elizabethan Age.[94] Therapeutic
optimism at the political level was an important precondition for the
generous dispensation accorded to psychiatry by the Mental Health
Act 1959.[95]

[92] P. Sedgwick, p. 206.
[93] B. Wootton, *Social Service and Social Pathology*. London: Allen & Unwin, 1959,
p. 211 *et seq.*
[94] For an illuminating psychiatric flight of fantasy regarding future dynamic
modernization of the mental health services see D. C. Maddison, 'Blueprint for a
Model Psychiatric Hospital of the Future', in H. Freeman and J. Farndale (eds.),
Trends in the Mental Health Services. London: Pergamon Press, 1963, p. 94.
[95] For comments on the relationship between the Mental Health Act 1959 and the
concept of the therapeutic community and Social Psychiatry see Dr Maxwell Jones'
'Introduction' in R. N. Rapoport, *Community as Doctor*.

9 The Mental Health Act 1959: II The Evolution of a New Legal Framework

THE Royal Commission on the Law relating to Mental Illness and Mental Deficiency, appointed in 1954 by the 1951–5 Churchill Government, was broadly based and possessed considerable professional expertise and experience. An interesting link with the Macmillan Commission was provided by the fact that its Chairman, Sir Eustace Percy (1887–1958), had actually served on the earlier body for a short time before becoming President of the Board of Education in the 1924–9 Baldwin administration. The consolidation of the medical profession's hegemony in the field of mental treatment, and the increasing antipathy toward legalism, was reflected in the balance of professional representation on the Commission. Whereas in 1924–6 a radical shift away from the late nineteenth-century preoccupation with legal safeguards had been achieved despite a legal chairman and a predominance of lawyers over doctors, in 1954–7 the Chairman was neither legal nor medical in background and medical exceeded legal representation by four to three. The Royal Commission consisted of Sir Russell Brain, a neurologist and President of the Royal College of Physicians; Lady Hester Adrian (1899–1966), a member of the Council of the Magistrates' Association, and daughter of Dame Ellen Pinsent, who had been a force in the National Association for the Care of the Feeble-Minded; Mrs Bessie Braddock (1899–1970), the Labour MP; Dr T. P. Rees, Medical Superintendent at Warlingham Park Hospital, who was actively engaged in the practice of open-door and other liberal therapeutic policies; Professor R. M. Jackson, author of *The Machinery of Justice in England*; Jocelyn Simon,[1] later Lord Simon of Glaisdale and then a barrister and Conservative MP; Sir Cecil Oakes (1884–1959), Deputy Chairman of the East and West Suffolk Quarter Sessions; Dr John Greenwood Wilson, first dual Medical

---

[1] Simon replaced Sir Harry Hylton-Foster (1905–65), also a barrister and Conservative MP, who assumed the office of Solicitor-General in November 1954.

Officer of Health for the Port and City of London; Dr David Thomas, and Mr Claude Bartlett.

Kathleen Jones has expressed the view that the Commission, despite its experience, was not particularly inspired or imaginative in the light of the state of therapeutic flux which dominated the practice of psychiatric medicine in the 1950s.[2] The Percy Commission was essentially weak in that its members, with the notable exception of Dr T. P. Rees, had little positive of their own to contribute. As a result they tended simply to adopt the proposals of the Ministry of Health and Board of Control which had been compiled by Frederick Armer, its Chairman, and Walter Maclay, a Senior Commissioner, and constituted a well-considered and coherent programme for legislative change.[3] In defence of the Commission, it could be said here that as the general direction of reform was predictable, only questions of design required to be settled. The Commission's terms of reference themselves indicated that its members should specifically consider the possibility of extending voluntary admission at the expense of certification.[4]

There was a considerable degree of consensus amongst the more important bodies giving evidence, such as organizations representing the medical profession and the Ministry of Health and the Board of Control, as to how the legal structure of admissions, detention, care, and treatment should be changed. The Commission at least attained a competent synthesis of a range of broadly congruent proposals which (apart from the suggested scheme of legal categorization of mentally disordered patients)[5] was remarkably little changed by Government and Parliament in the course of producing and debating the resultant Mental Health Bill. For example, the Commission, as we shall see,

[2] K. Jones, *A History of the Mental Health Services*, pp. 304–5.

[3] Interview with the author, 10 November 1975.

[4] Their remit was 'To inquire, as regards England and Wales, into the existing law and administrative machinery governing the certification, detention, care (other than hospital care or treatment under the National Health Service Acts 1946–52), absence on trial or licence, discharge and supervision of persons who are or are alleged to be suffering from mental illness or mental defect, other than Broadmoor patients; to consider, as regards England and Wales, the extent to which it is now, or should be made, statutorily possible for such persons to be treated as voluntary patients, without certification; and to make recommendations.'

[5] The Royal Commission recommended that the higher-grade feeble-minded, moral defectives, and other psychopathic patients should constitute one legal grouping, but the Government preferred the first category to be kept separate as the mentally subnormal, adopting a fourfold in place of the proposed threefold classification. See *Report of the Royal Commission on the Law Relating to Mental Illness and Mental Deficiency*, para. 186, and the Mental Health Act 1959, section 4.

adopted and developed the Socialist Medical Association's embryonic concept of review by a multi-disciplinary tribunal rather than initial judicial intervention as a safeguard for compulsory admissions into the major recommendation for a system of Mental Health Review Tribunals. This revolutionary idea did not feature at all in evidence from the Civil Service. The Percy Commission's brief was to 'modernize' the legislation governing mental treatment by equipping the mental health services to perform an expanded and more positively therapeutic role. This clear goal forged it into a body which from the outset proceeded on the basis of a commonly-held set of assumptions. This initial state of consensus owed something to the criteria of selection applied by the Government, for although lay and legal members were appointed, no aggressive advocate of greater formal legal safeguards was chosen as a counterweight to the professional preoccupation with therapeutic goals which could be expected from those actually working within the mental health services.

There is plenty of evidence of predisposition in the course of the Commission's examination of witnesses. When the very first set of witnesses, representing the Ministry of Health and the Board of Control, suggested the abolition of the magistrate for the detention of unwilling patients for up to twelve months, Lord Percy described the possibility as 'promising', although he did think that consideration would have to be given to the question of safeguards during that twelve months.[6] Just as members of the Commission made this sort of positive response right from the beginning to proposals for reducing the legal formalities surrounding detention in mental hospital, they were correspondingly harsh and persistent in their questioning of organizations who explicitly doubted the rectitude of compulsory admission being transferred essentially into the hands of the medical profession rather than legal or lay authorities. When the Society of Mental Welfare Officers attempted to argue for the expansion of the role of the duly authorized officer at the expense of the medical profession, emphasizing the relevance of social and other non-medical considerations to the question of detention, its representatives faced hostile interrogation.[7] Likewise, the Institute of Hospital Administrators, whose plea for the retention of judicial control of compulsory admissions was met with the charge that they were

[6] *Royal Commission on the Law Relating to Mental Illness and Mental Deficiency: Minutes of Evidence*, Question 220.
[7] Ibid., Questions 1, 147–62.

engaging in abstract political philosophy and failing to base their evidence on their professional experience.[8] The legal members also demonstrated their support for the abolition of judicial intervention before commitment. R. M. Jackson even participated in attacks on contrary proposals. His attitude was one of cautious and deferential questioning of recommendations for the reduction of legal safeguards allegedly based on clinical experience and it was only where legal protection was in danger of being radically undermined that he was trenchant or persistent.[9]

It is clear that the Commission was only concerned with safeguards at the level of providing potential patients with assurance that there were adequate legal channels for complaint and satisfying public opinion that there were suitable checks on the operations of the medical profession.[10]

Evidence presented to the Royal Commission

The Ministry of Health and Board of Control   The joint evidence of the Ministry of Health and the Board of Control was delivered to the Commission in two stages, the first in May 1954 at the commencement of its proceedings, and the second in March 1955. The witnesses were I. F. (later Sir Frederick) Armer, Chairman of the Board of Control and a Deputy Secretary at the Ministry of Health; H. R. Green, Legal Senior Commissioner with the Board of Control; and the Hon. Walter S. Maclay (1901–64), Medical Senior Commissioner with the Board of Control and Principal Medical Officer at the Ministry of Health.

Senior Civil Servants concerned with the administration of the mental health system could be expected to present the members of the Commission with a set of clear-cut proposals for the thoroughgoing reorganization of its legal framework, which would provide their deliberations with direction and create a reference point for the representations of later delegations of witnesses. In practical terms, the question of reappraising the legal structure had been current for a number of years, affording the senior administration the opportunity to develop a comprehensive and detailed policy. Historically, we have seen that the central bureaucracy played a more positive role

---

[8] Ibid., Question 3, 888.
[9] See his questioning of the British Medical Association, especially Questions 5, 358–79.
[10] See for example, *Report of the Royal Commission on the Law Relating to Mental Illness and Mental Deficiency*, para. 448.

than the medical profession itself in pressing for the philosophy of legalism to be at least modified, one reason being that it was not concerned directly with the impact of such a change upon the doctor-patient relationship. Surprisingly, however, in the first session of evidence, the Commission did not find itself confronted by any specific bureaucratic initiative. The Ministry of Health and Board of Control witnesses were remarkably cautious and tentative in suggesting reforms. In their written memorandum, they expressed their opposition to the deterrent potential of formal procedures under the Lunacy Acts and proposed the general principle of informality for willing patients, the reduction of formal procedures for unwilling patients to the minimum necessary for essential effective safeguards, and the assimilation of mental health administration in most respects to the rest of the health service. In the course of oral examination, they stressed that certification should be the last resort, reversing the assumption of the Lunacy Act 1890, and conceded that logically this required some new procedure short of certification. However, their position on the nature of this procedure was self-admittedly unformulated and it was only after lengthy exploratory questioning that the following clear statement of policy was elicited: 'We are suggesting that in our view it would be right and desirable to have a system whereby a person unwilling to receive treatment should in fact be detained perhaps up to twelve months by some procedure such as a temporary order procedure'.[11]

Thus the Ministry would only commit itself to extending the availability of the non-judicial temporary procedure to unwilling as well as non-volitional patients, and in fact at this stage resisted suggestions for the total abolition of prior magisterial intervention.[12] The witnesses' overall response to promptings from members of the Commission in favour of major liberalizations of the procedures for detention was reticent.[13] It is easy to conclude that they were deliberately vague as to how far formal legal safeguards should be sacrificed to therapeutic efficiency, and respectful towards the need to protect 'the liberty of the subject', in order to engineer fundamental legislative changes at the end of the day.[14]

[11] *Royal Commission on the Law Relating to Mental Illness and Mental Deficiency: Minutes of Evidence*, Answer 198: I. F. Armer.
[12] Ibid., Answer 209.
[13] Ibid., Answers 77 and 193.
[14] This interpretation was shared by Alexander Walk in interview with the author, 28 April 1977.

In their second appearance, the representatives of the Ministry of Health and Board of Control demonstrated much greater certainty, both in the content of their recommendations and the style of their exchanges with members of the Commission. In their 'Supplementary Memorandum' they set out in full the details of a procedure if unwilling patients were to be detained for a longer period than that permissible under existing legislation.[15] The procedure resembled that eventually adopted for admission for treatment under section 26 of the Mental Health Act 1959. Application would be made by a relative or the duly authorized officer, and supported by two medical recommendations, one from a practitioner specially approved by the local authority and the other from the patient's usual medical attendant, stating that the patient was mentally ill and in need of treatment. The application duly made would serve as authority for detention without judicial sanction and would be effective in the first instance for one year, but renewable at regular intervals. This procedure was envisaged as superseding certification and therefore dispensing with the participation of the magistrate in commitment entirely. Recourse to the judicial authority would only be available after admission, and then not until the elapse of six months 'to enable acute, short-term cases to be dealt with before intervention by a justice', 29 per cent of patients admitted under order being discharged within six months.[16]

These proposals were appreciably less deferential to concern for civil liberties than the remarks of the witnesses in their first cross-examination. They were designed to minimize application to an outside judicial authority, by rendering it optional rather than automatic, and by postponing it for a lengthy period subsequent to admission. The memorandum makes clear that because as many as 42 per cent of patients admitted under order were discharged within twelve months, that period would have been preferred to the recommended six months' delay before application to a Justice if medical considerations alone had been taken into account. Only its supposed unacceptability to public opinion prevented the adoption of such a proposal. Furthermore, the suggestion for the retention of some form of judicial involvement was made not because it was believed to have any intrinsic value as a safeguard but merely as a

[15] *Royal Commission on the Law Relating to Mental Illness and Mental Deficiency: Minutes of Evidence*, p. 898.
[16] Ibid., p. 900.

concession to tradition.[17] The upper echelons of the mental health bureaucracy were therefore ultimately in the forefront of those pressing for a radical excision from the system of formal procedures which, in the official view, impeded popular acceptance of the ideas of treatability and curability. Confident that consensus could be achieved on far-reaching reform, they felt prepared to recommend the total abolition of judicial intervention prior to commitment and this can only have had major influence on the Commission's decision to propose the same thing to the Government in its report.

Also of great importance, however, was the joint Ministry of Health and Board of Control evidence, at both appearances, in favour of a serious reduction in the role of the latter body—a reduction so great, in fact, as to border on a recommendation for its abolition and the absorption of its functions by the Ministry. Kenneth Robinson has described this as a watershed for the Commission and 'a most altruistic self-sacrifice'.[18] It was recommended that the Board's major function of inspecting mental hospitals as an independent body be transferred to the Minister of Health with the effect that they would be inspected on the same basis as other National Health Service Hospitals. Furthermore, it was proposed that the scrutiny of admission documents to see that all formalities had been complied with, a long-standing legal safeguard, be transferred away from the central authority and become a local responsibility. A residual role for the Board of Control was envisaged in its retention of discharge as a 'last court of appeal'.[19] For this purpose, it was thought desirable for it to have an institutionally separate identity 'for appearance's sake'.[20]

These proposals for the emasculation of the Board of Control as a strong, independent body with a function of scrutinizing the administration of the mental health system, with a view to the protection of 'the liberty of the subject', followed upon a gradual absorption into the Ministry of Health for all practical purposes since 1948, and ultimately upon the centralizing and professionalizing changes in the Mental Treatment Act 1930. The National Health Service reorganization deprived the Board of Control of most of its executive functions and left it largely with the task of monitoring the

[17] Id.
[18] Interview with the author, 2 April 1977.
[19] *Royal Commission on the Law Relating to Mental Illness and Mental Deficiency: Minutes of Evidence*, Answer 4,694.
[20] Ibid., Answer 4,700.

detention and treatment of individual patients as a check on abuses. But the scrutiny of admission documents, being restricted to checking documentary propriety, could not be a substantive safe-guard where the alleged facts did not match the real facts of the case. Thus the members of the Board were engaged in an enterprise which involved a great deal of time and effort but was realized to be of limited real value.[21] Naturally, they were dissatisfied with this situation and wished to divest themselves of the responsibility. Similarly, with the inspection of mental institutions they acted in effect as the agents of the Minister rather than as independent investigators. They had ceased, to the regret of many working in the mental health services, to issue long and detailed reports on individual hospitals. With dwindling functions, and geographically housed in the Ministry of Health itself, the Board of Control had already in practice become absorbed, and was willing to be integrated officially. Thus, when the time came, it acquiesced in its own dissolution.

In terms of facilitating the transition to a legal and administrative framework for the mental health system consonant with the post-war reorganization of the health and welfare services, the significance of the Board of Control's complicity in its own downfall was that it helped the Royal Commission to dispose of 'the institutional epitome of the old philosophy'.[22] The Board, although criticized from the other side for being under the sway of medical opinion,[23] represented to the modernizers the organizational complement of the Lunacy Act, concerned as it was with the minutiae of legal procedure and designed to guarantee respect for the 'liberty of the subject'. The transfer of its functions to the Ministry of Health and local health authorities could be seen as completing the administrative integra-tion embarked upon in 1946.

This aspect of the Ministry of Health and Board of Control's evidence was out of step with that of the medical profession. On the one hand greater integration was welcomed as further administrative validation of the profession's claim that mental disorder was a medical problem and to be treated as such. On the other, however, the absorption of the Board of Control into the Ministry of Health

---

[21] Ibid., pp. 22–3: Written Memorandum of the Ministry of Health and Board of Control, paras. 97–9.

[22] Kenneth Robinson in interview with the author, 2 April 1977.

[23] See especially, *Royal Commission on the Law Relating to Mental Illness and Mental Deficiency: Minutes of Evidence*, Evidence of the National Council for Civil Liberties.

appeared to threaten the position of psychiatry within medicine, leaving it with no separate voice and thus forcing it to compete with other specialties. In the course of questioning of the Royal Medico-Psychological Association representatives by members of the Royal Commission, one witness, Dr Tennent, phrased psychiatric reservations as follows: 'From the point of view of the medical side itself it is good ... but from the patient's point of view, certain of them feel now that they have no appeal to anybody other than the person running the hospital.'[24]

But when this picture of widespread dissatisfaction amongst patients was questioned, an underlying reason for disquiet was articulated by Dr Alexander Walk:

Even if not many patients are concerned about that particular point we are .... We find at all these levels (HMCs/RHBs) that psychiatry tends to be neglected and pushed aside and therefore we feel that it is not appropriate at Ministerial level either that psychiatry should merely be one of the subjects dealt with by the Ministry. We feel it should be safeguarded by having a certain autonomy at that level and we feel that the process of integration with the Ministry has gone so far as it is safe to allow it to go, or perhaps even a little too far.'[25]

The Royal Medico-Psychological Association's position was fully supported, and indeed more strongly emphasized, by the British Medical Association. Whereas the Royal Medico-Psychological Association's memorandum stated that 'The Board should be maintained in a position of relative independence',[26] the British Medical Association's reads 'The Board should be maintained in a position of complete independence as a central authority',[27] demonstrating that the profession as a whole was willing to endorse psychiatry's claim to enhanced status as a specialty. In the event, however, the view of the administration prevailed and the medical profession found itself overridden, although it continued to campaign for such an independent body, which has eventually been provided by the Mental Health Act 1983 in the form of the Mental Health Act Commission.

[24] See, for example, *Royal Commission on the Law Relating to Mental Illness and Mental Deficiency: Minutes of Evidence*, Answer 1,870.

[25] Ibid., Answer 1,873.

[26] Ibid., p. 291: Written Memorandum of the Royal Medico-Psychological Association, para. 199.

[27] Ibid., p. 1058: Written Memorandum of the British Medical Association, para. 211.

The Medical Profession   Just as the role of libertarian criticism in precipitating legislative reform was historically typical, so was that of the medical profession. In the light of the expectation of eventual reform of the Lunacy and Mental Deficiency laws, the Royal Medico-Psychological Association established subcommittees which embarked upon leisurely deliberations and produced tentative proposals. In 1949, a subcommittee examined and reported on the provisions of the Northern Ireland Mental Health Act,[28] which had been passed the year before and was widely regarded as a pioneering measure on which future British legislation might be roughly modelled. In 1953, another subcommittee drew up proposals for an amended legal framework for the treatment of mental disorder and psychopathy for submission to the Board of Control. The chairman of this subcommittee was William Rees Thomas (1887–1978), a Senior Commissioner of the Board of Control, and so the memorandum was in effect a submission to himself. Although the Association possessed links of this kind with the bureaucracy, in that certain key figures such as William Rees Thomas and Walter Maclay were both members of the Board of Control and members of the Association, it appears that they were not actively pressured to initiate steps towards the adoption of new legislation favourable to the psychiatric profession.[29] Both the Royal Medico-Psychological Association and

---

[28] The Mental Health (Northern Ireland) Act 1948, and to a lesser extent Eire's Mental Treatment Act 1945, were frequently cited as models for reform of the law in England and Wales in the course of the 1950s. Section 7 of the former Act provided for temporary admission along the lines of section 5 of the Mental Treatment Act 1930 in all compulsory cases in the first instance, certification being reserved for those failing to recover within two years. The legislation in Eire abolished judicial process for the reception of compulsory patients altogether. Another comparative influence was, as on previous occasions, the legislative structure in Scotland. In 1955 the Department of Health for Scotland published a White Paper, *The Law Relating to Mental Illness and Mental Deficiency in Scotland: Proposals for Amendment*, (Cmd. 9623). This aspired to 'bring present law and practice into line with current and more enlightened ideas of psychological medicine' (p. 3) and recommended the removal of certain restraints on voluntary treatment and the introduction of a new intermediate class of 'recommended patient', to be admitted without certification and a judicial order, designed to cover non-volitional cases.

[29] In an interview with the author, Alexander Walk maintained that there was not a systematic organized campaign to achieve specific legislative objectives, either through connections with the Board of Control, or by influencing Government or Opposition: the Royal Medico-Psychological Association had no direct links with Ministers or Shadow Ministers until these were forged in the late 1950s by Walk himself, as Secretary of the Royal Medico-Psychological Association's Parliamentary Committee from 1956, with Kenneth Robinson and Edith Summerskill on the Labour side to

the British Medical Association played a relatively relaxed role until the Royal Commission was appointed, after which they collaborated in drawing up comprehensive proposals for a new legislative code. The setting in motion of reform was not so much Kathleen Jones' 'affair of pressure groups',[30] or a concession to medical imperialism as a logical initiative for any government committed to the consolidation of Welfare State policies and whose timing was sensitive to agitated public opinion.

The role of the medical profession in influencing the Royal Commission in the direction of recommending a major shift from formal legal procedures in civil legislation for the mentally ill should not be overestimated. Although the Mental Treatment Act 1930 encouraged the profession to pursue a radical legal strategy of annexing the machinery of legal coercion and integrating it into the therapeutic process as the best method of harmonizing the employment of force with the claimed healing function of psychiatry, even in the 1950s many doctors were unhappy about assuming such control and preferred judicial or lay intermediaries to take the responsibility for custodial decisions. An increasing social and political consensus in favour of state interventionism favoured increasing medical unity behind demands for less legal and lay involvement in the procedures for the detention and treatment of mental patients, on the basis that positive efforts to promote the health of the nation required professional experts to be vested with greater legal powers, but there remained plenty of scope for disagreement amongst psychiatrists and within the profession generally as to how radical such demands should be, both in principle and in terms of what was adjudged to be politically possible.

The medicalization of psychiatric practices by the partial replacement of moral and disciplinary techniques with new physical treatments and some movement towards integration with general medicine promoted the solidarity of the profession as a whole with its psychiatric branch in its plea for fewer legal restraints in the treament of mental patients. The British Medical Association was, as in

achieve specific amendments of the Mental Health Bill. As Rees Thomas, a member of the Board of Control, had not warned the Royal Medico-Psychological Association of the imminence of the announcement, this tends to confirm the view that it was a political response to unwelcome pressure on abuse of mental deficiency legislation rather than simply a natural development in the course of the bureaucracy's long-term timetable for legislative reform in the mental health field.

[30] K. Jones, *A History of the Mental Health Services*, p. 153.

1924–6, fully supportive of the Royal Medico-Psychological Association in its evidence to the Royal Commission, as was the Royal College of Physicians. In fact, the British Medical Association and Royal Medico-Psychological Association committees responsible for drawing up recommendations possessed an overlapping membership and mutually influenced each other's work. They reached a general agreement apart from certain points of detail, these differences being attributed by the British Medical Association witnesses to the presence on their committee of a general practitioner and a public health doctor, which had allegedly 'widened their outlook'.[31]

Neither the Royal Medico-Psychological Association nor the British Medical Association, although arguing that certification should be a last resort, pressed for the total abolition of magisterial participation in the compulsory admissions procedures. They did, however, support the introduction of a two-year period of 'temporary treatment',[32] the full certification procedure being reserved for those still considered in need of treatment who were unwilling to remain voluntarily at the end of that period, and for those unable to be retained as temporary patients at the end of twelve months or during the second year as being unlikely to recover. The recommended safeguard against abuse of this procedure was an informal and optional judicial review,[33] which was not envisaged as being accompanied by any power of discharge.[34] The judicial authority would only be able to make advisory representations to the detaining authorities. Sir Cecil Oakes, one of the legal members of the Commission, was prompted to observe that this was tantamount to 'bringing in the judicial authority on the strict understanding that he should act in an utterly non-judicial way'.[35] Professor Jackson was also critical of the proposal and has later commented on the unhelpfulness of medical witnesses in solving the Commission's problem of a suitable safeguarding mechanism as a substitute for the judicial order.[36]

[31] See *Royal Commission on the Law Relating to Mental Illness and Mental Deficiency: Minutes of Evidence*, Answer 5,286.
[32] Ibid., p. 270: Written Memorandum of the Royal Medico-Psychological Association, para. 37 and p. 1,036: Written Memorandum of the British Medical Association, para. 45.
[33] Ibid., p. 271: Written Memorandum of the Royal Medico-Psychological Association, para. 41 and p. 1,036: Written Memorandum of the British Medical Association, para. 49.
[34] Ibid., Answer 1, 629.
[35] Ibid., Question 5, 372.
[36] In an interview with the author, 2 May 1977.

Although this aspect of medical recommendations may suggest a bid for medical monopoly of decisions affecting the patient's liberty, there are some indications of caution. When asked why the total abolition of the judicial order had not been recommended, the Royal Medico-Psychological Association's reply was that such a proposal would be too radical and would not be acceptable, and also that the contrast between certified and temporary status was of therapeutic value for temporary patients.[37] In proposing specific compulsory powers for detaining 'incurable' psychopaths, psychiatrists demonstrated their preparedness to assume a frankly custodial role, but at the same time they conceded that 'because such a measure, though not involving any new principle, does involve an extension of present custom and practice, safeguards of an exceptional nature (petition to a County Court) should be provided',[38] advice unheeded by the Commission. It is also evidence of a cautious approach to legal procedures that psychiatrists thought it necessary to seek specific legal authority to detain psychopaths at all. Previous legal difficulty in relation to this category had stemmed from doubts as to their certifiability under mental deficiency legislation, given that they were often of above average intelligence, or under lunacy legislation as they did not necessarily show any signs of the intellectual disorder regarded as characteristic of insanity. Although patients whose only 'symptoms' were persistent aggressive or irresponsible antisocial conduct were sometimes compulsorily institutionalized as 'moral defectives' or 'persons of unsound mind', by and large existing legal classifications do not seem to have been expanded beyond their intended meaning in order to invent the necessary legal powers. Rather, the medical profession waited for an opportunity to seek authentic powers through the appropriate official channels. They were also insistent upon the retention of the central authority's power of discharge as an ultimate safeguard for all categories of non-criminal mentally disordered.[39]

Thus it would seem that the medical profession, encouraged by social and political changes to feel more justified in making radical demands, and more confident of a sympathetic hearing from the

---

[37] *Royal Commission on the Law Relating to Mental Illness and Mental Deficiency: Minutes of Evidence*, Answer 1,641.

[38] Ibid., p. 289: Written Memorandum of the Royal Medico-Psychological Association, paras. 179–80, and p. 1,056: Written Memorandum of the British Medical Association, paras. 191–2.

[39] Royal Medico-Psychological Association, 'Comments on the report of the Royal Commission on Mental Health Law', 1957, p. 10.

Royal Commission than they had been in 1924, were prepared to commit themselves more ambitiously to the second legal strategy I have outlined: that of integrating the machinery of coercion in the therapeutic process. At the same time, there are indications of caution in relation to the removal of judicial safeguards which suggest a degree of sensitivity to the persistence of the libertarian tradition in social democratic politics. Furthermore, there was an undercurrent of concern within the profession still that if doctors became responsible for depriving patients of their liberty and the decision was no longer seen to be in lay or legal hands this would damage the doctor-patient relationship. This feeling was referred to on several occasions in the course of Parliamentary debates on the Mental Health Bill, notably by Dr A. D. D. Broughton, a Labour MP and psychiatrist who claimed, though this was not the view of the British Medical Association or the Royal Medico-Psychological Association, that there was widespread concern amongst doctors about their proposed new responsibilities. Labour's Arthur Blenkinsop, speaking in the course of the debate in Select Committee, was moved to state that 'It is not by any means the case that this is being pressed upon us by the professional group concerned as a matter of self-interest on their part. Not at all. In fact, on the whole the reverse would probably be true.'[40] This emphasis upon the reluctance of doctors, including both psychiatrists and general practitioners, to accept control of compulsory hospitalization procedures reinforces the argument that the medical profession did not play an 'entrepreneurial' role in relation to the Mental Health Act 1959. The only professional organization to articulate this particular grass-roots concern, however, was the Medical Practitioners' Union, a small association with a progressive reputation whose distinctive characteristic was self-conscious opposition to the medical élite whose views dominated the British Medical Association. Although mainly concerned with general practice, there were psychiatrists on its Council, who were typically drawn from local authority rather than private practice or the large teaching hospitals.

The position of the Medical Practitioners' Union on this issue was succinctly expressed in a letter to *The Times* from its Chairman, Bruce Cardew, criticizing aspects of the Mental Health Bill including the abolition of the judicial element prior to commitment:

[40] *House of Commons Debates*, Standing Committees, 1958–9, IV, col. 275 (26 February 1959). An alternative interpretation of Mr Blenkinsop's statement is that doctors were pressing Parliament for this change, but not out of self-interest.

The decision to detain compulsorily mentally ill . . . patients will be in the hands of the medical profession alone. The community accepts no responsibility. Many doctors feel that the basis of trust on which all psychiatric treatment must rest will suffer as a result of their having to assume administrative or executive functions.[41]

It was thought that members of the medical profession would be moving beyond their sphere of competence in accepting control of commitment, which incorporated social and other non-medical criteria.[42]

Why was it the Medical Practitioners' Union alone which voiced these medical reservations? First of all, the Medical Practitioners' Union's position was predictable, given its consistent opposition to any proposal emanating from the major medical organizations and construable as an exercise in expansionism on the part of the profession's élite. If the other professional associations did not express a similar view then one explanation might be that the misgivings may not have been so widespread as certain MPs and the Medical Practitioners' Union itself alleged. Kenneth Robinson referred in Parliament to the dissenting element as a small section of the psychiatric profession only,[43] and Alexander Walk has recalled that there was little trace of this attitude in the correspondence upon which the Royal Medico-Psychological Association's Memorandum of Evidence to the Royal Commission was based.[44] However, in relation to this latter point, as the total abolition of magisterial participation in commitment was not initially suggested by the British Medical Association or the Royal Medico-Psychological Association, it was only when the idea was officially recommended by the Commission in 1957 that opposition could be provoked from within the medical profession on grounds of anxiety for the future of the doctor-patient relationship.

Whatever the scale, these traces of a conservative legal strategy toward the resolution of the gaoler-healer contradiction in the ranks of the medical profession as late as the 1950s demonstrate that the increasingly general social consensus in favour of greater interven-

[41] *The Times*, 17 February 1959.
[42] A similar stance was adopted in evidence to the Bishop of Durham's Committee on Euthanasia: interview with Hugh Faulkner (a witness for the Medical Practitioners' Union before the Percy Commission), April 1977.
[43] *House of Commons Debates*, Standing Committees, 1958–9, IV, col. 290 (3 March 1959).
[44] In an interview with the author, 28 April 1977.

tionism, implying expanded legal powers for professional experts and the greater receptivity of Governments to delivering professionals concerned with social welfare from legal restraints, had not produced unanimity within the medical profession in favour of a radical legal strategy. It is difficult to determine whether particular sections of the profession were associated with particular attitudes on this issue.

It is clear that dissatisfaction was not confined to general practitioners: two of the doctors who adopted this position in Parliament, R. Bennett and A. D. D. Broughton, were in fact psychiatrists.[45] However, it seems to be true that the medical élite, removed from the realities of routine transactions with patients, entertained fewer reservations regarding the prospects of a radical legal strategy for purifying the medical image of psychiatric practice.

A final aspect of the medical profession's evidence which is of interest is the light which it sheds upon the uneasy relationship between doctors and mental welfare officers, and its inclusion of a strategy for instilling a more deferential attitude toward medical opinion in the developing contingent of mental health social workers.

The designation 'mental welfare officer' was adopted by the 'duly authorized officers' of local authorities who inherited the statutory duties of the relieving officers with the final breakup of the Poor Law in 1948. Their association amalgamated with that of the original mental welfare officers of voluntary associations working with the mentally deficient, to form the Society of Mental Welfare Officers in 1954. In the absence of an even remotely adequate supply of trained psychiatric social workers, the mental welfare officers developed aspirations to transform their traditionally narrow legal and administrative functions into a social-work role which would be respected as an integral contribution to the therapeutic rehabilitation of mental patients. However, in the exercise of their discretion not to follow medical advice, when carrying out their statutory duty under the Lunacy Act of making application to a Justice for certification, they had come into conflict with medical practitioners.

There was dissatisfaction amongst general practitioners over what was seen as presumptuousness on the part of a body of untrained local authority officers.[46] Medical evidence before the Commission was that mental welfare officers must learn to follow medical advice on the need for compulsory action being taken. Although it was

---

[45] *House of Commons Debates* 573, cols. 75–80 (8 July 1957).
[46] See *Royal Commission on the Law Relating to Mental Illness and Mental Deficiency: Minutes of Evidence*, Answer 5, 386: British Medical Association.

thought impracticable to compel mental welfare officers to do this,[47] it was urged that there be greater procedural constrictions to encourage them to do so.[48] The medical profession saw the solution in a trade-off, whereby they would support the mental welfare officers in their claims to professional recognition based upon a national system of training,[49] a matter recently considered in the Mackintosh Report (1951),[50] and soon to be supported by the Younghusband Report (1959),[51] provided mental welfare officers were prepared to accept the imposition of a definition of their role which did not threaten assumed areas of medical prerogative.[52]

Social Work   Local authority mental welfare workers with roots in Poor Law structures or voluntary organizations and not yet systematically trained, provided the community-based rank-and-file foundation for the establishment of a coherent social work component in the management of mental patients. The élite were the psychiatric social workers specially trained at the London School of Economics and Political Science, or Edinburgh and Manchester Universities, whose professional organization, the Association of Psychiatric Social Workers had 573 members at the time of giving evidence to the Percy Commission. Psychiatric social workers operated in institutional settings of a diverse character: some worked for local authorities in the community, but others functioned in mental hospitals, psychiatric departments of general hospitals, child guidance clinics, prisons, and approved schools. The representatives of the Association emphasized the particularity of their skills in their evidence to the Royal Commission. The Association did not, however, unlike the Society of Mental Welfare Officers, directly engage the medical profession by asserting the *greater* appropriateness of its skills in relation to particular areas of decision-making. Rather, it chose to stress the status of psychiatric social work by portraying it as being

[47] See ibid., Answer 1, 683: Royal Medico-Psychological Association.

[48] See ibid., p. 273: Written Memorandum of the Royal Medico-Psychological Association, para. 56.

[49] See ibid., Written Memorandum of the Royal Medico-Psychological Association, para. 54.

[50] *Report of the Departmental Committee on Social Workers in the Mental Health Services* (Cmd. 8260, 1951).

[51] *Report of the Working Party on Social Workers in the Local Authority, Health and Welfare Services*, 1959.

[52] See *Royal Commission on the Law Relating to Mental Illness and Mental Deficiency: Minutes of Evidence*, Question and Answer 5,393.

complementary to and enjoying parity of esteem with that of psychiatrists and psychologists:

[The psychiatric social worker's] work is distinguished from that of the other disciplines in that her professional concern is with the interaction between the patient's disturbed behaviour or illness and his immediate family background and wider social environment.[53]

The Association joined with other organizations of professional experts in decrying legalism in mental health legislation and arguing for greater procedural informality to reduce stigmatization and remove the punitive image of the existing processes.

The tension between mental welfare officers and doctors adverted to above raises the question of what theoretical perspective the former were bringing to bear on problems relating to the application of powers of commitment to mental patients. Although the 'uncharacteristic' positions periodically adopted by doctors and lawyers in relation to mental health legislation do not have a clear social-work counterpart, the evidence of the Society of Mental Welfare Officers does reveal an interesting ambiguity in the theoretical basis of their approach, reflecting their transitional position at this time between a legal-administrative and a social-work conception of their professional role.

In their evidence, they explicitly challenged the idea that compulsory hospitalization was essentially a medical decision. They cast doubt on the reliability of medical opinion and its expert status, and defended their discretion to disregard medical advice in the execution of their statutory duties. Such a militant position hardly seems an appropriate basis from which to launch a bid for admission to the 'mental health team'.

There were two strands to the argument of the Society of Mental Welfare Officers. The first strand was legal in origin, in that in claiming that a decision on compulsory hospitalization was not solely medical in nature, it stressed the fact that liberty was involved, and the corresponding need for lay intervention of some kind:

It has been suggested in some quarters that admission to hospital is a medical matter and no one else should be concerned in a decision to admit. We strongly hold that such a decision would be undemocratic ... and do not think that there is any precedent in holding that one profession alone should

[53] Ibid., p. 1,001: Written Memorandum of the Association of Psychiatric Social Workers, para. 3.

have virtually undisputed authority concerning the liberty of a very considerable number of people.[54]

Accordingly there was sympathetic comment on the role of the magistrate in certification and at points the mental welfare officers seemed to envisage for themselves a quasi-judicial layman's function to compensate for the reduction in the Justice's role which they expected to follow new legislation. Similar sentiments were expressed in the evidence of another organization representing mental welfare officers, the National Association of Local Government Health and Welfare Officers, whose position was strongly pro-judicial. The second strand was representative of the social approach and the desire of duly authorised officers to establish themselves as qualified social workers:

The Duly Authorised Officer is concerned with the patients in their social environment and on this question of an order takes into account the factor of the safety of the patient or of others, in considering whether the patient should be removed from his environment. That is the question at issue . . . not the question of the person's medical state, when it is a question of removing him.[55]

To some extent the Mental Welfare Officers succeeded in transporting their critique of the concept of medical control of the criteria of compulsion from the philosophical plane of libertarian conviction to the level of asserting a rival professional expertise based on thorough understanding of the social elements in patients' situations rather than 'narrow' clinical perceptions. In doing so, they disturbed the medical vision of the professional order which would follow upon the thorough integration of the mental health services in the institutional framework of the Welfare State.

Medical anxieties were aroused by the Royal Commission Report's enthusiastic endorsement of the principle of Community Care. Having supported the ideal of Community Care as a preventive strategy which would enable psychiatrists to expand their activities beyond the confines of the mental hospital, and having partly conceded the importance of the therapeutic environment and skills in the understanding of social relationships, they now had to provide

[54] Ibid., p. 196: Written Memorandum of the Society of Mental Welfare Officers, para. 4.
[55] Ibid., Answer 1,162.

renewed justification for their claimed special competence to play a leading role in translating it into practice.

Thus the Royal Medico-Psychological Association's comments on the Royal Commission's Report articulated an anxiety that in future the mental hospital might suffer from 'a prejudiced inequality of esteem, in which [it] is regarded as a necessary evil, while any and every service provided by a local authority is invested with the prestige of "Community Care", even when it is in fact institutional'[56] and regretted the 'insufficient recognition of the amount of psychiatric advice and direction which will be needed, especially in the many areas where mental health services are at present in a very rudimentary state, or where medical officers of health are without psychiatric experience or interest.'[57]

Debating the Precedence of Legal Safeguards

There was a widespread agreement on the need to informalize voluntary treatment and extend temporary treatment from one to two years, leaving certification as a last resort, and, if temporary status were to be available for resistant as well as non-volitional patients, then optional resort to a Justice after, rather than automatic review before, commitment was generally acceptable as a means to obviating stigmatization. However, more than a few bodies commented approvingly on the role of the lay magistrate. The Justices' Clerks Society,[58] the Justices for the County of Devon,[59] the National Association of Local Government Health and Welfare Officers,[60] the County Councils Association,[61] the Society of Medical Officers of Health,[62] and the Institute of Hospital Administrators[63] all expressly supported judicial intervention as a matter of principle. A typical statement was that of the County Councils Association: 'England is governed by laymen advised by experts, it is considered the best form of government.'[64]

---

[56] The Royal Medico-Psychological Association 'Comments on the Report of the Royal Commission on Mental Health Law', 1957, p. 8.

[57] Ibid., p. 9.

[58] *Royal Commission on the Law Relating to Mental Illness and Mental Deficiency: Minutes of Evidence*, Answer 952.

[59] Ibid., p. 240: Written Memorandum, para. 7.

[60] Ibid., Answer 2,299.

[61] Ibid., Answer 2,820.

[62] Ibid., Answer 3,310.

[63] Ibid., p. 728: Written Memorandum, para. 6.

[64] Ibid., Answer 2,820.

In most cases this position of principle did not affect the organizations' substantive recommendations in favour of a more restricted scope for judicial decision-making. Rather they produced an antipathy to the idea of abolishing the magistrate's role in commitment outright and support for ready access to some form of appeals procedure subsequent to compulsory admission. Exceptions to this were the Justices for the County of Devon's positive demand for greater judicialization of commitment procedures, and the view of the National Association of Local Government Health and Welfare Officers that any extension of temporary treatment would be dangerous.[65]

Reflecting the political ambiguity of libertarianism, the positions taken up by the different organizations were a complex fusion of politics and professional orientation. The Socialist Medical Association proposed a radical restructuring of procedural safeguards, involving multi-disciplinary tribunal review in order that 'justice should be seen to be done'. This was intended to facilitate extending the scope of admission for temporary treatment by defusing libertarian suspicion. The Society of Labour Lawyers made some not altogether dissimilar recommendations out of a more straightforward concern to safeguard civil liberties, especially those of the mentally deficient. While the socially progressive instincts of the former were to modernize and rationalize judicial safeguards as a tactic incidental to the medicalization of admissions processes, those of the latter were to deflect the mechanisms of the law to the advantage of the most vulnerable and powerless.

A number of arguments were advanced in criticism of magisterial determination of commitment in the course of evidence. The main critical themes were similar to those current in the period of the Macmillan Commission. There was concern that laymen were not competent to make what were increasingly seen as diagnostic judgments regarding the need or otherwise for compulsory hospitalization of the psychiatrically disturbed. This line of criticism was well expressed recently by Professor Jackson, one of the legal members of the Percy Commission, who had had experience as a magistrate and in that capacity been faced with deciding lunacy cases. Appreciating the deficiencies of the certification procedure from the point of view of due process—for example, the practice of duly authorized officers

---

[65] Ibid., Answer 2,299.

touring Justices to find one willing to make an order,[66] and the admissibility of hearsay evidence on doctors' certificates in the form of 'facts communicated by others'—he took the view that, as it stood, the determination was essentially diagnostic in character and therefore magistrates were being called upon to make decisions beyond their capabilities.[67] If the proceedings were to be altered so that they more closely resembled a judicial enquiry, then this would produce 'grotesque results' in that most patients' needs were primarily therapeutic rather than legal. Given the fact that after admission few patients were resistant to hospitalization, it would be the most logical, economic, and humane course to leave the judicial element until then, when a more adequate investigation could be made. Hence the tendency amongst those immediately concerned towards consensus in favour of reducing the scope of judicial procedures and in particular limiting or abolishing magisterial intervention prior to commitment. In accepting this view of certification as an inadequate protection for individual liberty,[68] the Commission was, according to Jackson, influenced by the strong opinion to that effect of the Commissioners of the Board of Control, who 'knew it on the ground', although certain witnesses seemed satisfied with the effectiveness of the magisterial proceedings in detecting and deterring abuses.[69]

We have seen that the judges themselves had been at variance on the question of the nature of commitment proceedings.[70] The Royal Commission, while noting that the administrative and judicial elements in the procedure were difficult to disentangle, largely accepted the view elaborated by Dr Alexander Walk in oral evidence on behalf of the Royal Medico-Psychological Association that the historical origins of judicial intervention lay not so much in concern for liberty as in administrative logic. A reversion to this weak, pre-1890 interpretation of the magistrate's role was favoured as late as the 1950s by those who desired to purge the mental health system of legalism. A British Medical Association witness before the

---

[66] Ibid., p. 240: Written Memorandum of the Justices of the County of Devon, para. 8.

[67] Interview with the author, 2 May 1977.

[68] *Report of the Royal Commission on the Law Relating to Mental Illness and Mental Deficiency*, para. 266.

[69] See, for example, *Royal Commission on the Law Relating to Mental Illness and Mental Deficiency: Minutes of Evidence*, Answer 2,313: the National Association of Local Government Health and Welfare Officers; Answer 998: the Justices' Clerks' Society.

[70] See pp. 210, 232.

commission was prepared to countenance the retention of a diluted form of judicial regulation of commitment provided the Justice was brought in 'less as a magistrate than as a man of some public standing'.[71]

A second line of criticism was the alleged superfluity of the certification process given the amplitude of other safeguards inherent in existing or proposed procedures. This was, of course, a powerful argument when coupled with the claim that the mere existence of legalistic forms of commitment had seriously adverse effects on patients and on the general effectiveness of the psychiatric service in terms of stigmatization. The sort of safeguarding mechanisms on which the critics could rely included the relative's right of discharge, the limitation to certain specified persons of the power to apply for compulsory admission, and the requirement of medical certificates, which amounted to what the Royal Commission called a stipulation of consensus amongst different descriptions of person on the need for commitment. A further argument was that, apart from any question of the legal need for judicial involvement given the structure of the admissions process and the procedures for monitoring patients once in hospital, the social need for safeguards in general had declined. Here it was possible to point to the relative infrequency of verified complaints of illegal detention, with its implication that the medical profession maintained high ethical standards, and the increasingly curative and therapeutic rather than custodial purpose of compulsory hospitalization. Most persuasive of all was the acknowledged overcrowding and understaffing of mental hospitals, which suggested that medical superintendents with responsibility for discharge would not detain patients for a moment longer than necessary, and indeed raised the contrary danger of premature return to the community.

Without entering into a discussion of the merits of these arguments or speculating on the degree of practical need which existed for legal safeguards, the debate was conducted along well-worn lines directly traceable to the scares of the nineteenth century. The threats supposedly posed to civil liberties by psychiatric practice in general and the availability of doctors' coercive legal powers in particular still tended to be conceived in terms of expert over-enthusiasm or conspiracies between doctors and relatives. This was true of some of the supporters of strong safeguards as well as those

[71] *Royal Commission on the Law Relating to Mental Illness and Mental Deficiency: Minutes of Evidence*, Answer 5,372.

who sought to portray the practical dangers as minimal. The Justices' Clerks' Society, to take an extreme example, exhibited a straightforward concern for the protection of the sane. Criticizing the tendency of the Ministry of Health and Board of Control to wish to contain or restrict the part played by the magistrate and judicial forms of procedure they contrasted the nature of their own position:

> They are looking at it, and I am sure quite properly looking at it—from the point of view of doing good to somebody who needs help. We are simply saying that those kind of people are in the very great minority in this country; there is a vast assembly of people who are perfectly sane, and the function of the magistrate is to make sure that the liberty of the subject is not interfered with.[72]

When the National Association of Local Government Health and Welfare Officers tried to argue that judicial safeguards ought to remain at established strength because the development of modern treatments such as leucotomy and Chlorpromazine carried with it the possibility that periods of detention might be used to change patients' entire personalities, the Chairman of the Commission reacted with hostility. He accused the witness of 'stating the consequences of certification in an extreme and alarming form'.[73] Yet, in effect, the Justice's order, although technically confined to detention, did place patients under medical control, and, as the witness pointed out, although it was the practice to obtain the consent of relatives to serious treatments it seems that the consent of detained patients themselves was not usually sought, and there was no developed legal procedure for the protection of their interests in this respect.[74] Further, section 16 of the Mental Treatment Act 1930 was regarded by the medical profession as giving substantive and procedural protection against legal actions by patients, extending to

---

[72] Ibid., Answer 992.

[73] Ibid., Question 2,304.

[74] See the description of the position regarding consent to treatment provided by Edith Summerskill, Labour Opposition Spokeswoman on Health, *House of Commons Debates*, Standing Committees, Session 1958–9, IV, col. 245. A National Association of Local Government Health and Welfare Officers' witness before the Percy Commission stated that they had 'yet to find a case where a certified patient [had] been asked whether he [was] willing to receive treatment': *Royal Commission on the Law Relating to Mental Illness and Mental Deficiency: Minutes of Evidence*, Answer 2,303.

the administration of treatments and even to voluntary patients.[75] The Commission, however, clearly regarded therapy as a medical province and made no recommendations for lay or legal participation in the supervision of the administration of serious treatments. Similarly, the 1959 Act laid down no clear procedures regarding psychiatric treatment and the legal position was afterwards open to conflicting interpretations, being singled out as one of the major defects of the Mental Health Act by its libertarian critics.

To the extent that there was appreciation that patients' liberties might be more threatened by default than by conspiracy and in particular by the debilitating effects of institutionalization, this was not perceived as a justification for the reinforcement of legal safeguards. While it was arguable that some voluntary mental patients might in effect be compulsorily detained because of informal constraints on their ability to enter or leave hospital, the view of the majority anti-legalist school, adopted by the Commission, was that this should be informalized completely and that informal status should be normal for non-volitional cases as well. The effect of this would, of course, be to deprive these patients of the formal avenues of review reserved for those positively resistant cases who needed to be subjected to compulsory powers. The solution to the problem of institutionally induced passivity or dependence was seen, consistently with the ascendant legislative philosophy, in new policies for the therapeutic management of mental hospital populations: that is, hospital authorities were to be encouraged to develop a prejudice in favour of treatment in the community, so that this would be preferred wherever possible. Community Care was to be the enlightened substitute for the obsessive legalism of Lord Halsbury.

Finally, of course, great emphasis was placed upon the argument that there was an urgent need to do away with judicial intervention, at least prior to commitment and in the form of automatic rather

---

[75] *Royal Commission on the Law Relating to Mental Illness and Mental Deficiency: Minutes of Evidence*, Answer 2,532: Royal College of Physicians. A detailed examination of the history of the procedural bar indicates that both before and after 1959 it was specifically concerned with actions arising out of alleged abuse of the compulsory procedures. On the position under the Mental Health Act see particularly the statement by Richard Thompson, Parliamentary Secretary, Ministry of Health, to the effect that the bar was designed to apply in respect of proceedings arising out of the application to patients of 'statutory or other clearly definable procedures' and did not extend to informal patients: *House of Commons Debates*, Standing Committees, Session 1958–9, IV, col. 755 *et seq.* In *R. v. Moonsami Runighian* [1977] Crim. LR 361 it was held that leave was not required under section 141 for proceedings against those who assaulted informal patients.

than optional review, because its quasi-penal symbolism and stigma-tizing consequences were a denial both of therapeutic rationality and humanitarian concern for its supposed beneficiaries. Subjection to what was seen by its opponents as this irrelevant ordeal was thought to be especially humiliating for the elderly, as they would be likely to die officially branded certifiably insane, with all the attendant stigma, simply because of the inevitable mental symptoms of senility. Stress was placed on the pervasiveness of the stigma of certification, which was alleged to create popular doubts as to the mental instability of the victim's family as well as the victim, and which could never be shaken off. The consequences in terms of more material considerations such as employment prospects were also used in argument. The contention of the opponents of the magistrate's role was that all these ramifications of stigma were attributable primarily to the procedure of certification rather than to insanity itself, or to the fact of compulsory powers being applied. As in the 1920s, responsibility was pinned on its association of permanent affliction and total status, and this view was accepted by the Royal Commission.[76] But again, those who urged careful consideration before moves were made to limit or abolish the role of the magistrate strongly maintained that the stigma was not inherent in the magisterial element in certifica-tion, but an emanation of the bizarre, irrational, and sometimes violent nature of insanity, and naturally attached with particular persistence to those so seriously affected that compulsory powers had to be employed.[77]

The Commission's sympathetic reaction to these arguments against judicial procedures prior to commitment was natural, since they either reinforced or themselves reflected the impetus towards the rejection of the central role of law in the mental health services which the Commission itself had been appointed to make concrete in the form of detailed legislative recommendations. The main problem facing the Commission, however, was not in finding ammunition against the Justice, or in mobilizing support for his abolition: it was in originating an acceptable alternative form of safeguard against illegal commitment. It was not politically possible to recommend a complete shift to reliance on other safeguards, such as a professional-family consensus, on the need for compulsory admission. Even if the

[76] *Report of the Royal Commission on the Law Relating to Mental Illness and Mental Deficiency*, para. 264.

[77] See, for example, *Royal Commission on the Law Relating to Mental Illness and Mental Deficiency: Minutes of Evidence*, Answer 982: the Justices' Clerks' Society.

evidence seemed to indicate a lack of great practical need for recourse to some external protective authority such as the magistrate, traditional concern for civil liberty was too strong. Yet, any safeguarding mechanism reliant upon the wisdom of lay or legal personnel would be open to the charge of lack of competence, and would have to be very carefully designed to avoid criticism on grounds of its potential for generating stigma.

The Concept of a Mental Health Review Tribunal

The concept of a panel with medical as well as legal and lay representation empowered to review compulsory admissions provided the Percy Commission with an ideal solution to this problem. This idea had surfaced in the course of the Macmillan Commission's collection of evidence. Sir Robert Walden, JP, asked whether he had any views as to an independent tribunal to investigate the mental state of detained patients, replied that it might be possible to have a Board composed of a medical expert, the Medical Superintendent, and a magistrate.[78] The eventual form in which this solution materialized in the Percy Commission's recommendations was a system of locally-based Mental Health Review Tribunals, each of which would consist of one or more medical members; non-medical members, who would be 'people with experience of judicial or administrative processes and knowledge of the social services [who] might include some people with legal experience, some JP's and others with more general experience',[79] and a legally-qualified chairman. The Commission envisaged that these tribunals would have no continuing power of discharge, but would review individual cases of long-term compulsory hospitalization at the option of the patient. Even then they would not act in an appellate capacity, but would review each case and determine whether the applicant's mental condition at the date of the hearing was such that some form of alternative treatment facility might be more beneficial or whether outright discharge might be justified.[80] There would be no obligation

[78] *Royal Commission on Lunacy and Mental Disorder, Minutes of Evidence*, I, Question 2,116 to Answer 2,121.

[79] *Report of the Royal Commission on the Law Relating to Mental Illness and Mental Deficiency*, para. 443.

[80] Ibid., para. 445. The Mental Health Act, section 123 gave the Mental Health Review Tribunals an all-or-nothing power of accepting or refusing the application for discharge, a point seized upon by its critics for operating as a pressure against discharge being granted: see L. O. Gostin, *A Human Condition Volume 1*. London: MIND (National Association for Mental Health), 1975 p. 63. The Mental Health Act 1983, section 72(3) has granted tribunals more flexible new powers.

on a tribunal to hold a formal or public hearing, to issue a public report of the proceedings in each case, or to make the contents of medical reports available to applicants. It was envisaged that there would not usually be legal representation, and there would be a right of appeal to the High Court on points of law only.[81]

The incorporation of medical representation in the safeguarding mechanism solved the problem of competence inherent in the former exclusively lay authority. This multi-disciplinary character of the tribunal, and the therapeutic rather than judicial nature of its functions, together with the optional form of review and its situation after commitment, also removed any potential for the stigmatization of applicants. There was no question any longer of all patients being subjected automatically to any process which resembled a court of law either before or after commitment, as any review would be at the request of a dissatisfied patient and would turn on therapeutic criteria. Because the hearing was after commitment it could be argued that it would be more extensive and therefore a more adequate investigation from the perspective of civil liberties.[82] The inclusion of medical expertise would meanwhile ensure a skilled examination in place of the routine and peremptory proceedings allegedly characteristic of certification.

The Commission seems to have been unsurely groping towards some such solution from early in the hearing of the evidence. In questioning the very first party of witnesses (the Ministry of Health and Board of Control) the Chairman canvassed the possibility of a statutory admissions committee with a judicial chairman.[83] However, the real breakthrough came with the evidence of the Socialist Medical Association. In its written memorandum it recommended the establishment of an Independent Tribunal for complaints in place of the jurisdiction of the Board of Control, which would make more thorough investigations.[84] In the course of questioning, the witnesses elaborated on the concept and expressed the view that, in general terms, the tribunal should be composed of representatives of the medical profession, the legal profession, and the public, that it might well be set up on a regional basis, and that to assist with assessing the

---

[81] *Report of the Royal Commission on the Law Relating to Mental Illness and Mental Deficiency*, para. 451.

[82] This argument was advanced by Christopher Mayhew in an interview with the author, 29 September 1975.

[83] *Royal Commission on the Law Relating to Mental Illness and Mental Deficiency: Minutes of Evidence*, Question 206.

[84] Ibid., p. 686, para. 18.

validity of complaints, it should have the power to call for independent psychiatric examination of patients. It quickly became apparent that the Socialist Medical Association had not fully decided what such a tribunal's functions might be. On the one hand it was to take over the investigation of allegations of all kinds from the Board of Control, and on the other it was envisaged as an appeals tribunal. It seems that complaints of unlawful detention were here being considered simply as one particular kind of allegation, albeit very serious, that merited investigation, and that they were not thought of as deserving any special apparatus of their own.[85] The witnesses specifically tendered their suggestion of tripartite representation as an attempted solution to magisterial feelings of inadequacy.[86] Although the Commission did not exactly lavish praise upon the Socialist Medical Association representatives when presented with the tribunal concept, their indebtedness is obvious. Nevertheless, the twin ideas of optional review and medical representation which were embodied in their proposal were logically obvious, and the administrative tribunal was a well-established mechanism for dispute resolution in social policy fields. To the extent that tribunals proceeded 'scientifically' rather than judicially, pursuing a bureaucratic rationality rather than emulating the courts, they reflected the same interventionist movement which had made the demise of the certifying Justice politically possible.

We have seen that the proliferation of tribunals within the structure of the Welfare State flowed from the negative role of the courts in proto-Welfare State social legislation producing a pronounced reaction against legalism. The expansion of the range and number of administrative tribunals accelerated after the Second World War, the Beveridge Report having endorsed the entrenched anti-legalism of existing social legislation. The National Insurance Act 1946, the National Insurance (Industrial Injuries) Act 1946, and the National Assistance Act of 1948 all depended upon systems of administrative tribunals. This apparently inexorable movement, based both upon the philosophy of the Welfare State and the immense weight of decision-making which its new structures generated, did not go unresisted by anti-bureaucratic conservative lawyers. The Franks Committee was appointed by the Lord Chancellor, Lord Kilmuir, in 1955 to examine the question of tribunals and enquiries,

---

[85] Ibid., Answer 3,650.
[86] Ibid., Answer 3,647.

following the Crichel Down affair, and reported in 1957.[87] Whilst recognizing the inescapable role of administrative tribunals within the legal and administrative system, the Committee's recommendations entailed a movement towards greater judicial control and legal involvement, in the form of extended rights of appeal to the Courts on points of law and extended rights of legal representation. The Mental Health Act did embody a right of appeal from Mental Health Review Tribunals on points of law[88] and legal representation was allowed following the implementation of the Franks Report by the Tribunals and Inquiries Act 1958 and as recommended by the Percy Commission itself. The legalism of the movement to judicialize decision-making by various strategies did not correlate with or generate concern to retain the Justice in certification or resistance to the introduction of Mental Health Review Tribunals, a circumstance which recalls the similar non-linkage of Hewart's revival of Diceyism in the late 1920s with the pockets of resistance to the non-judicial character of the 1930 Mental Treatment Act's Temporary Treatment Order. Indeed, one of the authors of a Conservative Political Centre pamphlet, *The Rule of Law*, published in 1955, which made proposals to increase judicial control on tribunals, was Derek Walker-Smith, the Minister of Health who steered through the Mental Health Bill. That the issues remained compartmentalized indicates that lawyers were continuing to fail to defend the role of the Justice in civil commitment because of its archaic and ineffective reputation as a safeguard in an area where the proposition that medical judgement should be trusted increasingly seemed self-evident. It was now even less a suitable territory for asserting the importance of the rule of law than it had appeared in 1930.

In terms of the transformation of mental health law, perhaps more important than the tribunal structure of the newly envisaged review authority or its medical representation was its new function. The tribunals were to be provided as a therapeutic back-up for the mental health services, not as an external, critical structure essentially based in an antagonistic discipline:

We should make it clear that these review tribunals would not be [there] to consider whether the patient's mental condition at the time when compulsory powers were first used was accurately diagnosed by the doctor signing

---

[87] *Report of the Committee on Administrative Tribunals and Inquiries*, (Cmnd. 218, 1957).

[88] Mental Health Act 1959, section 124(5).

the recommendations, nor whether there was sufficient justification for the use of compulsory powers at that time, nor to consider whether there was some technical flaw . . . some time must have passed and even in a short time the patient's condition may have changed.[89]

Tribunals would be concerned with deciding the therapeutically optimum course for the patient from the available alternatives. Patients' mental competence was prejudged by the very powers of the tribunal itself which made its proceedings exceptionally informal and discretionary. These powers were in fact explicitly justified by the Commission in terms of assumptions about the nature of those likely to apply: 'It must be recognized that a large number, possibly the majority of the applications to the tribunal will come from patients who are clearly mentally disordered.'[90]

By contrast, a judicial decision was considered suitable in cases of overriding the unwillingness of patients' relatives.[91] This discrimination reveals precisely the same legal division between sane and insane which was embodied in the Lunacy Act 1890. The insane were seen as possessing needs which could best be determined by skilled professionals, paternalistically concerned for their welfare. The sane alone possessed that autonomous individuality secured by legal rights and exercisable against others seeking to invade private sovereignty. The difference was that the Lunacy Act reflected concern for the sane and thus elevated legalism, while the Percy Commission's recommendations constituted a blueprint for equipping the mental health services with a legal framework within which therapeutic expertise held sway in the interests of a more efficiently waged war against the social and economic consequences of mental illness, and thus concentrated on the 'needs' of the insane. The proposed tribunals were to be a safeguard for individual liberty only in an attenuated sense. The Commission did not feel that any review was inherently necessary, given other safeguards present in the recommended compulsory procedures.[92] It was, however, important politically that there was some quasi-legal procedure so that justice could be seen to be done and the harmless nature of psychiatric activity underlined. Therapeutically, the presence of review tribunals also had its

[89] *Report of the Royal Commission on the Law Relating to Mental Illness and Mental Deficiency*, para. 445.
[90] Ibid., para. 448.
[91] Ibid., para. 496.
[92] Ibid., para. 438.

rationale as an outlet for the anxieties of troublesome 'paranoid' patients who were 'vexatious litigants'.

Even so, the proposal excited the fears of the medical profession. The Royal Medico-Psychological Association commented that:

It is essential that the proceedings should be of the nature of an independent review, i.e. a 'second opinion', and everything possible done to exclude an atmosphere of litigation. Anything resembling a public trial of insanity has always been recognized as harmful to the patient. In fact it is unlikely that the medical staff of hospitals would agree to take part in such proceedings; they would almost certainly prefer to discharge the patient. The Commission say that legal representation will not usually be needed. It is suggested that representation of any kind should not be allowed, unless there is a point of law involved.

In order to emphasize the reviewing, non-litigious nature of the proceedings, it would be better to avoid the term 'tribunal', which inevitably suggests the adjudication of a dispute. The designation 'Mental Health Review Committee' would be more appropriate.[93]

Having committed itself to a radical legal strategy, the medical profession was anxious to stamp a clear therapeutic image on the emergent review tribunal from the outset. This was perceptive, for although the Commission was at pains to stress at every point that the tribunals were not intended to perform the functions of appellate courts, they had the potential to be developed into a vehicle for legalistic interference with medical decision-making authority. The Franks Committee, reporting in 1958, introduced the watchwords of 'Openness, Fairness and Impartiality' into the functioning of tribunals as a defence against their overbureaucratization.[94] The conception of Mental Health Review Tribunals was vulnerable to future modification by such general movements within judicial administration or to a concerted attempt by lawyers or libertarians to use any facility for formal representation to seek to mould them into courts from inside. Nevertheless, the therapeutic emphasis in this initial conception is especially revealing of the underlying philosophy of mental health law which was to become enshrined in the Mental Health Act 1959.

The Percy Commission's Report and its Reception

The Royal Commission on the Law Relating to Mental Illness and

[93] The Royal Medico-Psychological Association, 'Comments on the Report of the Royal Commission on Mental Health Law', p. 5.

[94] See, R. M. Jackson, *The Machinery of Justice in England*, 7th edn. Cambridge: Cambridge University Press, 1977, pp. 122–56 on developments since 1958.

Mental Deficiency published its final recommendations in May 1957. On the subject of admission, the most sensitive indicator of the priority of legal safeguards—the Commission counselled reliance on informal admission to mental as to other National Health Service hospitals not only for those expressing positive willingness to accept treatment, but for all cases in which neither the patient nor his relatives raised positive objection.[95] Further, informal patients should not be required to provide formal notice in advance of self-discharge,[96] although there should be a procedure for transfer to formal status for sparing use in cases of emergency.[97] The Commission felt that the retention of compulsory procedures in the new era of informality was justified and invoked the existence of legislative powers to compel the physically sick by way of precedent.[98] However, it was emphasized that these procedures should only be activated as a last resort.[99] Decisions as to compulsory admission should be concentrated in medical hands, so that the normal procedure (for admission for twenty-eight days' observation or one year's treatment) would be an application to the receiving hospital by a relative or mental welfare officer supported by two medical recommendations and without judicial participation. It was felt that the critical decision that liberty should be withdrawn was a question requiring medical expertise which could not be left to a judicial authority, as under the procedures for certification, or, as under the Lunacy Act 1890 section 20, to the local authority duly authorized officer.[100] There should be provision for emergency admission for a similar period on the application of a relative or mental welfare officer supported by one medical recommendation.[101] Applications for admission should take the form of an authorization, rather than an order on the hospital to admit,[102] and hospitals should no longer be specially 'designated' or 'approved' for the reception of mentally disordered patients.[103] Patients found by the police should only be subject to

[95] *Report of the Royal Commission on the Law Relating to Mental Illness and Mental Deficiency*, para. 288.
[96] Ibid., para. 289.
[97] Ibid., para. 302.
[98] The Public Health Act 1936, sections 169–70 and the National Assistance Act 1948, section 47.
[99] *Report of the Royal Commission on the Law Relating to Mental Illness and Mental Deficiency*, para. 316.
[100] Ibid., para. 390.
[101] Ibid., para. 407.
[102] Ibid., para. 381.
[103] Ibid., para. 378.

powers of compulsion where liable to arrest under normal police powers. Stressing the desirability of optional review rather than automatic safeguards, given the disturbing effects of procedures for the protection of liberty on some patients,[104] the Commission advised the adoption of a system of local Mental Health Review Tribunals, as a substitute for prior judicial involvement in cases of long-term commitment. It was envisaged that these tribunals would operate on the basis of flexible procedure,[105] and that there would be an appeal to the High Court on points of law only.[106] The Review Tribunal's powers of discharge would be in addition to those vested in the nearest relative, the hospital staff, the Hospital Management Committee, and ultimately the Ministry of Health.[107] The Royal Commission also endorsed a movement away from institutional treatment settings towards Community Care,[108] and urged that County and County Borough Councils should be placed under a positive duty to provide community services for the mentally ill by the issue of a Ministerial direction' under section 28 of the National Health Service Act 1946.[109] Care in the community would normally be voluntary but the Commission did suggest procedures for guardianship which would be available in certain cases.[110] The Commission saw no need for central inspection of admission documents as a safeguard[111] and proposed the abolition of the Board of Control as a separate entity. Finally, the Commission proposed the re-enactment of the substantive and procedural protection given to doctors and others responsible for operating the legislation previously enshrined in section 16 of the Mental Treatment Act 1930.[112]

---

[104] Ibid., para. 388.
[105] Ibid., para. 488.
[106] Ibid., para. 451.
[107] Ibid., para. 438.
[108] Ibid., para. 601.
[109] Ibid., para. 715.
[110] Ibid., para. 411.
[111] Ibid., para. 257.
[112] The Royal Commission assumed a narrow view of the scope of protection afforded by section 16 of the Mental Treatment Act which does not dovetail satisfactorily with the outcome of *Pountney* v. *Griffiths* [1976] AC 314. The Commission clearly thought that the existing protection only applied to compulsory procedures, describing it as conferring protection 'for persons who take part in the certification or other procedures' and in calling for its re-enactment stated that it 'should apply to proceedings arising from any action, report or recommendation made in connection with the new compulsory procedures' (para. 490). This suggests that protection was not meant to extend to the day-to-day control of detained patients or to any aspect of the care of informal patients. See also *supra*, note 75.

The form in which these various recommendations were given statutory force by the Mental Health Act 1959 has already been elaborated.

There were only two significant respects in which the Conservative Government of 1955–9 departed from the recommendations of the Royal Commission on the civil side. Firstly, it was decided to attempt positively to define the condition of psychopathy as one of the categories of mental disorder subject to the provisions of the Act, and the category of subnormality was added to the Commission's proposed threefold classification of mental illness, psychopathy, and severe subnormality. Thus the definition and categorization of mental disorder was reorganized. Secondly, the Government refused to support its theoretical commitment to a shift from institutional to community mental health services by allocating specific capital grants to local authorities.

It is interesting to note that the Mental Health (Scotland) Act 1960, whilst being based upon the same fundamental orientation as the English Act in its stress on informal status for mental patients and the desirability of a movement toward community mental health services, differed significantly both in its retention of the role of the sheriff in approving compulsory commitment applications and in the establishment of the Scottish Mental Welfare Commission as an independent watchdog concerned with safeguarding the liberties of mental patients, both formal and informal, just as the English Board of Control was being discontinued. There was the particular irony that while Walter Maclay, as Senior Medical Senior Commissioner with the English Board, had been prominent in arguing for the abolition of the role of the magistrate in commitment and for the dismantling of special supervisory machinery, his brother John Maclay was called upon to defend the role of the sheriff and the need for a watchdog as the Minister responsible for presenting the Mental Health (Scotland) Bill in the House of Commons.[113]

We have seen that Scotland had distinct legislative traditions and a system which had historically commanded much greater public confidence for a number of different reasons, including its relative lack of dependence upon private commercial asylums and the greater effectiveness of its central administrative supervision. As a result, less formal methods of admission were able to be introduced much

---

[113] For the Government reasoning behind these provisions, see the speech of John Maclay, *House of Commons Debates* 617, col. 252 *et seq.* (9 February 1960).

earlier and were sustained. The role of safeguards did not become, as it did south of the border, a critical test of civil liberty. It may be that in the context of a more informal and trusted system, they did not acquire the same connotations of stigma and penality. These considerations help to explain why it was not a *sine qua non* of increasing state interventionism and a strategy of psychiatric expansion that in Scotland features that were legalistic by English standards should be dispensed with. It would seem that similar procedures developed different ideological resonances in the two distinct cultures as a product of differential historical, administrative, political, and legal development.

Publication of the Royal Commission's Report was a major contribution to a more general hastening of public interest in the question. On 19 February 1954, Kenneth Robinson had initiated the first general debate on the subject of mental health since the passage of the Mental Treatment Act in 1930 on a motion calling for greater resources. As Chairman since 1952 of the Mental Health Committee of the North West Metropolitan Regional Hospital Board, his interest had been stirred by the paradox of the importance of the issue of mental illness in terms of human misery and social and economic waste, and the marked neglect which characterized society's response. Although the Percy Commission had been appointed before the debate took place, it had created little stir, and there was scant reference to it in the course of the debate itself. Popular interest had been focused more on alleged abuses of mental deficiency legislation than on the general state of the mental health services. As the 1950s progressed, however, the pharmacological revolution, the spread of the open door policy,[114] and the appearance of experimental forms of care, together with the general discord between antiquated lunacy legislation and the new administrative and legal framework of the Welfare State, had the effect of broadening the discussion and began to break down some of the associations of fear and stigma which still attached to mental illness and to the services and institutions which had been created for mental patients. In addition, the National Association for Mental Health, founded in 1946, which launched a Mental Hygiene Campaign in April 1956, the Community Council for Health Education, and the Board of Control were engaged in efforts to convert the public to a 'modern' scientifically informed and socially tolerant attitude toward the mentally disordered.

[114] See *The Times*, 15 March 1956: 'The cult of the "open-door" is spreading rapidly throughout the mental hospitals of the country.'

Reaction to the Report was varied. 'Respectable' sections of the Press were enthusiastic: *The Times's* editorial which welcomed the Report provides a fine example of the transposition of liberal discourse to which earlier reference has been made. Entitled 'Bias for Freedom', it expressed the view that:

the plan offers well conceived protection for the individual; promises a big reduction in the use of compulsion; would stop the legal labelling of patients, especially children, now so offensive to public taste, and would remove unneeded shackles from the work of the mental health services.[115]

Other sections of the Press, castigated by R. W. Sorensen in the course of the House of Commons debate on the Royal Commission's Report as 'a few pockets of irresponsibility whose attitude is hopelessly old-fashioned and who pander to an appetite for sensationalism',[116] construed its findings as confirmation of allegations against the existing services, which was the last thing that the Commission's members would have wished. It was suggested that the ten to twenty thousand patients whom the Commission thought could be discharged were sane persons improperly detained, an interpretation condemned in Parliament as 'a gross perversion of the truth'.[117]

While the Medical Practitioners' Union and the National Council for Civil Liberties considered the Report's recommendations to be insufficiently liberal, in the sense that too much decision-making power was to rest in the hands of medical experts rather than lay or legal authorities, others were apprehensive that the result of their implementation would be the release of potentially dangerous patients into the community at the expense of considerations of public safety, and so criticized the Commission for an excessively zealous liberalism. These fears were given voice at the Annual Conference of the National Council of Women in October 1957 by Mrs C. Frankenberg, who accused the Commision of 'taking a grave risk with the safety of the public'.[118]

The Parliamentary reaction was broadly one of consensual acclamation, promising that the Report would shortly be translated into law without much difficulty. The main themes of the case in favour of the Mental Health Act 1959, as deployed by its Parliamen-

[115] *The Times*, 30 May 1957.
[116] *House of Commons Debates* 573, col. 38 (8 July 1957).
[117] *House of Commons Debates* 573, col. 87 (8 July 1957).
[118] *The Times*, 25 October 1957.

tary advocates, were: the need to assimilate the mental health services to general medicine; the rejection of automatic resort to compulsion; the abolition of quasi-penal procedures which perpetuated social stigma; the belief that in an age of curative treatments there was a much reduced danger that coercive powers would in practice be liable to abuse, and the shift from institutional to community-based care, achieving the social desegregation of the mentally disordered. These interlocking themes were justified ideologically as embodying the virtues of humanitarianism, liberalism, and scientific rationality.

Both the Labour and the Conservative parties had become so wedded to a social politics grounded upon the Welfare State philosophy that libertarian dissent was even more limited, fragmented, and theoretically confused than in 1930. It is difficult on primary examination to detect in the scattered opposition any firm basis for analytical generalization as to its political roots, and one is tempted to personalize the reasons behind dissent. An example is that of the two main critics of the provisions which dispensed with traditional legal safeguards—one was a former mental patient and the other hated doctors.[119] Such a disintegration of familiar alignments reinforced the general impression at the time that mental health law reform was a non-ideological affair. Nevertheless, it is possible, by isolating distinct tendencies of argument within the pockets of dissent on the issue of legal safeguards, to arrive at a more developed analysis of the political divisions accompanying the Mental Health Act's passage into law. The method used will be to place representative individuals who were frequent contributors to the debates along a spectrum ranging from whole-hearted support to seriously qualified support—there being no outright opposition. The arguments used can then be compared and an attempt made at categorization.

The spirit of bipartisanship which characterized Parliamentary debate on mental health legislation was well described at the end of the debate on the Percy Commission's Report in 1957 by R. W. Sorensen on the Labour side:

This has been a bipartisan debate, a fact which some people may deplore but I do not . . . . I think that this at least has been established in our discussion today, that all parties agree to what some of us would call the Socialist

[119] See Dr Donald Johnson, *House of Commons Debates* 605, col. 345 (5 May 1959) and Norman Dodds, *House of Commons Debates*, Standing Committees, 1958–9, IV, cols. 269–70 (26 February 1959).

principle and what others, no doubt, would call the ethical principle—the principle that we are responsible for the wellbeing of a considerable and important section of our community. Some of us, of course, wish to expand that principle elsewhere.[120]

The quotation is of interest because it indicates both that most Labour and Conservative MPs could agree on the need for a framework of legislation such as the Mental Health Act because of their common commitment to the principle of social responsibility for deprived minorities and that the general political differences between them were ones of degree. Mental health was not a sensitive area where interventionism was a matter for fierce disagreement, rather it was an area whose subsumption under Welfare State provision was accepted as necessary.

However, differences of approach became apparent in discussion of the detailed provisions of the Mental Health Bill. One resolute advocate of assigning questions affecting patients' civil liberties to doctors was Bessie Braddock. As a member of the Percy Commission, she was absolutely determined to protect the essence of its recommendations from the tampering amendments of those who failed to share her enthusiasm. She was particularly anxious that the principle of assimilating the procedures surrounding psychiatric to ordinary medical treatment should not be violated or diluted, and this led her vigorously to resist any attempted reintroduction of the old concepts of inspection of mental hospitals by independent visitors[121] and legal or lay participation in compulsory commitment decisions. She was quite prepared to make the type of absolute statement about the subject from which most MPs flinched, such as her exasperated expression of hope 'that we will get away from this insistence that there is someone who knows better than a doctor about what treatment is necessary for a patient.'[122]

Bessie Braddock's position was firmly that of the Royal Commission and the Government: that the mental health services must be integrated fully in the apparatuses of the Welfare State by equipping them with a new legal framework which facilitated rather than inhibited their performance of a preventative and curative role. As a Labour MP, she would support a Conservative administration

---

[120] *House of Commons Debates* 573, col. 87 (8 July 1957).
[121] *House of Commons Debates*, Standing Committees, 1958–9, IV, col. 15 (10 February 1959).
[122] Ibid., col. 302 (3 March 1959).

304 The Mental Health Act 1959 II

engaged in promoting a measure philosophically grounded in the interventionism of the Welfare State. Indeed, one would have expected the Labour Party, representing a more radical collectivism and subject historically to greater ideological influence from Fabian social theorists, to be more devoted to the reform than its Conservative sponsors. However, Labour MPs approached the question from a number of perspectives.

Perhaps the most interesting set of positions was that adopted by Kenneth Robinson, who, although a Labour member, author of a Fabian pamphlet on the mental health services,[123] and universally acknowledged as the Parliamentary pioneer of mental health reform, was a critic of the proposed legislation at certain key points, apparently from a libertarian point of view. He attempted to narrow the range of psychopathic patients liable to compulsory powers, to restrict the abridged emergency admission procedure to observation, to remove powers for censoring mail, especially in the case of informal patients, and to extend appeal for release to a Mental Health Review Tribunal to restricted criminal patients instead of leaving the discharge decision with the Home Secretary.[124] The rationale for pressing such amendments did not lie purely in a concern to inject greater safeguards for civil liberties in the Bill. Indeed, viewed from this angle, his position on its different provisions appeared self-contradictory. This was actually pointed out in Standing Committee by William Coldrick, the Labour and Co-operative Party member for Bristol North-East:

It is a little inconsistent that he [Robinson] should argue, as he has frequently done, that we should entrust to the medical superintendent and the medical practitioner the right to decide whether a person should be admitted to treatment and thereby have his general liberties restricted, while at the same time arguing that we ought not to entrust to the medical profession the responsibility of saying whether letters received by a patient would be detrimental to his form of treatment.[125]

His main concern, however, in relation to the issues of censorship and the position of restricted patients, was that the proposed law detracted from the assimilation of mental hospitals to general hospitals rather than prison. This is not to claim that libertarianism

---

[123] *Policy for Mental Health*, Fabian Research Series, 1958.
[124] Only the second proposition was conceded by the Government.
[125] *House of Commons Debates*, Standing Committees, 1958–9, IV, col. 400 (10 March 1959).

did not play some part in forming Mr Robinson's opinions, as witnessed by his stated opposition to censorship as a matter of principle,[126] but to point out that they did incorporate a strong strand of therapeutic rationality. To this extent, his outlook was not greatly at variance with that of Mrs Braddock.

Some other members, both Conservative and Labour, however, were not so committed to the scale of priorities represented by the new model of legislation, and shared a straightforward disquiet regarding its implications for civil liberties. In certain cases this disquiet was reflected in reservations and confusion combining awkwardly with a general inclination to support the measure. During Report Stage discussion of Clause 25 (Admission for Observation) Leslie Hale, Labour MP for Oldham West, commented:

The Clause, properly administered, under proper provisions by qualified people, may be of great service to many members of the community who need that service. I leave it with a little fear, a little wonder and a little anxiety, however, as to how far, if we do not watch the regulations carefully and if we do not ensure that they provide proper provisions, we may not have cases raised in this House in the years to come which will show that we have given a power which, unless it is watched, could become a possibly serious invasion of human liberty.[127]

Apart from one surprising vote in the House of Lords, which will be discussed shortly, support for amendments which challenged the fundamental assumptions of the Bill was, however, minimal. This was discovered to their cost by Donald Johnson, from the Conservative, and Norman Dodds, from the Labour side, who were seriously concerned about the consequences of the proposed changes from a libertarian perspective and who, throughout its Parliamentary passage, sought to restore former safeguards or strengthen the substitute procedures proposed by the Government. Their alliance underlined the fact that while there was bipartisan support for the Mental Health Bill, there was also a bipartisan distribution of doubts and reservations.

The two MPs had joined forces in May 1957, prior to the publication of the Percy Commission's Report, to embark upon a national tour in support of mental health reform in order to arouse public indignation at the 'appalling things going on under our

---

[126] Ibid., col. 394 (10 March 1959).
[127] *House of Commons Debates* 605, col. 274 (5 May 1959).

present antiquated laws'.[128] by which they meant cases of unjustified detention, and in 1958 had published a pamphlet, *Plea for the Silent*. The MPs expected the Commission to make radical recommendations for reform, but feared that, whatever Government was in power, its report would be pigeon-holed and forgotten. Appreciating the historical neglect of the mentally disordered, the MPs seem to have underestimated the powerful impetus to reform provided by the post-war transformation of social politics. When the Report appeared, they drew attention to the contrast between the mildness of its criticism of the existing services and the far-reaching nature of its recommendations for change.[129] Of course, there was no real contradiction here, and no need for the implication that the Commission had played down evidence of abuse to save official embarrassment. The strategy of minimizing resort to coercion and shifting the balance away from institutional care was justified on therapeutic rather than libertarian grounds. Closer inspection of the Report and the subsequent Bill, however, convinced them that, while it gave with one hand, it took back with the other, in that what they saw as valuable safeguards were put at risk. Norman Dodds was moved to state in Committee discussion of the Mental Health Bill:

> . . . I have a very heavy heart about this Bill, because when it was suggested that there was to be a new Bill, I believed that most of the provisions would largely be based on the fact that in the past so many bad decisions had been made over taking away the liberty of the individual. I came to the conclusion that every effort would be made to ensure that all possible safeguards were established before anyone at all was certified. Yet up to the moment there are fewer safeguards here than under the old Act . . . .[130]

Attempts were made to improve the Bill from this point of view, by *inter alia* providing a twenty-eight day observation period for all patients in the first instance, insisting upon review by a Mental Health Review Tribunal prior to compulsory admission for treatment, and writing elements of judicial procedure for the new tribunals into the Bill instead of leaving it as a matter of regulations to be made by the Lord Chancellor.[131] These efforts were, however, largely unsuccessful, for reasons which merit closer consideration.

---

[128] See *The Times*, 18 May 1957.

[129] *House of Commons Debates* 573, col. 82 (8 July 1957).

[130] *House of Commons Debates*, Standing Committees, 1958–9, IV, col. 294 (3 March 1959).

[131] These amendments, advanced in Committee, related to Clauses 25, 26 and 122 respectively.

Johnson and Dodds were very much in the historical mainstream of libertarian critics of the mental health system such as the earlier National Society for Lunacy Reform. Their passionate interest in the subject was focused firmly upon real or alleged abuses of the liberty of the patient (in both mental hospitals and mental deficiency institutions), but their theoretical analysis of the nature of these abuses and the type of reform required was poorly developed. Like the earlier Lunacy Law reform societies, Dodds and Johnson, in defining the threat to civil liberties posed by commitment powers, vacillated between more crude formulations, such as the time-honoured caricature of the 'mad scientists' incarcerating the sane, or the notion of conspiracy, and more sophisticated themes, later developed by Laing and Szasz into a full humanistic critique of modern psychiatric practice. In the Second Reading debate on the Mental Health Bill, Dodds actually reverted to the position of the legal profession in the late nineteenth century, emphasizing the humiliation of old people confined for social reasons having to associate with the insane, and calling for rigorous safeguards as the stigma of mental hospital was more serious than that of prison. However, Johnson at certain points was clearly concerned with the perspective of the 'consumer', and, being a former patient himself, demonstrated considerable perceptiveness concerning the predicament of the objects of the legislation. He also raised the question of the difficulties faced by patients in resisting treatments which they felt were not helping them, and identified the crux of doubts about the Mental Health Bill by insisting, in direct contravention of the view expressed by Derek Walker-Smith, steering the Bill through the Commons, that in the last analysis depriving mental patients of their liberty was not a medical matter of diagnosis but essentially a social question. They welcomed the humanitarian impetus toward the elimination of the stigma accompanying certification and other formal 'paper protections' provided in 1890. But they were suspicious of the medical profession, and perceived the helplessness of patients whose complaints could be discredited as paranoia or further mental symptoms. Thus they sought formal guarantees that liberty would only be lost after the requirements of due process had been fully and fairly observed.[132] The medical charge that placing legal-style procedures in the foreground would reimport a quasi-penal image and defeat the object of new legislation was not squarely

[132] *House of Commons Debates* 573, cols. 82–6 (8 July 1957).

faced. The two critics were in a difficult position: they welcomed the general reduction in the use of coercion which was now promised, and therefore had to accept the Bill's liberal credentials.[133] Nevertheless, the principled anti-legalism of its sponsors only made sense to them to the extent that it was directed at the abolition of the disabling total status of certified lunatic. Beyond that, in their own eyes it threatened the freedom of the individual. They lacked any sophisticated critique of medical conceptualizations of insanity, and failed to articulate an objection to the use of these conceptualizations as a justification for interventionist strategies of social reform. Accordingly, their libertarianism remained abstract and because it seemed inconsistent with the apparently worthy aims of the legislation, failed to do more than plant doubts and unsettle the mood of cross-bench accord and self-congratulation which generally reigned in the debate. Their opposition not only attracted numerically insignificant support but because of its theoretical deficiencies when contrasted with the seeming consistency of the arguments in favour of the broad structure of the Bill, and the apparent identification of the two MPs with dubious and extreme claims against the existing services, it tended not to be taken seriously.

A far more formidable opponent of the anti-libertarian tendencies of the Mental Health Bill was Baroness Barbara Wootton, recently raised to the Peerage and intellectually equipped to fight an incisive rearguard action in the House of Lords, as a prominent social scientist who had only in 1958 completed an influential criminological work incorporating a section devoted to analysis of the concept of mental illness.[134] Although she considered that the practical dangers were present rather more in the case of psychopathic and mentally subnormal patients, her analysis extended to the mentally ill as well.[135] The essence of Wootton's concern was the authoritarian tendency inherent in the modern movement towards reclassifying what had historically been moral problems as medical ones. In particular, she harboured fears in relation to the application of powers of compulsory hospitalization to the new category of psychopaths where the evidence of sickness was extreme anti-social

---

[133] *House of Commons Debates* 598, col. 794 (26 January 1959). See the speech of Norman Dodds, where he concludes 'I sincerely welcome the Bill because I believe that it is a big step forward. Nevertheless, I believe that individual liberty is in grave danger from the provisions in the Bill.

[134] B. F. Wootton, *Social Science and Social Pathology*, 1959.

[135] *House of Lords Debates* 217, col. 371 (29 June 1959).

conduct of a kind which had formerly been subject to official retaliation only in cases where the perpetrator had clearly broken the law and rendered himself liable to criminal penalties.[136] The proposed legislation raised the prospect of deviants (including alcoholics and homosexuals) losing their liberty in the absence of the commission of a criminal offence, and largely on the say of medical experts. Wootton's fears, shared by other members of the Lords, including Silkin, Pakenham, and Taylor, were expressed in the following speech in terms not dissimilar to those used by Thomas Szasz:

I know that the whole philosophy behind this Bill is to assimilate mental and physical illness, and in cases of severe mental disorder of any kind, whether illness or subnormality, that assimilation is possible. But I think that there is an element of romantic illusion in the belief that in all its manifestations, and particularly in those which are primarily concerned with anti-social behaviour, mental illness is of the same kind as physical disorder. It is not only a romantic illusion; I think it may be a dangerous illusion. It becomes a dangerous illusion if we allow persons to be detained indefinitely for long periods without judicial process, without the presence of any layman when the decision is made, without even the guarantee of a layman that the decision has been made consistently with the terms of the Bill.[137]

Thus, Baroness Wootton, whose political position was in general terms very much in the Fabian tradition, albeit a new incarnation of Fabianism having evolved beyond many of the concerns which absorbed the Webbs in the Edwardian period, was prepared to align herself with the Bill's libertarian critics and against the almost unreserved therapeutic optimism of its eager supporters. In the House of Lords debates, she reiterated the themes of her writings on mental illness in *Social Science and Social Pathology*: that the contemporary redefinition of moral as medical problems was taking place on the basis of insecure conceptual foundations, and that its implications, including its consequences for civil liberties, would have to be carefully monitored. Wootton's critique of the conceptual apparatus of psychiatry of course transcended the abstract libertari-

[136] Psychopaths had previously been detained under lunacy and mental deficiency legislation. The difficulty under the law prior to 1959 was that psychopathy was not assimilable to insanity because it did not imply intellectual disorder; neither was it straightforwardly assimilable to mental deficiency as many psychopaths were of normal or above average intelligence.

[137] *House of Lords Debates* 217, col. 394 (29 June 1959). The views of Thomas Szasz are considered in Chapter 10.

anism of spokesmen in the Commons and had more in common with the radical and penetrating analyses of Szasz and Laing than with the intellectual confusion, emotionalism, and sensationalism of the Lunacy Law reform societies. She spoke not as a campaigner on the isolated issue of patients' rights, but from the perspective of a social scientific critique of the medicalization of moral problems.

The question immediately raised is why Baroness Wootton, as a notable supporter of the Welfare State and a social scientist whose central theoretical enterprise was the development of a secure scientific basis for state action to eradicate social ills, should have adopted this position in the debate on mental health law reform. Barbara Wootton was a prominent member of the magistracy and so practical experience of commitment may have influenced her attitude, but, as we have seen, occupational background was no determinant of the positions adopted by individuals as to whether the process should be subject to medical or judicial control. The Magistrates' Association itself had originally supported the retention of the involvement of the magistrate in compulsory commitment procedures in its evidence to the Royal Commission:

The Council [of the Association] is convinced . . . that certification must remain. It is essential to maintain the basic principle of affording judicial protection to anyone suffering from mental disorder and mental deficiency, which involves care of the person and protection of his property while at the same time safeguarding the liberty of the subject . . . . We are aware of the stigma attached to certification, and of the resultant disabilities that may fall so heavily on relations and descendants particularly as regards insurance and emigration. Nevertheless we feel the advantages of certification outweigh these disadvantages.[138]

In order to reduce stigma, which flowed from the conditions themselves as well as judicial procedures, the Association recommended a programme of public education. However, Lady Adrian, who had been a member of the Royal Commission and was also a member of the Council of the Magistrates' Association, felt able to observe, when commenting on the Commission's recommendations in the Association's magazine shortly after the Report's publication that 'Our duties in connection with certification are never pleasant and are disliked by most magistrates and many will

---

[138] *Royal Commission on the Law Relating to Mental Illness and Mental Deficiency: Minutes of Evidence*, p. 354: Written Memorandum of Evidence of the Magistrates' Association, paras. 6 and 7.

welcome the prospect of relief from them.'[139] She also pointed out that those who felt they had performed a valuable service in checking unnecessary or improper confinement would have the opportunity to continue to serve this function as lay members of the new Mental Health Review Tribunals if they put themselves forward. By the time of the Act, the Association had come out in favour of the changes. Wootton herself actually preferred some other lay agency to the traditional lay Justice as a check on expert decision-making.[140]

An illuminating quotation from *Social Science and Social Pathology* sets her attitude to the concept of mental illness in perspective:

Without question . . . in the contemporary attitude towards anti-social behaviour, psychiatry and humanitarianism have marched hand in hand. Just because it is so much in keeping with the mental atmosphere of a scientifically-minded age, the medical treatment of social deviants has been a most powerful, perhaps the most powerful of humanitarian impulses; for today the prestige of humane proposals is immensely enhanced if these are expressed in the idiom of science. Indeed we might go so far as to say that, even if the intellectual foundations of current psychiatric science were exposed as nothing more than a fantasy, we might yet have cause to be grateful for the result of so beneficent a delusion. In all [my] criticism this aspect of the matter should not be lost to view.[141]

It seems that whilst Wootton shared some of the criticisms of the concept of mental illness later popularized by Thomas Szasz, her political conclusions from this analysis were widely different. Szasz's conservative libertarianism led him to see in a state psychiatry equipped with the conceptual apparatus of 'the myth of mental illness' the capacity to invade human liberty, undermine individuality, and erode moral responsibility in a way that presaged the creation of a uniform and passive collectivized society. Wootton's interventionism led her to approve the ascendancy of medical conceptualizations of insanity to the extent that they facilitated a preventive and curative, tolerant approach to mental disorder rather than a custodial and punitive one. On the other hand, unlike the 'assimilationists', who believed that it was only a matter of time before medicine conquered mental illness, she perceived that there were problems of subjectivism and cultural relativism which undermined

[139] H. Adrian, 'Mental Illness: The Royal Commission and the Work of Magistrates', *The Magistrate* xiii (1957), p. 103.
[140] *House of Lords Debates* 216, col. 715 (4 June 1959).
[141] p. 206.

psychiatric claims to scientific status, and grave problems of definition in equating anti-social behaviour with sickness. It was therefore her very occupation with the development of an adequate social scientific basis for progressive actions by the state that made her wary of the Bill's assumptions. She was prepared to condone the expansion of psychiatric activities and the attendant permeation of social, legal, and ethical thinking by medical concepts if these intellectual difficulties were appreciated and decision-making powers were not precipitately transferred into the hands of unaccountable quasi-scientific specialists.[142]

Debate in the House of Lords produced one surprising feature. An amendment proposed by Lord Silkin to reintroduce the Justice before compulsory commitment for treatment was only defeated by forty-one to twenty-two votes.[143] This contrasted with the negligible support similar moves attracted in the Commons. Furthermore, the division was along usual party lines, with mainly Conservatives, Unionists, and Liberals against the amendment, and Labour peers, together with one Liberal, voting in its favour.

It needs to be explained why concern for the civil liberties implications of the Mental Health Bill should have received greater expression on the Labour benches, and why this was more evident in the House of Lords. The Labour Party, as it is often said, owes more to Methodism than to Marx, or, one might add, Sidney and Beatrice Webb. The Nonconformist radicalism in its roots has provided an

---

[142] *House of Lords Debates* 216, col. 721 (4 June 1959). Baroness Wootton's fears were highlighted not so much by the provisions relating to mental illness as those relating to psychopathic personalities. It is not surprising that libertarian fears should have been most readily articulated in relation to the proposals for the application of compulsory powers to the new category of psychopaths. Whereas the concept of insanity being a mental illness had attained widespread cultural currency, the concept of extreme anti-social behaviour as a species of sickness was more alien. The only positive treatment available for psychopathic personalities was a moral education and the low chances of 'cure' ensured that such patients would be subject to a much more custodial regime than the mentally ill. There were parallels between perceptions of insanity in the late nineteenth-century period of therapeutic pessimism and those of psychopathy in the mid-twentieth century. Two psychiatrists, Dr Reginald Bennett in the Commons, and Lord Taylor in the Lords, were particularly outspoken about the difficulties of dealing with psychopaths. Lord Taylor preferred psychopaths to continue to be defined in moral terms and as a problem for the penal rather than the psychiatric system, given the lack of any specifically medical comprehension of or treatment for their problems. The distinctive characteristic of psychopathy being persistent anti-social behaviour, it raised in a particularly acute form the contradictions between gaoler and healer in the psychiatrist's professional role: *House of Lords Debates* 217, cols. 398–400 (29 June 1959).

[143] *House of Lords Debates* 217, cols. 389–90 (29 June 1959).

alternative source of ideology and the basis for a strong regard for civil liberties. As Finer *et al* express it: 'The Labour Party has inherited part of the tradition of nineteenth-century radicalism, a tradition which tempers Labour's collectivist policies with a bias against authority.'[144] This regard accordingly found expression on the Labour side in the debates on the Mental Health Bill. There is some evidence that there was more concern on the Labour than on the Conservative benches in the Commons as well: a straight division on Party lines took place on an official Labour amendment at the Report Stage to leave out provisions for censoring the letters of informal patients,[145] and Labour also applied successful pressure to restrict the emergency powers to admission for observation. That such libertarian concern was manifested in relation to more central issues in the Lords was perhaps a reflection of its subordinate political role.[146] In the Commons, bipartisan agreement on the basic structure of the Bill was celebrated as a confirmation of broad-based political commitment to the consolidation of the Welfare State, whereas in the Lords there was not the same adversarial spirit waiting to be temporarily healed amidst satisfying sentiments of trans-party accord. While Labour dissent on fundamentals in the Commons would have been a major moral defeat for the Bill, in the Lords it was treated more academically and hardly publicized. The more authoritative and persuasive presentation of arguments urging caution in relation to the Bill when contrasted with that of those put forward in the Commons could well explain the greater support obtained in the division lobbies. One would still have expected some votes to have been drawn from beyond Labour's ranks, but the Conservatives were whipped,[147] and unlikely to rebel on an issue attracting little political passion.

In general terms the relative absence of libertarian concern on the Conservative side, apart from being a reflection of the fact that it was a Conservative Bill, may be explained as follows. Once committed to

---

[144] S. E. Finer, H. B. Berrington and D. J. Bartholomew, *Backbench Opinion in the House of Commons 1955–59*. London: Pergamon Press, 1962, p. 97.

[145] This was defeated by 177 votes to 149: see *House of Commons Debates* 605, col. 338 (5 May 1959).

[146] See D. Ewins, 'The Origins of the Compulsory Commitment Provisions of the Mental Health Act 1959', p. 63.

[147] The fact that the major parties employed the whip on measures of reformism in social and personal morality such as the Mental Health Bill, the Street Offenders Bill, and the Obscene Publications Bill was itself controversial: see the letter of Jo Grimmond (Leader of the Liberal Party 1955–67), *The Times*, 24 January 1959.

the new post-war Welfare State order, the Conservatives were unlikely to develop a Szasz-style classical liberal critique of the collectivism of state psychiatric practices or to champion the sovereignty of the rule of law at the expense of an expansive mental health system based upon discretionary decision-making by therapeutic experts. By the 1950s, the retention of the legal structure of 1890, or its modification to improve the effectiveness of the safeguards provided, could only be interpreted as a hindrance to the pace of development achieved by the Welfare State. As M. J. Barnett remarks in his analysis of the emergence of the Rent Act 1957: 'Whatever their philosophic assertions, after 1957 control became the dominant note of their policy in many fields.'[148] The progressive wing of Conservatism, paternalistic, consensual, and reformist, and drawing upon the traditions of Shaftesbury and Disraeli, had been in the ascendant from the late 1940s and provided, in Harold Macmillan and R. A. Butler, the figures who dominated the party's leadership from the middle 1950s to the early 1960s.[149] Although the temporarily less dominant assertively individualist Right of Conservatism and the libertarian strands in Labour Party thinking provided the ideological soil in which objections to the priority of therapeutic effectiveness might grow, the consistency of the Mental Health Bill with the philosophy of the Welfare State ensured that dissent was overwhelmed. The spectrum of attitudes to the Bill in Parliament ranged, as we have seen, from Braddock's extreme assimilationism to the libertarian reservations of Johnson and Dodds, and of Baroness Wootton. But the debate was essentially within the confines of broad support for the well-meaning aspirations of the measure, and there were no notable victories in injecting more, or more effective safeguards. The result was that the Bill emerged as an Act much as it had been originally presented to Parliament, and the argument for more legal rights for patients was for a while buried until, reformulated by the sociological critics, it re-emerged as the basis for a radical attack on the Act's 'authoritarianism'.

[148] M. J. Barnett, *The Politics of Legislation*. London: Weidenfeld and Nicolson, 1969, pp. 232–3.
[149] S. E. Finer *et al.*, p. 98.

10 The Mental Health Act 1983: The New Legalism

THAT a quarter of a century after the Mental Health Act had supposedly marked a new era of enlightened mental health provision in which progressive developments would be liberated from the inhibiting restraint of legal controls inspired by negative suspicion of psychiatry, a new amending statute should be introduced to inject additional and in some cases radically new legal safeguards would have greatly surprised and dismayed members of the impressive professional and political consensus originally in its favour. The Act's proponents were infused with a profound sense of the inevitability and obviousness of the strategy they were pursuing. To them, legalism was inseparable from a punitive, scientifically uninformed view of mental disorder. Its installation as the prime motor of lunacy legislation in the late nineteenth century had been motivated by a desire to maximize the efficiency of civil commitment as a mechanism of social segregation and it was thought that modern medical and humanitarian enlightenment would make it impossible for such an approach to legislation ever to reclaim credibility. In its memorandum to the Royal Commission on the Law Relating to Mental Illness and Mental Deficiency the British Medical Association was confidently able to assert:

It is to be expected that, when the next Royal Commission studies mental law in another twenty years' time, it will be able further to relax the rules, both as to powers and safeguards, because the public's outlook will have made that an acceptable thing to do.[1]

The very opposite has, in fact, been the case. The liberal and humanitarian image which adorned the Mental Health Act at its inception became tarnished. Some of the criticisms to which it was subject were predictable from the beginning. There were complaints —usually provided by the case of mentally abnormal offenders guilty of serious crimes of violence whose release was the subject of a

[1] *Royal Commission on the Law Relating to Mental Illness and Mental Deficiency: Minutes of Evidence*, 1957, p. 1033: Written Memorandum of the British Medical Association, para. 23.

sensational campaign by the popular press—that those who designed the Act were over-optimistic and carried their liberal feelings toward the mentally ill to excess.[2] As a result, it was claimed, too many potentially dangerous patients were permitted to be at large in the community. This line of criticism was foreshadowed in October 1957 when the Annual Conference of the National Council of Women passed a resolution critical of the Percy Commission Report to the effect that 'the welfare of citizens should not be jeopardized for the problematical benefit of the mentally disordered'.[3] The Act was also criticized for failing to provide an adequate structure of finance for local authority mental health services so that in many localities there was little progress toward its goal of Community Care. Again this problem was anticipated. We have seen that it was the main Parliamentary criticism to which the Mental Health Bill was subjected, especially by the Labour Opposition.[4] What was surprising, however, was the vigorous and successful reaction against one of the very features of the Act which was most canvassed as civilized, liberal, and progressive, namely the substantial retraction of law from the regulation of psychiatric practice as an inappropriate and damaging medium within which to organize relationships between patients and mental health professionals and bureaucracies. As Margot Jefferys and Louis Blom-Cooper observed of the reaction against this assumption in their foreword to Larry Gostin's proposals for reform of the civil provisions of the Act in 1975:

Optimism has given way to scepticism if not pessimism. We are more aware of the complexities of human behaviour, of the unintended and unwelcome side-effects of well-intentioned statutory provision, of the differences in interest and outlook that lie behind an apparent consensus of approach to the treatment of the mentally ill ... any earlier complacency about the provisions of the Mental Health Act 1959 has evaporated.[5]

Before looking at the origins of this disillusionment, we shall consider its product, the Mental Health Act 1983, consolidating the Mental Health Act 1959 and the Mental Health (Amendment) Act 1982, which has restored formal legal safeguards to a central place in

---

[2] Of these, the case of Graham Young was perhaps the most significant: see A. I. Holden, *The St. Albans Poisoner.* London: Hodder and Stoughton, 1974.

[3] *The Times*, 25 October 1957.

[4] See Chapter 9.

[5] L. O. Gostin, *A Human Condition Volume 1*, pp. 6–7.

mental health legislation. The Act's reforming provisions are in considerable part attributable to proposals advanced by Larry Gostin, as Legal and Welfare Rights Officer and later Legal Director of MIND (National Association for Mental Health) in *A Human Condition*. In a civil context, the principal objectives of the MIND campaign were the introduction of stricter criteria for compulsory admission to mental hospital, the imposition of a more judicial character upon the procedures for reviewing commitment, the clarification and strengthening of patients' rights to resist unwanted treatments, the recognition of the need for some degree of formal machinery to protect the rights of informal patients, the reduction of restrictions of patients' civil freedoms, and the installation of an independent advocacy structure to monitor the observance of both patient and staff rights (the proposed Committee on the Rights and Responsibilities of Staff and Residents of Psychiatric Hospitals). All these have been achieved to some degree and in some form, and, taken together, they constitute a considerable revival of legalism, even though in important respects they have not fully satisfied MIND's demands.

The Mental Health Act 1983[6] first of all narrows and restricts the definition and classification of mental disorder for statutory purposes. Section 1(2) replaces the division of the mentally handicapped into the subnormal and severely subnormal with new concepts of mental impairment and severe mental impairment incorporating a behavioural criterion which must now be satisfied before the patient can be brought within the terms of the more serious detentionary powers under the Act. Impairment of intelligence and social functioning must be 'associated with abnormally aggressive or seriously irresponsible conduct', a precondition which already attached to the psychopathic category. This was a concession to MENCAP and other mental handicap organizations who had waged a sustained campaign in favour of the legislative dissociation of mental handicap from mental illness. However, a condition of 'arrested or incomplete development of mind' remains sufficient for the purposes

[6] For expositions of the current law as established by the Act, see B. Hoggett, *Mental Health Law*, 2nd edn. London: Sweet and Maxwell, 1984; L. O. Gostin, *A Practical Guide to Mental Health Law*. London: MIND (National Association for Mental Health), 1983. For critical commentaries see L. Gostin, 'Contemporary Social Historical Perspectives'; B. Hoggett, 'The Mental Health Act 1983', *Public Law* (1983), p. 172; D. Carson, 'Mental Processes: the Mental Health Act 1983', *Journal of Social Welfare Law* (1983), p. 195.

of admission for assessment or removal to a place of safety without this behavioural requirement.[7]

The introduction of a behavioural criterion may be interpreted as legalistic in that, unlike medicine, which is concerned with the treatment of the mentally disordered condition itself, law has normally focused upon the social implications of the manifestation of mental disorder in deviant conduct or incapacity. The consequence of this amendment is that the exercise of compulsory powers in relation to the categories of mental impairment and severe mental impairment is more closely correlated with anti-social conduct and with justifying the necessity for special legal powers to be applied. This does not affect the civil treatment of the mentally ill, with whom we are primarily concerned, but there is a further definitional change which does apply to this category, as it is made explicit by section 1(3) that a person is not rendered subject to be dealt with under the Mental Health Act solely by reason of 'sexual deviancy or dependance on alcohol or drugs'. The terms of the 1959 Act referred only to 'promiscuity or other immoral conduct'. Taken together these amendments emphasize that it is neither the mere existence of mental disequilibrium nor of deviant behaviour which activates the provisions of mental health legislation, but certain combinations of the two which justify special legal powers of psychiatric intervention.

A further restriction is placed upon the use of long-term compulsory detention in relation to mentally impaired and psychopathic patients in that section 3(2)(b) introduces a new test of treatability as a condition precedent of compulsory admission for treatment. It must now be demonstrated that treatment 'is likely to alleviate or prevent a deterioration of [the patient's] condition'. The Mental Health Act 1959 provided only that in relation to these categories the condition should require *or* be susceptible to medical treatment, or, in the case of the subnormal, other special care or training, before the patient could be classified as mentally disordered within the meaning of the Act.[8] This test underlines that in categories where the susceptibility of the condition to treatment may be at issue, long-term compulsory detention is not to be used for purposes of preventive custody. Whereas the precondition of abnormally aggressive or seriously irresponsible conduct would in isolation tend to convert the basis of the legitimacy of detention from paternalistic

[7] Mental Health Act 1983, sections 2, 4, 136. See B. Hoggett, *Mental Health Law*, pp. 54–5.
[8] Mental Health Act 1959, section 4(3), (4).

intervention toward a quasi-criminal sanction exacted in response to behavioural transgression, the treatability test attempts to ensure that the purpose of the detention, albeit one imposed in more restricted circumstances, is therapeutic rather than custodial.

The requirements attaching to compulsory admission and discharge under the Mental Health Act have been procedurally weighted in favour of the patient's liberty, both by alterations in the position of the various personnel who participate in the operation of the compulsory powers and by increasing the opportunities for tribunal review. In relation to the position of social workers in the compulsory commitment procedures, the Act envisages the introduction of a system of training to produce 'approved social workers' who, having passed an examination set by the Central Council for Education and Training in Social Work, will be able to carry out the more important statutory social work functions on a more specialized basis, thus, amongst other improvements, reducing the danger that applications will be made without due observance of the legal requirements designed to safeguard individual liberty.[9] This is part of a more general enhancement of the social work contribution to admissions procedures,[10] and to statutory processes more generally, as in the profession's representation on the Mental Health Act Commission and participation in multi-disciplinary review of treatment decisions made by psychiatrists. Such an increasing influence follows the social work profession's rapid expansion and its consolidation by the creation of a base in unified social service departments in the interval since 1959.[11]

The role of the nearest relative has been expanded and the term has been suitably redefined to help ensure that the person em-

[9] However, concentration of the responsibilities of mental welfare officers in the hands of approved social workers was not achieved at the date set by the Mental Health Amendment Act 1982 (28 October 1984) because of union opposition, and the shortage of approved social workers has led local authorities to adopt the expedient of designating appropriate social workers to carry out the relevant functions under the Act.

[10] Section 14 of the Act ensures some social work involvement in admission for assessment (formerly 'observation') or treatment by providing that, in cases where the nearest relative rather than the social worker has made the application, the hospital managers shall inform the local social services authority so that a social worker (who does not need to be approved) can be assigned to interview the patient and furnish them with a social circumstances report.

[11] See F. M. Martin, *Between the Acts*. London: Nuffield Provincial Hospitals Trust, 1984, Chapter 6, for a mental health oriented account of the development of the social work profession in the period separating the 1959 and 1983 Acts.

powered is the one most closely connected with the patient.[12] The authority of 'any relative' of the patient to make application for emergency admission, conferred by section 29 of the Mental Health Act 1959, has been withdrawn in favour of the nearest relative.[13] In the case of a patient admitted for assessment (formerly 'observation'), the nearest relative has now been accorded the same power of discharge already exercised on the terms elaborated in section 47 of the 1959 Act in respect of patients admitted for treatment.[14] The value of the nearest relative's right of discharge as a safeguard for the patient is, of course, problematic, as its exercise will be dependent upon the family situation, but it does provide an extra opportunity of release and affords a further external lever upon medical decision-making.

The duration of periods of detention under admission for treatment has been halved by the new Act: instead of one year in the first instance, followed by a further year and successive periods of two years, the periods are now six months, six months, and one year respectively.[15] This is one way in which opportunities for application to a Mental Health Review Tribunal for discharge have been significantly increased. Patients admitted for treatment have access to a tribunal once during each period of detention and the halving of these periods automatically doubles these occasions. It has additionally been provided that appeal to a tribunal will be available in the first fourteen days of admission for assessment under section 2, the reason being that it has now been clarified that admission on this basis does entitle the hospital authorities to administer treatment without the patient's consent. The most radical change in the scope of tribunal review, however, is that its basis has been converted from the selective one of responding to applications made on the initiative of patients to an automatic one, whereby if at the expiration of the period for making application a patient has not done so, then under section 68 of the Act the hospital managers are obliged to forward his case to a tribunal. It was estimated in debate on the Mental Health (Amendment) Bill that tribunal sittings would be increased from 904 in 1980 to about 4,500 per annum by this change.[16] Total

---

[12]   Mental Health Act 1983, section 26.
[13]   Mental Health Act 1983, section 4(2).
[14]   Mental Health Act 1983, section 23(2)(a). See however section 66(1)(g).
[15]   Mental Health Act 1983, section 20.
[16]   Kenneth Clarke, Minister of Health, *House of Commons Written Answers*, col. 457 (15 July 1982).

applications actually rose from 1,329 in 1982 to 3,445 in 1984 and are still rising, with the introduction of automatic review only accounting for part of this increase.[17] The tribunal system has also been strengthened by a major reform of its responsibilities regarding mentally abnormal offenders: tribunals themselves can now determine whether patients concerned in criminal proceedings and subject to restriction orders should be discharged, rather than merely advising the Home Secretary on the matter.[18] New Mental Health Review Tribunal Rules have increased the conformity of tribunal proceedings to principles of natural justice, augmenting, for example, the rights of patients and their representatives of access to documents, thus modifying the initially heavily therapeutic conception of the tribunal process.[19]

We have seen that as well as providing procedures for compulsory admission to mental hospital, the Mental Health Act includes provision for the exercise of compulsory powers in the community utilizing the concept of guardianship, which has played a significant part in the legal regulation of mental disorder since medieval times. This was one way in which the retention of residual coercive powers over mental patients could be married with the pursuit of the ideal of Community Care, but in practice the powers have been very sparingly used and concentrated overwhelmingly amongst the mentally handicapped rather than the mentally ill. In principle, the attractiveness of guardianship as a means of legal control of the mentally disordered has often been endorsed, for example by the Butler Committee on Mentally Abnormal Offenders in 1975,[20] but it has nevertheless failed to mature into a viable routine alternative to hospitalization. The 1983 Act has curtailed the powers of the guardian: instead of being vested with all the powers of a father over a child under the age of fourteen, as was the existing position,[21] only certain specific powers set out in section 8 are now conferred: the guardian can require the

---

[17] See *Biennial Report of the Mental Health Act Commission*, 1985, p. 28.

[18] Mental Health Act 1983, section 73.

[19] Mental Health Review Tribunal Rules (S.I. 1983 No. 942). For critiques of the operation of tribunals under the 1959 Act see C. Greenland, *Mental Illness and Civil Liberty*. Occasional Papers in Social Administration No. 38. London: Bell, 1970; P. W. H. Fennell, 'The Mental Health Review Tribunal: A Question of Imbalance', *British Journal of Law and Society* 4 (1977), p. 86. On the current law and practice of tribunals, see L. O. Gostin, E. Rassaby, and A. Buchan, *Mental Health: Tribunal Procedure*. London: Oyez Longman, 1984.

[20] *Report of the Committee on Mentally Abnormal Offenders*, (Cmnd. 6244, 1975), p. 200.

[21] Mental Health Act 1959, section 34(1).

patient's residence in a particular place, insist upon access being given to a doctor or social worker to visit him there, and enjoin the patient's attendance for medical treatment, occupation, education or training. Patients subject to guardianship have the same rights as informal hospital patients with regard to consent to treatment,[22] and the powers are not applicable to a person below the age of sixteen.[23] The liberation of the ward from the global parental overlordship of the guardian may be seen as a legalistic assertion of patients' rights, but it was intended to afford an incentive to local social services authorities to operate the guardianship procedures by streamlining the responsibilities entailed.[24] In practice, local authorities' concern about the resource implications of guardianship remains a factor and it is still only of marginal importance as a legal option.

It is apparent from this summary that the new Act has substantially bolstered formal legal safeguards. However, whilst the above provisions are addressed to problems which were already perceived as meriting statutory attention in 1959 and therefore revise established procedural mechanisms, those which we are about to consider grapple with problems which hardly surfaced in the debates which preceded the Mental Health Act and which therefore introduce quite new structures and procedures. The architects of the Mental Health Act made no attempt to formulate precise and explicit statutory provisions designed to crystallize the circumstances in which treatment for mental disorder could be imposed upon patients without their prior informed consent. Therapeutics were not conceived as a potential source of antagonism between doctors and patients, imposing an obligation upon the legislator to construct an appropriate set of legal rules for the resolution of disputes. Treatment was rather the goal of legislative provision, the benefit which legislation should seek to secure for the clients of the mental health services. However, from the vantage point of legalism, then temporarily dormant, psychiatric treatment is, after all, concerned

[22] Mental Health Act 1983, section 56.
[23] Mental Health Act 1983, section 7(1).
[24] This was an attempt to reverse the sharp decline in guardianship applications since 1959: the total number of the mentally disordered subject to guardianship in England and Wales had been 1133 on 31 December 1960, but was only 159 on 31 March 1974: see Department of Health and Social Security, *A Review of the Mental Health Act 1959*, London, HMSO, 1976, Appendix V. The great majority were mentally handicapped (134:25 in 1974), but a further problem with guardianship since 1983 is that now it is not mental handicap as such but mental impairment, including the presence of 'abnormally aggressive or seriously irresponsible conduct', which must be made out as the basis for an application: Mental Health Act 1983 section 7(2)(a).

with perceptual and behavioural modification. It may in addition be hazardous or produce unpleasant side-effects. Patients may not be prepared to co-operate in the administration of treatments which will produce such changes or which are potentially harmful. Thus, the imposition of treatment is as much an area where patients' rights are at issue as the activation of powers of detention. Furthermore, the validity of consent when given is itself problematic in the psychiatric context because of the presence of the mentally disordered condition itself, the effect of medication, and the pressures upon patients to accept treatments arising from medical claims to expertise and the unequal power relationship between patients and their professional custodians. These considerations are the foundation of Part IV of the Mental Health Act, 'Consent to Treatment'.

The Mental Health Act 1959, because its authors were concerned to reduce rather than to modernize formal legal safeguards, remodelled the procedures for compulsory admission and discharge without developing new safeguards to cope with the transformation of the mental health services from an essentially custodial to a more dynamically therapeutic function stimulated by the arrival, from the 1930s, of major, and often controversial, new treatments: psychosurgery, insulin treatment, electroconvulsive therapy, and new tranquillizing drugs. The Act, through its failure to confront the problem directly, created confusion as to the legality of treatment without consent in certain situations. The basic common law position is the same for psychiatric as for somatic medical treatment: physical interference constitutes a battery unless the real consent of the patient has first been obtained, except in cases of justification by urgent necessity, and failure to provide treatment on a properly informed basis may amount to actionable negligence.[25] In the case of admission for treatment under section 26 of the Mental Health Act 1959 it could be argued that because admission was 'for treatment' and was on a compulsory basis it was implicit that a detained patient's refusal to consent could be overridden by the responsible medical

---

[25] Although the House of Lords has recently made clear in *Sidaway* v. *Bethlem Royal Hospital Governors* [1985] 1 All E.R. 643 that English law does not accept the doctrine of fully informed consent that pertains in a minority of American jurisdictions, the state of the common law is complex, contentious, and uncertain on consent to treatment by the mentally disordered. The new Mental Health Act Commission has sought to identify the difficulties and propose solutions: see *Biennial Report of the Mental Health Act Commission*; the paper published by the committee responsible for drawing up the relevant section of the Code of Practice, *Consent to Treatment*, and the *Code of Practice* itself.

officer.[26] The Department of Health and Social Security took this view, but doctors seeking its advice were told that they ought to protect themselves if embarking upon a treatment attendant with risk by obtaining the consent both of the patient and of the nearest relative, even though the latter could be of no legal effect.[27] With regard to the treatment of patients detained under sections 25 and 29 'for observation', in relation to whom the Department adopted a similar position, it could be argued that this did not authorize treatment as distinct from observation and assessment, although section 25(2)(a) did refer to 'the detention of a patient in hospital under observation (*with or without other medical treatment*) for at least a limited period'.[28]

The Mental Health Act 1983 makes it clear that admission for the intermediate twenty-eight day period does authorize the administration of treatment and for the first time expressly confers the authority to impose treatment upon a patient against his will.[29] This serves as a significant quid pro quo for the medical profession who are also encumbered by the erection of a complex and intricate system of formal safeguards for the protection of patients which represents the high-water mark of legalism in the Act. The position regarding consent is now to depend upon the classification of the treatment to be administered, treatments being graduated in accordance with their gravity. Section 57 of the Act applies to the most serious types of medical treatment for mental disorder. Psychosurgery, defined as 'any surgical operation for destroying brain tissue or for destroying the functioning of brain tissue' is specified in the Act,[30] and others may be added by the Secretary of State by regulation, a power already activated in the case of hormonal implants for the purpose of reducing male sex drive.[31] Both of these treatments, which are rarely administered, can only lawfully be given with the consent of the patient *and* a second opinion. Unlike the other provisions in Part IV of the Act, which apply to detained

[26] Treatment would therefore have been given under the Mental Health Act rather than the National Health Service Act, members of staff responsible for it receiving the protection of section 141 of the former Act which placed substantive and procedural limitations upon a patient's right to legal redress for acts done in pursuance of its provisions.

[27] DHSS, *A Review of the Mental Health Act 1959*, pp. 40–1.

[28] Author's italics. See L. O. Gostin, *A Human Condition Volume I*, p. 122.

[29] The Mental Health Act 1983, sections 2(2)(a) and 63.

[30] Mental Health Act 1983, section 57(1)(a).

[31] Mental Health Act 1983, section 57(1)(b): Mental Health (Hospital, Guardianship and Consent to Treatment) Regulations 1983, reg. 16(1).

patients only,[32] section 57 applies also to informal patients. The extension of protection to informal patients, now embodied in section 56(2) of the 1983 Act, was one of *circa* two hundred instances in which the original formulations of the Mental Health (Amendment) Bill were altered in the course of its Parliamentary passage. It was incorporated on an amendment moved by the leading Opposition spokesman on the Bill, Terry Davis, and accepted by the Government, during consideration by the House of Commons after it had left the Special Standing Committee.[33] Section 57 is exceptional in that even though the patient consents, a second opinion is required, a significant intrusion into the doctor-patient relationship felt to be justified by the critical nature of the treatment in question. A medical practitioner other than the responsible medical officer must certify that the treatment should be given and a multi-disciplinary panel, consisting of the second medical practitioner and two non-medical members appointed by the Mental Health Act Commission established under the Act, must confirm that the patient's consent is valid. The medical practitioner, before giving his second opinion, must consult with two others who have been professionally concerned with the patient's treatment, one of whom must be a nurse and the other neither a nurse nor a doctor. It can be seen that these procedures multiply the personnel and disciplines statutorily engaged in the administration of psychiatric treatment in line with the long-established approach to decision-making at the admissions stage. In doing so they achieve a novel incursion into territory previously dominated by the medical profession and contribute to the legitimization of the partly competing professional claims of nurses, social workers, and clinical psychologists.

Section 58 governs rather less serious treatments where only the patient's consent *or* a second opinion is required. The forms of treatment affected are medicine given three months or more after the first administration and others specified by the Secretary of State, electroconvulsive therapy having been so specified.[34] The patient may consent to the treatment, in which case the reliability of the consent must be certified by the responsible medical officer or a doctor

[32] Part IV does not apply to all detained patients. The excepted categories in a civil context are those detained under three day sections: sections 4, 5(2) (or for six hours under section 5(4)), 135, and 136.

[33] *House of Commons Debates* 29, col. 77 (18 October 1982).

[34] Mental Health Act 1983, section 58(1)(a): Mental Health (Hospital, Guardianship and Consent to Treatment) Regulations 1983, reg. 16(2).

326 The Mental Health Act 1983

appointed for the purpose by the Secretary of State, or the treatment may be given on the basis of a second medical opinion, subject to the same obligations of consultation as in section 57.

These provisions are diluted by the contents of sections 59 and 62 of the Act. Section 59 allows consent or certificates under sections 57 and 58 to be given in respect of a plan or programme of treatment so that the requirements do not necessarily apply to each individual administration of treatment. Section 60 permits patients to withdraw consent in the course of such a plan of treatment, as they may prior to the completion of a particular instance of treatment, but section 62(2) introduces a provision whereby treatment can be continued pending compliance with section 57 or section 58 if the responsible medical officer considers that discontinuation would cause the patient serious suffering. Further, under section 62(1), treatments otherwise subject to the consent provisions of sections 57 and 58 are exempted from their requirements in certain circumstances of urgent necessity, provided the treatments concerned cannot be classified as 'irreversible' or 'hazardous'.

In respect of treatments which are not sufficiently serious to attract the requirements of section 57 or section 58, section 63 provides that they may be given without the patient's consent. However, it must be remembered that apart from the late extension of protection in the case of the most serious treatments to informal patients, Part IV of the Act only applies to detained patients, and then only to certain categories of detained patients. This means that in other cases the common law position survives. Thus the Act has not exhaustively defined the relationship between the power of the psychiatric profession to administer treatment and the right of patients effectively to withhold consent, although the Code of Practice drawn up by the Mental Health Act Commission provides guidance in this respect.[35]

The introduction of safeguards to restrict the powers of the psychiatric profession is one manifestation of legalism in the 1983 Mental Health Act. Another is the general reduction of immunities from suit in respect of the exercise of professional powers. Section 141 of the Mental Health Act 1959, re-enacting the substantive and procedural protection afforded by the Mental Treatment Act 1930,

---

[35] See footnote 25 *supra*. Section 118 obliged the Secretary of State to prepare a Code of Practice and specifically drew his attention to the need of mental health professionals for guidance in relation to the medical treatment of patients suffering from mental disorder: Mental Health Act 1983, section 118(1)(b).

section 16, provided that no civil or criminal proceedings should lie, even in cases of lack of jurisdiction, unless the act complained of was done in bad faith or without reasonable care, and that the prospective plaintiff must first apply to the High Court for leave to proceed, bearing the onus of showing substantial grounds for his contention that the act was wrongful in terms of these criteria. This protective provision has been interpreted expansively. In *Pountney* v. *Griffiths*,[36] the House of Lords agreed that it extended to the use of coercion by a Broadmoor nurse in his everyday responsibilities relating to the control and restraint of detained patients, and not just to the exercise of powers explicitly conferred by the Act. This protective fetter represents specific legislative intervention to shield staff (and especially the medical profession) by means of a general procedural bar without reference to the capacity of individual patients to undertake legal proceedings. The implied stereotype of patient as vexatious litigant on which this provision proceeds was rendered explicit by Lord Simon in his judgment in the Pountney case, when he described mental patients as 'inherently likely to harass those concerned with them by groundless charges and litigation'.[37] The Mental Health Act section 139 to some extent liberates psychiatric patients from the rigours of this procedural obstacle, and so strengthens their legal rights. The Secretary of State and District Health Authorities are removed from protection altogether and, in the case of criminal actions, the application for leave to proceed is now to be submitted to the Director of Public Prosecutions. The requirement to show substantial grounds as a precondition of leave to proceed with the action, first introduced in 1930 at a time when legalism was in retreat, is abolished. No further guidance as to the new threshold of proof to be reached is given in the section, but Donaldson, MR, has recently laid down, on the occasion of appeals by a Miss Winch who had been refused leave to proceed with negligence claims relating to her detention in hospital, that a prima-facie case does not have to be made out and it is enough to show that the complaint appears to deserve fuller investigation.[38]

Another reform which enhances patients' civil status is the statutory extension of the franchise to greater numbers of informal patients, although the position of detained patients is not similarly

---

[36] [1976] AC 314.

[37] At p. 329. But he did call for section 141 to be kept under review on account of the particular vulnerability of mental patients.

[38] *Winch* v. *Jones and Others*; *Winch* v. *Hayward and Others*, *The Times*, 16 July 1985.

improved. Section 4(3) of the Representation of the People Act 1949 debarred patients in mental institutions from using them as their address for electoral purposes. Like section 141 of the Mental Health Act 1959, this bar operated independently of the mental capacity of individual patients to exercise their votes. A limited reform has been introduced which allows voluntary patients to use their last or alternative non-hospital address, but insists upon postal voting and a prior unassisted declaration by the patient.[39]

A final major development which in some respects reflects the new legalism is the institution of a new statutory body to monitor, report on, and participate in the procedures designed to protect and fortify patients' rights. The new Mental Health Act Commission, consisting of a Chairman and ninety-one members, including doctors, lawyers, nurses, psychologists, social workers, and academics, was established by the Secretary of State, pursuant to the obligation imposed upon him by section 56(1) of the Mental Health (Amendment) Act 1982, as a special health authority under the National Health Service Act 1977, section 11. It took up its duties on 30 September 1983 when the reformed legislation came into force and has developed an administrative framework which comprises a Central Policy Committee and organizational division into three regions. The Commission's functions, laid down in section 121(2) and (7) of the 1983 Act, are: to review the care and treatment of detained patients; to appoint medical practitioners to give second opinions, and personnel, who may include its own members, for multidisciplinary review of consent to treatment under Part IV of the Act; to draw up a Code of Practice, and to review decisions to censor correspondence.

The concept of supervisory machinery concerned specifically with individual patients' rights and distinct from but answerable to the Department of Health and Social Security recalls the role of the Board of Control, especially in the years 1948–59 when it had lost its more purely administrative functions, and is also similar to the Mental Welfare Commission established by the Mental Health (Scotland) Act 1960,[40] and the seminal conception of the Mental Health Review Tribunal as floated by the Socialist Medical Associa-

---

[39] This was contained in the Mental Health (Amendment) Act 1982, section 62(2) and Schedule 2: see now Representation of the People Act 1983, sections 7(2)–(9).

[40] The wider remit of the Mental Welfare Commission was fixed by the Mental Health (Scotland) Act 1960, section 4. See now Mental Health (Scotland) Act 1984, section 3.

tion in its evidence to the Percy Commission before the 1959 Act.[41] It is a second instance, the first being multidisciplinary review of consent to treatment, of the injection of a substantially greater element of non-medical involvement in decisions affecting the liberty of patients. When the composition of the Mental Health Act Commission is compared with that of the Mental Health Review Tribunal, it is apparent that the perception of the range of disciplines appropriate to multidisciplinary scrutiny has expanded significantly since 1959, notably with the inclusion of nurses and clinical psychologists as well as social workers, who were already assured a statutory role by their participation in formal admissions procedures.

The Royal College of Psychiatrists did not regard the introduction of such a body as a threat. On the contrary, having been opposed to the abolition of the Board of Control in 1959, they had consistently advocated the reintroduction in England of a supervisory agency comparable to the Scottish Mental Welfare Commission, which could be expected to increase public confidence without importing the hard and fast restrictions proposed by MIND.[42] For MIND had aligned itself with the more aggressively libertarian notion of a legally-oriented advocacy system,[43] which would have a decentralized structure based on the situation of advocates in hospitals with regional and national support. The Government's model would seem to incline to the former conception and indeed their relative emphasis of a supervisory structure rather than legally entrenched patients' rights, which Kenneth Clarke, the Minister of Health actually condemned as 'legalism' when taken beyond fundamentals, has provided an explicit point of divergence from MIND's conception of a reformed legislative structure.[44]

Whether the new legalism makes any great practical difference depends to a significant extent upon how far the more critical and questioning sensibility toward psychiatry which has developed since the 1960s filtrates into the scrutiny of psychiatric practices with which the Commission is charged. The Conservative Government was careful in its selection of Commissioners, pointedly excluding Larry

[41] *Royal Commission on the Law Relating to Mental Illness and Mental Deficiency: Minutes of Evidence*, p. 686: Written Memorandum of the Socialist Medical Association, para. 18.

[42] Royal College of Psychiatrists, *Mental Health Commissions—The Recommendations of the Royal College of Psychiatrists*, 1981.

[43] See L. O. Gostin, *A Human Condition Volume 1*, pp. 130–5.

[44] K. Clarke, *House of Commons Debates*, Special Standing Committee, Twenty-first Sitting, col. 797 (29 June 1982).

Gostin himself as too radical. Nevertheless, the Commission has shown signs of activism. It was conceived as essentially to be concerned with the observance of the rights of detained patients, but section 121(4) of the Act provides that it may be directed by the Secretary of State to review the care and treatment of informal patients also. The extension of its potential responsibilities to embrace informal patients was one of the changes successfully pressed upon the Government in the Special Standing Committee on the Mental Health (Amendment) Bill and, along with the similar extension of part of the protection in respect of consent to treatment, reflected the concern of the Labour Opposition, shared by MIND, that the machinery in the Act should reach the great majority of mental patients who possess informal status (110,000: 6,500 in 1985). In fact, the Commission has made representations to the Secretary of State about the rights of informal patients, especially those *de facto* under detention in locked wards or rooms, and incapable patients considered to need greater protection in respect of treatment. This development belies the argument of opponents of the campaign to reform the 1959 Act who maintained that, with only a small and declining minority of patients being subject to compulsory powers, the scope for concern about patients' civil liberty was extremely restricted.

The new movement toward legalism which has just been documented has to be set in the context of the Act as a whole, and its limitations appreciated. The Act reflects not only a reassertion of legalism, but also the changing professional complexion of the mental health services in the period since 1959. These influences within the legislation are indeed linked because the non-medical professions involved in the care and treatment of psychiatric patients can be accorded increased recognition and prestige by their incorporation in the machinery for reviewing medical decision-making. The principal beneficiaries of this are social work, which has greatly expanded and developed since the Mental Health Act; clinical psychology, the expansion of which into mental hospitals developed from the late 1950s onwards, and nursing, which has been able to exert a greater influence on the development of the mental health services through more aggressive unionization.

Nurses are granted unprecedented recognition by the Act. Not only are psychiatric nurses to figure prominently in multidisciplinary consultation and review, but they are for the first time given the power to detain patients on their own initiative. Section 5(2) of the

Mental Health Act 1983 preserves the power of the medical officer in charge to detain an informal patient for three days pending activation of the procedures for formal admission. However, the appropriate medical officer may not be available and in the past this eventuality was sometimes guarded against by doctors providing nurses with signed, undated blank reports which they could use to detain an informal patient should the need arise.[45] As has so often been the case in the history of the mental health services, a practice designed to circumvent proper statutory procedure has been accorded legal recognition. Nurses have been granted a holding power valid for six hours.[46]

This may have consequences for the relationship between nurses and patients. On the one hand, nurses are the professionals in most immediate and regular contact with patients and as such are in a position to represent the interests of patients within the authority hierarchy of the mental health system—to operate as patient advocates. Further, they have the most direct interest in demanding more resources for the mental health services to improve working conditions and staff-patient ratios, and this provides the basis for an alliance between health service staff unions and organizations of patients. Radically progressive movements for the replacement of mental hospitals by democratic therapeutic structures, such as the Italian *Psichiatria Democratica*, naturally build upon this potential for solidarity.[47] But, on the other hand, nurses are also in the front line of the mental health system in its character as an agency of social control. It is they who actually apply the physical coercion upon which order within the system ultimately rests and in situations of understaffing the more custodial rather than the more progressive functions of nursing tend to predominate:

Institutionalized into the routines of ward life (as much as the long-stay patients but on the giving rather than the receiving side of the traditional services of the attendant), the mental nursing profession resists its own incorporation into a menial and unskilled role by stressing its link with the medical experience of its superiors; and this borrowed status, a moonlight over the inmate beds reflected from the imputed magnificence of the

---

[45] L. O. Gostin, *A Human Condition Volume 1*, pp. 20–1.

[46] Mental Health Act 1983, section 5(4). The nurse must be of the prescribed class: section 5(4), (7).

[47] On the relationship of law and Italian mental health practice see F. Basaglia, 'Problems of Law and Psychiatry: The Italian Experience', *International Journal of Law and Psychiatry* (1980), p. 17.

consultant (who is usually absent somewhere well below the horizon), draws its glory from the most mechanical, organic and unsocial traditions of medicine itself.[48]

Section 5(4) for the first time formalizes the role of the nurse as gaoler, accentuating the custodial aspect of the nurse-patient relationship, and it is interesting that while the Confederation of Health Service Employees unreservedly welcomed the six-hour holding power, the Royal College of Nursing reported a division of opinion amongst nurses and recommended a one-hour holding power only to the House of Commons Special Standing Committee.[49] The power has in practice been little used and Brenda Hoggett observes that no doubt nurses 'are most reluctant to jeopardise their relationship with informal patients by holding this sort of threat over them'.[50]

The recruitment of other professions into structures of multidisciplinary review, bringing to bear their own distinct (though internally contested) professional orientations, amounts to the provision of institutionalized opportunities for the tempering of medical judgment. Footholds are provided for radical critics of psychiatry within these professions to exert influence upon future directions of development, just as MIND, from the early 1970s, sought to use the opportunity for legal representation before Mental Health Review Tribunals as a lever for what might be called legal subversion, importing legal assumptions into a flexible and discretionary forum governed by a therapeutic rationality.[51] But the Act leaves the essential structures of mental health provision very much intact. The practice of psychiatry remains dominated by the medical profession. The injection of greater legal safeguards for the protection of patients against the excessive or unwarranted exercise of medical power does not alter this. As we saw in Chapter 1, legal mediation of medical decision-making may serve as a source of legitimation. Given the enduring controversy about the validity of psychiatry and about its credibility at the level of therapeutic results, legality, punctilious compliance with bureaucratic requirements, and preparedness to engage in inter-professional consultation provide substitute routes to

[48] P. Sedgwick, *Psycho Politics*, p. 234.
[49] *House of Commons Debates*, Special Standing Committee: evidence of the RCN and COHSE, cols. 87–8.
[50] B. Hoggett, *Mental Health Law*, p. 15.
[51] See, for example, L. O. Gostin and E. Rassaby, *Representing the Mentally Ill and Handicapped*. Sunbury: Quartermaine House, 1980, pp. 4–5.

public acceptance. Here, the actual form in which the principle of multidisciplinary review was enacted is significant. The Mental Health Act Commission has only advisory status, its terms of reference are initially limited to detained patients, and the protection of patients will depend to a large extent upon medical observance of a Code of Practice. The 1974–9 Labour Government's White Paper, published in 1978,[52] proposed that multidisciplinary panels should provide second opinions, rather than merely confirming the validity of consent and benefiting from consultation in new procedures for regulating the administration of controversial psychiatric treatments. The structure of the consent to treatment provisions in the new Act leaves essential decision-making powers in medical hands, and thus endorses medical claims, articulated chiefly through the Royal College of Psychiatrists, to exclusive competence in deciding upon the administration of medical treatments. The effect of insisting upon medical second opinions is to import the principle of professional self-regulation, which has produced public dissatisfaction in relation to the more exposed question of police accountability. The result reflects strong pressure from psychiatrists to resist more radical proposals. Instead of challenging the new legislative direction as a whole, the Royal College concentrated upon limiting the potential damage to professional interests of proposals to increase the regulation of psychiatric treatment, thus achieving the appearance of accountability without sacrificing real power. And of course, to the extent that power is redistributed, it is amongst mental health professionals: it is only a very limited step in the direction of the net reduction of professional power over psychiatric patients and is not inspired by any urge toward deprofessionalization.

Although a duty to provide after-care is conceded and the last resort status of commitment to hospital emphasized, the Government resisted the demand of MIND, the British Association of Social Workers, and others, accepted in the previous Labour administration's White Paper, for a 'crisis intervention service' as a community-based alternative to formal emergency admission to mental hospital, which would require new resources.[53] The measure can be seen as a convenient opportunity for a right-wing Conservative Government,

[52] Department of Health and Social Security, *A Review of the Mental Health Act 1959* (Cmnd. 7320, 1978).

[53] The Act was not perceived as being entirely devoid of resource implications. For example, Kenneth Clarke estimated the cost of the Mental Health Act Commission as £700,000 *per annum: House of Commons Debates* 20, col. 766 (22 March 1982).

334   The Mental Health Act 1983

wedded to austerity in the public sector, to appear to 'reform' the
mental health services by strategically limited concessions to the new
legalism, so that psychiatric hegemony was not seriously undermined,
without tackling head-on the substantive questions of the quantity
and quality of services.

Finally, before examining the new thinking which has influenced
the marked shift away from the complacent assumptions of 1959, it is
well to be reminded of the unintended consequences of legal
provisions. One question which has very much exercised the Mental
Health Act Commission in the two years since its inception is the
legality of the use of conditional leave under section 17 of the Act to
subject patients living 'in the community' to compulsory treatment.
While the Commission concludes that there is nothing wrong in the
genuine use of conditional leave as a means of assessing fitness for
discharge, with a condition of continuing treatment or else being
recalled to hospital, there is no legal basis for detaining under section
3 with a view to immediate conditional leave subject to compulsory
treatment in the community, or for renewal of the authority to detain
such a patient by merely nominal recall to hospital. Keeping patients
on a 'long leash' by such methods achieves *de facto* compulsory
treatment in the community, something which cannot be achieved by
invoking the guardianship provisions and which, though proposed by
B.A.S.W. in 1976 in the form of a Community Care Order, has been
specifically rejected. The result is the extension of hospital discipline
into the community: the community becomes an extension of the
hospital and a theatre for the exercise of self-arrogated medical
powers. This particular example of those in the field employing skill
in the manipulation of legal provisions has reopened the issue of
compulsory treatment in the community.[54]

MIND's Campaign for Patients' Rights

Although MIND's demands have not been met in full, it has been
claimed that approximately two-thirds of the provisions of the new
Act derive from the proposals advanced in *A Human Condition*.[55]
Whilst recognizing the role of other organizations in shaping the
legislation, an examination of MIND's campaign will help to uncover

[54] *Biennial Report of the Mental Health Act Commission*, 1985, pp. 25–27.
[55] See L. O. Gostin, 'Contemporary Social Historical Perspectives on Mental Health
Reform', note 4.

the nature of the Act's legalism, and to trace its immediate social origins.

The process of statutory reform began in the early 1970s, when MIND and the National Council for Civil Liberties became increasingly concerned with the issue of psychiatric patients' legal rights. In 1974, MIND established a multidisciplinary working party to review the Mental Health Act 1959 and subsequently created the full-time post of Legal and Welfare Rights Officer in recognition of the need for someone within the charity's organization to assume specific responsibility for following through the issues raised by the working party's deliberations. In 1975, MIND was afforded an official outlet for its representations, when an Inter-Departmental Committee, embracing the Department of Health and Social Security, the Home Office, the Lord Chancellor's Department, and the Welsh Office, was brought into being to examine the need for revisions of the Act. This review was mainly concerned with the civil aspects of the legislation, the Butler Committee on Mentally Abnormal Offenders having made recommendations in relation to Part V of the Act when it reported in October 1975. The Inter-Departmental Committee undertook its task in the light of two major independent critical analyses of the workings of the legislation, one by the Royal College of Psychiatrists and the other by MIND. The latter consisted of Larry Gostin's proposals, as the first Legal and Welfare Rights Officer of MIND, which were published in the two successive volumes of *A Human Condition*. In 1976, the Committee produced a consultative document,[56] to which MIND duly responded and this was followed in 1978 by the publication of the 1974–79 Labour Government's White Paper.[57] The Conservative Government elected in 1979 published its intentions in 1981[58] and enactment was finally achieved in the next year. In these latter stages of the emergence of amending legislation, MIND was intimately involved, along with the professional bodies, in shaping the final form in which reforms reached the statute book, both through engagement in consultation with the Department of Health and Social Security and through intense Parliamentary activity.

Explanations for MIND's campaign can be sought on a number of different levels. In terms of the contribution of individuals it was

[56] See note 24, *supra*.
[57] See note 52, *supra*.
[58] Department of Health and Social Security, *Reform of Mental Health Legislation*, (Cmnd. 8405, 1981).

important that in 1974 Tony Smythe, formerly of the National Council for Civil Liberties, was appointed MIND's Director, raising the degree of libertarian consciousness within the organization's leadership. From the point of view of evoking a Government response, it was helpful that, in David Ennals, MIND confronted a particularly sympathetic Secretary of State for Health and Social Services who was determined to further the process of achieving reform of the Mental Health Act.[59] The most productive individual contribution was, however, undoubtedly that of Larry Gostin, who, as its Legal and Welfare Rights Officer and later Legal Director, spearheaded MIND's campaign. It was of great significance for the character of MIND's influential proposals for reform that their architect should have been a lawyer by professional training and a citizen of the United States. The American culture is, of course, much more ingrained with legalism and constitutionalism than the British: civil rights tend to be formalized in conformity with a political tradition based upon a written Constitution. Moreover, in terms of Anti-Psychiatry, which was one of the theoretical sources of the revival of legalism, the British version tended to be a diffuse cultural movement of the Left, whose strategies were either too intimately personal or too socially cataclysmic to employ the piecemeal and ponderous machinery of the law, but its American counterpart was primarily inspired by Thomas Szasz, a conservative, who conceived legal change as paving the way for the rescue of mental patients from the clutches of the state psychiatric system, proposing the abolition of both civil commitment and the insanity plea.[60] Thus there has been an American influence at work in the translation of growing cultural scepticism about the validity and curative effectiveness of psychiatry into a concrete rearmament of patients with a stronger legal weaponry to combat the psychiatric power structure.

We have seen that this is not the first historical example of such a cross-cultural influence. Evidence concerning American lunacy legislation was before both the Dillwyn Committee and the Radnor Commission, and American developments were influential in the formation of the Mental Hygiene and Child Guidance movements. Comparative considerations have entered into the debate over the

[59] David Ennals succeeded Barbara Castle as Secretary of State in April 1976 at the commencement of the Callaghan administration and retained the office until Labour's defeat in the General Election of May 1979.

[60] See T. S. Szasz, *Law, Liberty and Psychiatry*, pp. 225–35.

merits of MIND's analysis of mental health legislation, and it has sometimes been argued (as has the exact reverse) that while greater legal protection for patients might be appropriate in terms of Gostin's experience of American conditions, it is inappropriate in the allegedly more enlightened British context.

The changing composition of MIND's staff not only illustrates the part played by particular individuals, but also the changing nature of the organization as a private charity channelling welfare resources to selected groups of the disadvantaged. Prior to the Welfare State, charities tended to see their function as the collection of funds and the distribution of largess, on the assumption that public provision would and should remain inadequate. Ideologically, their organizers extolled the virtues of voluntary effort and private bounty. With the advent of the Welfare State, however, charities have become greatly dependent upon public subsidy in the form of tax exemptions and state grants. Some voluntary organizations, such as the Child Poverty Action Group and Shelter, have been politicized, in the sense that they perceive the state as better able than themselves to make adequate direct provision for the disadvantaged and so have developed into interest groups applying pressure upon the State for greater resources for their clients. This entails a shift to a belief in comprehensive state provision, with voluntary organizations consigned to an indirect, representative role.[61]

The concept of representing clients *within* the Welfare State, rather than merely rendering supplementary services, has highlighted the issue of 'claimants' rights'. The egalitarian and paternalistic currents in the movement to create the Welfare State produced powerful bureaucratic structures charged with considerable administrative discretion and by the 1960s and 1970s its clients were increasingly organized in Claimants' Unions, tenants' associations, and other self-determined structures to challenge aspects of their relationship to the authorities paying out benefits or administering services which they perceived as stigmatizing and oppressive. These developments have disclosed to debate the question of the relationship between liberty and the Welfare State and law has been a not unnatural resort as a mechanism for supplying liberty with some degree of concrete definition. Law's reputation for conservatism, élitism, archaism, and mystification would have rendered it a

---

[61] M. C. Chesterman, *Charities, Trusts and Social Welfare*. London: Weidenfeld and Nicolson, 1979, pp. 353–4.

peculiarly inauspicious milieu through which to conduct efforts to enhance the status of welfare clients, but at least at the margins the legal profession and legal services have also been penetrated by the political transformations of the post-war decades. The 1960s and 1970s witnessed a crisis of legal order, a profound questioning of the capacity of the legal profession in its existing form to serve the requirements of British society in the era of the Welfare State and *a fortiori* of its suitability to assist in strategies for realizing the ideals of equality and social justice in which the Welfare State is widely perceived as having proved inadequate.[62] Extensions of the Legal Aid system, the growth of neighbourhood law centres, and the increasing presence of a social scientific component in legal education instanced developments flowing from and accommodating to this disquiet. Elements in the legal profession became more sensitive to the demand for legal expertise to be placed at the disposal of the clients of the Welfare State, in terms of legal advice, representation before administrative tribunals, and in the courts, and in broader political campaigns to reform Welfare State legislation.

The mental health services were not immune from these patterns of development. MIND's energies were significantly reoriented from traditional charitable activities toward a more active political engagement, and the notion of supporting patients' rights has become an organizing conception in its work. The appointment of a Legal Director, and the promotion of representation for the mentally ill and handicapped before Mental Health Review Tribunals by organizing training conferences, publishing a manual for representatives,[63] and the establishment of representation schemes, in addition to the campaign to change the Mental Health Act 1959 itself, reflected the growing prominence of legal amongst other types of support offered by MIND to psychiatric patients. In the same period, there was an influx of legal academics and practitioners, notably Louis Blom-Cooper, QC, into the field of law and psychiatry who were prepared to assist in the representation, research and advisory activities prosecuted under the auspices of MIND's Legal and Welfare Rights Department.

Such a reorientation did not pass unopposed from within the organization. Christopher Mayhew, its Presidential figurehead, at-

---

[62] See A. Hunt, *The Sociological Movement in Law.* London: Macmillan, 1978, Chapter 6; Z. Bankowski and G. Mungham, *Images of Law.* London: Routledge and Kegan Paul, 1976.

[63] L. O. Gostin and E. Rassaby, *Representing the Mentally Ill and Handicapped.*

tempted to distance MIND from the proposals of *A Human Condition* at the time of the publication of its first volume in November 1975, and he subsequently resigned.[64] Mayhew had been a passionate supporter of the original philosophy of the Mental Health Act and remained convinced of its virtues, resisting the birth of a new legalism in mental health legislation.[65] Anthony Clare, author of *Psychiatry in Dissent* and a well-known psychiatrist and broadcaster, also resigned, in 1981, from MIND's team of sympathetic practitioners. Externally, the newly overt political connotations of MIND's activities provoked a series of attacks from the Conservative MP, William van Straubenzee, in particular for Tony Smythe's allegations in December 1979 about the widespread improper use of unmodified electroconvulsive therapy at Broadmoor, which was within his constituency. Van Straubenzee proclaimed that 'no self-respecting Tory ought to subscribe a cent to its central funds' and expressed the view that it was 'handicapped by the professionals at present in charge of it'.[66] He pressured the Government to reduce its annual grant to the organization on this ground.[67]

The character of MIND's campaign can be further illuminated by an examination of the strategies it has employed to strengthen patients' legal protection. Representation before tribunals, the earliest focus of attention, provided an avenue for pursuing this objective without awaiting changes in either legislation or legislative regulations. The same can be said of litigation to test the extent of patients' rights in the domestic courts, even though this could end in adverse decisions, such as those on section 141 in *Pountney* v. *Griffiths* in the House of Lords and *Kynaston* v. *Secretary of State for Home Affairs* in the Court of Appeal.[68] But where the Act did not appear to protect fundamental civil rights, MIND took advantage of the opportunity to apply to the European Court of Human Rights in Strasbourg, thus closely linking the pursuit of litigation in individual cases to the broader political objective of forcing the British Government to change existing legislation. The Government's

[64] See his letter to *The Times*, 7 November 1975.
[65] A position he expressed strongly in an interview with the author, 20 September 1975.
[66] *House of Commons Debates* 997, cols. 744–6 (26 January 1981).
[67] If a charitable organization becomes too overtly political it ultimately stands to lose its charitable status, which in law is in principle incompatible with political purposes, by the Charity Commissioners removing it from the register. On charitable status and political purposes see *National Anti-Vivisection Society* v. *IRC* [1948] AC 31.
[68] [1982] Crim. LR 117 CA.

decision to shift the ultimate decision to discharge restricted patients detained under Part V of the Mental Health Act from the Home Secretary on the advice of a Mental Health Review Tribunal to the tribunal itself, embodied in section 73 of the Act, was compelled by the decision of the European Court in X v. *The United Kingdom* that section 65 of the 1959 Act contravened Article 5(A) of the European Convention on Human Rights, which had been ratified by the United Kingdom, by failing to provide patients subject to restriction orders with effective periodic judicial review.[69]

MIND's campaign against the Mental Health Act has not, however, been narrowly legal in character. The organization's rejection of the formalistic type of legalism inherent in Victorian Lunacy legislation was made clear at an early stage. In his Preface to the first volume of *A Human Condition*, Tony Smythe, MIND's then Director, expressed their policy in the following terms:

> We do not feel that a strictly legalistic approach would in itself be relevant to a human condition which is often complex and insufficiently understood and to a public service that is hard pressed for resources and adequately trained staff. Accordingly, in operating MIND's legal and welfare rights service we shall seek to integrate the different but complementary skills of lawyers, psychiatrists and social workers.

Similarly, Gostin has been sensitive to charges of legalism, a term with pejorative connotations of ritualistic legal formalism. In academic interventions in which he has sought to explain and justify the Act he has stressed that whilst law is not a creative discipline in the psychiatric context, in the sense of directly contributing to the therapeutic task, it does have diverse and valuable functions to

[69] X v. *United Kingdom*, application no. 6998/75 (1981) 4 EHRR 181. Article 5(4) provides that 'Everyone who is deprived of his liberty by arrest or detention shall be entitled to take proceedings by which the lawfulness of his detention shall be decided speedily by a court and his release ordered if the detention is not lawful.' The Government decided to opt for the Mental Health Review Tribunal to perform the function of this 'court', as opposed to the Crown Court or some specially appointed body: Lord Belstead *House of Lords Debates* 426, cols. 759–63 (25 January 1982). In the Lord Chancellor's Memorandum to the Special Standing Committee on the Mental Health (Amendment) Bill it was stated that a number of Circuit Judges would be appointed to Mental Health Review Tribunals specially designated to preside in restricted patient cases. In accordance with section 78(4) of the Mental Health Act 1983, the Mental Health Review Tribunal Rules now provide that the presiding legal member must be specially approved for this purpose and Circuit Judges and Recorders have been so appointed. The Home Secretary retains a power of discharge concurrent with that of the tribunal.

perform on behalf of mental patients. It can confer enforceable rights to psychiatric services in the spirit of an 'ideology of entitlement', as in rights to after-care and funding for legal representation before tribunals, and it can reinforce patients' civil and social status by securing their maximum retention of basic corollaries of citizenship such as freedom of correspondence, freedom of access to the courts, and the right to vote, as well as increasing the accountability of the psychiatric profession to its clients.[70]

This brings us to the question of the manner in which, in the course of the twentieth century, legalism itself as a philosophy of mental health legislation has come to be transformed in meaning. We might contrast two different ideal types of legalism, the traditional legalism exhibited in the Lunacy Act 1890 and a new legalism which inspired the critics of the Mental Health Act 1959. The older type of legalism may be described as a legalism rooted in a logic of repression, in a perception which is preoccupied with public order or social defence, and fundamentally condones the incarceration of the mentally disordered in isolated, disciplinarian institutions, characterizing them as dangerous elements who need to be placed under restraint for the security of the rest of society. In this view, compulsory procedures play the dominant role in the facilitation of treatment and voluntary status for patients is regarded as a marginal liberal concession. Whilst accepting the medical position that insanity is properly conceived as an illness, it invests mental disease with the property of contagion, a subversion of the humanistic import of the medical view prompted by the fear of insanity which orders the whole repressive model.[71] Since the medical view is conceded, doctors are allocated a substantial measure of autonomy in the hope they will bring about cures, but because the mentally ill are defined as a social threat and have to be confined, procedures for the trial and treatment of criminals are in principle to be extended to civil

Analogy.

[70] See L. O. Gostin, 'The Ideology of Entitlement: The Application of Contemporary Legal Approaches to Psychiatry', in P. Bean (ed.) *Mental Illness: Changes and Trends.* Chichester: John Wiley, 1983, p. 270.

[71] This assumption of the contagious nature of insanity is defined as an element in the contemporary popular (in the sense of non-specialist) view of the phenomenon in an article by Dr Ball in *L'Encéphale. Journal des Maladies Mentales et Nerveuses* reviewed by D. Hack Tuke in *Journal of Mental Science* 33 (1887–8), p. 140. It is also well illustrated in a speech drawing an analogy between insanity and smallpox delivered by F. Logan, MP, during the Second Reading debate on the Mental Treatment Bill 1929: see *House of Commons Debates* 235, col. 1003 (17 February 1930).

commitment on grounds of insanity. Just as procedural safeguards in a criminal trial are inserted for the protection of the innocent and comprise part of the armoury of rights and liberties which attach to law-abiding individuals as a badge of citizenship, so the safeguards which the advocates of this position would see built into the processes of civil commitment are calculated to protect the sane. The sane are perceived as deserving of protection from erroneous commitment because its consequences in terms of loss of liberty, loss of respect, and loss of livelihood are so drastic, and indeed comparable with those following conviction for an imprisonable offence. However, as far as those genuinely in need of psychiatric attention are concerned, social segregation and subjection to paternalistic and disciplinary regulation by medical experts are deemed fitting. Because the judicial safeguards against wrongful commitment are supported by this reasoning they tend themselves to be publicly perceived as penal in character and are infected with the stigma associated with a repressive system for containing the mentally disordered.

 The new legalism, in contrast, is part of a logic of resistance and is more authentically libertarian. The perception of the mental health services from which it flows shares with traditional legalism a common perception that they are primarily engaged in a social control function comparable to that carried out by the machinery for the management of crime, and rejects the medical preference, historically erosive of legal protection for patients, for a functional analogy with general medical services. But it differs in concluding that, given the social control functions of the system, its use of psychiatric coercion must be critically assessed in social, moral, and political, rather than medical terms. Medical conceptualization, terminology, and symbolism are criticized for legitimating dispensation with procedural safeguards conventionally accepted as demanded by natural justice in circumstances in which an individual faces loss of liberty. The increasingly voluntary basis of admission to hospital does not necessarily undermine this critique.[72] The presence of coercive powers as an ultimate recourse may render voluntarism nugatory in a significant number of instances. Furthermore, consent may derive from inertia, produced either by the mental illness itself or its treatment, or may indeed by devalued within the present perspective as merely a manifestation of individuals' internalization of psychiatric ideology. That is, in a culture in which the view is

[72] See, for example, L. O. Gostin, *A Human Condition Volume 1*, p. 16.

dominant that, for example, bizarre changes in perception or severe depression are to be comprehended as symptoms of illness, their sufferers will naturally reach for medical explanations and solutions. At this point, the new legalism takes on the character of a new paternalism, not only reinforcing the rights of the resistant, but reinterpreting the volition of those who apparently consent as induced collusion.

The intended beneficiaries of this augmentation of patients' rights are not the sane but the mentally disordered themselves, and the injection of greater legal machinery into coercive psychiatric processes of commitment, detention, and treatment is conceived as part of an attempt to encourage patients to accept greater responsibility in decisions affecting their lives and to improve their status as citizens. Abstracted from their traditionally repressive and segregatory setting and associated with the welfare legalism of an 'ideology of entitlement', it is not anticipated that legal safeguards will acquire stigmatory capacity. They should operate rather in harmony with the concept of Community Care by challenging the extent to which psychiatric patients are still institutionally confined.

Political and Theoretical Foundations of the New Legalism

Just as the post-Second World War consensus in favour of moderate social interventionism furnished the political climate for the Mental Health Act 1959, so the reassertion of legalism may be linked to the dissolution of this consensus, with the apparent exhaustion of social democracy and the renewed fashionability of versions of liberalism within both Conservative and Labour Parties. The former has seen the birth of the 'New Conservatism', marking an historic intra-party shift of ideology as significant for social welfare as that which brought about the New Liberalism at the turn of the century, but this time signalling the re-emergence rather than the eclipse of classical liberal values. The Poujadist-Friedmanite coup of 1975, which banished discredited Heathite intervention, has allowed liberal individualist social theory and philosophy to flourish within the Party, from the works of Adam Smith to those of Frederick Hayek. The Labour Party has also undergone a period of ideological self-examination, during which the relationship of the structures of the Welfare State to socialist objectives has been reassessed. There has been an increased sensitivity to the dangers of statism and bureaucratization and the legacies of Fabian social management and the Morrisonian model of public ownership have been challenged by a new awareness of the importance of accountability, democratic control, and self-determination, perhaps seen at its most advanced in the ultra-democratic, libertarian socialism associated with Tony Benn, whose politics are significantly reminiscent of traditional Radicalism. The parallel revival of liberalism in the two major parties has enabled a new consensus on the direction of mental health legislation to be built around the new legalism. As a detraction from the power of welfare state professionals in favour of the liberty of the individual it may be interpreted as anti-collectivist, as part of the reversion to nineteenth-century liberalism and 'Victorian Values' which is at the heart of the New Conservatism: there is, after all, some degree of affinity between the old and the new legalism, between the legalism of 1890 and that of 1983. The elevation of the rule of law against professional and bureaucratic discretion is an important common feature. But as the principal recipients of rights to legal redress are the late twentieth-century counterparts of the Victorian pauper lunatics, radicals on the Left can see the issue as one of shoring up the position of a particularly helpless and neglected section of the oppressed. MIND skillfully maintained this political ambiguity and support for the rights campaign was forthcoming from across the political spectrum, including Harvey Proctor on the Right of the Conservative Party and Michael Meacher on the Left of the Labour Party.[73]

The logic of resistance which informed the demands for a new legalism in mental health legislation emerged out of convergent developments in a number of disciplines. One of its sources was the body of literature and practice loosely termed Anti-Psychiatry, which evolved from the late 1950s to the early 1970s as an opposition to orthodox organically directed psychiatry, drawing external support, but rooted in psychiatry itself. In Britain, the main exponents of Anti-Psychiatry were R. D. Laing and David Cooper, who were both medically qualified psychiatrists.

Laing's early work applied existential psychological analysis of the perceptions of the psychiatrically disturbed in a humanistic attempt to render madness empathetically rather than clinically intelligible.[74]

[73] It was no doubt on the basis of this experience of coalition building that Larry Gostin, in his subsequent post as General Secretary of the NCCL, felt able to attempt the recruitment of support for civil liberties issues generally in the Centre and on the Right in an effort to break what he considered to be their dangerous over-identification with the Left. This strategy foundered on the conflict between supporters of individual and collective trade union rights in the 1984–5 Miners' Strike, bringing about his resignation, closely followed by his return to the United States.
[74] See R. D. Laing, *The Divided Self*. London: Tavistock, 1960.

He then turned his attention to the role of the dynamics of the family in generating confused and baffling behaviour in its members, thus transferring the location of disorder from the presenting individual to the primary social unit of which that individual forms a part.[75] This insight contributed to the acceptance of family therapy as an important weapon in mainstream psychiatry and social work. By the late 1960s, Laing was advocating the positive therapeutic value of 'the voyage into madness' as a self-healing process which should not be disturbed by the insensitive intervention of doctors utilizing their irrelevant resource of a training in physical medicine. He saw madness as a reaction of withdrawal from the irrationality of the social order as a whole, which imposed a profound alienation upon its members.[76] Together with David Cooper and others, he developed experimental forms of psychiatric practice which were more radically democratic than, but in the traditions of, the influential progressive work of Dr Maxwell Jones at Belmont Hospital in the 1950s.

The later work of Laing and Cooper was situated in the cultural critique launched by the New Left, inspired by the ideal of free spirited, expressive individuality in revolt against what one of its mentors, Herbert Marcuse, described as the 'comfortable, smooth, reasonable democratic unfreedom'[77] of advanced capitalist societies. This movement sought to expose the ideological underpinnings of social institutions conventionally considered to be removed from political discourse. One area exposed to political debate in this way was psychiatry, which was interpreted as a coercive apparatus devoted to the resocialization of those whose perceptions failed to conform to the dominant definition of reality which served the interests of welfare capitalism. Within this perception, madness could be characterized as a heroic revolt against the mental and spiritual alienation of confinement within the realms of experience permitted by the social and political order. The position of mental patients in the West was not so different therefore from that of the clients of Soviet psychiatry. Overtly political organizations of patients were formed with programmes related to this analysis: in Britain the Mental Patients Union pledged itself to 'challenge repressive

[75] R. D. Laing and A. Esterson, *Sanity, Madness and the Family*. London: Tavistock, 1964.

[76] R. D. Laing, *The Politics of Experience and the Bird of Paradise*. Harmondsworth: Penguin, 1967.

[77] H. Marcuse, *One Dimensional Man*. London: Sphere, 1968, p. 19.

psychiatric practice and its ill-defined concepts of "mental illness" '[78] and proclaimed that 'psychiatry is one of the tools that capitalism uses to ensure that frustration and anger against the repressive system is internalized'.[79] Counterparts of this organization included in the United States the Mental Patients Liberation Front, and in West Germany the Socialist Patients' Collective, founded by Baader-Meinhof anarchists at Heidelberg University in 1972.

We have already noted above that British Anti-Psychiatry was not concerned in any very direct way with legal reform, but its impact should be credited with some general responsibility for the dissatisfaction with the psychiatric philosophy of the Mental Health Act which gained so much momentum in the 1970s. In addition, the work of Thomas Szasz, an American psychiatrist of psychoanalytic persuasion, whose Anti-Psychiatric writings directly engage the implications of the critique of orthodox psychiatry for law, has been influential in Britain. In a series of highly polemical and iconoclastic analyses,[80] Szasz developed his now familiar central thesis that 'mental illness' is a label attached to a range of 'problems in living' which, although in logic only of metaphorical status, is treated as being their origin in actuality. In this sense, mental illness is a myth; it does not exist. The result of this category mistake, he claims, is that the psychosocial, ethical, and legal issues raised by these problems are distorted by illogical conceptualization in medical terms. Szasz perceives the medicalization of ethical dilemmas as dehumanizing and subversive of man's personal moral responsibility. In his view, the 'ideology of insanity' which underlies psychiatry is fundamentally totalitarian in that (apart from private practice) it serves the socio-economic interests of the state and legitimizes the confinement in mental hospitals, or 'concentration camps of the mad', of those who are committed to an 'officially forbidden image or definition of reality'. The conception of insanity as a disease analogous to physical illness, therefore, ultimately poses a political threat to freedom of choice: 'It thus seems possible that where fascism and communism have failed to

[78] 'The Declaration of Intent of the Mental Patients Union'.

[79] 'An Introduction to the Mental Patients' Union'. For a collection of similar views see Radical Therapist/Rough Times Collective, *The Radical Therapist*. Harmondsworth: Penguin, 1974. See also P. Brown (ed.), *Radical Psychology*. London: Tavistock, 1973 and P. Sedgwick, *Psycho Politics*, pp. 227–8, 239.

[80] See especially, *The Manufacture of Madness*, in which he argues that the concept of witchcraft fulfilled a similar function in medieval times to that of mental illness in modern civilization and compares psychiatric methods of diagnosis with those employed to determine guilt by the Inquisition.

collectivize American society, the mental health ethic may yet succeed.'[81]

This last quotation reflects Thomas Szasz' ideological position as a classical liberal, a kind of Milton Friedman of the political economy of mental disorder, who advocates the replacement of 'institutional' or 'community' psychiatry, subservient to the State, by a free enterprise 'contractual' psychiatry, catering to its psychiatric consumers on the basis of market exchange. This liberation by means of the cash nexus would be supported by the dismantling of paternalistic legislation and the restoration of the full rigours of the rule of law as the framework for psychiatric practice.[82] Szasz locates mental patients within and not beyond the field of common humanity and holds that they must be treated as autonomous and capable of exercising moral and legal rights along with the sane. In his view their position is comparable to the civil and political subjugation of America's black population and requires a similar civil rights campaign. The formalism and abstraction of Szasz' position reflects his classical liberal concern with the pursuit of equality of citizenship as the political foundation for the operation of the market.

The definitions of liberalism and humanitarianism to which Szasz subscribes are irreconcileable with those of post-war mental welfare legislation. They do, however, have clear affinities with Laing's critique of orthodox psychiatry. They also correspond in some degree to those which underlie Ivan Illich's position that in Western culture medical practice generally is based upon organizing concepts which objectify individuals by transforming them into clinical cases and which have the effect of depriving them of crucial areas of personal autonomy, thus performing a 'disabling' function.[83] Indeed, Irving Zola has argued that in its role as an institution of social control 'psychiatry has by no means distorted the mandate of medicine, but . . . is following instead some of the basic claims and directions of that profession'.[84] It is particularly interesting to note the parallels between Illich and Szasz in the light of Vicente Navarro's claim that behind the anarchist rhetoric, Illich's proposed solution to structural iatrogenesis (doctor-induced illness)—the

---

[81] T. S. Szasz, *Ideology and Insanity*. Harmondsworth: Penguin, 1974, p. 48.

[82] T. S. Szasz, *Law, Liberty and Psychiatry*, pp. 225–35.

[83] See I. Illich, *et al.*, *Disabling Professions*. London: Marion Boyars, 1977; *Medical Nemesis*. London: Calder and Boyars, 1975.

[84] I. K. Zola, 'Medicine as an Institution of Social Control', *Sociological Review* 20 (1972), p. 487.

deprofessionalization and debureaucratization of medicine and the reassertion of individual personal responsibility for health—constitutes nothing other than a return to the market model.[85]

A second source of alternative visions of mental illness and psychiatric practice has been the development of fresh sociological perspectives within deviance theory. In a reaction against the then dominant correctionalist orientation in criminology and deviance theory which services the social control requirements of the state and is predicated upon social control assumptions, from the 1950s onwards some sociologists began to generate critical perspectives on the agencies of social control and to evolve more subjectivist and empathetic accounts of deviance. The most important tendency within the sociology of deviance in this respect was the societal reaction perspective pioneered by Edwin Lemert, whose major work *Social Pathology* appeared in 1951. Lemert's argument that 'sociopathic phenomena', including mental disorder, were not inherently deviant, but simply differentiated behaviour meeting with socially and culturally conditioned disapproval, leading to social penalties, rejection, and segregation,[86] and that the social reaction played a part in shaping and, ironically, actually perpetuating and increasing 'primary' deviance suggested that mental illness was not a 'given', but socially constructed and plastic. It is interesting that he used a brief historical analysis of social control of the mentally disordered in the United States as an illustration of the operation of his theory.[87]

Prominent in the application of this perspective to the treatment of the mentally ill was the work of Thomas Scheff. Drawing on Lemert's concepts of primary and secondary deviation, he constructed a theory of mental illness as 'residual deviance':

There is always a residue of the most diverse kinds of violations [of cultural norms] for which the culture provides no explicit label.... For the convenience of the society in construing those instances of unnameable rule-breaking which are called to its attention, these violations may be lumped together into a residual category: witchcraft, spirit possession, or in our own society, mental illness.[88]

[85] V. Navarro, 'The Industrialization of Fetishism or the Fetishism of Industrialization: A Critique of Ivan Illich', *Social Science and Medicine* 9 (1975), p. 351.
[86] E. Lemert, *Social Pathology*. New York: McGraw-Hill, 1951, p. 22.
[87] Ibid., pp. 410–11.
[88] T. J. Scheff, *Being Mentally Ill*. Chicago: Aldine, 1966, pp. 33–4.

Scheff claimed that residual rule-breaking often occurs in people who retain the status of normal persons and is usually transitory, but that in a relatively few cases it will precipitate a crisis, become a public issue, and at this point the individual will be invested with the stereotyped social role of madman. It is his radical conclusion that among residual rule-breakers labelling is the single most important cause of careers as mental patients.

By proposing that it is merely another category of socially disapproved behaviour, this mode of analysis has helped to undermine the accepted wisdom that mental illness is a species of disease. Its effect is to suspend the scientific status of the medical view and to suggest that the conceptualization of aberrant or bizarre behaviour in medical terms may be sufficiently accounted for, both in terms of its historical emergence and of its role in contemporary social order, by sociological methods of explanation. This emphasis upon psychiatry as social control has addressed attention to the role of medical rhetoric in obscuring the social, political, and economic expediency of psychiatric activities and urged sociologists to look beyond the role of humanitarian impulse and technical psychiatric progress in producing mental health reform to the social functionality of psychiatric practices. This reorientation was complemented by the emergence in the 1960s of a more 'appreciative' or 'naturalistic' vein within the sociology of deviance, associated particularly with the work of David Matza,[89] which elevates the place of deviants' own subjective accounts in the sociological understanding of deviance. Perhaps the most influential presentation of the psychiatric system from the vantage point of mental patients has been Erving Goffman's *Asylums*,[90] which brilliantly documents the strategies by which the experience of enclosure in the alien universe of the mental institution is negotiated by its inmates.

Another academic discipline in which the treatment of psychiatry has been subject to upheaval is history. Psychiatric history as a province in which psychiatrists, such as Richard Hunter or Alexander Walk, record the emergence of madness into the light of modern medical science, has been challenged by a critical revisionist history which is not dependent upon psychiatric ideologies.[91] Within this

---

[89] See, for example, D. Matza, *Becoming Deviant*. Englewood Cliffs, New Jersey: Prentice-Hall, 1969.

[90] E. Goffman (Chicago: Aldine, 1962).

[91] See especially, R. Castel, *L'Ordre Psychiatrique: l'age d'or de l'alienisme*. Paris: Editions de Minuit, 1976; M. P. Foucault, *Madness and Civilization*; '*I Pierre*

history, broadly, psychiatry is conceived as a site of power and knowledge with complex cultural, political, and economic supports. Psychiatric medicine's status as a science is not assumed, but treated as a product of historical development, with focus upon the historical contingency of psychiatric ascendancy, the structure of psychiatric discourse, the strategies of the medical profession in laying claim to the psychiatric territory, and the specific contribution of psychiatric apparatuses and practices to the perpetuation and development of socio-political orders. The seminal work in the area of the history of psychiatry, Michel Foucault's *Madness and Civilization*, by its sheer imaginative breadth and an epistemological preoccupation which transcended established academic disciplinary boundaries, encouraged the rewriting of psychiatry's past to flourish as an interdisciplinary enterprise. Also contributory has been the strong reaction against economic determinism within modern Marxism and the emergence of critical cultural studies based upon analysis of the structure of thought and language as a major intellectual current within the European Left.[92]

That these radically critical perspectives on psychiatry were able to prosper was partly a reflection of the state of the profession and the mental health services themselves. The imaginative and experimental social orientation within post-war British psychiatry failed to redirect the energies of the profession as a whole. Rather, in the 1960s, there was a reassertion of organicism. Although there were those, such as Anthony Clare, who were exponents of a more open, subtle, and eclectic psychiatry, the historic insistence upon a more narrow definition of the psychiatrist's responsibilities endured, and this enhanced the force and credibility of Anti-Psychiatric broadsides. Whilst the status of psychiatry within medicine was reinforced by the translation of the Royal Medico-Psychological Association into the Royal College of Psychiatrists in 1971, repeated scandals about the treatment of patients in particular hospitals, the uneven development of community services, and only limited advance beyond pre-1959 therapeutic technologies combined to depress public confidence.

Riviere ... '. New York: Pantheon Books, 1978; D. Rothman, *The Discovery of the Asylum*. Boston: Little, Brown, 1971; A. T. Scull, *Museums of Madness*; 'Museums of Madness: Lunacy in Britain 1800–1860', University of Princeton PhD thesis, 1974; 'From Madness to Mental Illness: Medical Men as Moral Entrepreneurs', *Archives Européennes de Sociologie*, 16 (1975), p. 218; R. Smith, *Trial by Medicine*.

[92] See, for example, P. Q. Hirst and P. Woolley, *Social Relations and Human Attributes*. London: Tavistock, 1982.

Psychiatry's mission to medicalize madness was faced with serious theoretical challenges—philosophical, sociological, and historical—which far exceeded the effectiveness of the protestations of earlier outlets for unease such as the National Society for Lunacy Reform. The moral and control implications of psychiatric power were systematically exposed and criticized—psychiatry's 'bad conscience' was put on public trial. Furthermore, the renewed professional challenge posed by psychologists and the readiness of many social workers to take on board perspectives drawn from the radical literature constituted new difficulties for the preservation of psychiatric hegemony in the mental health sector. The civil liberties debate and the consequent reform of legislation have presented frameworks within which medically-based psychiatry has had to negotiate the multifaceted problems set by the sea change in attitudes to its remit since 1959. This amounted to nothing less than a serious erosion of the authority attached to the battery of organizing concepts founded on the proposition, to borrow Sedgwick's phrase, that mental illness *is* illness, which had sustained its legal progress for most of the century.

The study of the past teaches us that it is difficult to predict the future of mental health legislation. However, it would seem that legalism is resorted to at times of pessimism or uncertainty about how society should respond to the problems posed by mental disorder. Faith in procedure provides a substitute for conviction as to the 'solution' to these problems. As Unger, in *Law in Modern Society*, argues in relation to the emergence of the modern western legal order, the rule of law serves as a framework for stability where there are competing social interests none of which is sufficiently powerful to gain permanent ascendancy. So in the field of mental health, rival professional interests and philosophical perspectives are maintained in balance by means of the complex legal procedures and structures of the Mental Health Act 1983. The generation of a new therapeutic certainty capable of commanding broad social and political support would be the most powerful answer to the new legalism.

Bibliography

The main primary sources for the study were statutes, cases (these are both listed at the beginning of the volume), bills, parliamentary debates, Annual Reports of the Lunacy Commissioners and the Board of Control, Ministry of Health, Home Office, and Lord Chancellor's Office papers at the Public Record Office, *The Lancet*, the *British Medical Journal*, the *Journal of Mental Science* and *The Times*. I was given access to the papers of MIND and also received helpful material from Dr Walk on behalf of the Royal College of Psychiatrists (including the RMPA's 'Comments on the Report of the Royal Commission on Mental Health Law', 1957) and from the Mental Patients' Union (including 'An Introduction to the Mental Patients' Union' and 'The Declaration of Intent of the Mental Patients' Union'). The following reports and secondary sources are either referred to in the footnotes or have been of particular value:

Report of the House of Commons Select Committee on Lunatics, 1860.
Report from the House of Commons Select Committee on Lunacy Law, 1878.
Special Report of the Commissioners in Lunacy to the Lord Chancellor on the Alleged Increase of Insanity, 1897.
Report of the Interdepartmental Committee on Physical Deterioration, (Cd. 2175, 1904).
Report of the Royal Commission on the Care and Control of the Feeble Minded, (Cd. 4202, 1908).
Report of the Royal Commission on the Poor Laws and Relief of Distress, (Cd. 4499, 1909).
Report of the Committee on the Administration of Public Mental Hospitals, (Cmd. 1730, 1922).
Report of the Proceedings of the Conference convened by Sir Frederick Willis on Lunacy Reform, 1922.
Report of the Committee on Insanity and Crime, (Cmd. 2005, 1923).
Report of the Royal Commission on Lunacy and Mental Disorder, (Cmd. 2700, 1926).
Report of the National Society for Lunacy Reform, 1926.
Report of the Proceedings of a Conference on Mental Health, National Council for Mental Hygiene and Tavistock Square Clinic, 30 October–2 November 1929.
Report of the Proceedings of a Conference on Mental Treatment, held by the Board of Control with others on the implementation of the Mental Treatment Act, 22 and 23 July 1930.
Report of the Departmental Committee on Voluntary Mental Health Services, 1939.

Report of the Committee on Social Insurance and Allied Services, (Cmd. 640, 1942).
Report of the Departmental Committee on Social Workers in the Mental Health Services, (Cmd. 8260, 1951).
The Law Relating to Mental Illness and Mental Deficiency in Scotland: Proposals for Amendment, (Cmd. 9623, 1955).
Report of the Royal Commission on the Law Relating to Mental Illness and Mental Deficiency, (Cmnd. 169, 1957).
Report of the Committee on Administrative Tribunals and Inquiries, (Cmnd. 218, 1957).
Report of the Royal Commission on the Law Relating to Mental Illness and Mental Deficiency: Implications for Local Authorities and the General Public, Proceedings of a Conference held at Church House, 6 and 7 March 1958.
Report of the Working Party on Social Workers in the Local Authority, Health and Welfare Services, 1959.
Report of the Committee on Mentally Abnormal Offenders, (Cmnd. 6244, 1975).
A Review of the Mental Health Act 1959, Department of Health and Social Security, 1976.
A Review of the Mental Health Act 1959, (Cmnd. 7320, 1978).
Mental Health Commissions—the Recommendations of the Royal College of Psychiatrists, 1981.
Reform of Mental Health Legislation, (Cmnd. 8405, 1981).
Biennial Report of the Mental Health Act Commission, 1985.

SECONDARY SOURCES

Abel-Smith, B., and Stevens, R. B.,*Lawyers and the Courts: a sociological study of the English legal system 1750–1965*. London: Heinemann, 1967.
Adrian, H., 'Mental Illness: The Royal Commission and the Work of Magistrates', *The Magistrate* xiii (1957), p. 103.
Archbold, Sir J. F., *Lunacy*. 4th edn. Ed. S. G. Lushington. London: Shaw and Sons, 1895.
Atiyah, P. S., *Accidents, Compensation and the Law*, 3rd edn. London: Weidenfeld and Nicolson, 1980.
Balint, M., *The Doctor, His Patient and the Illness*. London: Pitman, 1957.
Bankowski, Z., and Mungham, G., *Images of Law*. London: Routledge and Kegan Paul, 1976.
Barnett, M. J., *The Politics of Legislation: the Rent Act 1957*. London: Weidenfeld and Nicolson, 1969.
Barton, R. W., *Institutional Neurosis*. Bristol: John Wright, 1959.
Baruch, G., and Treacher, A., *Psychiatry Observed*. London: Routledge and Kegan Paul, 1978.
—— 'Towards a Critical History of the Psychiatric Profession', in D. Ingleby (ed.), *Critical Psychiatry: the politics of mental health*. Harmondsworth: Penguin, 1981, p. 120.

Basaglia, F., 'Problems of Law and Psychiatry: The Italian Experience', *International Journal of Law and Psychiatry* (1980), p. 17.

Bastide, R., *The Sociology of Mental Disorder* (trans. J. McNeil). London: Routledge and Kegan Paul, 1972.

Bateson, G. (ed.), *Perceval's Narrative: a patient's account of his psychosis 1830–2*. London: Hogarth Press, 1962.

Bean, P., 'The Mental Health Act 1959: Some Issues Concerning Rule Enforcement', *British Journal of Law and Society* 2 (1975), p. 225.

——— *Compulsory Admissions to Mental Hospitals*. Chichester: John Wiley, 1980.

Beirne, P., and Sharlet, R., 'In Search of Vyshinsky', *International Journal of the Sociology of Law* 2 (1981), p. 153.

Bentham, J., *Panopticon*. London: Payne, 1791.

——— *Works*, ed. J. Bowring. Edinburgh: Tait, 1843.

——— *Introduction to the Principles of Morals and Legislation*, ed. J. H. Burns and H. L. A. Hart. London: Methuen, 1982.

Beveridge, W. H., *Pillars of Security and Other Wartime Addresses*. London: Allen and Unwin, 1943.

Blacker, C. P., *Neurosis and the Mental Health Service*. Oxford, Oxford University Press, 1948.

Blackstone, W., *Commentaries on the Laws of England*. 16th edn. Ed. J. T. Coleridge. London: Butterworths, 1825.

Bottomore, T., *Austro-Marxism*. Oxford: Clarendon Press, 1980.

Bowden, T., *Beyond the Limits of the Law*. Harmondsworth: Penguin, 1978.

Brabel, S., and Rock, R., *The Mentally Disabled and the Law*. Washington: American Bar Foundation, Mental Health Law Project, 1971.

Brand, J. L., 'The Parish Doctor: England's Poor Law Medical Officers and Medical Reform 1870–1900', *Bulletin of the History of Medicine* 35 (1961), p. 97.

——— 'The National Mental Health Act of 1946: A Retrospect', *Bulletin of the History of Medicine* 39 (1965), p. 231.

Brenner, M. H., *Mental Illness and the Economy*. Cambridge Mass.: Harvard University Press, 1973.

Briggs, A., *Victorian Cities*. London: Pelican, 1968.

Brown, J., 'Charles Booth and Labour Colonies 1889–1905', *Economic History Review* 21 (1968), p. 349.

——— 'Social Judgements and Social Policy', *Economic History Review* 24 (1971), p. 106.

——— 'Social Control and the Modernization of Social Policy 1890–1929', in Thane, P. (ed.), *The Origins of British Social Policy*. London: Croom Helm, 1978, p. 126.

Bucknill, J. C., *The Care of the Insane and their Legal Control*. London: Macmillan, 1880.

——— 'The Abolition of Proprietary Madhouses', *The Nineteenth Century* 17 (1885), p. 263.

Bunbury, H. (ed.), *Lloyd George's Ambulance Wagon: being the memoirs of William J. Braithwaite 1911–1912*. London: Methuen, 1957.

Burn, W. L., *The Age of Equipoise: a study of the mid-Victorian generation*. London: Allen and Unwin, 1964.

Butler, T., *Mental Health, Social Policy and the Law*. London: Macmillan, 1985.

Campbell, C. Macfie, *Destiny and Disease in Mental Disorders*. New York: W. W. Norton, 1935.

Campbell, C. N., 'Legal Thought and Juristic Values', *British Journal of Law and Society* 1 (1974), p. 21.

Campbell, T., *The Left and Rights: a conceptual analysis of the idea of socialist rights*. London: Routledge and Kegan Paul, 1983.

Carlen, P., *Women's Imprisonment: a study in social control*. London: Routledge and Kegan Paul, 1983.

Carson, D., 'Mental Processes: the Mental Health Act 1983', *Journal of Social Welfare Law* (1983), p. 195.

Castel, F., Castel, R., and Lovell, A., *La Société Psychiatrique Avancée*. Paris: Editions Grasset, 1979.

Castel, R., *L'Ordre Psychiatrique: l'age d'or de l'alienisme*. Paris: Editions de Minuit, 1976.

Chambliss, W., and Seidman, R. B., *Law, Order and Power*. New York: Addison Wesley, 1970.

Chesney, K., *The Victorian Underworld*. Harmondsworth: Penguin, 1970.

Chesterman, M. C., *Charities, Trusts and Social Welfare*. London: Weidenfeld and Nicolson, 1979.

Clare, A., *Psychiatry in Dissent: controversial issues in thought and practice*. 2nd edn. London: Tavistock, 1980.

Clark, D. H., *Administrative Therapy: the role of the doctor in the therapeutic community*. London: Tavistock, 1964.

Clarke, P. F., *Liberals and Social Democrats*. Cambridge, Cambridge University Press, 1978.

Coates, D., *The Labour Party and the Struggle for Socialism*. Cambridge, Cambridge University Press, 1975.

Cockton, H., *The Life and Adventures of Valentine Vox the Ventriloquist*. London: Robert Tyas, 1840.

Colaiaco, J. A., *James Fitzjames Stephen and the Crisis of Victorian Thought*. London: Macmillan, 1983.

Collini, S., *Liberalism and Sociology: L. T. Hobhouse and political alignments in England 1880–1914*. Cambridge, Cambridge University Press, 1979.

Cooper, D., *The Death of the Family*. New York: Pantheon, 1970.

Cosgrove, R. A., *The Rule of Law: Albert Venn Dicey, Victorian Jurist*. London: Macmillan, 1980.

Cotterrell, R., *The Sociology of Law: An Introduction*. London: Butterworths, 1984.

Coulter, J., *Approaches to Insanity: a philosophical and sociological study.* London: Martin Robertson, 1973.

Cullen, M., *The Statistical Movement in Early Victorian Britain: the foundations of empirical social research.* Brighton: Harvester Press, 1975.

Dalton, H., *Practical Socialism for Britain.* London: Routledge, 1935.

Dangerfield, G., *The Strange Death of Liberal England.* London: Paladin, 1970.

Defoe, D., *Essay upon Projects*, London, 1697. Reprinted Menston: Scolar Press, 1969.

Dicey, A. V., *The Law of the Constitution.* 10th edn. London: Macmillan, 1959.

_____ *Lectures on the Relation between Law and Public Opinion during the Nineteenth Century.* London: Macmillan, 1914.

Dickens, C., *Little Dorrit.* Harmondsworth: Penguin, 1967.

Dickson, D. T., 'Bureaucracy and Morality: An Organizational Perspective on a Moral Crusade', *Social Problems* 16 (1968), p. 143.

Donnelly, M., *Managing the Mind: a study of medical psychology in early nineteenth-century Britain.* London: Tavistock, 1983.

Donzelot, J., *The Policing of Families.* London: Hutchinson, 1979.

Dowse, R. E., *Left in the Centre: the I.L.P. 1893–1940.* London: Longmans, 1966.

Dreyfus, H. L., and Rabinow, P., *Michel Foucault: Beyond Structuralism and Hermeneutics.* Brighton: Harvester Press, 1982.

Durkheim, E., *The Division of Labour in Society.* New York: Free Press, 1964.

Eckstein, H., *Pressure Group Politics: the case of the B.M.A.* London: Allen and Unwin, 1960.

Edwards, A. H., *Mental Health Services: Law and Practice*, 5th edn. Ed. L. O. Gostin. London: Shaw & Sons, 1986.

Egret, J., *Louis XV et L'Opposition Parlementaire 1715–1774.* Paris: Armand Colin, 1970.

Elton, G. K., *The Tudor Revolution in Government: administrative change in the reign of Henry VIII.* Cambridge, Cambridge University Press, 1953.

Emy, H. V., *Liberals, Radicals and Social Politics 1892–1914.* Cambridge, Cambridge University Press, 1973.

Ewins, D., 'The Origins of the Compulsory Commitment Provisions of the Mental Health Act 1959'. University of Sheffield MA thesis, 1974.

Fears, M., 'Therapeutic Optimism and Treatment of the Insane' in R. Dingwall *et al.* (eds.), *Health Care and Health Knowledge.* London: Croom Helm, 1977, p. 66.

Fennell, P. W. H., 'The Mental Health Review Tribunal: A Question of Imbalance', *British Journal of Law and Society* 4 (1977), p. 86.

_____ 'Justice, Discretion and the Therapeutic State', University of Kent MPhil. thesis, 1979.

_____ 'Law and Psychiatry: The Legal Constitution of the Psychiatric System', *Journal of Law and Society* 13 (1986), p. 35.

Fine B. (ed.), *Capitalism and the Rule of Law.* London: Hutchinson, 1979.

Finer, S. E., Berrington, H. B., and Bartholomew, D. J., *Backbench Opinion in the House of Commons 1955–59*. London:Pergamon Press, 1962.

Finnane, M., *Insanity and the Insane in Post-Famine Ireland*. London: Croom Helm, 1981.

Foot, M., *Debts of Honour*. London: Picador, 1980.

Foucault, M. P., *Madness and Civilization: A history of insanity in the Age of Reason*. New York: Vintage Books, 1973.

—— *'I, Pierre Riviere, having slaughtered my mother, my sister and my brother . . . ': a case of parricide in the 19th century*. New York: Pantheon Books, 1975.

—— *Discipline and Punish: the birth of the prison*. London: Allen Lane, 1977.

Fraser, D., *The Evolution of the British Welfare State*. London: Macmillan, 1973.

Freeden, M., *The New Liberalism: an ideology of social reform*. Oxford: Clarendon Press, 1978.

—— 'Eugenics and Progressive Thought', *Historical Journal* 22 (1979), p. 645.

Freidson, E., *Profession of Medicine: a study of the sociology of applied knowledge*. New York: Dodd, Mead, 1970.

Garland, D., 'The Birth of the Welfare Sanction', *British Journal of Law and Society* 8 (1981), p. 29.

—— *Punishment and Welfare*. Aldershot: Gower, 1985.

George, V., and Wilding, P., *Ideology and Social Welfare*. London: Routledge and Kegan Paul, 1976.

Gilbert, B. B., *The Evolution of National Insurance in Great Britain: the origins of the Welfare State*. London: Michael Joseph, 1966.

—— *British Social Policy 1914–39*. London: Batsford, 1970.

Goffman, E., *Asylums: essays on the social situation of mental patients and other inmates*. Chicago: Aldine, 1962.

Gostin, L. O., *A Human Condition Volume 1: The Mental Health Act from 1959 to 1975: observations, analysis and proposals for reform*. London: MIND (National Association for Mental Health), 1975.

—— *A Human Condition Volume 2: the law relating to mentally disordered offenders: observations, analysis and proposals for reform*, London, MIND, 1977.

—— *A Practical Guide to Mental Health Law*, London, MIND, 1983.

—— 'The Ideology of Entitlement: The Application of Contemporary Legal Approaches to Psychiatry', in P. Bean (ed.), *Mental Illness: Changes and Trends*. Chichester: John Wiley, 1983, p. 27.

—— 'Contemporary Social Historical Perspectives on Mental Health Reform', *Journal of Law and Society* 10 (1983), p. 47.

Gostin, L. O., and Rassaby, E., *Representing the Mentally Ill and Handicapped: a guide to Mental Health Review Tribunals*. Sunbury: Quartermaine House, 1980.

Gostin, L. O., Rassaby, E., and Buchan, A., *Mental Health: Tribunal Procedure*. London: Oyez Longman, 1984.

Grace, C., and Wilkinson, P., *Sociological Inquiry and Legal Phenomena*. London: Collier Macmillan, 1978.

Grant-Smith, Rachel, *The Experiences of an Asylum Patient*, ed. M. Lomax. London: Allen and Unwin, 1922.

Greenland, C., *Mental Illness and Civil Liberty: a study of Mental Health Review Tribunals in England and Wales*. Occasional Papers in Social Administration, 38, London. Bell, 1970.

Griffith, J. A. G., *The Politics of the Judiciary*. 2nd edn. London: Fontana, 1981.

Gusfield, J., *Symbolic Crusade: status politics and the American temperance movement*. Urbana: University of Illinois Press, 1963.

Halévy, E., *A History of the English People in the Nineteenth Century, V: Imperialism and the Rise of Labour 1895–1905*. 2nd edn. London: Ernest Benn, 1929.

Halmos, P., *The Faith of the Counsellors*. London: Constable, 1965.

Harris, D. R., *et al.*, *Compensation and Support for Illness and Injury*. Oxford: Clarendon Press, 1984.

Harris, J., *Unemployment and Politics: a study in English social policy 1886–1914*. Oxford: Clarendon Press, 1972.

—— *William Beveridge: A Biography*. Oxford: Clarendon Press, 1977.

Hay, D., 'Property, Authority and the Criminal Law' in D. Hay *et al.*, *Albion's Fatal Tree: crime and society in eighteenth-century England*. London: Allen Lane, 1975.

Hay, J. R., *The Origins of the Liberal Welfare Reforms 1906–14*. London: Macmillan, 1975.

Hayek, F. A., *Law, Legislation and Liberty*. London: Routledge and Kegan Paul, 1982.

Heuston, R. F. V., *The Lives of the Lord Chancellors 1885–1940*. Oxford: Clarendon Press, 1964.

Hewart, LCJ, The Rt. Hon. Lord, *The New Despotism*. London: Ernest Benn, 1929.

Hindess, B., and Hirst, P. Q., *Pre-Capitalist Modes of Production*. London: Macmillan, 1975.

Hirst, P. Q., *Social Evolution and Sociological Categories*. London: George Allen and Unwin, 1976.

—— 'Law, Socialism and Rights', in P. Carlen and M. Collison (eds.), *Radical Issues in Criminology*. Oxford: Martin Robertson, 1980, p. 92.

Hirst, P. Q., and Woolley, P., *Social Relations and Human Attributes*. London: Tavistock, 1982.

Hodgkinson, R. G., 'Provision for Pauper Lunatics, 1834–1871', *Medical History*, 10 (1966), p. 138.

Hoggett, B., 'The Mental Health Act 1983', *Public Law* (1983), p. 172.

____ *Mental Health Law*. 2nd edn. London: Sweet and Maxwell, 1984.

Holden, A. I., *The St. Alban's Poisoner: the life and crimes of Graham Young*. London: Hodder and Stoughton, 1974.

Honigsbaum, F., *The Division in British Medicine: a history of the separation of general practice from hospital care 1911–1968*. London: Kogan Page, 1979.

Hunt, A., 'Perspectives in the Sociology of Law', in P. Carlen (ed.), *The Sociology of Law*. University of Keele, Sociological Review Monograph 23, 1976, p. 22.

____ *The Sociological Movement in Law*. London: Macmillan, 1978.

Hunter, R., and Macalpine, I., *Three Hundred Years of Psychiatry 1535–1860: a history presented in selected English texts*. London: Oxford University Press, 1963.

Illich, I., *Medical Nemesis: the expropriation of health*. London: Calder and Boyars, 1975.

____ *et al.*, *Disabling Professions*. London: Marion Boyars, 1977.

Ingleby, D., 'Mental Health and Social Order' in S. Cohen and A. Scull (eds.), *Social Control and the State: historical and comparative essays*. Oxford: Martin Robertson, 1983, p. 141.

Jackson, R., *The Chief: the biography of Gordon Hewart, Lord Chief Justice of England 1922–40*. London: George G. Harrap, 1959.

Jackson, R. M., *The Machinery of Justice in England*. 7th edn. Cambridge: Cambridge University Press, 1977.

Johnson, T. J., *Professions and Power*. London: Macmillan, 1972.

Jones, K., *A History of the Mental Health Services*. London: Routledge and Kegan Paul, 1972.

____ 'The Limitations of the Legal Approach to Mental Health', *International Journal of Law and Psychiatry* 3 (1980), p. 1.

Jones, M., *Social Psychiatry: a study of therapeutic communities*. London: Tavistock, 1952.

Jordan, B., *Freedom and the Welfare State*. London: Routledge and Kegan Paul, 1976.

Kahn, P., *et al.*, *Picketing: industrial disputes, tactics and the law*. London: Routledge and Kegan Paul, 1983.

Kinsey, R. M., 'Marxism and the Law: Preliminary Analyses', *British Journal of Law and Society* 5 (1978), p. 202.

____ 'Karl Renner on Socialist Legality' in D. Sugarman (ed.), *Legality, Ideology and the State*. London: Academic Press, 1983, p. 11.

Kittrie, N., *The Right to be Different: deviance and enforced therapy*. London: John Hopkins Press, 1973.

Kovel, J., 'The American Mental Health Industry', in D. Ingleby (ed.), *Critical Psychiatry*. Harmondsworth: Penguin, 1981, p. 72.

Laing, R. D., *The Divided Self*. London: Tavistock, 1960.

—— *The Politics of Experience and the Bird of Paradise*. Harmondsworth: Penguin, 1967.

Laing, R. D., and Esterson, A., *Sanity, Madness and the Family: families of schizophrenics*. London: Tavistock, 1964.

Larson, M. S., *The Rise of Professionalism: a sociological analysis*. Berkeley: University of California Press, 1977.

Lemert, E., *Social Pathology*. New York: McGraw Hill, 1951.

Lewis, G., *Lord Atkin*. London: Butterworths, 1983.

Lockyer, R., *Tudor and Stuart Britain 1471–1714*. London: Longmans, 1964.

Lomax, M., *Experiences of an Asylum Doctor*. London: Allen and Unwin, 1921.

Lord, J. R., 'American Psychiatry and its Practical Bearings on the Application of Recent Local Government and Mental Treatment Legislation', *Journal of Mental Science* 76 (1930), p. 456.

Lubenow, W. C., *The Politics of Government Growth: early Victorian attitudes towards state intervention 1833–1848*. Newton Abbott: David and Charles, 1971.

McBriar, A. M., *Fabian Socialism and English Politics 1884–1918*. Cambridge: Cambridge University Press, 1962.

McCandless, P., 'Liberty and Lunacy: the Victorians and Wrongful Confinement', *Journal of Social History* 5 (1978), p. 366.

MacDonagh, O., 'The Nineteenth Century Revolution in Government: A Reappraisal', *Historical Journal* 1 (1958), p. 52.

MacDonald, M., *Mystical Bedlam: madness, anxiety and healing in seventeenth century England*. Cambridge: Cambridge University Press, 1981.

MacKenzie, D., 'Eugenics in Britain', *Social Studies of Science* 6 (1976), p. 523.

—— Review Article, *British Journal for the History of Science* 11 (1978), p. 90.

—— 'Karl Pearson and the Professional Middle Classes', *Annals of Science* 36 (1979), p. 138.

Macleod, R., 'Medico-Legal Issues in Victorian Medical Care', *Medical History* 10 (1966), p. 44.

Macmillan, H. P., *Law and Other Things*. Cambridge: Cambridge University Press, 1938.

Maddison, D. C., 'Blueprint for a Model Psychiatric Hospital of the Future', in H. Freeman and J. Farndale (eds.), *Trends in the Mental Health Services: a symposium of original and reprinted papers*. London: Pergamon Press, 1963, p. 94.

Manchester, A. H., *A Modern Legal History of England and Wales 1750–1950*. London: Butterworths, 1980.

Manning, D. J., *The Mind of Jeremy Bentham*. London: Longmans Green, 1968.

Mapother, E., 'Mental Treatment under Modern Regulations', *Mental Hygiene* (1935), p. 126.

Marat, J. P., *Plan de Legislation Criminelle*. Paris, 1790.

Marcuse, H., *One Dimensional Man*. London: Sphere, 1968.

Marshall, T. H., *Citizenship and Social Class, and other essays*. Cambridge: Cambridge University Press, 1950.

—— *Social Policy in the Twentieth Century*. London: Hutchinson, 1970.

Martin, F. M., *Between the Acts: community mental health services 1959–1983*. London: Nuffield Provincial Hospitals Trust, 1984.

Marx, K., *Capital: a critique of political economy*, volume 1, ed. F. Engels. Tr. S. Moore and E. Aveling. London: Lawrence and Wishart, 1970.

Matza, D., *Becoming Deviant*. Englewood Cliffs, New Jersey: Prentice Hall, 1969.

Mellet, D. J., 'Society, the State and Mental Illness, 1790–1890: Social, Cultural and Administrative Aspects of the Institutional Care and Control of the Insane in Nineteenth Century England'. University of Cambridge PhD thesis, 1978.

Middlemas, K., *Politics in Industrial Society: the experience of the British system since 1919*. London: Deutsch, 1979.

Midwinter, E. C., *Victorian Social Reform*. London: Longmans, 1968.

Miliband, R., *Parliamentary Socialism: a study in the politics of Labour*. London: Merlin Press, 1972.

—— *The State in Capitalist Society*. London: Weidenfeld and Nicolson, 1969.

Miller, P., 'The Territory of the Psychiatrist', *Ideology and Consciousness* 7 (1980), p. 63.

—— 'Psychiatry—the Renegotiation of a Territory', *Ideology and Consciousness* 8 (1981), p. 97.

Miller, P. and Rose, N., (eds.) *The Power of Psychiatry*. Cambridge: Polity Press, 1986.

Morris, A., *et al.*, *Justice for Children*. London: Macmillan, 1980.

Mowat, C. L., *The Charity Organization Society 1869–1913: its ideas and work*. London: Methuen, 1961.

Navarro, V., 'The Industrialization of Fetishism or the Fetishism of Industrialization: A Critique of Ivan Illich', *Social Science and Medicine* 9 (1975), p. 351.

Nelken, D., 'Is there a crisis in Law and Legal Ideology?', *Journal of Law and Society* 9 (1982), p. 177.

Norris, V., 'The Mental Hospital Service and its Future Needs: A Statistical Appraisal', *The Lancet* 2 (1952), p. 1172.

Palmer, J., and Pearce, F., 'Legal Discourse and State Power: Foucault and the Juridical Relation', *International Journal of the Sociology of Law* 11 (1983), p. 361.

Parris, H., 'The Nineteenth Century Revolution in Government: A Reappraisal Reappraised', *Historical Journal* 3 (1960), p. 28.

Parry, N., and Parry, J., *The Rise of the Medical Profession: a study of collective social mobility*. London: Croom Helm, 1976.

Parry-Jones, W. Ll., *The Trade in Lunacy: a study of private madhouses in England in the eighteenth and nineteenth centuries*. London: Routledge and Kegan Paul, 1972.

Pashukanis, E. B., *Law and Marxism: A General Theory* (trans. B. Einhorn, ed. C. Arthur). London: Ink Links, 1978.

Patel, I. L., 'Treatment or Punishment? A Nineteenth Century Scandal' *Psychological Medicine* 6 (1976), p. 143.

Pearson, G., *The Deviant Imagination: psychiatry, social work and social change*. London: Macmillan, 1975.

Peay, J., 'Mental Health Review Tribunals: Just or Efficacious Safeguards?' *Law and Human Behaviour* 5 (1981), p. 161.

—— 'Mental Health Review Tribunals and the Mental Health (Amendment) Act', *Criminal Law Review* (1982), p. 794.

Pelling, H., *A Short History of the Labour Party*, 5th edn. London: Macmillan, 1976.

Perkin, H., *The Origins of Modern English Society 1780–1880*. London: Routledge and Kegan Paul, 1969.

Pimlott, B., *Hugh Dalton.* London: Jonathan Cape, 1985.

Pinker, R., *Social Theory and Social Policy*. London: Heinemann, 1971.

Pope, H. M. R., *A Treatise on the Law and Practice of Lunacy*, 2nd edn. Ed. J. H. Boone and V. de S. Fowke. London: Sweet and Maxwell, 1890.

Porter, R., 'Being Mad in Georgian England', *History Today* 31 (December 1981), p. 42.

Radical Therapist/Rough Times Collective, *The Radical Therapist*. Harmondsworth: Penguin, 1974.

Raleigh, T., 'The Lunacy Laws', *Law Quarterly Review* 1 (1885) p. 157.

Rapoport, R. N., *Community as Doctor: new perspectives on a therapeutic community*. London: Tavistock, 1961.

Reade, C., *Hard Cash: a matter-of-fact romance*. London: Sampson Low, Son, & Marston, 1863.

Rees Thomas, W., 'The Unwilling Patient', *The Lancet* (1952) 2, p. 972.

Reiss, S., 'A Critique of Thomas S. Szasz's *The Myth of Mental Illness*', *American Journal of Psychiatry* 128 (1972), p. 1081.

Reynolds, S., and Woolley, B. and T., *Seems So! a working-class view of politics*. London: Macmillan, 1911.

Rheinstein, M. (ed.), *Max Weber on Law in Economy and Society*. Cambridge, Mass.: Harvard University Press, 1954.

Robinson, K., *Policy for Mental Health*. Fabian Research Series, 1958.

Rosen, A. M. (ed.), *Mental Health and Mental Disorder: a sociological approach*. International Library of Sociology and Social Reconstruction: Routledge and Kegan Paul, 1956.

Bibliography 363

Rose, N., 'Unreasonable Rights: Mental Illness and the Limits of the Law', *Journal of Law and Society* 12 (1985), p. 199.

—— *The Psychological Complex: psychology, politics and society in England 1869–1939.* London: Routledge and Kegan Paul, 1985.

—— 'Psychiatry: The Discipline of Mental Health', in P. Miller and N. Rose (eds.), *The Power of Psychiatry.* Cambridge: Polity Press, 1986.

—— 'Law, Rights and Psychiatry', in P. Miller and N. Rose (eds.), *The Power of Psychiatry.* Cambridge: Polity Press, 1986.

Rosen, G., *Madness in Society: chapters in the historical sociology of mental illness.* London, Routledge and Kegan Paul, 1968.

Rothman, D., *The Discovery of the Asylum: social order and disorder in the New Republic.* Boston: Little, Brown, 1971.

Rusche, R., and Kirchheimer, O., *Punishment and Social Structure.* London: Russell and Russell, 1968.

Saul, S. B., *The Myth of the Great Depression 1873–1896.* London: Macmillan, 1969.

Scheff, T. J., *Being Mentally Ill: a sociological theory.* Chicago: Aldine, 1966.

Scruton, R., *The Meaning of Conservatism*, 2nd edn. London: Macmillan, 1984.

Scull, A. T., 'Museums of Madness: Lunacy in Britain 1800–1860'. University of Princeton PhD thesis, 1974.

—— 'From Madness to Mental Illness: Medical Men as Moral Entrepreneurs', *Archives Européennes de Sociologie* 16 (1975), p. 218.

—— *Museums of Madness: the social organization of insanity in nineteenth century England.* London: Allen Lane, 1979.

—— 'Moral Treatment Reconsidered: Some Sociological Comments on an Episode in the History of British Psychiatry', in Scull (ed.), *Madhouses, Mad-Doctors and Madness.* London: Athlone Press, 1981.

—— *Decarceration: community treatment and the deviant—a radical view.* 2nd edn. Cambridge: Polity Press, 1984.

Searle, G. R., *The Quest for National Efficiency: a study in British politics and political thought 1899–1914.* Oxford: Basil Blackwell, 1971.

—— *Eugenics and Politics in Britain 1900–1914.* Leyden: Noordhoff, 1976.

—— 'Eugenics and Politics in Britain in the 1930s', *Annals of Science* 36 (1979), p. 159.

—— 'Eugenics and Class', in C. Webster (ed.), *Biology, Medicine and Society 1840–1940.* Past and Present Society. Cambridge: Cambridge University Press, 1981, p. 217.

Sedgwick, P., 'Mental Illness is Illness', *Salmagundi* 29 (1972), p. 196.

—— *Psycho Politics.* London: Pluto Press, 1982.

Shklar, J. N., *Legalism.* Cambridge, Mass.: Harvard University Press, 1964.

Sigerist, H., *Civilisation and Disease.* Ithaca, New York: Cornell University Press, 1944.

Skultans, V., *Madness and Morals: ideas on insanity in the nineteenth century*. London: Routledge and Kegan Paul, 1975.

—— *English Madness: ideas on insanity 1580–1890*. London: Routledge and Kegan Paul, 1979.

Smith, P., *Disraelian Conservatism and Social Reform*. London: Routledge and Kegan Paul, 1967.

Smith, R., *Trial by Medicine: insanity and responsibility in Victorian trials*. Edinburgh: Edinburgh University Press, 1981.

Stanton, A. H., and Schwarz, M. S., *The Patient and the Mental Hospital: a study of institutional participation in psychiatric illness and treatment*. London: Tavistock, 1954.

Stedman-Jones, G., *Outcast London: a study in the relationship between classes in Victorian Society*. Oxford: Clarendon Press, 1971.

Stevens, R. B., *Law and Politics: the House of Lords as a judicial body 1800–1976*. University of North Carolina Press, 1978.

Sutherland, E. M., 'The Diffusion of Sexual Psychopath Laws', *American Journal of Sociology* 56 (1950), p. 142.

Swazey, J. P., *A Study of Therapeutic Innovation: chlorpromazine in psychiatry*. Cambridge, Mass.: M.I.T. Press, 1974.

Szasz, T. S., *The Myth of Mental Illness: foundations of a theory of personal conduct*. London: Paladin, 1972.

—— *The Manufacture of Madness: a comparative study of the inquisition and the mental health movement*. London: Paladin, 1972.

—— *Law, Liberty and Psychiatry: an inquiry into the social uses of mental health practices*. London: Routledge and Kegan Paul, 1974.

—— *Ideology and Insanity: essays on the psychiatric dehumanization of man*. Harmondsworth: Penguin, 1974.

Tawney, R. H., *Equality*, 5th edn. London: Unwin Books, 1964.

Taylor, A. J., *Laissez-faire and State Intervention in Nineteenth Century Britain*. London: Macmillan, 1972.

Taylor, I., Walton, P., and Young, J. *The New Criminology: for a social theory of deviance*. London: Routledge and Kegan Paul, 1973.

—— *Critical Criminology*. London: Routledge and Kegan Paul, 1975.

Theobald, H. S., *The Law Relating to Lunacy*. London: Stevens and Sons, 1924.

Thompson, E. P. *Whigs and Hunters: the origin of the Black Act*. London: Allen Lane, 1975.

Timms, N., *Psychiatric Social Work in Great Britain 1939–1962*. London: Routledge and Kegan Paul, 1964.

Titmuss, R. M., *Essays on the Welfare State*. London: Allen and Unwin, 1958.

—— *Commitment to Welfare*. London: Allen and Unwin, 1968.

Tooth, G. C., and Brooke, E. M., 'Trends in the Mental Hospital Population', *The Lancet*, 1 (1961), p. 710.

Treble, J. H., 'The Attitude of the Friendly Societies Towards the Movement in Great Britain for State Pensions', *International Review of Social History* 15 (1970), p. 266.

Trevor, A. H., 'The Mental Treatment Bill 1923', *Transactions of the Medico-Legal Society*, xvii (1922–3), p. 181.

Tuke, D. H., Review of Scandinavian and French Literature, *Journal of Mental Science*, 33 (1887–8), p. 134.

Tuke, J. B., 'Lunatics as Patients not Prisoners', *The Nineteenth Century*, 25 (1889), p. 596.

Tumanov, V. A., *Contemporary Bourgeois Legal Thought: a Marxist evaluation of the basic concepts*. Moscow: Progress Publishers, 1974.

Twining, W., and Miers, D. R., *How to Do Things with Rules*, 2nd edn. London: Wiedenfeld and Nicolson, 1982.

Unger, R. M., *Law in Modern Society: toward a criticism of social theory*. New York: Free Press, 1976.

Venables, H. D., *A Guide to the Law Affecting Mental Patients*. London: Butteworths, 1975.

Walker, N., *Crime and Insanity in England: Volume 1*. Edinburgh, Edinburgh University Press, 1968.

Walker, N., and McCabe, S., *Crime and Insanity in England: Volume 2*. Edinburgh, Edinburgh University Press, 1973.

Webb, B., and Webb, S., *English Poor Law Policy*. London: Longmans Green, 1910.

—— *English Poor Law History Part II: the last hundred years*. London: Longmans Green, 1929.

Weber, M., *The Theory of Social and Economic Organization*. New York: Free Press, 1964.

Weiss, P., *The Persecution and Assassination of Marat as Performed by the Inmates of the Asylum of Charenton under the Direction of the Marquis de Sade*, 2nd edn. London: Calder and Boyars, 1966.

Wells, H. G., *The New Machiavelli*. London: John Lane, 1911.

Whitehead, T., *Mental Illness and the Law*. Oxford: Basil Blackwell, 1982.

Williams, B., 'The Idea of Equality', in P. Laslett and W. G. Runciman (eds.), *Philosophy, Politics and Society*, Second Series. Oxford: Blackwell, 1962.

Williams, G. L., 'The Criminal responsibility of Children', *Criminal Law Review* (1954), p. 492.

Woodroffe, K., *From Charity to Social Work in England and the United States*. London: Routledge and Kegan Paul, 1962.

Wootton, B. F., *Plan or No Plan*. London: Gollancz, 1934.

—— *Social Science and Social Pathology*. London: Allen and Unwin, 1959.

Yeo, S., 'Working-Class Association, Private Capital, Welfare and the State', in N. Parry, M. Rustin, and C. Satyamurti (eds.), *Social Work, Welfare and the State*. London: Edward Arnold, 1979, p. 48.

Zola, I. K., 'Medicine as an Institution of Social Control', *Sociological Review* 20 (1972), p. 487.

Index

374   Index